The History of Maidstone ... - Primary Source Edition

J M. Russell

Nabu Public Domain Reprints:

You are holding a reproduction of an original work published before 1923 that is in the public domain in the United States of America, and possibly other countries. You may freely copy and distribute this work as no entity (individual or corporate) has a copyright on the body of the work. This book may contain prior copyright references, and library stamps (as most of these works were scanned from library copies). These have been scanned and retained as part of the historical artifact.

This book may have occasional imperfections such as missing or blurred pages, poor pictures, errant marks, etc. that were either part of the original artifact, or were introduced by the scanning process. We believe this work is culturally important, and despite the imperfections, have elected to bring it back into print as part of our continuing commitment to the preservation of printed works worldwide. We appreciate your understanding of the imperfections in the preservation process, and hope you enjoy this valuable book.

THE

history of Maidstone

BY

J. M. RUSSELL.

WITH ILLUSTRATIONS.

MAIDSTONE:
WILLIAM S. VIVISH, 28, KING STREET;
FREDERICK BUNYARD, 29, WEEK STREET.
LONDON: SIMPKIN, MARSHALL, & Co.
1881.

ALL RIGHTS RESERVED.

DA
690
.M2
R91
1881

Buh

PREFACE.

This work was first given to the public in monthly parts; and now that it is about to be published in its complete form, I desire to tender my thanks for the kind help I have received during its progress through the press. I must especially acknowledge my indebtedness to Mr. Edward Hughes, who suggested reproductions of some of the effaced or altered features of old Maidstone, and who has afforded me much valuable information on the recent history and topography of the town and neighbourhood. My thanks are also due to Mr. William Tarbutt, of Cranbrook, for his kindly co-operation; to Mr. Robert Hovenden, of Heathcote, Croydon, for access to his excellent library of Kentish books and pamphlets; and to the Town Clerk of Maidstone (Mr. Herbert Monckton) for permission to examine the Corporation records, and for facilitating the courteous assistance of the Museum officials.

Pencil drawings by William Alexander, Thomas Charles, and Edward Pretty have been copied for the majority of the lithographs. I am indebted to Mr. Hubert Bensted for elaborate tracings of the "House in High Street" and the "House in Bank Street," needful for the photo-lithographic reductions; to Mr. F. W. Ruck for the difficult drawing of the "Old Mitre and Fire Office;" and to Mr. F. J. V. James for the reduced copy of Charles's sketch of the Prisons in King Street. The rest, with two exceptions, I owe to the friend who induced me to venture to illustrate, trusting that absence of artistic execution might be excused by archæologists in the satisfaction at getting reliable record of such scraps of the past.

J. M. R.

December 8, 1881.

CONTENTS.

	PAGE
INTRODUCTORY	1

CHAPTER I.

MAIDSTONE DURING THE MIDDLE AGES.—Roman Remains—Derivation of the Name—Maidstone in the Eleventh Century—Meetings on Penenden Heath—Ancient Courts of Assize—The Hundred—The Manor—Newark Hospital—Convent of Franciscans—The Old Bridge ... 7

CHAPTER II.

THE THREE KENTISH REBELLIONS.—Wat Tyler and Jack Straw—Breaking into Maidstone Gaol—Death of Tyler—The Rising under Jack Cade—Wyatt's Rebellion—Allington Castle—Wyatt and his Adherents at Maidstone: the Queen's Troops sent against them—Victory of the Insurgents: their Advance upon London—Surrender of Wyatt: his Death ... 33

CHAPTER III.

ST. MARY'S CHURCH—THE COLLEGE OF ALL SAINTS.—The Archiepiscopal Palace—St. Mary's Church—Goulds Chantry—Rectors of Maidstone—License for Archbishop Courtenay's Foundation—Erection of the College—Death of the Archbishop: his Place of Burial—Endowments—Description of the College Buildings—Masters of the College—Wotton's Tomb—The College Dissolved—Pensions to Priests—Revenue of the College: its Domain Lands ... 70

CHAPTER IV.

THE CHURCH OF ALL SAINTS.—Archbishops at the Palace—Chantries—The Reformation—The Rectory vested in the Crown—Sale of the Church Plate and Vestments—The Parish Register—The Rood of Grace—Burning of Martyrs in the Fair Meadow and elsewhere—Grant of the Tithes to the See of Canterbury—The Perpetual Curates: Augmentation of their Stipends—Sequestration of the Living—Thomas Wilson, the Puritan Incumbent—The Tithes of Maidstone—The first Vicar ... 96

CHAPTER V.

ALL SAINTS' AND OTHER MAIDSTONE CHURCHES.—The Fabric of All Saints' Church—Its Architecture—The Organ Loft—Organs, Ancient and Modern—The Original Roof—The Church Re-Pewed—Destruction of the Spire—Bells and Bell Ringing—Monuments in the Church—Funeral Regulations—The Chapel of St. Faith—Ancient Chapels—Recently-erected Churches ... 124

CHAPTER VI.

NONCONFORMITY IN MAIDSTONE.—The Dutch Refugees—John Gifford, the Baptist—Prosecutions under the Conventicle Act—Ministers Ejected in 1662 The Early Baptists at Tovil and Maidstone—Simon Pine—Joseph Wright as Medical Practitioner, Prisoner, Mayor, and Baptist Minister—The Old Presbyterian Congregation—George Swinnock, the Preacher and Author—The Week Street Congregation—Other Dissenting Chapels 146

CHAPTER VII.

THE FRATERNITY OF CORPUS CHRISTI.—Gift of the Hall in Earl Street—The Fraternity sanctioned by the Crown—The Brotherhood Hall—Number of Brethren and Sisters at various times: their Annual Contributions—Rent-roll of the Fraternity—The Annual Accounts—Chantry in All Saints' Church—Feasts on Corpus Christi Day—List of Wardens—The Fraternity Dissolved—Hall and Lands Purchased by the Town 162

CHAPTER VIII.

THE GRAMMAR SCHOOL.—Founding of the School—The Original Endowment—The First Master—Benefaction by William Lamb—Qualifications of Scholars—The Master's Salary—School Orders—Payments by Scholars—Gunsley's and Davy's Bequests—Annual Visit of the Corporation—The Master convicted of Manslaughter—Eminent Scholars: Horne, Smart, and Pond—New School Premises—Lubbock and Randall Scholarships—The Charity Commissioners' Scheme 172

CHAPTER IX.

MUNICIPAL AND PARLIAMENTARY HISTORY.—The Portreve and his Brethren—Incorporation of the Town—The first Charter revoked—The second Charter—Representative Burgesses in Parliament—Curious By-Laws—Early Creation of Freemen—The third Charter—How Corporation Meetings were announced—Andrew Broughton: his share in the Death of Charles I.—The fourth Charter—The Kentish Petition of 1701—Five Justices Imprisoned by the House of Commons—Thomas Bliss—Disputes between the Corporation and the Inhabitants—The Corporation Dissolved—The fifth Charter—Corporation Feasts—The sixth Charter—New Town Hall—The Corporation Rent-roll in 1822—Non-Resident Freemen—Parliamentary and Municipal Reform... 183

CHAPTER X.

ANCIENT STATE OF THE TOWN.—Leland's Visit—The Manor of Maidstone—Manors of East Lane and Wyke—Population in 1572—Sanitary Condition of the Town—The Plague The Bear Ringle—The Queen's Players—Conduits in the High Street—Benefactions to the Poor—Fearful Ravages of the Plague—Letter-carrying in the Seventeenth Century—The King's Mead—Visit of Samuel Pepys—Population in 1695—The Poor-Rate Smallpox Population in 1782—The Streets Paved and Lighted—Street Nomenclature—Old Inns and Taverns 217

CHAPTER XI.

MAIDSTONE DURING THE CIVIL WAR—STORMING OF THE TOWN.—The Kent Assizes in 1642—Petition to the Parliament—A Committee of Members sent down to Maidstone--Petition to the King, and Suggestions to the House of Commons—The King's answer—Agitation in 1643—Cause of the Kentish Rising in 1648—Lord Fairfax commissioned to suppress the Rising—Main body of the Royalists at Rochester—March of Fairfax to the Medway—Maidstone stormed—Fairfax leading his troops to the Attack—No Relief from Rochester—Surrender of the Defenders Pacification of Kent—Maidstone Men at the Trial and Execution of the King—Old Soldiers—The Fairfax family 245

CHAPTER XII.

COURTS AND PUNISHMENTS.—Early Courts and Prisons—The Court House—Preparations for the Assizes—Old Legal Punishments—The Upper and Lower Court Houses—The County Prison and the Brambles—Cases at the Quarter Sessions during the Commonwealth—Trial of Witches—Tragedy at Lees Court—Cases at the Assizes in Charles II.'s reign—County Prison and Bridewell in King Street—First person executed for Sheep-stealing—Demolition of the Lower Court House Riot at the County Prison—Visit of John Howard—State Trial at the Town Hall Number of Prisoners tried at the Assizes—List of Executions on Penenden Heath - Public and Private Executions 275

CHAPTER XIII.

TRADE OF THE TOWN.—Kentish Ragstone—The Walloon Settlers in Maidstone—Manufacture of Cloth and Linen Thread—Early Cultivation of Hops—The Medway Traffic—Municipal Survey of the River—Issue of Tokens—Wages in 1698—General Trade of the Town—Hop-growing and Hop-picking—Fruit Cultivation—Brewing and Distilling—Paper-making—Fairs and Markets—Market Buildings 307

CHAPTER XIV.

OLD HOUSES AND OLD FAMILIES.—The Mote—Vinters—Park House—Buckland—Shales Court - Kingsley House—Digons—Jordans Hall—Old Houses in the High Town - Hunter's House The Old Theatres—The Palace—The Astley Family—Sir John Astley's Will—Astley House—Thomas Bliss - Broughton's House—Earls Place—Chillington—The Maplesdens - Nicholas Barham's Will—The Charles Family—Julius Brenchley—The Museum and Public Library 332

CHAPTER XV.

SOME INCIDENTS OF BYGONE TIMES.—A Monster—Wonderful Crop of Wheat—Visit of Henry VI.—Terrific Storm—Smuggling - Capture of Sturgeons - Military Encampments on Coxheath—The Troops Reviewed by the King—General D'Hilliers at the Bell Hotel—Review of Kentish Volunteers in the Mote Park—Equipment of Maidstone Volunteers in George the Third's Reign—Precautions against Invasion—The last great County Meeting on Penenden Heath 363

CONTENTS.

CHAPTER XVI.

ENDOWED CHARITIES AND CHARITABLE INSTITUTIONS.—William Hewitt—Sir Henry Cutt—Robert Gunsley—Alexander Fisher—Robert Rowland—Sir John Banks—Thomas Bliss—The Workhouse—Maidstone Union—Mrs. Duke—Edward Hunter—William Gill—John Brenchley—Sir Charles Booth—Mrs. Wright—Mrs. Carter—Thomas Robert Cutbush—Thomas Edmett—The West Kent General Hospital—The Ophthalmic Hospital 376

CHAPTER XVII.

MAIDSTONE WORTHIES.—Edward Lee—John Hall—John Jenkins—Sir Jacob Astley—William Shipley—William Woollett—William and James Jefferys—William Alexander—William Hazlitt 387

CHAPTER XVIII.

RECENT PROGRESS.—Old and New Roads—Houses on the Bridge—Population in 1821—Introduction of Gas—The Coaching Days—Railways—Alexander Randall—Water Supply—The New Bridge—Drainage of the Town—Population in Decennial Periods—Conclusion 399

APPENDIX 409

ILLUSTRATIONS.

	PAGE
Maidstone in 1722	*Frontispiece*
Sir Thomas Wyatt the Elder	46
East Side of St. Faith's Green	*to face* 142
St. Peter's Chapel and Entrance to Newark House	,, 144
The Brotherhood Hall	,, 164
Kingsley House	,, 241
The Court Houses and Market Place, 1623	,, 280
The County Prisons, King Street	,, 286
Hunter's House	,, 303
The Market Cross and Conduit	,, 314
Pruned Filbert Tree	324
The Market Place, 1820	*to face* 330
The Old Mote House	,, 335
The Old Mitre and Fire Office	,, 343
House in Bank Street	,, 345
House in High Street—Lower End of High Street	,, 346
House in High Street	,, 351
Houses in Week Street	,, 353
Earls Place, Earl Street, corner of Havock Lane	,, 355
Houses at East End of Bridge East View	,, 400
Houses at East End of Bridge - West View	,, 402
The Old Bridge, 1797	,, 407

THE HISTORY OF MAIDSTONE.

INTRODUCTORY.

A HUNDRED and forty years ago, the Rev. William Newton, of Wingham, in Kent, published a small volume which, if we consider the sources of information then within reach of the local chronicler, formed a fairly comprehensive epitome of the history and antiquities of Maidstone. Several books have since been printed, in which particular subjects connected with the town have been treated with more or less of detail. But a full and consecutive History of Maidstone, exhibiting a picture of its rise and progress, its past and present condition, has not been published.

In the following pages an endeavour has been made to supply this want. Local records, Kentish literature, and such of the treasures of the British Museum and the Public Record Office as were thought likely to throw fresh light on the subject, have been examined, and a mass of material has been brought together from all quarters.

Maidstone, the county town of Kent, is situated on the river Medway, in the centre of the county, almost midway between London and Dover. Passing the town of Tonbridge, the river, for fifteen miles, flows in a north-easterly direction, between meadows and hop gardens, and then, by a rounded curve, changes its course to the north-west. On the bend of the Medway thus formed stands the Town of Maidstone. It is built, for the most part, on picturesque declivities which slope down to the river, and is environed by a country which presents the variegated beauty of hill and dale. Wherever the eye rests there are orchards and hop plantations; but the view to the north-east is impeded by the bold chalk ridge of the North Downs, two miles from the town. Long shady walks lead past blooming gardens, or through rich farms, till they end in some sleepy village or hamlet; or you come upon homesteads sunning themselves on gentle eminences, or buried out of sight among the hops and the fruit trees.

The annals of Maidstone are replete with circumstances of historical interest. A record which carries the memory back to the Norman Conquest, and even to the epoch of the Roman occupation, comprehends a multiplicity of changes. Casting the eye rapidly over the twilight period of antiquity, we shall follow Maidstone as it emerges from the brighter light of the fourteenth century, and advances, by many noteworthy stages, into the sunshine of our own times. In the course of the narrative we may catch a glimpse of devout pilgrims, weary and foot-sore, seeking succour at the Hospital of St. Peter and St. Paul; and we shall see that institution suppressed, in order to augment the endowments of the College which Archbishop Courtenay founded here in the closing years of his life. We shall note the germ of modern municipal government in the good order enforced by the Portreve and his Brethren. Nor shall we omit to notice that the exertions of the chief magistrates of those days were in all probability zealously seconded by numerous trade guilds or brotherhoods, and by the powerful Corpus Christi Fraternity which then existed. Possessing much landed property, the Fraternity once a year feasted in magnificent style in the old Hall at the bottom of Earl Street, and the exact statement of the price of each commodity supplied for these festivals, adds much to our knowledge of the domestic and social economy of our forefathers in the fifteenth century.

One cannot fail to observe that the history of the town is in some measure bound up with the history of English rebellions. Wat Tyler and his followers, in the first intoxication of a transient success, entered the town by a path long after known as Tyler's Lane, and broke into the gaol which stood at the upper end of the High Street, setting the prisoners at liberty. There were Maidstone men who joined in the revolt under that designing Irishman, Jack Cade, and were slain by the sword, or handed over to the hangman. Rather more than a century later, Sir Thomas Wyatt, after parting with wife and babe at his Castle of Allington, rode into the High Street, one stormy morning in January, and unfurled the banner of rebellion. Victory glimmered for a moment on his arms, and then all was closed on the scaffold at Tower Hill. A melancholy fate for the son of the witty diplomatist—the sweet singer who adorned the early literature of England—old Sir Thomas, who, "courtier of many courts," yet

> loved the more
> His own grey towers, plain life and letter'd peace,
> To read and rhyme in solitary fields,
> The lark above, the nightingale below,
> And answer them in song.

In 1648, when the struggle between the King and the Parliament was approaching its tragic close, Maidstone hoisted the royal colours, and in the cloudy sunset of a June evening, the valley of the Medway resounded with the roll of musketry and the clang of arms. General Fairfax, with his veteran troops, had moved down upon the town. The streets were barricaded, and the trainbands and other brave men of Kent offered a furious resistance to the soldiers of the Parliament; but after four or five hours' fighting, they were driven at midnight into All Saints' churchyard, where they surrendered.

Most ancient of the ancient buildings in the town, All Saints' Church is rich in associations of the past. It is Maidstone history in petrifaction—a local record in stone and lime. Grey as a rocky coast washed by the surge of ages, the venerable fabric has witnessed every important event during five hundred years. It was built at a time when the last of the Plantagenets was sitting upon the English throne, and when Maidstone was an insignificant market town, whose inhabitants subsisted chiefly by agriculture, and long before the cultivation of hops had been heard of. It has seen the opulent establishment of the College in the height of its glory, of which only the crumbling fragments are visible to us. It has seen grave and stately processions accompanying successive prelates to the Palace. It has seen the partial rebuilding of Allington Castle, and it has seen the moated pile become a ruin. Nor has it escaped the effects of the great religious movements that have shaken England to its centre. It has been filled with Popish shrines and rolling incence; it has been despoiled by malcontents, and defaced by Puritans. Yet it remains, a noble monument of the past, and so long as the sound of its bells for prayer echoes along the valley, so long may congregations continue to worship within its sacred walls.

If a criminal sought refuge in All Saints' Church, he received "protection of sanctuary." But the means also existed for effectually punishing offenders against the public peace. The cucking-stool was a frequent source of expense, and the stocks and the pillory were constantly in need of repairs. There was a "cage" for rogues and vagabonds in the High Street, but it does not appear to have fully answered its purpose, for in 1654 it was removed to "the void place beside the Great Bridge stairs." The judges and the bar rode the circuit. At the Kent Assizes there were invariably great numbers of prisoners for trial, and many were condemned to death. The names of footpads figured conspicuously in the gaol calendar; and indeed it was no uncommon thing for travellers to be brought to a halt on country roads by a person, with a black vizard, flourishing a pistol, and bidding them to give up their purses. But there came a time when the robber, without his mask, was brought before the judges at Maidstone, and eventually put in a waggon, with a coffin in it, and drawn to Penenden Heath, there to be handed over to the executioner.

And there are other matters besides—mournful episodes, and incidents of a varied and familiar character—which also illustrate the customs, as well as the spirit, of by-gone times. In the tyrannic reign of Mary, seven men and women, one of them a blind maiden, were one morning dragged along the High Street to the Fair Meadow, where they suffered a cruel death for their religious opinions. Occasionally, actors or players performed in the Meadow, but as the Puritan spirit grew they waned in public favour. To those whose regard the Corporation wished to win, gloves or sugar-loaves, or some such gift, were presented, and sometimes the honorary freedom of the borough was conferred upon them. One of the mayors of the town was Andrew Broughton, who acted as clerk of the court which tried and condemned Charles I., and who built a large house, which still exists, in Earl Street, where he resided till the eve of the Restoration, when he fled to the Continent. The industrious Pepys, one cold morning in March, visited Maidstone, and having obtained a view of the town from the battlements of the church tower, repaired to his inn at the top of Gabriel's Hill, where he was served with a fish dinner, which he no doubt "mightily" enjoyed. Down this hill there often walked a little boy, William Woollett by name, destined to become the most eminent engraver of his time. Hazlitt was born and for a short time resided here. When the protracted war with France was still in progress, George III., resplendent in gold lace, with a long train of attendants, rode through the town, on his way to the Mote Park, to review the assembled Volunteers of Kent. A sumptuous repast was served in the Park, and the King, with his family, and surrounded by his principal Ministers of State, was greeted with the huzzas of thirty thousand spectators. The day was a memorable one, and that evening, as the hop gardens glowed in the setting sun, every road leading from Maidstone was covered with post-horses and creaking coaches, and with homeward-bound pedestrians who had come hither to see the "good old King."

This summary may serve to indicate the variety of interest that surrounds the subject. As regards the plan or arrangement which has been followed in this work, it should be stated that the first chapter comprises an outline of the history of the town from the earliest times down to the end of the fourteenth century. After that date, the history is divided into sections, each section completing to some extent its particular portion of the subject. An anxiety to avoid frequent repetitions, and to facilitate the association of connected facts, has dictated this arrangement.

CHAPTER I.

MAIDSTONE DURING THE MIDDLE AGES.

Roman Remains—Derivation of the Name—Maidstone in the Eleventh Century—Meetings on Penenden Heath—Ancient Courts of Assize—The Hundred—The Manor—Newark Hospital—Convent of Franciscans—The Old Bridge.

THE claim of this locality to the site of the Roman station Vagniacæ, mentioned in the "Itinerary" of the Emperor Antoninus, has been from time to time advanced, and the opinions elicited have usually differed very widely. Camden believed Maidstone to be Vagniacæ, chiefly on the ground that its position corresponded, as he affirmed, with the distances implied in the Roman stages between London and Richborough. In that opinion he has been followed by Gale, Burton, and other antiquaries. The late Rev. Beale Poste, of Tovil, about twenty years ago wrote an elaborate paper to prove that a Roman road went through Maidstone to the Weald, fixing the site of the lost station at a point in the immediate vicinity of Springfield Paper Mill.* Other writers have taken different views; one has placed Vagniacæ at Southfleet, and another has suggested Aylesford as a probable

---

* "Archæologia Cantiana," vol. i.

site, while a third commentator has so far gone astray as to persuade himself that Maidstone, and not Rochester, was the Durobrivæ of the Romans. To these diverse views should be added the hypothesis of one who is especially qualified to express an opinion. "Although it appears to me," says Mr. C. Roach Smith, "that we are more justified in placing Vagniacæ near Springhead, yet I think a Roman road ran near or through the site of Maidstone, probably direct from London, ... and that it branched off in one direction to Rochester, in another towards Loose and Sutton Valence, and that it had vicinal ways, as indeed all the main roads must have had."* The whole question is involved in obscurity, and while it gives full scope for ingenious conjecture, one can afford, in examining it, to be deferential rather than dogmatic.†

Lambarde, our earliest Kentish topographer, says: "Forasmuch as I find not this place above once named in any ancient history, and but seldom mentioned in any ancient records that I have seen, I dare not pronounce any great antiquity of it."‡ But though Maidstone may not have been a military station of the Romans, there is reason to believe, from its important local position and from ancient remains which have been found, that it was a place of some consequence during the Roman occupation of this country. These relics may here be noted. In 1715 several Roman urns and bottles were discovered at the lower end of Earl Street, and urns were also found in Havock Lane towards the end of the last century, and at St. Faith's Green in the year 1819. About the latter date, part of a Roman shield, a

---

* "Archæologia Cantiana," vol. x., p. 171.
† Mado, another Roman station, has also been supposed to refer to Maidstone.
‡ "Perambulation of Kent," written in 1570, and published in 1576, p. 195.

brooch, and several coins, were unearthed near the site of Wheeler Street. Between the months of November 1859 and March 1860, while a piece of ground was being trenched at the back of the present Grammar School, at a point about five hundred yards west by north of All Saints' Church, more than two dozen human skeletons were dug up, as well as about a hundred and fifty Roman urns and coins. In 1822 a small image of bronze and a lamp, both Roman, were found in a garden adjoining St. Peter's Church. Newton tells us that while some men were at work at Vinters, in the early part of last century, they came upon what was considered to be a Roman burying place. Remains of Roman villas have been found in the neighbourhood of the town—one at Little Buckland, and others in proximity to the London and Chatham Railway bridge, Barming Church, and Allington Castle. In 1870 the foundations of a residence, clearly traceable to the Roman period, were excavated in a hop garden near Upper Stone Street, on the left of the Loose Road in going from the town, and a little beyond the junction of the road to Tovil. The walls of several rooms could be traced with great distinctness, and appeared to have formed parts of an extensive villa.

Let us next notice the name of Maidstone. The Romans, during their occupation, did not trouble themselves with the names of places, and Taylor remarks that we rarely find any place in Britain denoted by a name which is merely Roman. They conquered, but the Saxons who succeeded them were more bent on colonising the country, and they regulated the names of places by their own language, and with reference to their position. Maidstone in Saxon times was called *Medwegestun*, meaning "Medway's town." Lambarde tells us that in an ancient Saxon book which he had seen on the bridge-work at Rochester, it was written *Mægwanstane*, "that is to say, the mighty or strong stone, a name (belike) given for the quarries of hard stone there." In Domesday Book, which dates from the eleventh century, the name is given as *Meddestane*, which means, says Newton, the "mid town, or town in the middle of Kent;" while in the law reports of Edward I.'s reign it is spelt *Maydenestan*, which has been supposed to signify the "town of maidens," an idea which is also wittily embodied in an ancient Latin rhyme.* Now when we consider that the Saxons, like other nations, frequently named their places from contiguous rivers, there can be little hesitation in concluding that Maidstone derives its name from the Medway, being, in fact, Medway's town, or the town on the Medway.†

What the appearance of Maidstone was during the succeeding centuries of Anglo-Saxon rule, when Kent was the free prey of any lawless tribe, and how its inhabitants were affected by the evangelising movement of St. Augustine and his monks, as, in the remote years of the Heptarchy, they journeyed from Canterbury, singing their Latin litanies, it is impossible to ascertain, since no information of any description has come down to us. Yet when we remember that a great and decisive battle was fought near the spot where Kit's Coty House stands, it may be inferred that the little rude village, scattered, as Maidstone would then be, along the eastern bank of the Medway, passed through many vicissitudes, the peculiarities of its situation affording easy access to the ruthless invader.

As we approach the close of the eleventh century, we are able, with the aid of Domesday Book, to penetrate with some degree of success the bewildering mists of eight hundred

---

* The old seal of Maidstone represents a maiden standing on a stone.
†Kilburne, in his "Survey of Kent," 1659, says that Allington Castle was called the "Castle of the Medway."

years. The survey of Domesday, made by order of William the Conqueror in the years 1085 and 1086, supplies some interesting details respecting Maidstone, and if the obsolete and somewhat ambiguous terms in which these particulars are described should tend to increase the difficulty of elucidating them, we may still form a pretty distinct idea of the state of things which then existed. Prior to the Norman invasion, the value of land here as elsewhere in Kent was exceedingly low. In the reign of Hardicanute, the last of the Danish line of English sovereigns, the annual value of Maidstone manor was £12, and it was estimated at £14 in the year 1066, when Edward the Confessor died. Twenty years later a decided change for the better had been brought about. The venerable Lanfranc, Archbishop of Canterbury, was lord of the manor, as well as of several other manors in this district. The manor of Maidstone had risen to the yearly value of £35 10s. It is entered in Domesday for ten sulings or solins, a measure of land peculiar to Kent, from *sul*, a plough. As a suling may have been equal to 160 acres, it is probable that 1,600 acres represent the extent of land thus enumerated. Of these, the demesne lands, reserved for the archbishop's immediate use, appear to have amounted to more than 900 acres, the remainder being held under him by three knights in military service. There was arable soil sufficient for thirty teams, in addition to twenty-three acres of meadow, and woodland for the pannage of fifty-three hogs. Upwards of a hundred persons were engaged in agricultural pursuits. On the archbishop's holding there were twenty-five villains, or compulsory tenants, whose rents were paid chiefly in agricultural services, twenty-one bordars, or labourers, and ten serfs; while thirty-two villains, ten bordars, and ten serfs were employed on the knights' land. We have also a brief account of other branches of labour in which the inhabitants were engaged, mention being made of two saltworks, and several mills and fisheries. The latter, for which capacious weirs were required, formed one of the minor industries of those times. "Sticks" of eels were often tendered for rent, a stick containing twenty-five eels. The entry in Domesday Book, relating to Maidstone, runs thus:—

"The archbishop holds Meddestane. It answers for ten sulings. There is the arable land of thirty teams. In demesne there are three teams; and twenty-five villains, with twenty-one bordars, have twenty-five teams. The number of serfs, ten. There are five mills of 36s. 8d.; two fisheries of 270 eels. Of meadow there are ten acres; and wood of thirty hogs. A church there.

"Of this manor three knights hold of the archbishop four sulings, and have there three and a half teams in demesne. Thirty-two villains, with ten bordars, have six teams. Number of serfs, ten. They have a mill of 5s.; thirteen acres of meadow; two and a half fisheries of 180 eels; two saltworks; and wood of twenty-three hogs.

"In aggregate value, in the time of King Edward, the manor was worth £14; when he received it, £12. The demesne of the archbishop is now worth £20; that of the knights, £15 10s. The monks of Canterbury have 20s. every year from two tenants of this manor."

A comparison of some of the above figures with those in Domesday referring to other manors in this part of Kent, shows the relative superiority, more or less, of Maidstone in the year 1086. If, for the sake of simplicity, we take the value of the manor at £36, we find that this sum was £5 less than the yearly value of the manor of East Farleigh, £4 more than Boxley, £9 more than Aylesford, and £32 more than either East Barming or West Malling. The number of villains and bordars engaged on Maidstone Manor was eighty-eight; fifty-nine were employed at Boxley, forty-five at Aylesford, eleven at West Malling, thirteen at East Barming, and as many as 108 at East Farleigh. Nor are we without the means of forming an opinion as to the provision made for public worship. It is not improbable that the church which is mentioned as existing at Maidstone was the building which was dedicated to St. Mary, and on or near the site of which the present church of All Saints was erected three centuries later. The only other churches in this district of which Domesday speaks were at West Farleigh, East Farleigh, and West Malling; and these were probably sufficient for the limited requirements of the time. The population was everywhere scanty. Maidstone consisted of but few houses, possibly not more than a hundred, which, according to the English custom, would be included in the archbishop's demesne. The whole population of Kent at this period has been estimated by Ellis, Henshall, and other expounders of Domesday, at about thirteen thousand.

Maidstone owed much of its importance to its river and its central position in the county. The advantages which it possesses in this respect were early recognized. The first county courts and county meetings were held on Penenden Heath,* a common lying partly in the parish of Maidstone and partly in Boxley parish, about a mile to the north-east of the town. Penenden has many ghastly memories. The name signifies in Saxon the "place of penalty."† Long before the Norman invasion malefactors received their sentence and were also executed there, and down to the year 1830, with occasional intermissions, criminals convicted of capital offences were hanged on the heath. It is stated in Domesday that if the landed proprietors in the county "shall be warned to convene at a shiremote, they shall go to Penenden, not farther." The shiremote or sheriff's court was held on the

---

* From the root *pen*, a head or point. In England hills bearing this name are numerous.

† Greenwood's "Epitome of County History," 1838, vol. i., p. 174.

heath three times a year, and the attendance of the bishops earls, provosts, and other dignitaries was rendered compulsory. Before the chief men thus assembled, the principal civil and criminal cases were brought, and such as were beyond the competence of the Hundreds, which were important divisions for the administration of justice. The late Mr. Larking believed that a mound still to be seen in the grounds of Foley House—formerly part of the heath—marks the spot on which these ancient courts were held.*

Every reader of Kentish history has a vivid recollection of a famous court which met on the heath in the year 1076. Odo, Bishop of Bayeux, and Earl of Kent, had from time to time by an unscrupulous exercise of power, appropriated lands belonging to the See of Canterbury, until his possessions had enormously increased in extent and value, including the manors of Otham, Thurnham, Wateringbury, Boughton, West Farleigh, and other lands in this part of the county. He was the uterine brother of William the Conqueror, and being also a personal favourite of the king, was at first entrusted with the government of the country during the latter's temporary absence in Normandy. A daring and avaricious minister, careful of his own aggrandizement, he had abundant opportunities for enriching himself at the expense of others. But Archbishop Lanfranc, who had succeeded to the See six years before, also stood high in the king's favour, and irritated by Odo's extortion, he at length represented to his Majesty the injury sustained by his church. William saw the reasonableness of the appeal, and forthwith directed an inquiry to be made by his leading prelates and advisers.

The place of meeting was Penenden Heath, and there

---

* "Domesday Book of Kent," 1869, by the Rev. L. B. Larking, M.A.

on the appointed day the great personages assembled. The king was represented by Geoffery, a Norman bishop. Two other bishops were present, Arnost of Rochester, and Ægelric of Chichester, who was renowned for his extensive knowledge of the law, and who, on account of his advanced age, was by royal mandate conveyed thither in a waggon. Richard de Tonbridge, the eldest son of a Norman baron, who was the owner of East Barming and many lordships, and Hugh de Montfort, who had fought by the King's side at the battle of Hastings, and whose descendants distinguished themselves in the Crusades and the wars of the barons, also attended to lend the weight of their great influence. The presence of William de Arces, Haimo Vicecomes, and other barons of the king and the archbishop, with many tenants of the bishops, completed the representative character of the assembly. Lanfranc was present to plead the cause of his church, while Odo, in person, defended himself from the accusation of the injured primate. The trial lasted three days, and the decision was given in the Archbishop's favour. He recovered several of the original possessions of the See, not only from Odo, but from two other tenants-in-chief of the King, Radulfus de Curva Spina and Hugh de Montfort, and the liberties existing between the church and the Crown were defined and established. Lambarde observes that the example of this illustrious assembly led to other meetings on the Heath, and he seems to imply that no public gatherings were previously held there, but he is mistaken, since it is known that even before the Conquest county courts and other meetings were held on Penenden Heath. This was the last cause tried on the heath involving the rights of the church.

It should be observed that the civil division of the county was into Laths, Hundreds, and "boroughs." The Lath is peculiar to Kent, and is synonymous with a "rape" in Sussex, and a "riding" in Yorkshire. It was divided into Hundreds, and the Hundreds again were divided into boroughs. Many a chapter has been written on the Hundred, but nearly all ending in conjecture, though bearing witness for its name to a division of number and population. It is of very great antiquity, far earlier than the days of King Alfred. On the authority of the survey of Domesday, we know that Maidstone was a Hundred, and that it formed part of the Lath of Aylesford, as at the present day. The Hundred of Maidstone included that parish, and the parishes of Boxley, Detling, Loose, Linton, East Farleigh, East and West Barming, with their churches, and part of the parishes of Bearsted, Hunton, Marden, and Staplehurst.

Thus Maidstone not only had its shiremote, or superior court for the whole county, but its Hundred court for the local business of the Hundred. The king was the supreme judge, and the final appeal was to him. Itinerant judges did not exist under Anglo-Saxon sovereigns, who often sent their commissioners to assist in the administration of justice. The jurisdiction of these local courts was, however, greatly restricted towards the end of the twelfth century, when the practice was adopted of sending Justices to each county for the purpose of holding courts of assize. These Justices in Eyre, as they were called, at first performed their journeys once every seven years, but after the passing of Magna Charta they made the circuit of the kingdom once a year. These courts were first held at Canterbury and Rochester, and sometimes at Maidstone, East Greenwich, Dartford, Sevenoaks, and the Lowry of Tonbridge as a distinct liberty. One of the Justices in 1343 was Sir John Lord Cobham, brother-in-law to Archbishop Courtenay, and who then possessed the manor of Chillington. Fifteen days' notice of the

Justice's arrival was given, and by an arrangement between the sheriff, coroners, and constables, on the one hand, and the knights on the other, two classes of juries appear to have meanwhile been chosen out of the Hundreds, viz., a jury of inquiry, who probably fulfilled the duties discharged by our constabulary or Justices of the peace; and an accusatory jury, whose duty it was to sit in judgment on the prisoners, or to exercise the functions of our grand jury.* A fine sight it must have been to see the Justice's cavalcade proceeding to the assize town where his commission was to be executed. Preceded by the circuit-porter, bearing in his hand a goodly ebony wand, rode the clerks of the judge, gentlemen well skilled in the curious Norman-French and Law-Latin of the day. They were followed by the grave clerk of assize and his officers, with well-secured saddle bags. Then came the Justice, riding upon a mule, and clothed in a long red coat of the finest broadcloth, the sleeves and collar being thickly embroidered with gold. A train of serving-men, with three or four sumpter-horses, wound up the procession.

It was the duty of the Justice before he quitted the town, to assess tallages upon the inhabitants, either collectively or individually, for the benefit of the Crown; and customs upon the import and export of goods, as well as a right of taking two casks out of each freight of wine, were at one time exacted These imposts, which were irregularly levied, caused no little public annoyance. Attempts were sometimes made to evade them, and from the Plea Rolls we learn that in the reign of Henry III., cloth and wines were sold in Maidstone "contrary to assize," one of the offenders being a linen draper. How the recalcitrant tradesmen were chastised we are not told, but it may be presumed that their interview

---

* "History of the Weald of Kent," by Robert Furley, vol. ii, p. 171.

with the judge at the next assize was not particularly agreeable.

In those days, however, and for long afterwards, there were lawful ways of escaping the wrath of "my lord the king's justice." We read in the Plea Rolls, for instance, that about the middle of the thirteenth century, five persons were implicated in the murder of a man in the neighbourhood of Maidstone, and one of them took refuge in the church. This refers to the "benefit of sanctuary," which afforded protection for a limited period to criminals fleeing to a church or certain boundaries surrounding it. While the protection thereby given often enabled criminals to defy the civil power, it was not unfrequently the means of preserving the innocent, and, in the case of guilty persons, of giving time for the first heat of resentment to pass before redress could be sought. Closely connected with this privilege was the practice of "abjuration of the realm," which permitted the criminal who took the benefit of sanctuary, to go in penitence, within forty days afterwards, before the coroner, and to take an oath to quit the country, and not return without the king's licence. A port was assigned to him for embarcation, to which he must immediately repair, with a cross in his hand, knowing that the penalty for returning without the royal permission, was death.

There are several instances of the exercise of these privileges in Maidstone between the years 1241 and 1255. One Ralph Cobbe put himself into the church, confessed that he was a thief of many thefts, and abjured the realm before the coroner; and a similar course was followed by another person, who had killed a woman by striking her on the head with a club. Again, Juliana de Budehurst, who had participated in a murder, was imprisoned in the archbishop's gaol at Maidstone, but escaped therefrom to the church at

Detling, and confessing her guilt, abjured the realm before the coroner. It is also recorded that a person who was accused of murder took refuge in Maidstone church, and then absconded, and that another person was apprehended on the same charge, and immured in the archbishop's prison, but escaped, and putting himself in the church here, confessed the deed. An amusing case is related of a collision of authority between the bailiffs of the king and the archbishop. A person in Maidstone Hundred was in debt to the Crown, but as he seems to have disputed the claim, the king's bailiff brought matters to a crisis by distraining upon his property. No sooner were a number of cattle seized, than the archbishop's bailiff sent several men to re-take them, or, failing that, to take the king's bailiff. But the order was adroitly executed upon themselves, for the king's bailiff, with the assistance of his clerk and others, captured the archbishop's men. He then drove the cattle towards Rochester, and remained for the night at Wateringbury. On the morrow, however, reprisals were exacted. Other men from the archbishop's demesne re-took the cattle, and led several of the king's party captives to Maidstone. At the same time they seized a plough, yoked with oxen, on the land of the king's bailiff, in the Hundred of Brenchley, and brought it to Maidstone, where it was detained until the demands of justice were satisfied. The king's bailiff was afterwards beaten with a stick round Maidstone church on three Sundays—a form of corporal punishment which doubtless had the merit of being roughly effective.*

The manner in which the laws were administered in the Hundreds in the thirteenth century occasioned many abuses. An obnoxious practice which had long prevailed was the farm-

---

* Plea Rolls, temp. Henry III.

ing out of the appointments of sheriff, coroner, and of other officers, to the highest bidder. It is not surprising that under such a system taxes were illegally imposed, and that lands were sometimes taken from their lawful owners by rapacious escheators. So notorious and intolerable had these practices become, that when Edward I. succeeded to the throne he commanded an inquiry to be made into the rights of the king and the excesses of coroners, escheators, sheriffs, and other servants of the Crown. The reports of the royal commissioners are given in the Hundred Rolls for the year 1274, and Mr. R. Furley, in his "History of the Weald of Kent," has been at much pains to reproduce and elucidate such of them as relate to a large part of the county. From the portion of the Roll which refers to the Maidstone Hundred, we gather that the manor of Maidstone, which formerly, as we have seen, belonged to the archbishop, had been seized by the escheator, in name of the Crown, without the king's authority. Particulars are also given as to the nature of the tenure by which some of the lands in the Hundred were held. Thus we read that one William de Borveling held an estate *in capite*, *i. e.*, immediately of the Crown; and that the heirs of John le Walays held Weavering Street in "sergeanty." In feudal times there were two descriptions of sergeanty—petty sergeanty, a species of tenure at a nominal rent, consisting of some small implement of war, as a bow or a pair of spurs; and grand sergeanty, the form apparenty alluded to here, which involved attendance on the king in war, and at other times when summoned. The record is as follows:—

"This Hundred is in the Archbishop's hands, and when it is amerced before the Justices in Eyre, the king has a fourth part.

"The Lord Osbert de Lungchamp, knight, holds certain land called Ovenhelle [Overhill] by the service of following the king in his army into Wales for forty days at his own cost, with one horse of the value of 5s., and with one sack of the value of 6d., and with a bottle to the same sack. The heirs of John le Walays hold land called Weveringe in sergeanty by the same service. The Abbot of Boxle does not permit the heirs of Weveringe, who hold that sergeanty, to have common in the pasture of Pynendenne [Penenden Heath], whereby the sergeanty is diminished every year to the value of 5s. William de Borveling holds a fee of the king *in capite*.

"The Abbot of Boxle has withdrawn all his tenants from the Hundred courts of the king at Merdenne and Cranebroke, who were wont to do suit there, for sixteen years past and more.

"Christ Church [Canterbury] has withdrawn its tenants of Bademindene from Brenchesle [Brenchley] Hundred, those of La Knocke and Chilintune from Merdenne Hundred, and those of Stokebery from Twyferde Hundred.

"The Archbishop and Prior of Christ Church have royal liberties.

"The Abbot of Begeham receives 20s. from the fee farm of Detling, which would be to the king's damage if the wardship of the heir of the Lord of Becking were in the king's hands by vacancy of the archbishopric.

"The manors of Maydenstan, Ferlygh, and Lose, and a certain manor of the Prior of Christ Church, were seized into the king's hands by the escheator, without the king's precept."

The seizure of Maidstone manor here referred to, might have been an illegal one; but Philipott suggests, though without giving a reason, that the manor had ceased to be a part of the ecclesiastical domains upwards of seventy years before this time.* We have not been able to find any confirmation of Philipott's assertion; and it can hardly be assumed that the manor had changed hands at the date he mentions. It was about this time that William de Cornhill presented a house at Maidstone to the See of Canterbury, as a residence for the archbishops. Domesday Book tells us that the

---

* "Villare Cantianum," 1659, p. 228.

archbishop was in possession in the year 1086; it is certain that he held lands here in the thirteenth and fourteenth centuries; and we know that the manor was finally alienated from the Church in the reign of Henry VIII. Moreover, the growing ecclesiastical importance of Maidstone, and the warm interest evinced in its welfare by succeeding primates, culminating in the erection of a splendid Church and the establishment of the College, militate against the supposition that the manor had, for any considerable length of time, become the property of the Crown or of a private individual.

Down to the reign of Henry III. there had been no ecclesiastical establishments in the town.* But in the year 1260 Archbishop Boniface founded a hospital at Newark, in the West Borough,† in honour of Saints Peter and Paul.‡ In ancient times hospitals differed in their aim and scope from modern institutions of that name. They were intended for the shelter and refreshment of travellers, as well as the support of the helpless and indigent. This one at Maidstone was established for the benefit of poor pilgrims. Connected with it, there is reason to suppose, was a small chapel, a beautiful specimen of the Early Pointed style, which, after remaining in a dilapidated state for a long series of years, was in 1836 restored and enlarged into the present church of St. Peter. The Hospital was doubtless a convenient place of resort for the numerous pilgrims who made

---

* Gervase of Canterbury, in his Chronicle, as edited by Dr. Stubbs, and published in 1879, says that in the year 1196 Archbishop Hubert proposed to found a church of secular priests at Maidstone, but owing to the opposition of the monks the project was abandoned.—"Chronica Gervasii," vol. ii., p. 537. Dr. Stubbs observes that Gervase became a monk in 1163, and if, as he supposes, Gervase was brother to Thomas de Maidstone, another Monk, the family from which they sprung may, he thinks, be referred to this town. "Maidstone," he adds, "was not an unlikely place to have furnished a contingent of monks to Christ Church."

† Poste, p. 1; Newton, p. 31.

‡ Tanner's "Notitia Monastica," p. 224.

pious journeys to the shrine of Thomas à Becket. It was, if we may judge from records in the Lambeth Registers, moderately endowed. Its annual value is stated to have been £5 6s., and the tithes of the chapels of East Farleigh, Linton, and Sutton-by-Dover were appropriated to its use. The managing body of the Hospital consisted of a master and brethren, whose corporate existence was secured by letters patent. Stephen de Wingham was one of the brethren sometime during the last half of the fourteenth century. The following is a list of masters, with the date of their appointment:—

Robert de Bradegare	1272
William de Sele	1282
Michael de Wydewode	1304
John de Englichman	1311
Thomas Jordan	1312
John de Waltham	1324
William de Maldon	1326
Martin de Ixning	1333
Richard de Norwich	1349
Simon de Bredon	1357
Thomas Yonge	1372
William Bisynge	1377
John Ludham[*]	1380

Corrodies or pensions were regularly granted out of the revenue of the Hospital, the recipients being usually persons who were or had been in holy orders. Philip de Milton was a recipient in 1353, Hugo Cayley in 1361, Robert Goldclne in 1365, William Chaundler in 1363, John Wales, of Sevenoaks, and John Speckhawk in 1368, John Walleys, of Sevenoaks, in 1369, William Colbrook and John Cozens, an old servant of the archbishop, in 1376, and Roger Cornwaile in 1380. John de Waltham, who had been master for two years, was granted an annual pension on the 11th of July

---

[*] Also previously master of the Hospital of St. Thomas, at Canterbury.

1326. One of the registers at Lambeth Palace states that on the 4th of January, 1280, a letter was written to the master of the Hospital, empowering him to sequestrate the revenues of the church of Maidstone. There is also preserved at Lambeth Palace the will, dated 1389, of John Ludham, one of the Masters. From this we learn that John Whyteclyve, an intimate friend of Archbishop Islip, was a great benefactor to the Hospital. Whyteclyve was vicar of Mayfield from 1361 to 1380, warden of Canterbury Hall, Oxford, in 1365, and subsequently prebendary of Chichester. While on a visit to Maidstone in 1383 he was taken suddenly ill at the house of William Topclyve, at Shoford,* which appears to have been situated on the east side of the town. Topclyve had in the previous year obtained a license from the crown to castellate or fortify his house, which had been damaged by the rebels under Wat Tyler.† The illness of Whyteclyve rapidly assumed a mortal form, and at midnight on the 12th of November his friends were summoned to his bedside to receive his directions regarding the disposition of the property, which he wished to be devoted to pious uses, for the good of his soul. By his own desire, he was buried in the chapel of the Hospital at Maidstone. At the time of his death Whyteclyve was rector of Horsted Keynes, near East Grinstead.

Another religious house, though of a different order, was established at Maidstone early in the fourteenth century, namely, a monastery or convent of Franciscans. There is some doubt as to the precise date of the foundation, but the

---

* According to an indenture in the Public Record Office, dated February 6, 1552, the "manor of Shoford," with other lands in the neighbourhood of Maidstone, was sold by William Rooper, of Eltham, for £207 to William Warham, of Southton, Sir Anthony St. Leger, K.G., of Ulcombe, and John Lennard, of Chevening.—Close Rolls, 481.

† In the will of John Wodehull, rector of Orpington Church, A.D. 1382, William Topclyve is named as one of his executors.

year 1331 has, with some plausibility, been mentioned. Among the Letters Patent of Edward III. is a license for the building of an oratory and mansion at Maidstone, for which purpose two messuages and six acres of land were conveyed to the guardian and brethren of the institute. This is further alluded to in the supplement to Dugdale's "Monasticon," which states that the monastery was founded by the king and his brother the Earl of Cornwall. Beyond these meagre statements, nothing is known of the foundation. It is generally supposed to have stood at the top of Gabriel's Hill, where a vault and other remains of what must at one time have been a building of some consequence, may still be seen. In 1670 this house was rated at 1s. for the parish church assessment. Down to the beginning of last century it appears to have been in a tolerable state of preservation, and Newton mentions that the owner of it used to say that in his deeds it was called the Priory or Friary. It is probable that the brethren belonging to the convent here were transferred to Walsingham, in Norfolk, whither in 1345, says Hasted,* Edward III. obtained leave of the Pope to remove many of the Franciscans.

Permanent surnames were not much in use until after the Norman Conquest, when persons were often designated from their habitations. Ralph de Maidstone, reputed to have been born here, is described by Wike as "Vir magnæ literaturæ et in theologiâ nomanitissimus;" he was consecrated Bishop of Hereford in the year 1234. Five years after, he exchanged his mitre for a cowl, and became a Franciscan at Oxford; he finally retired to a convent at Gloucester, where in 1245 he died. John de Maidstone was dean of Lincoln in 1274.† In 1311 Walter de Maidstone obtained the king's

---

* "History of Kent," vol. iii., p. 117, fol. edit.; see also Stevens's "Supplement to the Monasticon," vol. i., p. 155.

† John de Maidstone was a monk of Canterbury in 1239.—"Monumenta Franciscana."

license to fortify his mansion at Maidstone; he was possibly identical with the person who, bearing the same name, was bishop of Worcester in 1317. Walter de Maidstone was sub-dean of Lincoln in 1329. Another person of the same name, a monk in Faversham Abbey in 1367, was afterwards canon of Christ Church, Canterbury. One Walter de Maidstone annexed the church of Powyke to the Priory of Great Malvern. In the last decade of the thirteenth century, Robert de Maidstone owned a portion of the revenue attached to the church of Romsey, in the archdeaconry of Winchester*; he was subsequently canon of Winchester. William de Maidstone was abbot of Faversham Abbey in 1366.† Among the noted writers of Kent in the fourteenth century were Radolfus and Richard Maidstone. The latter, who was born here, was a monk of the order of Carmelites, at the Friars, Aylesford, where he died in 1396, and was buried in the cloister of that monastery. One of the valets of Edward I. was William de Maidstone, of whom it is stated that he was sent with important despatches to the Court of Rome, and died on the journey thither. In 1397 Thomas de Maidstone was canon of the Priory of Leeds, in Kent; he is mentioned in a bull of Pope Boniface IX. as being one of a party of canons and other ecclesiastics who laid violent hands on John de Stapley, a monk in the Abbey of St. Albans. Clement de Maidstone was a retainer of Richard Scrope, and wrote an account of the martyrdom of that prelate. John de Maidstone was dean of Chichester in the year 1400; and the same name occurs

---

* His portion was taxed by the Pope at £20.—"Taxatio Ecclesiastica."

† There was formerly an altar tomb in Ulcombe church to the memory of William de Maidstone, inlaid with his portraiture and armorial bearings in brass, and dated 1429. A person of this name was esquire to Lady Despenser in 1405, and offered to support by combat that lady's charges of high crimes against the Duke of York.

in a list of archdeacons of Bedford and Oxford for the fifteenth century.*

The Archbishops of Canterbury are reputed, not without reason, to have been generous benefactors to the town. We have seen that in the early part of the thirteenth century they began to pay frequent visits to the place, which under their friendly auspices was gradually developing its physical resources and increasing in population. It has been shown that at the close of William the Conqueror's reign the manor was valued at £35 10s. In the course of the two succeeding centuries it greatly increased in value, for we find in the Pope's taxation of the See in 1291†, that the manor is returned at £93 16s. 11d., while the church of Maidstone with its chapels is taxed at £106 13s. 4d., exceeding all the other churches in the diocese, except Minster in the Isle of Thanet and Reculver.

Thirty years before the latter date, the inhabitants had received a fresh proof of the favour with which they were regarded by the archbishops. In 1261 Archbishop Boniface obtained a grant from Henry III. to hold a weekly market at Maidstone, on a piece of ground called Petrisfield, a corruption of *Peter's*-field, one of the Saints to whom the Hospital was dedicated. Markets and fairs were then held in churchyards, or near them.‡ The document by which this privilege was conferred is still preserved, one of the

---

* Nathaniel Bacon, a member of the Long Parliament, and who is supposed to have been the author of an anonymous work on the government of England, for which the publisher was outlawed, married Elizabeth Maidstone. John Maidstone was in 1644 agent to the Earl of Manchester, general of the Parliamentary forces. On March 24, 1659, he wrote a long letter on the civil war to John Winthorp, governor of Connecticut; which letter is printed among Thurloe's State Papers.

† "Taxatio Ecclesiastica."

‡ In the Maidstone Museum there is a charter, bearing date of 1413, by which the relict of John Fuller, of Maidstone, grants a messuage, situated in "the market," to Richard Propechaunt, of Maidstone, and Robert Vyne, of East Sutton.

witnesses who signs it being John Mansell, afterwards rector of St. Mary's. It directs that the market is to be held on Thursday, on which day, singularly enough, the market is still held. Subsequent grants have confirmed the original license, but there is no reason to suppose that the day has ever been changed. The market quotations of Maidstone and the neighbourhood are curious. In the latter part of the thirteenth century, an ox could be bought for 15s.,* and the price of horses ranged from 10s. to £1 each. Six pounds of wheat sold for a penny, but in 1356 wheat brought 6s. per quarter. In 1320 oats averaged from 2s. to 3s. 6d. per quarter; and about the same time beer, such as it then was, made without hops, and spiced with pepper and other condiments, was retailed at a penny a gallon. A good ploughman could be had in 1270 for 6s. or 7s. a year, and an excellent bailiff for 10s., exclusive of diet.† The charges for the conveyance of goods were in proportion. About the year 1330, three thousand tiles were conveyed from Maidstone to Leeds—five miles—for 3s., while the cost of conveying four carrots [cart-loads] of lead from the Thames to Maidstone, and from Maidstone to Leeds, was 8s.

But though substantial advantages may have accrued to the neighbourhood from the institution of a weekly market, the difficulty of passing freely across the Medway at all times of the year was probably felt to be a hindrance to the general progress of the town.‡ Accordingly a stone

---

* This would probably be equal to £25 in our present money. £10 or £20 was then reckoned a fair income for a gentleman. Thirty-five or thirty-six may be a proper multiple, in order to bring the prices given above to a level with those of the present day.

† " History of Agriculture and Prices in England," by Professor Rogers.

‡ Ferry boats must have been in use on the Medway for centuries before even a wooden bridge was built, when the only means of conveying to Maidstone and Rochester the oak timber felled in the Weald was by rafts. In the fourteenth century the erection of bridges was encouraged by grants of ecclesiastical indulgences to the wealthy laity.

bridge, wide enough for one vehicle to pass at a time, was built over the river. It had nine low pointed arches, which were in course of time reduced to five in number, and converted into the semi-circular form.* The exact date of this improvement has baffled the researches of every Kentish historian and antiquary. Lambarde, who wrote, it should be remembered, upwards of three hundred years ago, says: "Of the bridge I can find no beginning, but I suspect that it rose by the archbishops, who were not only owners of the Palace, but lords and patrons of the whole town and church also. Neither is it unlikely," he adds, "that it received help from Archbishop Courtenay, of whom it is recorded [by Leland] that he builded at Maidstone somewhat besides the College." Similar inferences have been drawn by subsequent writers, and a survey of the surrounding circumstances seems to point to the conclusion that the bridge was constructed in the fourteenth century. It was about this time that Maidstone rose into ecclesiastical distinction. The archbishops had from an early period maintained here a gaol for the confinement of offenders belonging to the Hundred and adjoining districts; and the meadow on the other side of the river, opposite the Palace, was the archbishop's park, which was leased out for pasturage.† On the site of the old palace, a building of goodly dimensions had been raised. Towards the close of the century a College of secular canons was founded, for which a palatial structure was erected; while the ancient parochial church of St. Mary was built anew, and dedicated to All Saints. Almost concurrently the Hospital was dissolved,

---

* Clement Taylor Smythe's Collection of MSS., printed papers, &c., in Maidstone Museum, vol. iii., fol. 194.

† In the year 1258 Robert de Hugham held under Archbishop Boniface six acres of meadow at Maidstone, worth annually about 6s. 6d.

and its endowment merged into that of the new and larger monastic institution.

These changes mark a distinct epoch in the history of the town. The archbishops indeed would appear to have been the prime movers in every great work, and it is not unreasonable to suppose that, some years before the erection of the College and All Saints' Church, the bridge was built in order to facilitate communication between the eastern and western portions of the parish. There can be little doubt that the undertaking received much assistance from them. This view is borne out by the fact that the heavy tax which had previously been imposed on Maidstone for the repair of the timber bridge at Rochester was abolished in the reign of Richard II, through the munificence of Sir John de Cobham and Sir Robert Knolles, who built a bridge of stone over the Medway at Rochester, and, with other donors, endowed the corporation of the Bridge Wardens with large estates for its maintenance. When it is also considered that during the demolition of the bridge at Maidstone in 1879, a silver coin of the reign of Edward III. was found in the original portion of the structure, some distance below the roadway, we may conjecture that the bridge dates from the fourteenth century.

It may well be thought that local prosperity was aided materially by the erection of a stone bridge. Workmen were busy in the quarries around Maidstone, and the ragstone which was dug here was already celebrated for its enduring qualities. The freestone of Maidstone was used in the building of a private house in London in 1355. In a lease of Packman's Wharf, Thames Street, made in that year, the lessee, Richard Wyllesdon, covenants to make cellars seven feet high, and to build above them a chief dwelling-place, viz., a hall forty feet in length and twenty-four feet wide, and a parlour, kitchen, and buttery, the material to be employed being Maidstone ragstone. For the repair of Rochester castle in 1367 Ralph Crompe, of Maidstone, supplied 1,850¼ tons of stone, and was paid for the same £37 0s. 2¼d.; and Hugh Stace, another stone-dealer, quarried 2,289¼ tons, for which he charged £47 13s. 11½d., at 5d. per ton. With the spanning of the Medway by a stone bridge, a fresh impetus was doubtless given to the industry of these primitive quarrymen.

Publicity by litigation was not unknown, and in the Lansdowne Collection the particulars are given of a number of local cases tried at Westminster in the reign of Edward II.[*] In one of these cases, Alice and Walter de Frendesbury, and Emma, wife of Walter, were the plaintiffs, and Thomas le Taillur, the defendant; the matter in dispute being the ownership of a messuage, with appurtenances, in Maidstone. Thomas, we are told, admitted the right of the plaintiffs, and granted the property to them and to the heirs of Walter, and received £5 for the concession. In another case, Hamo de Tancto was the plaintiff, and Richard le Mareschal, of Benyngton, and Johanna, his wife, the defendants, when Hamo set up a claim to eight acres of land, three-parts of a messuage, and a moiety of one acre of wood, in East Farleigh and Maidstone. Eventually the defendants admitted the claim, and granted the property to Hamo and his heirs, and received for themselves and the heirs of Richard £10 for the concession. In a third case John le Bretoun and Alice his wife, sued John Attehelle and Agnes his wife, in reference to the ownership of a tenement, twelve acres of land, and an acre of wood, in the parish of Maidstone. Here again the defendants admitted the right of the plaintiffs, but the grant

---

[*] See "Archæologia Cantiana," vols. xii and xiii.

was made to the former, by service of a rose at the Nativity of St. John the Baptist, and after their death the property was to revert to John and Alice and to their heirs. There is a monotonous similarity in all the cases, and to state the bald facts of each of them would only weary the reader without adding appreciably to his knowledge.

CHAPTER II.

THE THREE KENTISH REBELLIONS.

Wat Tyler and Jack Straw—Breaking into Maidstone Gaol—Death of Tyler—The Rising under Jack Cade—Wyatt's Rebellion—Allington Castle—Wyatt and his Adherents at Maidstone: the Queen's Troops sent against them—Victory of the Insurgents: their Advance upon London—Surrender of Wyatt: his Death.

THE first of these rebellions broke out during the minority of Richard II., and cast a dark shadow on the year 1381. Although in Kent the system of land tenure was in some respects less rigorous than that which prevailed in other counties, yet the feudal customs were pressing with great severity upon the people. As the serf of the lord of the soil, the agricultural labourer was sold with the stock on the land, or as a separate chattel. His children were in bondage like himself, and could be claimed by his master at any time. There were in towns free workmen and free labourers, but their number was small. Acts of Parliament fixed the wages of all classes of workmen and labourers; and any man who quitted his work without leave was promptly apprehended and put in the stocks. An ordinance made about the year 1370 directs that saddlers, skinners, and tanners shall be "chastised for charging excessively." Against these oppressive laws and customs a spirit of resistance was secretly growing up among the common people, and only waited a fitting opportunity to declare itself. Another fruitful cause of disaffection was the manner in which the taxes were collected. These were not only oppressive in themselves, but the burden of them was greatly increased by the tax-gatherers, who farmed them from the Crown, and who strove, for their own aggrandisement, to make them yield as large a sum as possible. In 1381 a poll-tax was levied on all persons above the age of fifteen. The tax was intended to defray the cost of the war with France, and was viewed with extreme repugnance by the majority of the labouring classes.

Such was the state of things when Sir Simon Burley rode into Gravesend, and seeing one of the townsmen, claimed him as his slave. The man denied that he was ever a slave to any one, and the inhabitants protested against his removal. Sir Simon affirmed that he was the son of one of his female slaves, and disregarding the entreaties of the crowd, ordered his guard to take him to Rochester Castle. No sooner had the arrogant knight left the town than portentous murmurs were heard, followed by the cry of "Down with the tyrants!" The inhabitants, vowing vengeance on all lords and owners of land, resolved to join the men of Essex, who had already risen in arms, in anticipation of assistance from "the brethren" who were also in revolt in the Eastern Counties. Before sufficient time had elapsed for the excitement created by this provoking incident to subside, another offence was given to the men of Kent. A tax-gatherer called at the house of John of Dartford,[*] and

---

[*] Rapin, Baker, Hume, and Lingard all differ as to the name and designation of this person.

demanded the poll-tax. John was at work roofing a house, and his wife paid for him and herself and their two servants or apprentices, but claimed exemption for her daughter, as being under the taxable age. This exemption the agent refused to allow, and asserted that the girl had passed her fifteenth year. The woman protested, and appealed to her neighbours in support of her statement; but the collector would listen to no testimony, and was behaving in an unseemly manner towards the girl, when a friend ran off and told John what was going on at his house. John was not to be trifled with. Seizing his massive helving hammer, he hurried home, where he found a crowd assembled, and before the tax-collector had time to draw his sword, he struck him a blow on his head with his hammer. The man fell dead. No one uttered a word of remonstrance. The spectators looked on in approving silence. John told them, in a few forcible words, that his cause was theirs, and he knew that at heart every one of them was burning with indignation at the unjust laws by which they were governed. The air quivered with acclamation. John had begun the struggle for freedom.

The flame of insurrection, thus ignited at Gravesend and Dartford, spread with astonishing rapidity. From every part of the county, the men of Kent rallied to the cry of "King Richard and the true Commons." Indifferently armed—most of them, indeed, carrying only such homely weapons as came first to hand—they were led to Rochester and Canterbury, where they compelled the Mayor and Corporation to join them, and as they proceeded to London—there, as they alleged, to make their own terms with the king—they were numerously reinforced. Two individuals among them had already been conspicuous for the vehemence of their opinions, their personal audacity, and the restless energy of their character. These were Wat Tyler and Jack Straw, known by tradition to almost every one. It has been said that Wat Tyler was a native of Dartford, but as Stow, who wrote in the sixteenth century, calls him "Tighler of Maidstone," he was probably in the earlier years of his life connected in some way with this town.* An unscrupulous demagogue, daring to temerity, and not without a certain rough and ready ability for controlling masses of men, he had inspired the confidence, as he had inflamed the passions of the insurgents. They accordingly chose him for their leader. Scarcely less bold and desperate was Jack Straw, who became one of Tyler's lieutenants. Tradition relates that he was born in a cottage at Pepingstraw, in Offham parish, hence the name he assumed.

Almost every town in Kent was at the mercy of the insurgents; and poor and ignorant as they were, one is not surprised that their heads were turned by the temporary possession of power. John Gower, the prosaic and voluminous Kentish poet, who was a contemporary of Tyler, has set forth the evils of the time in his Latin poem, the "Voice of One that Crieth," and minutely describes the miseries attendant upon the rising. The insurgents went from place to place, committing all sorts of excesses, burning books and records, houses and colleges, making prisoners of landowners and lawyers, and cutting off the heads of others, getting drunk on the wine which they found in the cellars of castles and mansions, and compelling earls, barons, and knights to attend upon them in the capacity of servants. They reached Maidstone on the 11th of June; and besides causing much destruction to property, and killing the beasts that were grazing in the archbishop's park, they put several persons to death. They

---

* Lingard, in his "History of England," vol. iii., p. 143, also calls him of Maidstone. Hasted, vol. iv., p. 723, says his real name was Walter Hilleard.

also set at liberty all the prisoners in the archbishop's gaol, among the latter being John Ball, who had several years previously been condemned to perpetual imprisonment for preaching heretical doctrines. Ball seems to have begun his preaching about 1360, and six years later he attracted the attention of the authorities. Archbishop Langham ordered every one under pain of excommunication to withdraw from his sermons, and Ball himself was summoned before his grace to answer for matters "touching the salvation of his soul." Whatever the result of this examination may have been, it appears to have had little effect on Ball, who continued as before to proclaim the doctrines of Wickliffe in the market places and churchyards. The new archbishop, Simon de Sudbury, was, however, so alarmed by his conduct that he ordered him to be seized and imprisoned for life at Maidstone. The advance of the rebels in the summer of 1381 afforded a happy release to Ball. He became one of themselves, either by choice or compulsion, and acted as their field chaplain. His self-esteem was immoderately flattered by Wat Tyler, who promised, if things went well, to promote him to the See of Canterbury. But for the present, Wat had more pressing business on hand. He triumphantly led his followers from town to town. Subsequently they mustered in force on Blackheath, where they were joined by men from Essex and the Eastern Counties. Here they were harangued by Ball, who took for his text the distich,

> When Adam delved and Eve span,
> Where was then the gentleman?

The insurgents had so far overcome all opposition. They felt that the game was pretty much in their own hands. The Court was overawed, and London was in a ferment of excitement. Thinking resistance vain, the king promised acquiescence with Tyler's demands, which included a general pardon, freedom of commerce, and the abolition of slavery. A party of the insurgents had meanwhile sacked the Temple, released the prisoners in Southwark gaol, and burnt many houses. They had also broken into the Tower, and murdered the archbishop, the Prior of St. John's, and several noblemen.

But this career of riot and bloodshed was shortly to come to an end. To many of the insurgents, whom King Richard had succeeded in propitiating, charters of enfranchisement were granted, and they returned to their homes. But Wat Tyler still remained at the head of several thousands of Kentishmen, and the king, encountering him at Smithfield on June 15, invited him to a conference. In the course of the interview, Sir John Newton joined his majesty, and Tyler, fancying him an interloper, objected to his presence. A quarrel ensued, in which Tyler's dagger was snatched from his hand by Newton. The king instantly ordered his arrest, and a party of soldiers arriving, Sir William Walworth, the Lord Mayor, drew his sword and struck Tyler, who, before he could recover himself, was slain. Deprived of their leader, the insurgents became dispirited, and confusion spread quickly among them. The king now perceived his opportunity, and heading the populace, led them to Islington, where Sir Robert Knolles and a body of well-armed soldiers had been secretly drawn up for his protection. He granted charters of freedom to the insurgents, and partly by cajolery, partly by force, they were either induced to quit the metropolis, or were made prisoners.

When tranquility was restored, the charters were revoked by the king, and commissions were issued for the trial of the ringleaders. Punishment was meted out without stint or mercy, and an Act of Indemnity was passed to hide the acts of the officers of the Crown. Jack Straw was arrested in London and executed. In the presentments of the juries are recorded the names of many of the insurgents.

Henry and John Twysden, John Warner, of Smarden, William Shethere, William Sandre, and John Godegron, of Cranbrook, Richard Brewer, John Michelot, John Cogger, and James, sometime servant to John Soleyn, of Canterbury, were among those who were indicted for breaking into the prison at Maidstone. William Brown, of Boxley, and John Webbe, of Maidstone, were charged with having risen against the king and the people, and feloniously slain John Stonhelde, of Maidstone, and John Godmot, of Bordenn. Another presentment, dated October 8, states that Thomas Harding, mason, of Linton, and others, rose in arms at Linton, and threatened to burn Maidstone; they also forced men to join them, and conspired against the king, the sheriff, and others. Indictments were likewise preferred against Richard Barbour and John Hosyere, of Maidstone, and several men from Loose and East Farleigh. Harding and a number of other prisoners were convicted and sentenced to be executed, but the sentences do not appear to have been carried out. Others were acquitted. John Cote, mason, of Loose, turned king's evidence, and his confession gave colour to a suspicion that the Duke of Lancaster was concerned in the rebellion. The irrepressible John Ball, instead of being made Archbishop of Canterbury, fled northwards, but was overtaken at Coventry and conveyed to St. Alban's, where he was hanged, drawn, and quartered, his quarters being set up at four different places. A rather hot-headed canon of Leicester, in Richard's reign, describes Ball as "the divider of ecclesiastical unity, the stirrer up of discord between the clergy and laity, the indefatigable tower of unlawful opinions, and disturber of Christ's church."

The insurrection was the most democratic movement known in England up to that time; but the people got nothing by it. A statute was passed, fixing a low scale of wages; exorbitant demands were made for taxes; and the labourers were reduced to a state of bondage worse than before.

Scarcely had the chequered events of that short-lived revolt died out of the memory of the oldest inhabitants of Maidstone, when another popular rising occurred, throwing the county again into commotion. The prolonged rivalry between the houses of Lancaster and York, and the murder of the Duke of Suffolk, had given rise to much discontent and intrigue in the reign of Henry VI., and one of the political adventurers of the time was an Irishman named Jack Cade. Little is known of Cade's personal history, except that he was an illegitimate relation of the Duke of York, and had been obliged, for crimes committed in this country, to seek refuge in France. On his return to England, he found the nation disquieted and chafing under the abuses of the time. Early in the summer of 1450 he determined to champion the cause of the people of Kent. But a better name than his own was needed to conjure with, and to evince his affinity with the Duke of York, he called himself John Mortimer. First publicly stating his intentions in the neighbourhood of Ashford, he gave the signal for a general rising on the 24th of May. The magic of the name of Mortimer at once rendered him popular. He had soon under his command many thousands of Kentishmen. Three of his followers were Richard Culpeper, of East Farleigh, a member of a well-known family, now extinct; William Beale, and John Fisher, carpenter, of Maidstone, who may have belonged to the families of Beale and Fisher, which were long associated with the municipal affairs of the town. Robert Est and Richard Dyne, of Maidstone, and John Chamberlain or Smethcote, of East Farleigh, who came forward and threw in their lot with Cade, would also appear, from the incidental mention of their names in local records, to have been men of some social position. Other inhabitants of Maidstone who swelled the ranks of the insurgents were Richard Manney, mason, John Baker, yeoman, John Mason, waxchandler, Richard Sabin, John Colney, Stephen Colvey, goldsmith, William Finch, tailor, Robert Shaile, Richard Wood, Thomas Ellis, sen., and Thomas Ellis, jun., husbandmen, John Aston, yeoman, and Thomas Carter, draper.

Without loss of time Cade and the insurgents, numbering upwards of 20,000, marched towards London, and encamped on Blackheath, whence they opened communications with the citizens. The king, surprised at the celerity of their movements, sent to enquire why they had left their homes. Cade replied in a paper, entitled "The Complaint of the Commons of Kent," in which he asserted that the people were robbed of their goods for the king's use, that misgovernment had banished justice and prosperity from the land, and that the men of Kent were especially ill-treated and overtaxed. In another paper, headed "The Requests by the Captain of the Great Assembly in Kent," he complained that the free election of knights of the shire had been hindered, and demanded that Crowmer, the sheriff of Kent, and Lord Say, the lord-lieutenant, should be punished for their malversations, and that the king should resume the grants of the Crown which the corrupt persons who filled the high offices at court fattened on, the sovereign being thereby compelled to live on taxation. To the court these demands appeared preposterous, and on the 11th of June an army, under the command of Sir Humphrey Stafford, was sent against the insurgents. The latter, who had been reinforced by small contingents from Sussex and Surrey, thereupon retreated as far as Sevenoaks, where they were attacked by the royal forces, who were signally defeated and their commander slain. Elated by his victory, Cade once more advanced, and finally encamped on

Blackheath. He then despatched a messenger to the court, promising that as soon as the grievances of his followers were redressed they should lay down their arms. A large proportion of the citizens of London had from the first looked with a kindly eye upon his enterprise, and the effect of this timely overture was to increase public feeling still more in his favour. At length the king's soldiers refused to fight against their countrymen—an evidence of disaffection which it was impossible for the Privy Council to ignore. It was consequently deemed prudent to convey Henry for safety to Kenilworth.

The court made some trifling concessions, but the insurgents were unappeased, and on the 2nd of July they entered the city without opposition. Cade published stringent orders against plunder and violence, and for two days he maintained the strictest order, his men being withdrawn from the city at night and lodged in the fields. But a consciousness of undisputed authority produced a desire for revenge. Lord Say, Crowmer, and several unpopular citizens were dragged to Cheapside, where their heads were cut off. The wealth of London, too, excited the cupidity of the insurgents, who plundered some houses, and so alarmed the populace that the latter secretly determined to prevent their entrance into the city on the morrow. While Cade and his men were in the fields, they got news of the plan laid against them, and during the night of the 5th of July they made an attack on London bridge, slashing in two the ropes of the drawbridge, and cutting down the men who where guarding it. The assault was sharply delivered, but the citizens fought bravely, and being assisted by a detachment of soldiers from the Tower, repulsed the assailants with great slaughter. So complete was the defeat that Cade despaired of rallying his men. The majority were satisfied with a promise of pardon, and returned to their homes. Cade, with a few devoted adherents, fled towards the coast, and a price being set upon his head, he was hotly pursued by an esquire named Alexander Iden, who came up to and killed him at Heathfield Sussex, on the 11th of July. On the 15th his body was brought to the metropolis, where it was quartered, and his head was stuck on the gatehouse of London Bridge as a terror to traitors.

The more prominent of his adherents were tried and executed, but to the indistinguishable rank and file the royal clemency was extended. Maidstone was one of the towns pardoned, and the names of a number of the inhabitants appear in the official list of Kentishmen whose conduct was condoned.*

A hundred years elapsed before the peace of the town was again disturbed by a spontaneous act of the men of Kent. The detestation with which the nation regarded the projected marriage of Queen Mary with the Archduke Philip of Spain, in the year 1554, induced Sir Thomas Wyatt, of Allington Castle, to head an insurrection in the county, with a view to prevent the alliance. But before entering into the details of that foolish rising, it may be well to give some account of its leader, his family and place of residence.

The picturesque ruin of Allington Castle, situated on the west bank of the Medway, at a bend of the river about a mile and a half north of Maidstone, is an object of pensive interest to the tourist who visits this part of the valley of the Medway. Looking out of history upon him, it starts a recollection of its past owners—how one, who had endured the miseries of the Tower, came thither at last under the smile of his sovereign; how another, in the interludes of a

---

* Patent Rolls, 28th Henry VI. (part two).

courtly life, often found leisure to indite a pretty sonnet to some "ladye faire;" and how a third held secret counsel with trusty friends within those broken and ivygrown walls, and parted here with his wife on the eve of his ill-starred enterprise, never again to return. The more ancient part of the castle has been in a state of delapidation for two hundred and fifty years.* It originally consisted of a quadrangle, surrounded by a moat, with round towers at the corners, and smaller intermediate towers. The outer walls, as well as several of the interior walls, are still standing, and enclose a considerable area. The massive gateway, with its square spandrel and square-headed window, retains the chiselled groove of the old portcullis, and deviates but slightly from the ordinary style of mediæval gatehouses. Part of the building, which is now roofless and overrun with ivy and Virginia creeper, has been converted into a farm-house, which looks almost as picturesque as the castle itself.†

A fort stood on the site of the present ruins in Saxon times, and having been destroyed by the Danes, was rebuilt after the Conquest. Passing in succession into the hands of Odo, bishop of Bayeux, Earl Warren, kinsmen of William I., and Lord Fitzhughes, it became the property of Sir Giles Allington, after whom both the castle and the parish were henceforth named. The estate continued in the Allington

---

* The later portions of the building were evidently inhabited in the seventeenth century. In the Allington parochial register, which dates from 1630, the following entry occurs: "1631.—Elizabeth Best, daughter of John Best, the younger, of Allington Castle, baptised May 20." At the Kent Assizes in 1678 a young woman who had been employed at Allington Castle as a domestic servant, was sentenced to be executed for causing the death of her new-born infant by throwing it out at one of the upper windows of the castle.

† This alteration was made in 1829. The western portion of the castle also had previously been fitted up as a farm house; but about forty years ago this was dismantled, the roof torn off, the floors taken away, and the material used for the building of peasants' cottages.

family until the middle of the thirteenth century, when it was held by Sir Stephen de Penchester, Lord Warden of the Cinque Ports, who had fought in the Crusades. Penchester greatly improved the castle, and in the year 1280 obtained a license from Edward I. to fortify and embattle it. The tower called Solomon's tower was built during his ownership. He died without male issue, and the estate descended to Henry de Cobham, of Rundale, and then to Robert Brent, whose grandson sold it in 1493 to a representative of a wealthy family from Southange, Yorkshire. This was Henry Wyatt, who attached himself to the rising fortunes of the Duke of Richmond, afterwards Henry VII. For this offence he was imprisoned in the Tower, where, according to his epitaph on the family monument in Boxley church, he was fed by a favourite cat, which brought him daily a pigeon from a neighbouring dovecot. On the accession of Henry, he was knighted and constituted a member of the Privy Council. He was one of the executors of that monarch's will, and also stood high in favour with Henry VIII. When Cardinal Wolsey returned from his embassy to France in 1527, Wyatt entertained him at Allington. The Abbot of Boxley appears to have been a frequent visitor at the castle; and it is related, that being detected one day presuming too freely upon his position, Lady Wyatt ordered him to be put in the stocks. Sir Henry, being subsequently called upon by the Privy Council to answer for his wife, replied, "If any of you had done what that Abbot did, she would clap you into the stocks also." He died in 1538, and was succeeded by his eldest son Thomas, who was born at Allington in 1503.

Educated at St. John's College, Cambridge, and married to Elizabeth Brooke, daughter of Lord Cobham, at the age of seventeen, Thomas soon proved himself well qualified to follow in the footsteps of his father. Of fine manners and cultivated mind, he possessed a form in which, says his friend the Earl of Surrey, "force and beauty met." He spoke French, Italian, and Spanish fluently, and became a consummate courtier, far-sighted and dexterous in the management of affairs. His numerous estates in Kent and elsewhere included the Mote, the Abbey and lands of Boxley, the Friars, the manors of East Farleigh, Hunton, Boughton, and East Peckham, and the estate of Sheals Court and other lands in the neighbourhood of Maidstone. At the marriage of Anne Boleyn he officiated as ewerer. In 1536, having incurred the disfavour of the Duke of Suffolk, he was committed to the Tower, but was soon released, and received the honour of knighthood. In the following year he was made sheriff of Kent, after which he went for two years on a mission to the court of Spain, where he acquitted himself with great tact and ability. On his return he, in June 1540, entered into a contract with the king, whereby he parted with a number of his lands in Maidstone and elsewhere, receiving in exchange other estates in Kent and Surrey. He was then despatched to Paris as English ambassador, and afterwards, being accused of carrying on a treasonable correspondence with Cardinal Pole, he was again committed to the Tower, where he was harshly treated. When the charge was preferred against him he was, however, acquitted, and in 1542 the king, to mark his sense of Wyatt's innocence, bestowed upon him several valuable estates, and created him high steward for life of the manor of Maidstone.

Sir Thomas Wyatt the Elder.
From the original by Hans Holbein.

Wyatt was a wit as well as a poet. It is stated that he encouraged Henry to proceed with his divorce of Queen Catherine, notwithstanding the opposition of Rome, remarking to him that "it was very strange a man could not repent, when he had done amiss, without asking the Pope's leave." But wishing now to withdraw himself from public life, he lived for the most part retired at Allington. He improved and partly rebuilt the Castle.* After the anxieties of diplomacy and the perils of court intrigue, the repose which his secluded country seat afforded came as a congenial change. He had acquired a considerable reputation as a poet. His poems are generally on amatory subjects, formed upon Italian models. They are remarkable for their purity of thought and expression, and mark a distinct stage in the history of English literature. His satires, as well as his paraphrase of David's penitential psalms, also possess genuine merit. In his quiet retreat at Allington he wrote much, and in the intervals of study he used to hunt in the park and woods, and shoot with his bow.†

But his retirement was not to be of long duration. In the autumn of 1542, a Spanish embassy being expected at London to arrange for a war with France, Henry ordered Wyatt to meet the mission at Falmouth, and conduct it to the metropolis. He met with unfavourable

---

* A newspaper published in 1848 says that in the refection-hall of the castle there might then have been seen the mantelpiece where once the faggot blazed, and on the entablature the initials "T. W. 1538," denoting the spot where old Sir Thomas warmed into verse.

† A MS. volume of family papers, referred to in the "Gentleman's Magazine" for 1850, mentions that Sir Thomas brought up a lion's whelp and an Irish greyhound at the castle, and made playmates of them; they used to wait at the gate or hall-door for his coming home, and testify their delight at his return by the most violent demonstrations. At last, as the lion's whelp grew in courage and strength, these evidences of attachment became rather dangerous; and as on one occasion he ran roaring at his master, and springing fiercely upon his chest, he must have seriously injured him but for the greyhound, which, leaping on his back, pulled him down, when Wyatt drew his rapier and slew the whelp on the spot.

weather, and riding too fast, overheated himself. Arriving at Sherborne, Dorsetshire, he was seized with fever, and expired on the 10th or 11th of October. His remains were buried there, though no inscription marks the spot. Fifteen years after his death his poems, together with those of the Earl of Surrey, were published in London, and they have since gone through many editions.

The poet was succeeded at Allington by his only son, Thomas, who was born about the year 1521. His wild and riotous habits had induced his father to promote his marriage with Jane, daughter and co-heiress of William Hawte, of Bourne, when he was about his sixteenth year. This does not appear to have improved him, as some years later he was imprisoned in the Tower for disorderly conduct in London, and for breaking windows with stones shot from a cross-bow. There is an interesting memento of his connection with Allington in Aylesford Church, where a palimpsest brass records the death and burial of John Savell, a faithful servant of his. From an early age Sir Thomas devoted himself to military pursuits. After a tour through Spain he raised a body of troops at his own expense, and did good service at the seige of Landrecies in 1544. In the following year he was placed in command at Boulogne, where he displayed so much energy and military talent that the Earl of Surrey, in a despatch to Henry VIII., tells the king that "for hardiness, circumspection, and natural disposition to the war," there were few officers to compare with him. He continued in honourable service on the continent till 1550, when Boulogne was restored to the French. During the next three years he passed most of his time at Allington, but the national changes which ensued, and the dangers that were apprehended on the death of Edward VI., had the effect of turning his thoughts in a new direction.

The Reformation had been making steady progress in England, and with the accession of Mary in 1553 the Protestants were anxious to prevent a relapse to Romish practices. But one of the first acts of that queen was to effect a reconciliation with the Pope, and to restore the old religion. The violent reaction of public feeling which so sudden a change produced was aggravated in an extraordinary degree by the announcement of Mary's intention to espouse Philip of Spain. In the hope of silencing the clamour of the people, Philip was made to agree, in the articles of marriage, that the administration of government should remain entirely in the hands of the queen and her ministers. Still the nation was intensely dissatisfied. It was stated that the King of Spain, with a view to ultimately gaining possession of England, would allow his son to agree verbally to any terms, and that if the match was permitted the Inquisition and other forms of Spanish tyranny would be established in this country.

Excited though they were by these and other alarming reports, the majority of the people nevertheless "thought that as the evils of the Spanish alliance were only dreaded at a distance, matters were not yet fully prepared for a general revolt." But there were others who, says Hume, believed that it would be safer to prevent than to redress grievances, and they accordingly entered into a conspiracy to rise in arms and declare against the Queen's marriage. Sir Thomas Wyatt was to take the field in Kent, and Sir Peter Carew in Devonshire; while the Duke of Suffolk, with the latent design of placing his daughter, Lady Jane Grey, on the throne, undertook to raise the Midland counties. The plot was concocted in London, and though every means was taken to avoid publicity, the secret got wind. This was fatal to their designs. The conspirators had decided that the rising should not take place till midsummer, after Philip's arrival in England, but they felt that it would be imbecility now to postpone action. They therefore determined that matters should be brought to a crisis without delay. Having completed their arrangements with all possible haste, they quitted London for their respective destinations.

Wyatt reached Allington Castle in the second week of January 1554. He was popular amongst the people of Kent, and at his instigation meetings hostile to the Queen were held on Penenden Heath, and at other places in the county. In the short time that remained for maturing his preparations, no effort was spared to secure the support of his friends. At his request, Anthony Norton, of Trosley, called at the castle on the morning of the 23rd of January. Norton found Wyatt sitting in his parlour by the fire. During the subsequent conversation Robert Rudstone, of Boughton Monchelsea, Alexander Fisher, and another gentleman, arrived. The prospects of the rising were talked over with much earnestness and animation, and Fisher asked Norton to get William Tilden, draper, who had been mayor of Maidstone two years before, to secure the services of the yeomen living in the neighbourhood of the town. Norton, before leaving, was offered a cup of beer in the hall, and then the parson of Allington accompanied him out of the castle.* Wyatt and his confederates resolved to set up the standard of rebellion at Maidstone, on Thursday, the 25th of January.

Tennyson, in his "Queen Mary," depicts the scene at Allington when this important decision was taken. Anthony Knyvett, of Chedington, is present, and in a burst of passion, Wyatt exclaims:

---

* Domestic State Papers, vol. iii.

Down scabbard, and out sword! and let rebellion
Roar till throne rock, and crown fall. No, not that:
But we will teach Queen Mary how to reign.
Who are those that shout below there?

KNYVETT: Why, some fifty that follow'd me from Penenden Heath in hope to hear you speak.

WYATT: Open the window, Knyvett; the mine is fired, and I will speak to them.

Men of Kent, England of England, you that have kept your old customs upright while all the rest of England bow'd theirs to the Norman, the cause that hath brought us together is not the cause of a county or a shire, but of this England, in whose crown our Kent is the fairest jewel. Philip shall not wed Mary; and ye have called me to be your leader. I know Spain. I have been there with my father; I have seen them in their own land; have marked the haughtiness of their nobles, the cruelty of their priests. If this man marry our Queen, however the Council and the Commons may fence round his power with restriction, he will be king, king of England, my masters; and the queen, and the laws, and the people, his slaves. What! shall we have Spain on the throne and in the Parliament. Spain in our ships, in our forts, in our houses, in our beds?

CROWD: No! no! no Spain.

A PEASANT: But, Sir Thomas, must we levy war against the Queen's grace?

WYATT: No, my friend: war *for* the Queen's grace—to save her from herself and Philip—war against Spain. And think not we shall be alone—thousands will flock to us. The Council, the Court itself, is on our side. And if we move not now, yet it will be known that we have moved; and if Philip come to be king, O, my God! the rope, the rack, the thumbscrew, the stake, the fire. Forward to London with me! forward to London! If ye love your liberties or your skins, forward to London!

On the evening of January 24, Wyatt sent a message with a letter to the sheriff, Sir Robert Southwell,* of Mereworth, inviting him and Lord Abergavenny to join the rising. Southwell returned a verbal answer, denouncing Wyatt as a traitor, and advised the messenger, whom he knew to be an honest man, to remain loyal to the Queen. The man delivered his message to Wyatt, and returning to the sheriff, served loyally under him during the rebellion.

Next morning, as arranged, Wyatt left Allington on his

---

* Froude, vol. v., p. 323, says that Southwell had been among the loudest objectors in Parliament to the marriage.

fatal exploit. As he rode out of the castle gate, his wife brought her infant of only a few weeks old to him, and as he kissed it, he said, "Thou mayest prove a very dear child to me." Fancy may picture him, amid the clatter of arms and tramp of horses, casting a wistful eye back to the old home, with its garniture of trees:

> Ah, gray old castle of Allington, green field
> Beside the brimming Medway, it may chance
> That I shall never look upon you more.

He was accompanied by Sir Henry Isley, of Sundridge, owner of Vinters, Thomas Isley, of Boxley, George Maplesden, of Digons, Maidstone, and other gentlemen. It was market day at Maidstone, and the town was throbbing with excitement. As Wyatt and his small band galloped into the High Street, cheer upon cheer greeted them. The leader stopped in the centre of the street, near the spot on which the Russian cannon now stands, and surrounded by his men, unrolled a bulky parchment, from which he read, with stentorian voice, "A Proclamation agreed unto by Thomas Wyatt, George Harper, of Sutton Valence, Henry Isley, knights,[*] and by divers of the rest of the shire, sent unto the Commons of the same." The proclamation denounced the intended marriage, and stated that a hundred armed Spaniards had arrived at Dover, and were already at Rochester. No mention was made of religion, but it was promised that the Queen was to be specially exempt from violence. The inhabitants were solicited as neighbours, friends, and Englishmen, to aid in the defence of their country's liberties, and urged to repair to the various towns for the purpose of securing help. "And please, Sir Thomas, is your quarrel against the Queen?" asked one of them. "No," was the reply, "I have no wish to injure her Majesty." Several

---

[*] Harper and Isley had each been sheriff of Kent in the previous reign.

persons then shook him by the hand, and promised to stand by him. Wyatt was a Roman Catholic, and many of his lands had belonged to the religious houses which were suppressed by Henry VIII. A leading inhabitant assured him that though he loved pottage well, yet he would sell his spoons and plate rather than the cause should fail, and added, "I trust you will restore the right religion again." "Hush!" whispered Wyatt, "you must not name religion, for that would withdraw the hearts of many."*

Wyatt remained in the town overnight, and next day proceeded to Rochester. By this time his force amounted to fifteen hundred men. Seizing the castle, the insurgents destroyed the western extremity of the bridge, and fortified the eastern side of the city. Wyatt sent messengers to his supporters at a distance to join him without delay. The church bells were rung, and the proclamation was published, in every town. Penshurst castle, during the absence of its owner, was rifled of its armour. Parties of the insurgents went hither and thither with drums beating. Lord Abergavenny, the sheriff, and other known royalists, were declared to be traitors. The impetuous Knyvett, as he jumped into his saddle, vowed that he would achieve his purpose or die in the field.

Hostilities were now fairly commenced, as far as Wyatt and his followers were concerned, and it remained for the adherents of the Queen to evince their loyalty by a prompt display of well-directed energy. But it was no secret that several members of the Privy Council were strongly opposed

---

* The following entry appears in the Chronicle of old Charles Wriothesley, who died in 1559:—"The 25 of Januarie tydynges were brought to the Lorde Maior by Sir John Gage, Lorde Chamberleyn to the Queene, that Sir Thomas Wyet with certayn rebels were up in Kent, about Maydstone. Whereupon a Courte of Alldermen was called immediatelie in the forenoone; and that night the Lorde Maior rode to peruse the watch of the citie, and so everie night after two Alldermen to ride to peruse the said watches," p. 107.

to the forthcoming marriage, and tacitly wished that the rising in Kent might induce Mary to withdraw from her engagement with Philip. A select body of troops, if sent at once against the rioters, might have crushed the rebellion in its infancy; but the Council dallied, and apathy prevailed in high quarters. Under these circumstances, and believing that if Philip came over and married her all would be well, the Queen at the outset trusted to her loyal subjects in Kent to keep the insurgents in check. Nor was her trust altogether misplaced. The sheriff, finding the inhabitants of Maidstone in favour of the rising, did not attempt to disperse the force which assembled there on the 25th, but on the 27th he met Lord Abergavenny and other gentlemen and yeomen at Malling, and addressing the people as his "loving friends and neighbours," denounced Wyatt's proclamation, and in the name of the Queen, offered a free pardon to such of the offenders as would return to their homes within twenty-four hours. Shouts of "The Queen!" followed this address. Placing sentries in the market place and at each of the entrances to the village, the royalists retired to rest for the night; but sleep was not long to be enjoyed. Soon after midnight an alarm was given that Sir Henry Isley and five hundred men from the Weald were on their way from Sevenoaks to join Wyatt at Rochester. A hurried consultation was held at Malling, and Southwell penned a letter to London, urging the Privy Council to direct the Lord Warden and other gentlemen of East Kent to repair to Rochester. He then called his supporters together, numbering about six hundred yeomen, and went in pursuit of the insurgents. Approaching Wrotham Heath, the sound of drums was heard, and their fluttering ensigns were seen in the distance. Lord Abergavenny, with a detachment, moved rapidly forward, and encountered them in Blacksole field. They were evidently desirous of avoiding an engagement, but the main body of the royalists coming up, shots and arrows were exchanged, and a tough skirmish ensued, the insurgents being put to flight, and sixty prisoners taken.

This encounter inspired the sheriff and his men with fresh courage, and brought to their ranks many of those Kentishmen who were still hesitating between loyalty and treason. One of the new comers was William Coleman, an Ightham blacksmith. He told Sir Robert Southwell that about six o'clock one morning, William, eldest son of Sir Henry Isley, came to his forge to have his horse shod, and tried to persuade him to follow Wyatt. "The Spaniards," said Isley, "are coming into the realm, with harness and handguns, and will make us worse than conies, and viler." The blacksmith was too stolid for his visitor. "Coleman, if thou beest a good fellow, stir and encourage all thy neighbours to rise against these strangers. I go to Maidstone, and return again shortly." "Sir," quoth the smith, "these be marvellous words; we shall be betrayed if we stir." "No!" said Isley, as he mounted and galloped off, "the people are already up in Devonshire and other places, and we shall have help enough."

The Queen had meanwhile issued a proclamation in which Wyatt, Suffolk, Carew, and others acting with them, were held up to popular condemnation, and the sheriffs and mayors in the disturbed parts of the country were called upon to proclaim them traitors. Five hundred men were summoned to arms in Gloucestershire; but the Privy Council still refused to sanction a general levy of troops, and her Majesty had only her guard on whom she could rely for personal protection. In this dilemma she appealed to the Lord Mayor for assistance, and the Corporation at once responded. Five hundred men raised in the city were placed under the command of the Duke of Norfolk, and these, with the Queen's guard, proceeded to Gravesend. A herald was then despatched to Rochester, offering a free pardon to Wyatt and as many of the insurgents as would lay down their arms within twenty-four hours. When the herald reached Rochester bridge he was not permitted to cross, and in answer to his message, Wyatt stated that he and his men had done no wrong and required no pardon. But scarcely had the herald returned to his destination before Sir George Harper, who held the command conjointly with Wyatt, quitted the camp, and presenting himself to Norfolk at Gravesend, begged the Queen's pardon. Harper advised the duke to advance against the insurgents without delay, as he would find no resistance. Before acting on this advice, Norfolk wrote to the Privy Council, communicating the news of the successful attack in Blacksole field, and stating that he had induced Harper to desert the insurgents; that his forces had been reinforced by about three hundred men from East Kent, and that on the following day, the 29th, he hoped to be at Rochester. About this time also the sheriff wrote to the Council. He said that Wyatt had sent his couriers to noble personages in Sussex, Surrey, Essex, and Suffolk, to stir up the people, and that he and Lord Abergavenny hoped to stop the passage of the insurgents from Essex into Kent. He doubted whether Lord Cobham was to be trusted, seeing that he was Wyatt's uncle, and suggested that the Duke of Norfolk should move forward either to Rochester or Maidstone.

While these matters were in progress, the insurgents at Rochester were beginning to lose heart. The citizens of Canterbury had declared against them, and a reward of £100 a year in perpetuity was set upon their leader's head. It is said that Wyatt was seen to weep,* and

* Rapin, vol. ii., p. 37.

that he meditated flight to a foreign country. Proctor, a contemporary writer, tells us that while in this despairing mood, he called for a splendid coat which he had quilted full of "angels"—gold coins—not long before, in anticipation of a possible reverse of fortune.* The weather, however, was too boisterous to admit of an escape by water, and the rapid march of events left little time for hesitation.

Norfolk, with six or seven hundred men, was advancing from Gravesend. The duke had seen much hard service in his time, and forty years had passed since he, as Earl of Surrey, cut up the Scottish army at Flodden. He was now an octogenarian, and it is not perhaps surprising that under the influence of such cross-currents of feeling as were agitating the nation, the grey-headed old soldier failed to rouse a spirit of loyalty and confidence amongst his men. In point of numbers his force was far inferior to that under Wyatt, and Captain Brett and several of his lieutenants were suspected of being in secret league with the insurgents. For this reason he was urged to delay his advance until the arrival of the sheriff, the Lord Warden of the Cinque Ports, and a contingent which was expected from East Kent. But he continued his march, and about four o'clock in the afternoon of the 29th he found himself within canon-shot of Rochester bridge. He placed himself in front of his men, and prepared for an assault. A stiff breeze was blowing, and the cold was intense. Across the water, a party of the insurgents were seen watching their movements. The duke gave orders to disperse them; but while a gun was being placed in position, Sir Edward Bray galloped up, shouting that the Londoners were changing sides. Before the duke had time to realise the full meaning of Bray's words, he

---

* Account of the Rebellion written by John Proctor, schoolmaster of Tunbridge, in 1554.

saw Captain Brett and Sir George Harper advancing with all their men. Brett suddenly stopped, and raising his sword, said, "Masters, we are going to fight in an unholy quarrel with our friends and countrymen, who seek only to preserve us from the dominion of foreigners; wherefore I think that no English heart should oppose them, and I am resolved for my own part to shed my blood in the cause of this worthy captain, Master Wyatt." Cries of "A Wyatt! a Wyatt! we are all Englishmen!" went up from his comrades. Norfolk saw that he was betrayed, and putting spurs to his horse he galloped off with Lord Arundel and a few others towards Gravesend; while Wyatt with a party of troopers dashed forward, and cried out, "As many as will tarry with us shall be welcome; as many as will depart, let them go." Nearly the whole force deserted, and eight brass guns and Norfolk's baggage fell into the hands of the insurgents. Most of the duke's private attendants took service under Wyatt.

Norfolk's misfortune, as may be supposed, affected in very opposite ways the fortunes of the two parties in the struggle. The venerable general, with a handful of troops, continued his retreat to London. Lord Abergavenny and the sheriff were left almost alone in the county. The latter, who was at Maidstone, hurried to Malling, and thereafter posted to the Privy Council for instructions. Sir Thomas Cheyne, the Lord Warden, wrote to the Council, stating that the abominable treason of the Londoners had infected the whole population, and that he was no longer sure of any one. Wyatt, on the other hand, was in high spirits, and sent a letter to the Duke of Suffolk informing him of his success. He next held a council of his chief men at Rochester, and urged the adoption of a more aggressive attitude. He proposed that the person of Southwell, the sheriff, should be secured, but this being opposed, it was finally resolved to march at once upon London, capturing on the way Cooling Castle, close by Gad's Hill, the seat of Lord Cobham.

This nobleman had held aloof from the rising, but on hearing of Norfolk's disaster, his sons came into Rochester, and Wyatt forwarded to him a letter with a request that he also should join them. But instead of replying to Wyatt, Cobham wrote to the Duke of Norfolk, telling him that the insurgents relied upon the pensioners, the guards, and the London populace for assistance. He said he had a few men at his disposal, who were armed with black-bills, and asked for instructions as to what he should do with them. Having decided to treat Cobham as an enemy, Wyatt ordered a party of the insurgents to repair to Cooling Castle, while he proceeded with the main body to Gravesend. The castle was attacked on the morning of the 30th, and Cobham, after a stout resistance, was taken prisoner, and carried off to Wyatt. Just before surrendering, however, he found time to inform the Privy Council of what had occurred. He stated that his castle was assaulted in a most forcible manner, that he defied the insurgents as traitors, and defended himself as best he could for six hours. He had but four or five hand guns, four spikes, and some black-bills, and the assailants having battered the gates with their ordnance, and slain several of his men, the latter began to mutiny, and he was compelled to yield. He added that he knew his loyalty was suspected, but that he intended to remain faithful to her Majesty.

The same evening Abergavenny wrote to the Council, acknowledging the receipt of a letter requiring him to follow in the track of Wyatt and his associates. He said that on the previous night he had assembled two thousand men at Maidstone, and was marching them towards Rochester, when they heard of the defection of Norfolk's force. The whole of his men thereupon deserted, many to Wyatt, and others to their homes, while he was obliged to seek refuge, with his servants, in the sheriff's house at Mereworth, where he expected to be immediately attacked. He concluded his letter by regretting the action pursued by the duke in marching to Rochester without having previously communicated with him. The Lord Warden, writing the next day to Abergavenny, declared that he was prepared to shed his heart's blood in the defence of the Queen, and promised to meet him at Rochester, on the 4th of February, with as many men as he could procure.

When the insurgents reached Dartford, their numbers had greatly increased. One authority has estimated them at two thousand men, another at three thousand, and a third at from twelve to fifteen thousand. Though the last of these figures is evidently much beyond the mark, it is clear that at this stage Wyatt had a considerable force under his command. And so forcibly did this fact present itself to the Queen, that she sent her Master of the Horse and two loyal members of her Council to confer with the leader of the insurgents. Wyatt, who usually wore his name in large letters on the front of his cap, had placed his ordnance at the west end of the town, and thither he went forth, pike in hand, to meet them. Replying to their request as to what would satisfy him, he demanded the Tower and the Queen's person, and required that the Council should be changed. A parley ensued, during which he denied that he was a traitor, and affirmed that he had assembled the men of Kent to prevent the realm being overrun by Spaniards.

The interview ended, and the Queen's representatives returned to St. James's. Now was the time for Wyatt to have struck an effective blow. The city gates were open, and the citizens were ready to welcome him. But he dawdled by the way, and allowed the favourable moment to pass. Having spent two days in moving forward from Dartford, he remained another day at Dartford Strond, and suffered three of his prisoners to escape. On the 3rd of February he arrived at Southwark, which surrendered without opposition. While there the news of his confederates' failure in other parts of the country reached him. His letter to the Duke of Suffolk had been intercepted, and had led to the duke's arrest, and his confinement in the Tower. The rising in Devonshire was suppressed, and Sir Peter Carew had fled to France. These tidings were extremely disheartening to the insurgents, who had already begun to grumble at their prolonged inactivity.

Still Wyatt lingered; and the Queen, emboldened by imminent danger, seized her sceptre, and rode through the streets of London to the Guildhall, where she addressed a crowded audience of the citizens. She told them that her subjects in Kent had risen in rebellion in consequence of her intended marriage, and announced that if the country was opposed to the union, she was quite prepared to withdraw from it. The appeal was successful. Next day twenty thousand men were enrolled, and placed in different parts of the city. Mary's cause was now in the ascendant, and might have continued so but for the action of certain members of her Council, who, knowing that in spite her words to the contrary her heart was set upon Philip, declared that they were still opposed to the Spanish match Strange fluctuations of public opinion were occasioned by these announcements, affecting the London train-bands as well as the insurgents, many of whom deserted to the train-bands, while parties of the latter passed over in turn to the insurgents.

On the day of his arrival at Southwark, Wyatt resolved to make an attempt to examine the defences of London Bridge, with a view to facilitating his entrance into the city. About midnight he cautiously made his way to the bridge, and breaking down a wall, passed into the porter's lodge. The porter was asleep, but his wife and family were awake. Wyatt commanded them not to stir, as they valued their lives, and leaving his men to guard the house, he proceeded to the draw-bridge, which was cut away. Torches were flaming on the city side, and amongst several moving figures he recognised the Lord Admiral, the Lord Mayor, and other officers in consultation about the defence of the bridge. He returned to his confederates, telling them that there was no way in that direction into the city. Proposals were then made to effect an entrance by Kingston-on-Thames, or by Aldgate, Wyatt himself suggesting a return into Kent to attack the force which they knew to be marching towards London under the sheriff and his supporters. It was, however, decided that they should march for Kingston Bridge, and crossing the Thames, enter London by Hyde Park. But two more days elapsed before any attempt was made to act upon this decision. In the interval, Wyatt continued to communicate with his friends within the city, who promised to stand by him should he reach Ludgate by daybreak on the 7th. Having reimbursed those of his men who had sustained loss by following him, he at length pushed out of Southwark on the 6th, with a force which had dwindled to fifteen hundred men. The strictest order was maintained, property being, with one or two exceptions, scrupulously respected. He led his little band through the marshes of Lambeth and Wandsworth, and reached Kingston about four o'clock in the afternoon.

The wildest excitement prevailed in the city. Judges and lawyers wore armour under their robes, and every man provided himself with means for his own protection. Precautions against surprise had been taken by cutting off all communication across the river. The bridges, for fifteen miles, were broken down, and the boats secured on the city side. The Queen was advised to fly, but refused. "Whatever happens," she was heard to say, "I am the wife of the Prince of Spain; crown, rank, life, all shall go, before I will take any other husband."

Wyatt found that only about thirty feet of the wooden bridge at Kingston had been destroyed, and that the gap could be filled up without great difficulty. It was perceived that one of the vessels moored on the other side of the river would exactly answer the purpose, but a guard of three hundred royalists looked menacingly across the water. The royalists attempted to dispute the passage, and Wyatt's guns were turned upon them. A few well-delivered rounds compelled them to retire, and two or three Medway sailors plunged into the water, swam to the opposite side, and procured a barge. After several hours' work, the bridge was repaired, and late in the evening the insurgents passed over it in torchlight unopposed. Their numbers had now increased to four or five thousand men. Driving in the advanced post at Brentford, they continued their march upon the city, but under conditions which, it was evident, must seriously diminish their chance of success. The night was cold and wet, and their movements were exceedingly slow. To add to their embarrassment, a gun-carriage broke, and an hour was lost in repairing it. It was thus impossible for them to keep their appointment at Ludgate, and several of Wyatt's chief supporters saw that failure was inevitable. This afforded another opportunity for Sir George Harper. Thinking to save his head, and restore his tarnished name to the favour of his sovereign, he rode off to St. James's and announced the approach of the insurgents.

The Queen instantly called a council of war, and it was decided to allow Wyatt and his men to enter the city and then surround them. At four o'clock in the morning, the train-bands were ordered to muster immediately at Charing Cross. By eight o'clock ten thousand men were under arms.

Several hours later,* Wyatt, at the head of his small force, reached Hyde Park Corner. He wore high boots and spurs, a hat of velvet embroidered with broad bone-work, a shirt of mail with light sleeves, and a vest handsomely trimmed with yellow lace. His men, now reduced to about two thousand, were badly armed, and looked weary and draggled, after their protracted and cheerless march. Wyatt flourished his sword and led them on. As they emerged from Hyde Park Corner, a troop of cavalry rushed out from a by-way and cut them in two. In the struggle about one hundred of the insurgents were killed, many were wounded, and four hundred were captured. Meanwhile Wyatt and three or four hundred men were advancing towards Ludgate. The streets were lined with people, who looked on with almost breathless eagerness, but made no effort to stop them. At St. James's they separated, Wyatt and a small party fighting their way along Pall Mall, not without loss, while another party, under Knyvett, took the direction of Westminster. Wyatt pressed bravely on, and at Charing Cross, where the Lord Chamberlain, with a thousand pikemen, was stationed, a lucky incident enabled him to pass. Seeing the insurgents coming up, Edward Courtenay, the young Earl of Devon, turned his horse towards Whitehall, and above the shouts and imprecations the voice of Sir

---

* In his Chronicle, Charles Wriothesley, who was probably an eye-witness, says it was two o'clock before Wyatt reached the Park.

Thomas Cornwallis was heard crying, "Fie! my lord, is this the action of a gentleman?" Courtenay took no notice, and as he galloped off, calling "Lost! all is lost!" the guards were seized with alarm, and fled in the utmost confusion. Knyvett's men shot a few arrows at them as they entered the gates of Whitehall, and hurried on for Charing Cross; but their way was closed by a company of archers, and a fierce hand-to-hand fight ensued, in which sixteen of the insurgents were slain.

Wyatt continued to advance. Passing along the Strand, Temple Bar was thrown open to him. At the old Fleet bridge three hundred royalists stood under arms, but offered no opposition. The moment his approach was observed, Ludgate was closed. Stating that "the Queen had granted all their petitions," he demanded to pass. "Avaunt! traitor, thou shalt have no entrance here," answered the Lord Admiral. Wyatt felt that the day was lost. Of the ardent band of knights, yeomen, and peasants who had followed him from Allington a fortnight ago, only twenty-four now stood by him. Wheeling round his horse, he plunged through the crowd, and endeavoured to fight his way back to Temple Bar. But being completely hemmed in by cavalry, he dismounted, and in despair sat down upon a bench opposite the Bell Sauvage Yard. "Sir," cried a bystander, "ye were best to yield; the day has gone against you; perchance ye may find the Queen merciful." Sir Maurice Berkeley then rode up, and summoned him to surrender. Wyatt at once threw away his sword, and to save him from the hands of enraged royalists, Berkeley took him up upon his horse.* Knyvett, Brett, and others also surrendered. The prisoners were carried back to Westminster, and the Queen, in a flutter of joyous excitement, stood at a window in the

---

* Baker's "Chronicles of the Kings of England," p. 319.

F

Palace and saw them borne off in a barge to the Tower. When the tumult had subsided, a slight reaction in favour of Mary set in, and the nobility flocked to St. James's to offer their congratulations.

During the next few days Sir Henry Isley, Thomas Culpeper, and many others were apprehended. The sheriff of Kent wrote to the Privy Council on the 10th of February, stating that he had secured Richard Parke, Wm. Smythe,* William Green,† Alex. Fisher, William Tilden, Peter Maplesden, and others, and had sent " such as were of substance " to Allington Castle, and set a guard over them; the poorer prisoners he had committed to Maidstone gaol; he pointed out that Sir George Harper, in addition to his residence at Chart, had also a house in London, where many of his valuables were to be found. In a postscript he added that he had himself taken charge of Allington, and had delivered the custody of the mansions of Harper, Thomas Culpeper, Robert Rudstone, and Sir Henry Isley, to several faithful adherents of the Queen. A special commission was issued for the trial of the prisoners in London. Harper, Rudstone, Knyvett, Walter Mantell, sen., of Monk's Horton, Walter Mantell, jun., of Canterbury, Captain Brett, Culpeper, and other ringleaders were arraigned on the 15th of February. The indictments also included the names of the young Cobhams, Thomas Isley, John Nayler, of Maidstone, Edward Wyatt, of Allington, and Robert Fuller and John Swinnock, of Maidstone. As the prisons were filled, the forms of an ordinary trial were dispensed with in the case of the humbler offenders, who were dragged forth in batches to places of execution. Nearly one hundred were executed in London, and on the 18th twenty-three were hanged in

---

* Smythe was a jurat of Maidstone in 1559, and mayor in 1564.
† Green was mayor in 1560; he died in 1569.

Kent.* Towards the end of February, several of the ringleaders were also sent into the county for execution. Sir Henry Isley,† with his brother, and Thomas and William Mantell were hanged at Maidstone; Anthony and William Knyvett, with another of the Mantells, at Sevenoaks; and Captain Brett and others at Rochester. Lord Cobham's two sons were condemned, but not executed, as was also Robert Rudstone, who afterwards had his estates restored to him. Sir George Harper likewise appears to have escaped with his life. Hume speaks of him as one of the persons of distinction whom Philip, immediately after his marriage with Mary, in hopes of gaining popularity, discharged from the Tower. Several hundreds of the insurgents, with ropes about their necks, were conducted before the Queen at Whitehall, and, falling on their knees, received her pardon. A royal commission was subsequently issued empowering twelve gentlemen to set at liberty such of the offenders as were in the different gaols in Kent, and to compound with them according to the nature of their offences. Among those who were thus released from prison were William Tilden and John Hall, an eminent surgeon, of Maidstone.‡ As a punishment on the town for joining in the rebellion, the Privy Council revoked the Charter which had been granted in the previous reign, and Maidstone remained in a state of disfranchisement for five years.

Wyatt's trial was from time to time delayed, as Mary's advisers hoped to extort from him a confession implicating

---

* Wriothesley's Chronicle, p. 112.

† "1561.—The 14 May was bered [buried] in Saint Pulker's parryche my lade Esley, the wyff of Sir Henre Esley, knight of Kentt, the wyche he came in with Sir Thomas Wiat, knight, by Queene Mare's days, and he was hanged and drane and quarted, and ys hed sent unto Maydston and set apone."—Diary of Henry Machyn, citizen of London, temp. 1550-63, p. 258.

‡ Tilden died in July 1561, and Hall in October 1568; both were buried at All Saints' Church.

her sister Elizabeth in the rebellion. He had to some extent compromised that princess, and Lady Wyatt was appealed to, with a promise that if her husband would make a further confession, his life should be spared. The trial at length took place on the 15th of March. Wyatt pleaded guilty, and admitted that he had written to Elizabeth, advising her to remove as far as possible from London, and that he had verbally received her thanks. This did not satisfy the court, and when sentence of death was passed upon him, he was given to understand that he might still earn his pardon if he would criminate the princess. On the 17th, Elizabeth wrote to the Queen, denying Wyatt's statement. Wyatt remained in the Tower until nine o'clock on the morning of the 11th of April, when he was led out for execution on Tower Hill. He made certain observations on the scaffold, which, though ambiguous in their import, were accepted by the spectators as amounting to an acquittal of Elizabeth from any share in the rising. His head was then struck off, and afterwards set on a pole in a field near Hyde Park, but was soon stolen by some of his partisans;* whilst his body was quartered, and hung in chains at four different parts of the city.

The Queen allowed Lady Wyatt to retain possession of the manor of Boxley, and a portion of the adjoining land; but the other extensive estates which had hitherto belonged to her family were forfeited. A lease of the castle and manor of Allington was in 1568 granted by Queen Elizabeth to John Astley, Master of her Jewels. Wyatt's son George was in 1570 restored in blood by that Queen, and became the owner of Boxley manor and other estates. He died in 1624, and was succeeded by his eldest son Francis, who was knighted, and was twice governor of Virginia, dying in

* Grey Friars' Chronicle, p. 89.

1644. His granddaughter married Sir Robert Marsham, Bart. Edwin Wyatt, who resided at Chillington House, was serjeant-at-law. He represented Maidstone in Parliament from 1685 to 1688, and was recorder of the borough from 1688 to 1690. The estates were, in 1753, devised by the last of the Wyatts to Robert, second Lord Romney.

CHAPTER III.

ST. MARY'S CHURCH—THE COLLEGE OF ALL SAINTS.

The Archiepiscopal Palace—St. Mary's Church—Goulds Chantry—Rectors of Maidstone—License for Archbishop Courtenay's Foundation—Erection of the College—Death of the Archbishop: his Place of Burial—Endowments—Description of the College Buildings—Masters of the College—Wotton's Tomb—The College Dissolved—Pensions to Priests—Revenue of the College: its Domain Lands.

A CHURCH existed at Maidstone as early as the eleventh century, but we have no record of its ministers until the time of King John. A grant in one of the Charter Rolls of that king's reign mentions that William de Cornhill was rector of Maidstone in the year 1205. Cornhill belonged to a family occupying a high position in the county. Two or three years after the above date, desiring to exemplify his devotion to the Church, he gave his mansion here as a residence for the archbishops.

This mansion, since known as the Palace and also as the Manor House, was originally of modest dimensions. Archbishop Ufford, in 1348, caused the whole or the greater part of it to be pulled down, and commenced to erect a larger and more commodious building; but death overtook him when he had worn the pall only six months. During the still shorter career of his successor, little progress appears to have been made with the Palace, and it was not until Simon Islip was appointed to the See that the work was brought to completion. Having sued the administrators of Ufford for dilapidations, and received £1,100, he pulled down a house belonging to the archbishopric at Wrotham, and bringing the materials to Maidstone, used them in the building of the Palace. It is said that for this and similar objects he obtained a license from the Pope to raise a subsidy in the diocese, to be levied at the rate of 4d. in the mark (13s. 4d.); but as his officers only showed the license to the clergy without reading it, he extorted a full tenth from many of the people. However that may be, to Islip belongs the credit of having finished the erection of the Palace, which afterwards became a favourite occasional residence of the archbishops. Some portions of the fabric yet remain, but the present building, which has undergone considerable alteration in modern times, belongs to later periods.*

Of the church of which Cornhill was rector little is known. That it was the ancient parish church of Maidstone, dedicated to St. Mary, we have no reason to doubt, there being, so far as can be ascertained, no other building in the parish which was used at the beginning of the thirteenth century for the purposes of public worship.† The church of St. Faith, of which the visible remains disappeared about twenty years

---

* "History and Antiquities of the Collegiate Church of All Saints," by John Whichcord, architect, 1845.

† The license for the foundation of the College speaks of St. Mary's as the "parish church." In the year 1367 John Stoyl made his will, which was subsequently proved in St. Mary's church, and in which he makes use of these words:—"I leave my body to be buried in the parish church of St. Mary of Maydeestone, and I leave to the high altar there 10s., and to the work of the same church 20s." He left 40s. to the "chapel of St. Faith."—Langham's Register, 120, a.

ago, was probably not then in existence. An inscription found on one of the old pillars attached to it would seem to fix the date of its erection to the year 1272.* Lambarde mentions the principal buildings in the town, but makes no allusion to St. Faith's, and the general silence of contemporary writers in this respect justifies the belief that, from an architectural point of view, it was not a building of much consequence. It was apparently a free chapel, but at any rate it appears to have been subordinate to St. Mary's, which was unappropriated, the rector receiving both the great and small tithes. St. Mary's was a rich benefice, as is proved by the taxation roll of Pope Nicholas IV., in which the living is returned at £106 13s. 4d., the chapels of Detling and Loose being then annexed to it.

Philipott states that a chantry was established in the church by Roger de Vinters about the year 1366, and that it was endowed with the estates of Goulds and Shepway, which, in the reign of Charles I., became a part of the Mote estate. Beale Poste admits that such a chantry existed, but doubts whether it was founded by Vinters, and affirms that its endowment consisted of Goulds only, Shepway having been already in lay hands. An ancient manuscript in possession of the Dean and Chapter of Canterbury, however, corroborates while it also corrects Philipott's statement. The chantry was established under the will of Robert Vyneter, of Maidstone, in 1369, as set forth in a royal license granted to his executors in that year.† It was endowed with lands, mills, &c., to the amount of £20 per annum, for the support of two priests to celebrate masses for the souls of the founder and his friends; but the names of the lands are not given. As

---

* Poste, p. 98.
† Historical MSS. Commission, Fifth Report. Vyneter also founded a chantry at Canterbury.

the altar, however, afterwards became known as Goulds chantry, it is probable that the rents of that estate were included in the grant for its maintenance. Vyneter was one of the conservators of the peace for Kent in 1344, and is believed to have resided on the estate since called Vinters.

We glean from the Lambeth Registers other scraps of information respecting St. Mary's. A letter was sent by the archbishop to the Prior and Chapter of Christ Church, Canterbury, in 1296, admonishing them to provide oil and wax for the celebration of the Lord's Supper in the church of Maidstone. Ordinations frequently took place in the church; one was held in 1313, two in 1318, one in 1320, and another in February 1368, on which latter occasion Archbishop Langham ordained twenty-six youths. The names of the following rectors, with the year of their admission, are extant:—

William de Cornhill	1205
John Mansell	1263
Ralph de Farnham	1279
Nicholas de Knowle	1288
Stephen Haselingfelde	1310
Thomas de Keresbrooke	1326
Hugh Polegnini	1367
Robert Sibthorpe*	1381
Robert Fynchcook†	1393
William de Tyryngton‡	1394
Guy de Mone	1395

Three of these rectors were subsequently promoted to high positions in the Church of England. Cornhill was consecrated bishop of Litchfield and Coventry in 1215. John

---

* It is worthy of note that in his will he says, "I commend my soul into the hands of my Lord Jesus," thereby discarding the then universal formula of commending his soul to the Virgin Mary.

† Also rector of Otham, near Maidstone.

‡ He was prebendary of Lincoln, and may probably be identified with William de Tyryngton, to whom in 1370, Nicholas, rector of Orpington, bequeathed his silver beads and manuscripts.

Mansell, who was held in high esteem by Henry III., was a noted pluralist, and received various testimonies of the royal favour. He was prebendary and chancellor of St. Paul's, prebendary of Wells and Chester, provost of Beverley, and treasurer of York, besides holding other clerical appointments. Nor were the offices conferred upon him confined to the church. He subsequently became Constable of the Tower, Chief Justice of England, and Keeper of the Great Seal. Of this extraordinary individual it is related that in a battle between the English and French, he took an eminent Frenchman prisoner; and it is also stated that when Alexander III. of Scotland and his consort visited England, they accepted his invitation to dine with him in London, on which occasion an immense company was magnificently entertained, 700 dishes being served. He ultimately, however, fell into disfavour with the Court, and Newton tells us that he died abroad in a poor and wretched condition. Guy de Mone was one of the executors under Archbishop Courtenay's will. A prebendary of Lincoln, he became bishop of St. David's in 1397, and dying at Charlton, in Kent, on the 31st of August 1407, was buried in the abbey church of Leeds.

Mone was the last rector. A few months prior to his incumbency, Archbishop Courtenay had obtained a license from Richard II. to establish a college of secular canons at Maidstone, and to convert St. Mary's into a collegiate church. The license is dated the 2nd of August 1395, at Leeds Castle, where the king was then staying. It states that the College is to consist of one master or warden, and as many fellow chaplains and other ministers as in the discretion of the archbishop shall be thought necessary, and empowers him to assign to them, for their support, the advowson of the parish church of St. Mary, with its chapels, and also the revenues of the Hospital at Newark, with the tithes of the chapels of Linton, East Farleigh, and Sutton-by-Dover annexed to it; provided that the alms hitherto paid to the poor at the Hospital shall continue to be paid at the College.* In the same year the rectory of Maidstone was appropriated to the College by a bull of Pope Boniface IX.

It will be convenient in this chapter to deal only with the history of the College, reserving the Church and its annals for separate treatment. Having received the royal sanction, Courtenay appears to have lost no time in turning the project into practical shape. He gave orders for the demolition of St. Mary's Church, and the erection, apparently on the same spot, of the church of All Saints. Simultaneously, a few yards to the south of All Saints' Church, he commenced to build an imposing edifice for the use of the master and priests, and others connected with the College, the ruins of which now form as interesting a specimen of fourteenth century architecture as may be seen in England. In order to defray the expenses of so costly an undertaking, he acquired a license from the Pope to tax all benefices within his province to the extent of 4d. in the pound. The Bishop of Lincoln, however, considering the imposition unjust, refused to make the collection in his diocese, and appealed to the Pontiff. Courtenay was then staying at his Palace at Maidstone, and while the appeal was pending, he was prostrated by fever. His illness increased, and he expired here on the 31st of July 1396, at the age of fifty-three.

As to the place of Courtenay's burial, some uncertainty prevails, but the general opinion of recent writers upon the subject is that he was interred at Canterbury. The archbishop had in his will expressed a wish to lie, at his death,

* Dugdale's "Monasticon," vol. vi., p. 1395. The Hospital was dissolved in August 1397.

with his ancestors, in the nave of Exeter Cathedral. While on his death-bed, however, he altered his intentions, and on the 28th of July added a codicil, stating that he did not consider himself worthy to repose in any cathedral or collegiate church; and he therefore directed that he should be privately buried in the churchyard of Maidstone,* in a spot previously pointed out to his esquire, John Boteler. When his death occurred, preparations were no doubt immediately made to give effect to his last directions as to his funeral. But according to an obituary kept by the monks of Christ Church from 1486 to 1507,† the king happened to be at Canterbury at the time, and overruling the codicil, decreed that the obsequies should take place within the Cathedral. The archbishop's body was consequently removed to Canterbury on the 4th of August, and there interred in the presence of the king, the nobles, the bishops and clergy, and eight or ten thousand spectators. "It was," says Dean Hook, "a public funeral conducted on a scale of great magnificence."

The evidence sometimes advanced in favour of the archbishop's burial at Maidstone chiefly rests upon the testimony of a Latin inscription which was formerly to be seen on the marble slab to Courtenay's memory in the chancel of All Saints' Church. The slab is 11ft. 5in. in length by 4ft. 2¼in. wide, and originally formed the tablet of an alter-tomb, four feet high; but after the Reformation, being found to obstruct the passage through the main aisle, it was lowered, and inserted nearly level with the pavement.‡ Weever visited the church sometime before 1631, and copied the inscrip-

---

* Hook's "Lives of the Archbishops," vol. iv., p. 393; "Archæologia Cantiana," vol. i., p. 179.

† Parchment marked D 12—2; the obituary is also confirmed by the supplement to Thorn's Chronicle.

‡ Newton, p. 71; Poste, p. 87.

tion,* which was, he says, "inlaid with brass about the verge" of the stone, the still existing indentations demonstrating that an archbishop's effigy and other ornaments also occupied its surface. This inscription may be literally translated thus:—

Behold, a reverend (man) William Courtenay by name, who had willed himself to be buried here, in the present place, which he had already built from the foundation, and dedicated to All Saints in token of honour. The last day of July was to him the end of life, in the year one thousand three hundred ninety and five. Consider what this mortal sometime (was), but now thus! How great also was this man while he bore his limbs warm! He (was) primate of the Father; chief of the clergy, and (his) lineage high: very handsome in body and (his) reason shining with wisdom. The son of the noble Earl of Devon, he was a renowned doctor of the laws, whom fame made illustrious. The town of Hereford, famous London city, and Canterbury, three Sees together, (were) a glory to him. Let honour be given; therefore he became chancellor (of Oxford). In all respects a holy father, he was a wise minister, for he was bountiful, cheerful, chaste, pious, and modest; magnanimous, just, and so great a friend to the poor. And because, O Lord, this man was a good shepherd of Christ, we pray that with Thee he may enjoy comfort. Amen.

---

* Nomine Willelmus en Courtnaius reverendus,
Qui se post obitum legaverat hic tumulandum,
In presenti loco quem jam fundarat ab imo;
Omnibus et sanctis titulo sacravit honoris;
Ultima lux Julii sit vite terminus illi,
M ter C quinto decies nouoque sub anno,
Respice mortalis quis quondam, sed modo talis,
Quantus et iste fuit dum membra calentia gessit.
Hic primas patrum, Cleri Dux et genus altum,
Corpore valde decens, sensus et acumine clarans.
Filius hic comitis generosi Devoniensis,
Legum doctor erat celebris quem fama serenat,
Urbs Herefordensis, polis inclita Londoniensis,
Ac Dorobernensis, sibi trine gloria sedis,
Detur honor fit Cancellarius ergo.
Sanctus ubique pater, prudens fuit ipse minister,
Nam largus, letus, castus, pius atque pudicus;
Magnanimus, justus, et egenis totus amicus.
Et quia Rex Christi pastor bonus extitit iste,
Sumat solamen nunc tecum quesumus. Amen.

Both the inscription and the monument fix the chancel as the place of the archbishop's interment, whereas, in the codicil of his will, the churchyard is expressly mentioned. Nor does the epitaph positively state that he was buried here, but only that he had ordered it in his will. Again, the year of his death is given as 1395, instead of 1396—an unusual mistake in an ancient inscription, though it may be due to a confusion of the astronomical with the ecclesiastical year.* On the strength of this inscription, Weever supposed that Courtenay's body lay at Maidstone; but when speaking of Canterbury Cathedral, he says, " I find here in this church a monument of alabaster at the feet of the Black Prince, wherein, both by tradition and writing, it is affirmed that the bones of William Courtenay lie entombed; and I find another to the memory of the same man at Maidstone."† The Canterbury monument is without an inscription, but has the archbishop's effigy, in pontifical dress, lying at full length upon it.

The Rev. Samuel Denne, an antiquary of some repute, a hundred years ago, was a stong disbeliever in the authenticity of the entries in the Canterbury records, contending that they were mere forgeries by the monks in order to exalt the reputation of their Cathedral. In 1794, at his instigation, the ground under the slab in Maidstone church was excavated in his presence,‡ the perpetual curate of All

---

* On this point Mr. J. G. Waller, one of our most distinguished ecclesiastical antiquaries, has kindly favoured me with his opinion. "I don't know," he writes, " whether it is possible that the blunder of a year could have arisen from a mistake in computing from January instead of the 25th March. For instance, a year beginning January 1395 would, after March 25, be 1396. I have no doubt this is how the error has arisen. Such errors are numerous enough in our historians, but I should hardly have expected it in an old inscription."

† "Funeral Monuments," p. 225.

‡ The slab, which had previously stood an inch or two above the pavement, was then inserted level with the floor.

Saints' the master of the Grammar School, and other persons being also present; and in a letter to a friend, dated August 1799, he gave an account of what he saw. After removing the earth to a depth of 5ft. 6in., a human skeleton was found. "The skull, the collar-bone, and the bones of the arms and legs were," he wrote, "in their proper positions. Some of the ribs had sunk on the vertebræ, but appeared through their whole length at their due distances; the teeth were remarkably well set, and seemed to be complete." Mr. Denne fully believed the remains to be those of Courtenay; yet no episcopal ring or crosier was found to identify them with those of a prelate—a fact which renders the exhumation unfavourable to the theory that the archbishop's body was interred here.[*]

After Courtenay's death, the building of the College was continued by his successor, Archbishop Arundel, and by the close of 1397 the work may have been completed. In the previous year the king, by his letters patent, dated Sept. 15, had granted to the master and priests the advowson of the church of Crundall, near Wye, with the reversion of the manors of Trimworth and Fannes in that parish, then held by Henry Yevele for life; and, on the 8th of June 1406, Henry IV. granted to them the manor of Wittersham, with its appurtenances, consisting of 7 messuages, 3 cottages, 156 acres of land, 59 acres of pasture, 27 acres of wood, 34 acres of marsh, and other lands and tenements in the parishes of Maidstone, Loose, Boxley, and Hoo.

Colleges of this description existed at a very early period. At the time of the Norman Conquest, the secular canons had to give way to the mendicant orders; and it was not until there was peace, and commerce and arts began to

---

[*] Dean Stanley, in his "Historical Memorials of Canterbury," observes that Courtenay "lies at the Black Prince's feet," p. 151; also pp. 226-7.

flourish, that colleges of secular priests were again established. Canons were of two kinds, secular and regular. The secular were so called because they conversed in *seculo*, abroad in the world, and discharged spiritual offices to the laity. They were instituted for the more efficient performance of divine service, and lived under much less strict rules than the friars and monks. At the Maidstone College, a master and several canons were maintained, as well as a number of chaplains, singing men, and choristers. The robe worn by the master was a scarlet gown and hood, lined with sarcenet of a lighter hue. Services were held daily in All Saints' Church, where the seats and stalls of the clergy are still prominent objects of interest.

Unfortunately, no pictorial representation of the College in perfect condition has been preserved, and certain portions of the remaining building are so incorporated with modern additions and alterations that it would be difficult to precisely ascertain its original dimensions. But during the building operations conducted by Lord Romney in the beginning of 1845, the modern parts of the structure were partially removed, and the ancient distribution of the rooms could be traced with a very close approach to accuracy.*

The College was built in the Perpendicular style. As the ruins indicate, it was fortified, like all important institutions five hundred years ago, to resist any sudden attack. Faced with squared Kentish ragstone, the gateway tower is battlemented, and is entered in the north front by a groined archway. It is 55ft. long, 25ft. wide at the base, and about 45ft. high to the battlements. The main archway is 8ft. 11in. wide and 19ft. high, while the smaller one adjoining, for foot passengers, is 4ft. wide. On entering the vestibule, the first room to the right is 32ft. 6in. by 12ft.

---

* Beale Poste's "History of the College of All Saints."

10in., with a fire-place and two windows, and appears to have been the hall or refectory. The next apartment is 18ft. 8in. in length, also with a fire-place and two windows, and was apparently the kitchen. Then there was the scullery 15ft. long, with one window, and a passage adjoining 4ft. wide. This passage communicated with the tower next the river, the floor of which is 16ft. 10in. by 12ft. 1in. Upstairs, beginning at the end of the building where we commenced, was a bedroom 16ft. 6in. by 15ft. 6in., in a line with which were three apartments, one 15ft. 8in. long, the second, possibly the infirmary, 18ft. 1in. in length, with two windows and a fire-place, and the third, 15ft. 10in. long, with one window and no fire-place, and a passage 4ft. 9in. wide, whence a stone spiral staircase leads to the upper room of the river tower. This upper apartment has four windows, and may have been the treasury or muniment room. Another staircase conducts to the roof, which forty years ago was tiled, and ended in a peak, surrounded by battlements.

A cloister below, and a corridor above, ran the whole length of these apartments. The cloister was 5ft. 10in. wide, built of timber on a dwarf wall, and divided in compartments between stout uprights or pillars. In each compartment was a mullion joined to an arched heading from either pillar. The corridor, which was over the cloister but extended rather wider, was formed of open framework, the compartments varying from 7ft. 1in. to 8ft. 3in., from centre to centre of their respective uprights. In the cloister there were several inscriptions, and one near the kitchen door, which was obliterated in 1837, was written in Lombardic characters, and was thought to have been the 49th verse of Psalm cxix, as rendered in the Vulgate.

Returning to the gateway tower, we find over the arch

a room 50ft. by 21ft., with a large fire-place at the eastern end; it has three well-proportioned windows looking towards the church, two smaller windows in the opposite direction, and one towards Knightrider Street. On the right hand side of the outer entrance is an apartment 13ft. 3in. by 11ft. 11in., with one window and no fire-place, which may have been a vestibule or an almonry. A spiral stone staircase leads to the bedroom above, over the doorway of which are inserted, with a graver, the characters, "Arc'p'copus Ws. O.," being the initials of the founder. On the left hand side of the gateway was the bakehouse of the College. The room measured 18ft. 1in. by 11ft. 2in., and was provided with four windows. Traces formerly existed showing that an oven of great magnitude had joined to the side walls. An adjacent meadow was called the bakehouse mead, as appears by a certificate of the College, dated 1546, and by a recital of lands in a private Act of Parliament passed in 1698.

The master's house is believed to have stood towards the river, but the original structure has been disfigured by various additions and interior alterations. It appears to have consisted of four rooms, viz., a parlour, a withdrawing room, and two sleeping apartments. The beams in the ceiling of one of the rooms were handsomely fluted and moulded, and when the papering was removed from the withdrawing room in May 1845, ornaments of leaves and baskets of flowers, painted in many colours, were seen. The original walls were 2ft. 6in. thick. A part of the building which stands about forty yards to the rear of the front gateway has been called the master's tower; it is nearly 14ft. square, inside measurement, and the opening through it is embraced by a single arch, beautifully moulded. An interior staircase conducts, by sixteen steps, to an upper room, which is 14ft. 5in. square.

The distance between the front and the back or south gateway is about a hundred and forty yards. The back gatehouse, of which only a fragment remains, measured 32ft. 2in. by 18ft. 10in., and had carriage and footway arches similar to those of the principal entrance. There was a doorway in the river wall which communicated with a bridge over the Medway to the archbishop's park, now known as the Lock Meadow. During the alterations thirty-six years ago, the foundations of other parts of the College were discovered, but owing to their decayed and imperfect condition, their former appropriations could not be surmised.

It may here be stated that the ancient building at the south end of Mill Street is thought to have belonged either to the Palace or the College—more probably to the latter; in which case it might have been occupied by the College servants, or by the poor persons and children to whom the master and priests were forced by their endowments to give £10 a year in alms, as appears by a return made to the Crown in 1535. The building is 146ft. long by 26ft. in width. A flight of sixteen steps, with a mouldering oak railing, leading to the front floor, is boldly corbelled out from the face of the front wall, and covered with a pent-roof. This is an excellent example of the external staircases by which the upper chambers of a certain class of houses were approached in the fourteenth century.*

We will now proceed to notice the masters and clergy of the College. The first master was Sir John Wotton,† who was canon of Chichester, and rector of Staplehurst in 1393. He died on the 31st of October 1417, and his will, as preserved in the Lambeth Library, shows that he was a man of

---

* Parker's "Mediæval Domestic Architecture."

† "Sir" or "Dominus" was commonly applied to priests until the Reformation, and was no indication of knightly rank.

large substance. He bequeathed sums of money to the churches of Maidstone, Loose, Detling, East Farleigh, Linton, Sutton, and Staplehurst, and also to several of these parishes for distribution amongst the poor people. Being opposed to the sumptuousness of funerals in those days, he left the following directions to his executors. "I will that only five wax tapers, each of the weight of ten pounds, in honour of the five wounds of Christ, be burning, with becoming furniture, in the obsequies round my corpse; one of which to be placed by my heart, to point my mind to God, and the rest to be burning about my corpse in the form of a cross. And that twelve torches only be prepared and borne before my body while it is being carried to the church. And when my body has been deposited in the appointed place, I will that the said twelve torches be extinguished, and afterwards that they be lit at the mass, and burn until the entire mass is finished; that they be then borne away with the funeral, in sign of light eternal, until my body be buried, and afterwards that they remain with the wax tapers in the said church, to the honour of God, until they are expended."

His remains were interred in All Saints', and it is evident from his will that he had fixed upon the identical spot on which his monument now stands as that where he wished to be buried. The monument is at the back of the sedelia, facing the south-east entrance, and has often been ascribed to Archbishop Courtenay, because it bears his arms. It is richly canopied, and a slab of Bethersden marble retains the indentations of a brass pourtraying the master in his robes, and encompassed by the epitaph—"Hic jacet Dominus Johannes Wotton, rector ecclesiæ parochialis de Stapilhurst, canonicus Cicestrensis, and primus magister hunjus Collegii, qui obiit ultimo die Octobris 1417." The painted subjects in the recesses are curious as specimens of artistic colouring at the beginning of the fifteenth century, when even in Italy the art of painting was comparatively young. One of them delineates an archangel, supposed to be Gabriel, with the figures of St. Katherine and St. Mark; and another represents two figures, believed to be Thomas á Becket, the patron saint of Canterbury, and Richard de la Wyche, the canonised bishop of Chichester. On the canopies are the arms of Archbishop Arundel, and also those of the College and of Christ Church.

Wotton was succeeded at the College by John Holond, LL.D., who was instituted on the 8th of March, 1418, and died in the following year. Of several of the masters little is known. Roger Heron was admitted August 7, 1419, and resigned in 1430; William Duffield held office until 1441; John Darrell, admitted July 8, 1441; Peter Stackley, LL.B., admitted 25th June, 1444; Robert Smyth, admitted December 6, 1450, and died in 1458; Thomas Boleyn, LL.B., admitted November 24, 1458, became canon of St. Roche, Luxemburg, and died in 1470; John Freston, admitted in 1470, and resigned in the same year. John Lee, who was appointed on the 2nd of May, 1470, died in 1494. Several small legacies are mentioned in his will. He bequeathed certain of his effects to the College, and gave to six priests 3s. 4d., to the priests of the Church 4d., to two parish priests 4d., to four choristers 8d., and to thirteen poor persons 1d. each. It is interesting to note that he also left £10, to be divided in equal parts, and bestowed as marriage gifts on five maidens living in the parish of Maidstone.

The next master was John Comberton, D.D., who was appointed June 4, 1494. He died in 1506, and bequeathed 20s. to the College, 10s. for the repair of All Saints' Church, 6s. 8d. for the repair of St. Faith's Chapel, and 10s. for the repair of the roads between Stone Street and Tovil, besides other legacies. His successor was collated to the mastership on the 17th of April, 1506. This was William Grocyn, who was the friend of Erasmus, the enlightened and vigorous promoter of the Reformation. Grocyn had completed his Oxford studies in Italy, and held high rank as a scholar, Erasmus speaking of him as being singularly learned and one of the most judicious divines in England. Besides being master of the College he was vicar of East Peckham from 1511 to 1517, and in the latter year he was preferred to the church of St. Lawrence, Old Jewery, London. Dying in 1519, at the age of seventy-seven, he was buried at the end of the stalls in the high choir of All Saints'. By will he devised certain lands for the support of the College. Grocyn, it is said, introduced Erasmus to Archbishop Warham.

Some improvements in the institution were obviously intended at this juncture, as the primate, in one of his letters to the Duke of Buckingham, writes that he has an urgent appointment at Maidstone in June 1519, concerning the reformation of this College. Grocyn was succeeded by Thomas Penyton, who was admitted on the 5th of October, 1519. The next and last master was John Lease, LL.D. He had been educated at New College, and was rector of Biddenden, afterwards Vicar-general to the archbishop, and prebendary of St. Paul's. His name appears in a list of subscribers to a loan to Henry VIII. in 1542. He died in 1557, and was buried in the chapel of Winchester College, of which he was a fellow.

The College was dissolved about the year 1546, when its domain lands became the property of the Crown. A pension of £48 16s. 8d. appears to have been bestowed upon John Lease, the late master, and life pensions were also granted to a number of priests. The following is a list of those who were in receipt of pensions at the commencement of Mary's reign, but whether they were all connected with the College, or were chantry priests, we cannot discover. William Olane, John Godfrey, and Thomas Wood (sub-master), received £6 13s. 4d. each; George Denham, £6; John Porter (sacristan), Thomas Warde, and William Rix, £5 each; George Pryour, John Parker, Arthur Butler, Thomas Pynde (who died in 1549), and Richard Rede, £4 each; William Clere, Arthur Barton, and John Weston (who died in 1551, and was buried in All Saints' churchyard), £2 13s. 4d. each; John Ware, John Pyersbie, and Thomas Huggarde, £2 6s. 8d. each; Jacob Killingrewe, Henry Sturgeon, Edward Cowdrey, and Richard Turner, £2 each.

There is no record of the annual value of the College prior to 1535. In that year Henry VIII. resolved to transfer the first-fruits and tenths of all benefices and ecclesiastical institutions from the Pope to the Crown, and that they might be collected to their full value he caused a valuation roll to be drawn up. This roll, known as the "Valor Ecclesiasticus,"* is at the Public Record Office, and the returns of the College are therein given in considerable detail. The items are these:—

Site of College, with all arable, pasture, and meadow land belonging thereto, in Maidstone and Horwash	£8	10	0
From the sale of woods in the parishes of Maidstone, Boxley, Barming, and Aylesford, besides the fuel of the Hospital of the said College, and of the farmer of Buckland	0	13	4
Farm of Buckland, with all lands lying in the West Borough (Westree), let out to farm	14	13	4
Farm of the manor of Chillington, with the dominical lands belonging to the same, formerly of the rectory of Maidstone, the annual rent of Assize belonging to the said manor, and the profits of the Court in ordinary years	2	18	3
Lands and tenements in Maidstone, let out to farm	12	16	3
Lands let out to farm in Hunton, Marden, Boxley, Weavering, and Halstow within the Hundred of Hoo	5	3	0
Carried forward	44	14	2

* Vol. i., pp. 75, 76.

Brought forward £44	14	2	
Tenths or profits of the rectory of Maidstone, with the chapels of St. Faith, Detling, and Loose, the predial tithes, personal oblations, and other emoluments 61	6	8	
And of the farm of two messuages and divers lands belonging to the said chapels, with the predial tithes, personal oblations, and other emoluments pertaining to the same 20	6	8	
Farm of the rectory of East Farleigh and of certain lands there.. 10	13	4	
Farm of the rectory of Linton (Lylyngton) and of certain lands there 11	0	0	
Farm of the chapel of Sutton............................ 5	11	8	

	£	s.	d.
„ „ manors of Trimworth and Fannes, with dominical lands annexed thereto	18	13	4
Rents belonging to the said manors	14	16	8¼
Profits of the Court in ordinary years...............	0	3	4
„ „ sale of wood belonging to the said manors, besides the fuel for the farmer there....	1	10	0

	£	s.	d.
	35	3	4½
Farm of the manor of Wittersham, with the dominical lands, sale of wood, and profits of the Court	16	16	1
The Lord Archbishop of Canterbury for serving the rectory at Northfleet	6	13	4
Total revenue........................... £	212	5	3½

The "deductions" from this sum are as follows:—

Rents paid—

	£	s.	d.
To the Archbishop from the Manor Court of Maidstone	9	2	11
To the Prior of Christ Church, Canterbury, from the Court of East Farleigh	1	9	5½
To the Prior of Leeds..................................	1	8	2
To the Abbot of Bello (Battle?)	0	12	8
To the Abbot of St. Augustine, without the walls of Canterbury	0	8	10
To the Abbot of Boxley	0	4	4
To Sir Henry Isley..................................	0	3	2
To Lord Grey	0	3	0
To the lord of Preston (at Faversham?)	0	2	0
To Thomas Weldish, of Linton	0	1	9
To the Court of Paulster (Wittersham?)	0	1	2

	£	s.	d.
	13	17	5½
In procurations to the Lord Archdeacon.....................	0	10	0
Pension to the vicar of Linton	2	13	4
„ two chaplains serving the chapels of Detling and Loose	16	0	0
Corrodies distributed to five poor persons from the foundation ..	10	0	0
Obits of Archbishop Courtenay, founder of the College, and of its benefactors...	1	13	4
„ Masters John Wotton and Galfrid Malstone	3	0	0
Fee to the seneschal of the Court	1	10	0
„ „ auditor	1	0	0
„ „ collector of the College rents......................	2	13	4
Total deductions .... £	52	17	5½

Deducting this amount from the revenue, the gross income of the College for the year 1535 was £159 7s. 10d. About ten years after the above survey, the king resolved to suppress all the colleges, monasteries, chantries, and religious guilds in the kingdom; and with this view the Maidstone College property was re-valued by a royal commission. The report of the commissioners differs from the foregoing in but few particulars, the gross annual value being returned at £208. The College was then dissolved, its lands being vested in the Crown.

If we now follow the history of the College property, we shall find much curious information respecting the the situation and extent of the lands which belonged to the institution, the persons by whom they were occupied, and the names of localities in and around Maidstone in the middle of the sixteenth century. It will be impossible to do so, however, as minutely as could be wished, inasmuch as the ancient volumes which contain the particulars of the sale of these lands are in many parts illegible from having been saturated with water during the conflagration in which both Houses of Parliament were destroyed in 1834, when these and other valuable records were thrown into the street.

The first transaction preparatory to the dissolution was an indenture made on the 30th of November 1537, by which Archbishop Cranmer exchanged with Henry VIII. the manor of Maidstone, and also the advowson of the College and Church of Maidstone, for various lands in other parts of the county. Three years afterwards the king negotiated an exchange of property with Sir Thomas Wyatt the elder. The deed by which this was effected is dated June 14, 1540, and slightly curtailed is as follows:—

Sir Thomas Wyatt grants and sells to the king the various estates of Shales Court, Okington, Rundall, Timberwood, Rainetoft, Milton, and Pole in Kent; the parsonage of the church of Milton; and estates in the towns and parishes of Shorne, Higham, Chalk, Milton, Southfleet, Denton, Stone, Darenth, and Swanscombe, in the county of Kent. Also the following parcels of land in the parish of Maidstone, viz., Hillfields,* twenty acres, in tenure of William Reeve,† of Maidstone; land called John Tolset's croft, five acres; one parcel of land adjoining to Sharnoll Cross, by estimation three acres, in tenure of Henry Cheeseman, in Maidstone; a parcel of land called Caryng,‡ and the profits of the fair yearly there, for standing upon the same, in tenure of Wm. Parker; a parcel of land of two acres behind St. John's chapel,§ and a garden at the same chapel; a garden, tenement, and two parcels of land at Whitfield Cross, in Maidstone, containing four and a half acres, in tenure of William Maundy; a saffron garden,‖ one acre, in tenure of Thomas Lorkin, in Maidstone; a shop and shambles in High Street there, in occupation of Thomas Bennet, butcher, and a yard and one rood of ground in occupation of Peter Capper; a tenement called Maundy's tenement and garden, in occupation of Peter Mapleeden; a wharf lying before Wingham's house; a messuage in tenure of William Lilly,¶ in Maidstone; the messuage called Shepway Court, with appurtenances, in Maidstone, in tenure of Thomas Nash, and all the houses and buildings thereto belonging; one parcel of land called Shepway field, twenty acres; Longcroft, five acres; Shebrome, sixteen acres; Kington field, Nokefield and Little Nokefield, sixteen acres; Little Whitfield, four acres; a parcel of land at Mangrovett,** five acres; twenty acres of land at Shepway Hothe, with appurtenances in Maidstone, in tenure of Thomas Nash; five acres and three roods adjoining Shepway Hothe, being parcel of the said messuage called Shepway Court, in Maidstone; one messuage called Dynes, in Maidstone, in holding of William Smyth. And the said Sir Thomas Wyatt covenanteth to the king that the said lands are of the clear yearly value of £207 19s. 3d., over and above all reprises, and besides the soil of the woods (i.e., the rent of the same in depasture) and yearly wood sales, which are covenanted to be of the value of £38 19s. 10d. Reserved to Sir Thomas Wyatt £6 10s. 3d., due to the manor of Maidstone for the said lands, and several other quit-rents due to other manors.

Then follows a list of properties granted in consideration of the above by the king to Sir Thomas, including the abbey and vicarage of Boxley, with the lands attached, and lands at Weavering Street, Harbourland, Teston, Aylesford, East and West Malling, &c., the whole being of the clear yearly value of £200 19s. 10d., exclusive of certain rents reserved.

---

* In the will, dated 1618, of James Franklyn, of Maidstone, his lands called Hillfields, containing twenty acres, are mentioned.
† One of the jurates named in the first Charter of Incorporation granted to the town.
‡ The Fair Meadow is doubtless a part of Caring, which consisted of sixteen acres, and was previously let by the archbishop to the Abbot of Boxley at 16s. per annum, as stated in the Maidstone Manor Book of 1509.
§ This chapel is believed to have stood in Stone Street.
‖ Saffron, which was used for dying, but is now superseded by chemical inventions, was formerly much cultivated.
¶ William Grocyn, master of the College, was godfather to William Lilly, and left him 5s. in his will. In the middle of the sixteenth century, one William Lilly, a staunch Protestant, occupied the house still standing at the south-west corner of Havock Lane.
** Now the site of the new cemetery.

With the death of Sir Thomas Wyatt, in 1542, many of his possessions appear to have reverted, by sale, exchange, or otherwise, to the Crown. Thus we find by a deed, dated August 23, 1547, that Caring, with the profits of the market, Lorkin's saffron garden, Whitfield, Shepway Court, consisting of ninety acres, and Shales Court, comprising about three hundred acres, were granted to Sir Walter Hendley, knight, sergeant-at-law. There are also enumerated in the grant ninety-four acres of land called Stonerock, Shernold's croft, consisting of eighteen acres, and other lands, lately the property of the archbishop. Among the latter is the manor of Oldborough, which is sometimes spoken of as Great Oldborough and Little Oldborough, the former consisting of twenty-four acres, and the latter of three fields containing twelve acres. Oldborough is mentioned in one of the deeds as being "in Maidstone," but its exact site has not been ascertained.

After remaining more than two years in possession of the Crown, the site of the College and its domain lands were purchased for £1,081 18s. 1d. by George Brooke, Lord Cobham, of Cobham Hall. In a deed, dated the 10th of May 1549, the particulars of the purchase are thus set forth :—

> The entire site of the late College of All Saints, in Maidstone, with all its rights and appurtenances; three barns and two orchards adjacent to the said site, consisting of three acres; and all the houses, structures, garden grounds, pools, fish-ponds, &c., within the precinct of the said College, and all the lead in and upon the roofs of the said buildings. Also twelve plots of arable land, amounting to a hundred acres, lying in Maidstone, Loose, and elsewhere; thirteen acres of pasture land, in Maidstone; eighteen acres of meadow, and the bakehouse mead, three acres; and lands called Horwash in Detling and Boxley, late in occupation of the master of the College, and afterwards demised to Walter Herenden. Also the following among other messuages and lands let to hire, viz., a tenement and garden near the great bridge in Maidstone, in the occupation of John King; four cottages at Newark,* in the occupation of poor persons; a tenement with

---

* These were chargeable with a rent of 20s., and were not therefore almshouses.

garden at Gabriel's Hill, in occupation of Robert Balser;* a messuage and garden in Mill Lane, in occupation of David Barham; a barn called Burleys, and an orchard and piece of ground at Cloverhouse, six acres, in Maidstone, in occupation of Thomas Huggarde; lands with appurtenances in occupation of Thomas Nicholson; lands and tenements called North and South Buckland; lands in West Borough and other parts of Maidstone, in tenure of Simon Smythe; five pieces of land in West Borough in occupation of John Weston, † or assignees; a tenement and parcel of land at Newark; a piece of land called Shepherd's Close, consisting of two acres; land in occupation of George Piene; two pieces of land at Boxley; annual rents of Assize, with their appurtenances, in Maidstone, amounting to 16s. a year; twenty-seven acres of land, parcel of the manor of Chillington; three tenements in Mill Lane, in occupation of John Melbourne, John Morley, and Clement Ludde; four tenements and garden at the Cliff, near the rivulet [Len], in Maidstone, in occupation of poor persons; ‡ a house and shop in Middle Row, occupied by Agnes Warden; houses and lands in West Borough, in occupation of William Ryse and Walter Herenden; two acres in Maidstone, occupied by William Bassock; six acres of land near Poll Mill, § in Maidstone, occupied by Richard Tomlyn; a house and garden in High Street, in occupation of Thomas Cook; and the manor of Chillington: the whole under this head amounting to the yearly value of £44 16s. 5¼d.

When the monasteries and other religious houses were dissolved, persons, designated "Ministers," were appointed by the Crown to collect the revenues, and they rendered a yearly account of all monies which came to hand. The accounts of the College of Maidstone for the year 1549 are in some parts not decipherable, whilst several of the amounts mentioned were not received, a portion of the property having, as we have seen, been granted to Lord Cobham. William Tilden, afterwards concerned in Wyatt's rebellion, was one of the local collectors. The items are thus specified:—

For site of the College and divers lands and tenements £65 1 11
Rents of the manor of Chillington 2 11 5
  ,, ,, lands in Boxley parish 2 2 0
  ,, ,, meadow at Weavering 0 2 0
Tithes of land in West Borough, belonging to the rectory 5 0 0
  ,, ,, the north-west part of Maidstone parish 9 0 0
  ,, ,, at Loddington 6 0 0
  ,, ,, in occupation of College, with oblations of the rectory 32 1 0

* He was mayor in 1562 and again in 1569. John Balser, who filled the office in 1578, and acted as chamberlain on several occasions, is mentioned in 1575, in deeds of Shales Court, as a draper. He owned land near the town, and the right was reserved to him to use a pond at the top of Stone Street, which was filled in about the end of last century.
† In another document Weston's five pieces of land are described as "three, called Upperdyke and Netherdyke, and two, lying near Bower wood." He is called John Westenbury in the Corporation records, setting forth the grant to Cobham.
‡ These were not almshouses, as in 1546 they paid a rent of 17s.
§ Situated on the Len, a short distance beyond the present Turkey Mills.

	£	s.	d.
Lands in occupation of Lord Cobham	6	0	0
St. Faith's churchyard	0	6	8
Tithes of the chapel of Detling	7	6	8
,, ,, ,, Loose	5	13	4
Rents belonging to the chantry of Goulds in Maidstone church	12	0	5½
,, ,, late Fraternity of Corpus Christi	41	0	8
,, ,, property in the parish of Staplehurst, &c.	0	10	1
Parsonage house, &c., at East Farleigh	10	13	4
,, ,, Linton	11	0	0
Portion of the tithes of Sutton, near Dover	5	6	0
Manors of Trimworth and Wittersham, and land at Marden and Halstow (including arrears)	47	6	0

The following payments are noted:—

	£	s.	d.
To Collector for rectory of Maidstone	2	14	0
,, Lord Cobham for hire of house for curate (apparently at Maidstone)	1	5	0
,, another Collector	2	13	4
,, clerks for collecting and writing accounts	0	4	0
,, John Wardrope, curate of Detling, besides profits and oblations of vicarage (which had been granted to him for life)	2	13	4
,, pension of curate of Maidstone for three-quarters of the present year (granted by Walter Mildmay)	10	0	0
,, Thomas Pyne, his assistant, for the same period	5	13	4
,, salary of John Weston, steward *	3	0	0

The grant of the lands belonging to Goulds chantry, and of other property, was purchased for £360 13s 4d. by Sir George Blagge and Richard Goodryke, on February 8, 1550. More detailed reference will be made to the chantries in connection with the history of All Saints' Church, but it may be noted here that the grant included the manor of Goulds,† and also Jordan's orchard, near Wren's Cross, in Maidstone, which was formerly attached to the mansion of Jordan's Hall, in Stone Street.

The next grant, dated 13th June, 1550, is from Edward VI. to Sir Thomas Wyatt the younger, conveying the following lands lately in possession of his father and of the See of Canterbury:—The manor of Oldborough, the archbishop's park, Padde's ‡ fulling mill, a parcel of land at the end of the

---

* The Weston here referred to was lessee of the manors of Trimworth and Fannes, and proprietor of land called Bydews in Maidstone; he died in 1564. William Lane was another steward of the College.

† Robert Lamb was lessee of the estate in 1598.

‡ Evidently the origin of Padsole, where a fulling mill formerly stood.

great bridge, a barn in the Bower, a rood of land in Fant, and "our rectory and church of Maidstone, and our chapels of Loose and Detling, and all lands belonging to the said rectory in Maidstone, Loddington, Detling, and Loose; and all jurisdictions and liberties in as free and ample a manner as enjoyed by any of the archbishops of Canterbury, by Sir Thomas Wyatt, deceased, or by the custos or guardians of the College of Maidstone," together with the annual rent of £3, payable by the mayor and commonalty of Maidstone; which manors, rectory, lands, &c., are of the annual value of £118 6s. 5d., and are hereby granted to the said Sir Thomas Wyatt, he paying an annual rent for the same of the said amount, and also the stipends of the curates of Maidstone, Loose, and Detling.

A further grant, from the king to Lord Cobham, of a portion of the College property was made on the 29th of February 1551. Lands in the Hundred of Hoo, formerly belonging to Sir Thomas Wyatt the elder, are therein described, and likewise a fulling mill and a parcel of land in occupation of George Piene, in Maidstone. Nearly three years after this, on December 8, 1553, an indenture was framed between Cobham and Wyatt the younger; it states that as there has been suit and variance between both parties as to which of them shall of right possesses the tithes arising from the lands of the College, Cobham, by the advice of his learned counsel, fully acknowledges the right of the same to be in Sir Thomas, as owner of the parsonage of Maidstone. Seven weeks after this indenture was signed, Wyatt headed the Kentish insurrection with which his name is associated.

Lord Cobham, by a contract dated June 18, 1562,[*] let to John Jackson, citizen and founder, of London, at a rent of

---

[*] Close Rolls, 651.

£45, the site of the College and other messuages and lands in the tenure of John Bennet, William Green, George Piene, and Simon Smythe. The College and domain lands continued in possession of Cobham's family until 1603, when his grandson, Henry Brooke, for conspiring to place the Lady Arabella Stuart on the throne, was sentenced to death, and only reprieved on the scaffold. After this event, the interest for life in the property, as we learn from a document dated May 13, 1604, was given to Frances, Countess of Kildare, wife of Lord Cobham, daughter of Charles Howard, Earl of Effingham, and who had been before married to the Earl of Kildare. The reversion was granted to Lord Salisbury, who had married Henry Lord Cobham's sister, and who died in 1619, his wife dying in 1628. Continuing in the Salisbury family for two or three generations, the estate passed in 1656 to Diana, daughter of Robert Cecil, brother to the Earl of Salisbury. It was subsequently much neglected, through this lady having only a life interest in it, and in 1698 a private Act of Parliament was passed to enable it to be invested in trustees for her benefit. The College property was afterwards purchased by Sir Robert Marsham, Bart., and the Earl of Romney, his descendant, is the present owner.

CHAPTER IV.

THE CHURCH OF ALL SAINTS.

Archbishops at the Palace—Chantries—The Reformation—The Rectory vested in the Crown—Sale of the Church Plate and Vestments—The Parish Register—The Rood of Grace—Burning of Martyrs in the Fair Meadow and elsewhere—Grant of the Tithes to the See of Canterbury—The Perpetual Curates: Augmentation of their Stipends—Sequestration of the Living—Thomas Wilson, the Puritan Incumbent—The Tithes of Maidstone—The first Vicar.

WHEN the College was established at the close of the fourteenth century, the church, with its chapels, was appropriated to the new foundation; and the stalls in the choir, with their richly worked canopies, and the twenty-eight massive oak seats in the chancel, are interesting memorials of the connection which for a hundred and fifty years existed between them. While All Saints' remained a collegiate church, the archbishops occasionally resided at the Palace for several weeks at a time, and the splendid retinue which in those days accompanied the chief bishop of the province formed a highly picturesque feature of his visits to the town. Archbishop Arundel was a frequent visitor, and completed the work of building the church which his predecessor had begun. We find him, on the 16th of May, and again on the 18th of

September 1407, conferring holy orders in All Saints' Church, by ordaining as a deacon, and afterwards as a priest, his friend Philip Morgan, who, several years later, became Bishop of Worcester, and, in 1425, Bishop of Ely. Archbishop Stafford, like Courtenay, ended his life at the quaint old building overlooking the Medway; he died on the 25th of May, 1452, and was buried at Canterbury. In 1458, Archbishop Bourchier was at the Palace, when Bishop Peacock, for affirmations which had been pronounced heretical, was ordered hither to receive his last sentence. Cranmer honoured Maidstone with his special regard, and left in his note-book a memorandum in which he speaks of it as one of the considerable towns in his diocese where learned clergymen, with adequate stipends, ought to be placed.

Previous to the Reformation there were several chantries in All Saints' Church, and indications of them are still to be found. In the east end of the north chancel aisle two steps ascend to what was no doubt an altar, and in the south wall of the chancel and nave there are the remains of two piscinæ. A chantry was founded in the church, in the first half of the fifteenth century by the brotherhood of Corpus Christi, and a priest celebrated mass daily for the souls of the deceased brethren and sisters. There was another chantry of which nothing is known, except that it was dedicated to St. Mary. The services connected with Goulds Chantry, founded in St. Mary's Church by Robert Vyneter, were continued in All Saints' Church, and one of the chancel aisles was in all probability the site of the altar. In the grant of the endowment of this chantry to Sir George Blagge and Richard Gooderyke in 1550, eight farms or other pieces of land are mentioned as belonging to it, and the names of the tenants are given. The dwelling-house of the priest, with orchard and garden attached, also referred to in

H

the grant, stood on the south side of Knightrider Street. An entry in the Lambeth Registers states that in March 1521 John Brede was appointed to the chantry. The last officiating priest was John Godfrey, who had been a canon of Boxley Abbey, in consideration of which he received a pension of £4 on the dissolution of that house.

Archbishop Arundel in 1406 founded a chantry in the church in honour of St. Thomas; and the duty of the priest, for whose maintenance the sum of £6 13s. 4d. was annually appropriated from the rent-charge on the great tithes of Northfleet, was to pray for the souls of the founder and of all deceased believers.* The episcopal registers of Canterbury make mention of yet another chantry in All Saints' Church. They were carefully examined by Beale Poste, and he observes that in one of them he found a notice, under date of 1417, of the "foundation of a chantry in the Collegiate Church of All Saints, Maidstone, by John Wotton," master of the College. Of the name of the chantry he could find no trace. There are records, however, of several appointments to the "perpetual chantry at the altar of St. Katherine" in Maidstone Church, and in the absence of other evidence, it may be surmised that they refer to the endowment attributed to Wotton. Richard Smith was appointed to the chantry of St. Katherine in 1462, and Thomas Shelton in 1463; and the latter dying in the same year, the vacancy was filled by Thomas Lott. We thus have accounts of four or five chantries in All Saints' Church, but at the dissolution in 1547 only two of them appear to have remained, namely, those of Goulds and the Corpus Christi Fraternity.

When the College was founded, Archbishop Courtenay

* The priest was also required by the archbishop's will to take part in all the solemn processions in the church, on which occasions he was to be dressed in vestments provided at the founder's expense.—Historical MSS. Commission, Fifth Report.

annexed to it the tithes of Maidstone, as well as those of the parishes of Detling and Loose, and in return for this the master and fellows became responsible for the spiritual ministrations of the three parishes. The advowson of the church had been from time immemorial in the gift of the archbishops of Canterbury, but in 1537 Archbishop Cranmer exchanged it with Henry VIII. When, ten years later, the chantries and colleges were suppressed by Act of Parliament, All Saints' ceased to be a collegiate church, and the rectory, with the chapels of Loose and Detling, were vested in the Crown, but the church was left, as heretofore, for the use of the parish, the grant of it being confirmed by the third Charter of Incorporation.

In fulfilment of Henry VIII.'s policy for seizing a portion of the revenues of the Church, the advisers of his youthful successor made a general order empowering royal commissioners, in conjunction with local committees, to examine and sell the plate, bells, and vestments belonging to all cathedrals and churches in the country, and to allow the churches to retain only what was necessary for the decent administration of the sacraments, and for the performance of divine service according to the Protestant and more simple form of worship. The proceeds of the sale were to be delivered to treasurers appointed by the Crown; but in the case of Maidstone, owing probably to the intervention of Sir Thomas Wyatt or some other eminent person, the town was permitted to expend the money derived from the sale of the church goods, in the purchase of St. Faith's chapel and burying-ground, and the lands and Hall of the Corpus Christi brotherhood, then dissolved—the Hall being afterwards converted into a free school. The local committee consisted of about ninety of the inhabitants, including the curate and churchwardens; but from an early stage of the transaction there was a want of unanimity among them. No doubt the majority were fully persuaded that if a free school and other valuable property could be obtained on such advantageous terms, a great boon would be secured to the parish, but there were others who shrank from the idea of the town becoming a party to what they regarded as a sacriligious proceeding. The latter were not without many active supporters in the parish, and the differences of opinion had risen to the dimensions of a serious dispute, when the following letter, dated September 14, 1548, was received from the Duke of Somerset, who was Protector for a few months during the minority of the king:—

To our Loving Friends the Inhabitants of Maidstone.

We commend us unto yo, and understanding that, being purposed amongst yo to doo sum things that may tend to a common benefit and a charitable act, a fewe of yo, to the number of eighte persons, should not be so well bent to it as the rest are, we therefore have a desire that things of charitie and good acts might procede universally in the realme; so would we be lothe to hear that a fewe should be hinderors of the same when the greeter number upon honest consideracons determyn anything to the furtherance thereof, and in that respect myndeng the advancement of Godd's honour and things lawdable in a common welthe, we expect yo to be of as good mynde and conformities to doo together the thinge which ye shall perceive mete and convenyent amongst yo.—Thus fare ye hertily well, from, Syrs, your loving friend, SOMERSET.

This letter had the desired effect, and the church plate and vestments having been sold, the sum of £200 was thereby realised. The purchase of St. Faith's chapel and burying-ground, the Hall in Earl Street, and the lands formerly belonging to the Guild of Corpus Christi, was then completed, and confirmed by the Charter granted to the town in the same year.

An inventory of the "goods, plate, jewels, bells, and ornaments" in the church, as made before the royal commissioners, is preserved among the Corporation muniments. There is a long list of the articles which were sold, many of them being very ancient, the gifts from time to time of the archbishops and other pious friends of the church. Upwards of forty silk and velvet vestments of various colours, green, red, white, blue, and black, some embroidered, are mentioned; and also about thirty embroidered copes of blue and crimson velvet, and of crimson, blue, and white silk; besides several embroidered white silk and blue and crimson altar cloths. "Latten [brass or bronze] candlesticks and other like stuff of latten, which cometh to the weight of ccc. save x. lbs.," are stated to be worth 54s. 4d. The whole inventory concludes thus:—

	lb.	oz.
The great pax [crucifix] of silver and gilt, weighing	6	5
Two silver and gilt basins	7	2
Two silver and gilt censers	3	3
A silver and gilt cross	5	1
The lesser gilt pax	1	2
A pair of silver candlesticks	5	11
A silver shype, with a little spoon	1	15
Two little paxes of silver	0	13
A little silver bell	0	8
A pair of small cruets and a silver censer ring	0	13
A gilt chalice	1	0
A gilt chalice	1	5
A gilt chalice poell	1	7
One other gilt chalice	1	3
A chalice, with pome, double gilt	1	1
Three pipes and eleven knobs of silver	3	9

All this abovesaid was delivered by William Collet [sexton] unto the churchwardens and others of the said inhabitants in the presence of William Crew, constable, Nicholas Mellow, Thomas Edmonds, Alexander Fisher, James Barret, John Smith, Thomas Baker, John Lilly, William Kemp, and Rydrock, the writer thereof.

Certain of the said church plate having the founder's arms which remaineth in the hands and custody of William Collet:—

	lb.	oz.
A gilt cross, with a foot, weighing	8	3
Two great candlesticks of silver and gilt	9	4
Pair of great censers of silver and gilt	6	7
A great pax, gilt	2	5
Two cruets of silver and gilt	0	13

And also remaineth in the hands and custody of the said William Collet the chrismatory of silver and two chalices.

The more part of the residue of the said goods, plate, jewels, bells, and ornaments were delivered into the custody of William Collet, as by the inventory aforesaid thereof made more plainly doth appear; and the said William Collet delivered part of the said goods, &c., unto James Barret, William Tilden, Thomas Goar, and to others, as he saith he will more plainly declare for his discharge before the king's majesty's commissioners.

Also there remaineth in the custody of Thomas Haggard and James Collet a certain piece of linen called a veil, and other things, value 20s. 10d.

Also there was stolen out of the said church of Maidstone by night in the 5th year of the king's majesty's reign that now is, of the goods, &c., aforesaid, one cope and other things, which the said William Collet can more plainly declare.

There were then "in the steeple, five bells and one little bell called the morrow-mass bell." These were put up for sale with the other articles, and were bought in for the use of the church. The plate and vestments, as may be supposed, passed into various hands, a "holy water stoup of silver" coming into the possession of a linendraper.

When the temporary excitement caused by these doings had passed away, the town began to experience the ill effects produced by the alienation of the great and small tithes. During the existence of the College, services had been regularly held in the church by the master and priests; but now that only a small stipend, with the oblations, obventions, &c., was allowed for the perpetual curate, the parishioners, Hasted tells us, suffered much from the scantiness of such provision for a person properly qualified to undertake the cure of so large and populous a parish. Having been for three years vested in the Crown, the rectorial revenues, with the tithes of Detling and Loose, were, in June 1550, granted by Edward VI. to Sir Thomas Wyatt the younger, who undertook to pay the stipends of the perpetual curate and his two assistants.

The first minister of All Saints' of whom we have any separate account was John Porter, who on the dissolution of the College, received a pension of £5 a-year. To Porter we are indebted for the first parochial register of baptisms, marriages, and burials, which he commenced on the 3rd of September 1542, the mandate for keeping parish registers having been issued four years previously. The Maidstone register was discontinued during Mary's reign, but with the accession of Elizabeth it was resumed. Porter appears to have held the living of Crundale in 1555. Some years later he was included among the Popish recusants whom the Ecclesiastical Commissioners thought fit to confine within certain bounds. He was ordered to remain in Maidstone or in any other part of Kent, the city of Canterbury excepted, and to report himself periodically to the high sheriff of the county. Ecclesiastical affairs becoming more settled, he made his peace with the governing powers, and died as curate of Loose in 1562.

Shortly before Porter became " parish priest," as he signs himself in the register, an extraordinary sensation was created by the exposure of what was called the "Boxley Rood of Grace." It was no secret that the monks had been leading vicious lives under cover of their cowls and hoods, and the public feeling against image-worship was every day growing more intense. An image set up in the neighbouring Abbey of Boxley had for years attracted numerous pilgrims, as well as much wealth in offerings to its shrine; but just before the Abbey was dissolved, a suspicion got abroad that the image was false and that its miracles were pretended. John Hooker, a preacher of Maidstone, one day in February 1538, was prompted by curiosity to walk over to the Abbey; he saw, attached to a crucifix, a figure that sometimes moved its head, eyes, and lips, and bent its body to express the receiving of prayers, while other gestures were made to signify the rejection of them. A few days after this a Maidstone man, named Partridge, visited the image, and discovered that it was moved by mechanical means. It was immediately seized and brought to Maidstone, where it was exhibited in the market place. Then it was carried to London, and examined by the king, a special performance of its motions being given before the court. The "Rood" was subsequently taken to St. Paul's Cross, where, the performance having been repeated, it was burned in the presence of a concourse of the citizens, and a sermon was preached by the Bishop of Rochester on the wickedness of praying before images. It turned out that this ingeniously-devised figure had been made in France by an English mechanic.*

Porter was succeeded at All Saints' in 1548 by Richard Awger, who was the first perpetual curate of Maidstone, and in that capacity signed the inventory of the church goods. He was also the first minister who was married at All Saints' after the passing of the Act which abolished compulsory celibacy, his marriage taking place in 1552. But he was not long to enjoy his wedded life in peace, for in the following year Mary came to the throne, and then commenced that relentless system of persecution which accompanied the temporary restoration of Romanism. Awger sought refuge in flight, as did also many of those who had taken part in the sale of the church plate and vestments. He was followed in the curacy by John Day, a man of violent Popish tendencies. In the spring of 1554, Sir Thomas Wyatt, for conspiring against the Queen, forfeited the rectory with the rest of his estates to the Crown. The advowson was thereafter granted to Cardinal Pole and his successors in perpetuity, while the tithes, which were then worth £81 per annum, were devised for a term of years to Christopher Roper, gentleman, of East Farleigh.

* "1538.—This yeare in Februarie there was an image of the crucifix of Christ which had been used of longe continuance for a great pylgremage at the Abbey of Boxley, by Maydestone, called the Roode of Grace. It was made to move the eyes and lipps by stringes of haire, which they would shewe a miracle, and never perceyved till now. The said Roode was set in the market place at Maydestone, and there shewed openly to the people the craft of moving the eyes and lipps, that all the people there might see the illusions that had beene used in the said image by the monks of the saide place, of manye yeares tyme out of mynde, wherebye they had gotten greate riches in deceavinge the people, thinckinge that the said image had so moved by the powere of God, which now playnlye appeared to the contrarie."—Wriothesley's Chronicle, p. 74.

Meanwhile, the change from Protestantism to the practices of Rome was gradually proceeding in Maidstone. The altar in All Saints' Church, which had been taken down in 1550, was set up again, and once more the mass was celebrated in all its gorgeousness. Peter Brown and other inhabitants who refused to conform to the change fled to the continent. John Denley, for several years a member of the Town Council, Patrick Packington, and John Newman,* a pewterer, while endeavouring to make their escape, were apprehended in Essex. Fox, in his "Book of Martyrs," says that a paper was found upon Denley containing the articles of his faith, "which he maintained with great resolution, disputing against the absurd doctrine of transubstantiation, and at length resisting it unto blood." Newman spoke in a like spirit, and told the Queen's Commissioners, by whom he was tried, that during the reign of King Edward he was daily instructed by continual sermons, showing him that there was no corporal presence in the bread and wine provided at the Lord's Supper. "The doctrine," he said, "was not believed by us on a sudden, but by continual prayer, which we offered unto God that we might not be deceived; but if the doctrine were true, that God would incline our hearts to receive it; or if it were not true, that God, through his preventing grace, would preserve and fortify us against the errors of it. We were convinced, through mature deliberation, with the concurrence and joint belief of our friends, that the labour of the preachers who instructed us was supported by the Word of God." These statements availed nothing, and Newman was burned at Saffron Walden, in Essex, on August 31, 1555. Packington likewise refused to recant, and he and Denley suffered at the stake at Uxbridge on the 8th

---

* Newman owned a piece of land in the West Borough, near the bridge, as appears by an indenture dated 1562.—Close Rolls, 848.

of July. Of Denley it is stated that "he was joyful even in the midst of the terrors of death, and sung a psalm when the flames raged about him; and though he was interrupted by a wretch that cast a faggot at him, which hurt him and drew blood from his face (upon which Dr. Story jeered, and said to the man who cast the faggot, that he had 'marred a good old song,') yet he soon raised himself again, and spread abroad his hands, and proceeded in singing the psalm, till his joyful soul took flight to the mansions of the blessed."*

During Mary's sanguinary reign the Brambles prison in the High Street was filled with those who refused to conform to the usages of Romanism. In July 1555 a recusant named William Mynge expired in the prison. Walter Appleby,† a Maidstone linendraper, and his wife Petronil, finding it impossible to live longer in the town, concealed themselves in the house of their friend William Wood, at Strood; but before a fortnight had passed, they were seized by their persecutors, taken before the Bishop of Rochester, and sent to Maidstone gaol.‡ Edmund Allin, miller, a well-to-do native of Frittenden, was also committed to prison. It is said that he entered into disputations with

* A few weeks previous to the martyrdom of Denley, John Bland, an East Kent minister, was a prisoner in Maidstone gaol; he was burned at Canterbury on the 12th of July.—Fox's "Acts and Monuments" (fourth edition), vol. 7, p. 295. Nor were these the only persons who, up to this time, had suffered here for their religious convictions. A cutler, Edward Walker by name, was burned at Maidstone in the year 1511. Archbishop Warham, in a letter dated 1522, speaks of a minister named Bradshaw, who was imprisoned at Maidstone for destroying certain writings against the doctrines of Luther which had been displayed at Boxley Abbey, and for disseminating seditious publications in the High Street, Maidstone. Thomas Hitten, another preacher, met with a less merciful fate. After being incarcerated and tortured for his religious opinions, he had fled beyond the sea, sustaining himself by working as a carpenter. Returning to Kent after an absence of several years, he was apprehended at Gravesend and brought to Maidstone, where, in 1530, he died at the stake.

† Appleby had been married at All Saints' Church in 1547.
‡ Fox's "Acts and Monuments," vol. viii., p. 729.

Sir John Baker, of Sissinghurst, a member of the Privy Council, and with two priests belonging to Staplehurst and Frittenden. The persons who apprehended him went to his house and took away a bag of money which they appropriated to their own use, but in the succeeding reign his executors appealed to the authorities, and the money was refunded.

In June 1557 the persecuting spirit of the time seems to have reached a terrible climax. On the morning of the 16th of that month two men and five women were burned at the stake—Walter Appleby and his wife; Allin and his wife Catherine; Joan Manning, the wife of a Maidstone victualler; Joan Bradbridge, a young woman of Staplehurst; and Elizabeth Lewis, a poor sightless girl, commonly called Blind Bess. Their prosecutors at the trial were Archdeacon Harpsfield, of Canterbury, Bishop Thornton, of Dover, and Sir John Baker; and the warrant for their execution stated that their opinions were "contrary to the determination of the dogmas of our Holy Mother, the Catholic Church, and especially concerning the sacrament of the Eucharist." The stake was set up in the Fair Meadow, and the faggots were piled round it by a bailiff named Dunk. A number of people, many of them weeping, assembled to witness the spectacle. Shortly before ten o'clock the seven martyrs were brought out of the prison in the High Street and led to the place of punishment. They were all tied, says an eye-witness, to one stake. Dunk said to Joan Bradbridge, when he was setting the wood about her, "Good Joan, forgive me thy death." Laying her hand on his shoulder, she replied, "Ah, Dunk, repent, repent, for though I forgive you, God's wrath is never forgotten." Then she turned to the onlookers and said, "What is it I hear?" She was assured that the clock was striking. "Thanks be to the Lord," she exclaimed; "by eleven we shall be with our

God." Looking towards the blind maiden, she observed, "Now, Sister Besse, be of good cheer; thou didst never see, but soon ye shall see the Lord Jesus Christ;" to which the blind maiden made answer, "I trust so." One of the spectators was John Day, the Popish incumbent of All Saints', who seized the occasion to deliver a sermon characterized by extraordinary vehemence of language, in which he reviled the poor creatures who were writhing in their death-struggle, declaring that they were lost, and charging them with Arianism and Anabaptism. The people were amazed at such violence of speech, and ventured to signify their dissent. Day was indignant. "Good people," he cried, "ye ought not in any wise to pray for these obstinate heretics, for, look! as ye see their bodies burning with material fire, so shall damnable souls burn in the unquenchable fire of hell everlasting." The sermon was repeated from the pulpit of All Saints' on the following Sunday; and from this time forth, Day, who had never been popular in the parish, was detested. Among those who were in prison at Maidstone in 1558 for adhering to the Protestant faith, were Catherine Knight, of Thurnham, Alice Snothe, of Biddenden, and Christopher Brown, of Maidstone; but on the death of Queen Mary in the same year, they were released.

When Elizabeth had been but a short time on the throne, England was again a Protestant country. The altar in All Saints' was finally displaced in 1560, though Day was still allowed to remain in charge. In that year the Queen granted the reversion of the rectorial revenues to the See of Canterbury, at which time they were valued as follows:—

The rectory, with the tenths	£36	0	0
The barn, and the tenths of the chapel of Loose	5	13	4
Carried forward....	£41	13	4

Brought forward	£41	13	4
The barn, tenths, and glebe of the chapel of Detling	7	6	8
The tenths in the north-east of Maidstone	9	0	0
The tenths of Loddington*	6	0	0
The tenths of Eastry	10	0	0
	£74	0	0
Deductions:—			
To the chief priest of Maidstone	£20	0	0
To the priest his assistant	6	13	4
To another chaplain there	6	13	4
To the curate of Loose....................................	2	13	4
To the curate of Detling...................................	2	13	4
	£38	13	4

It does not appear, however, notwithstanding these deductions, that there was for some years after this date more than one person appointed to officiate here, to whom the archbishop paid a stipend of £10.

There was about this time great irregularity in the management of the church, and a want of decorum on the part of many who attended the services. The Mayor and Jurates frequently intervened, and passed orders for the better regulation of public worship. Notice was given that persons who took dogs into the church were to be fined; and in 1562 an order of Burghmote was issued stating that the inhabitants were henceforth to "sit in the church of Maidstone in such places or seats as the churchwardens for the time being shall assign or appoint," and any offence against this rule was to be visited by a fine of 3s. 5d., to be levied on the goods or chattels of the person or persons so offending.

Many attempts were made to procure Day's removal from the curacy, but he was permitted to hold office till 1563. He did not long survive his dismissal, and was buried in All Saints' churchyard. Archbishop Parker speaks of him as a

---

* Loddington is an outlying part of Maidstone parish, situated about five miles from the church, and containing 567 acres and a few houses. "This hamlet has been from time immemorial treated as part of the Weald of Kent, and consequently the woodland in it is exempt from tithe."—Furley, vol. i., p. 122. Newton mentions that in his time there was a tradition that a chapel formerly existed at Loddington.

great frequenter of public-houses, and a man who led a scandalous life. It is not certain who the next perpetual curate was, but Day was probably succeeded by Thomas Tymme, who was for several years a preacher of Maidstone.

Those of the inhabitants who had sought safety on the continent, now returned to the town and resumed their former occupations. One of them was Peter Brown, a butcher, who continued for several years to take a prominent part in the municipal affairs of the borough. Dying in 1567, he left a sum of money for the purchase of a copy of the Scriptures, of the largest volume—probably Cranmer's or the Geneva Bible—to be placed in All Saints' Church and secured by a chain. His will, proved on the 2nd of February in that year, sets forth the bequest in these terms:—"Peter Brown, of Maydestone, bocher, testator, wills 26s. 8d. unto the buying of a great Bybill of the largest volume, that was used to be set in the nether end of the church of Maydestone, in the place where it was wont to be set in the time of the late King Edward VI.; and the same to be fast bound with a chain, to be free for all men to read for ever." *

The old allegiance to Rome having been thrown off, the Parliament of Elizabeth called upon the people to forswear the mass and the confessional, and to attend the Episcopal Church on Sundays and holidays. A person calling himself Faithful Cummin, who, while professing to be a zealous Protestant, was in reality a Dominican Friar, visited the town in April 1567, and held religious services at the Maidenhead Inn; but the news of his preaching coming to the knowledge of Archbishop Parker, he was ordered to appear before the Court of High Commission. The Court from time to time

---

* In 1660 the Corporation paid 6s. 6d. for six chains for the great Bible.

adjourned his case; and Cummin, not wishing further to commit himself, told his hearers at the Maidenhead Inn that he had received a divine command to go beyond the sea, for which purpose he obtained a sum of money, and departed. He was next heard of in the Low Countries, having been rewarded by the Pope with two thousand ducats for "teaching the English people to hate the new Liturgy."

The names of persons who refused to attend the Reformed Church were presented at the Quarter Sessions. In 1578 Henry Petil and his wife, Annie Hawkins, Thomas Hawkins the younger and his wife, and John Finch and his wife, all of the parish of Boughton, were reported "for that they have not come to church to hear divine service, as they ought to do, not this two years' day." Not long after this the name of William Abell, of a neighbouring parish, was also brought under the notice of the court. The churchwardens of Allington wrote in 1580 that "there is not any Popish sectuarie or recusant that doth forbear to come to our church of common prayer, or to hear God's word preached, so far as we know or can learn."

The next perpetual curate was Richard Storer, who, after several years of office, was in 1582 succeeded by Robert Carr. In the following year Archbishop Whitgift added £10 per annum to the incumbent's stipend, thus raising it to £20. Thomas Aierste, yeoman, of Maidstone, died in 1596, and left in the hands of his executors sufficient money to purchase a copy in English of Calvin's "Institutes of the Christian Religion," together with a chain for the fastening of it "to a desk at the lower end of the parish church of Maidstone, for the better instruction of the poor and simple therein."

Carr died in 1618, having been minister of All Saints' for thirty-six years, and his successor was Robert Barrell. The

Earl of Salisbury in 1619 set up a claim to the possession of the church, on the ground that it was a portion of the College property, of which he had become the owner. Lord Cobham, one of the former owners, had, it was said, claimed the church as his private property, though he had not instituted any legal proceedings. Salisbury revived the claim, insisting that St. Faith's must have been the parish church, and that All Saints' was merely a private chapel attached to the College. The Mayor and Jurates resisted this pretension, and in the end gained their case.

Barrell had been the nominee of the puritanic Dr. Abbot, Archbishop of Canterbury, and in 1623 he dedicated to him a pamphlet in which he professed to have "discovered" the "sandy foundations of the Papistical faith." In course of time, however, he associated himself with the High-Church party, which encouraged the nearest possible approach to the ceremonies and ornaments of Romanism. Crosses were again set up in All Saints', and the communion table became an altar. These and similar acts irritated the Puritans, who were a numerous body in the town; and that they might have in the neighbourhood a minister of their own choice, one of their number, Robert Swinnock, a jurate, bought the right of presentation to the living of Otham, near Maidstone, and in 1630 procured the settlement there of Thomas Wilson, a man of deep religious convictions and thoroughly Protestant sympathies. Swinnock and many other parishioners now left All Saints' and attended the services at Otham, where Wilson laboured with marvellous success. Between Barrell and Archbishop Laud on the one hand, and the Corporation on the other, several disputes arose, and one of these had to be settled by an appeal to the law. The church dues, as fixed by Barrell in 1636, were regarded as excessive; and the Mayor and Jurates, on behalf of a number of the parishioners, took up the matter, but were heavily fined by the archbishop's court.

An order for the erection of communion rails in All Saints' Church was the signal for another outburst of Puritan feeling. A petition from Maidstone and the neighbourhood was presented to the House of Commons, complaining that the clergy "have practiced and enforced antiquated and obsolete ceremonies," as standing at hymns, turning to the East, and "denying the sacrament of the Eucharist to such as have not come up to a new rail before the altar." In May 1640 a petition was also presented from the Puritans of Maidstone praying the House to take their grievances into consideration. They stated that the archbishop was the patron of the church, and received the tithes, but that he had "taken no further care of the inhabitants, continuing over them one Robert Barrell, his curate." Barrell, the petition set forth, sometimes preached only once in four or five weeks, and his substitutes on other occasions were not remarkable for their ability, a fact which was to be regretted, seeing that the petitioners had offered to choose and maintain "an able man." They further complained that Barrell rebuked Wilson of Otham for preaching twice on Sunday, and they accused Barrell of being "covetous and contentious" and "a common tavern hunter." The opposite party afterwards drew up a counter petition, but it was not presented, as the king's authority had been virtually superseded, and the civil war begun. A parliamentary order was, however, issued to arrest those who had been concerned in it, though no apprehensions appear to have been made; and the only consequence of the petition was the expulsion from the Town Council of several Jurates who had assisted in it and who had expressed themselves strongly in favour of the Royal cause.

In May 1643 Barrell was sent for by the House of Commons to answer for certain expressions derogatory of the Parliament which he had made use of in a sermon preached at All Saints' in the previous month. He sent a petition to the House of Lords on the 20th of May, praying that two attorneys whom he named might be assigned him as counsel for his defence against the charges brought against him by the Commons. On the 17th of June a petition was received by the Upper House from several inhabitants of Boughton Malherbe, stating that "Robert Barrell, a man of considerable estate, had not resided amongst them for twenty years, putting curates upon them of corrupt doctrine," and that he had also been "very remiss in preaching at his own church of Maidstone," and had "declared that the king's commands, even if illegal, ought to be obeyed;" for which reasons the petitioners prayed that the "profits of the living might be sequestered, and paid over to John Osborne, an orthodox and painful minister."* Barrell was subsequently ejected, and a motion was carried to sequestrate the curacy of Maidstone. The living was then placed under the orders of seven sequestrators.

Many of the monuments in the church were defaced or broken during the years of the civil war. On St. Bartholomew's Day a party of Puritan soldiers, having done much mischief in Rochester Cathedral, came on to Maidstone, the inhabitants being so alarmed that they closed their shops. A similar party of soldiers visited the town not long after this. It is probable that on these occcasions considerable damage was done to the interior of the church. From the circumstance also that in 1648, when the town was stormed by General Fairfax, the Royalists were driven into All Saints' at midnight, and that the church was made use of by the victors

---
* Historical MSS. Commission, Fifth Report.

as a place of lodgment for their prisoners, and possibly their wounded, it may be surmised that the Puritan soldiers, who detested fine places of worship, had little respect to spare, after the fury of the fight, for the brasses and monuments within the building.

It was natural that the ejection of Barrell should have raised the hopes of Wilson and his friends. There was a general expectation that the popular preacher of Otham would be asked to succeed him at All Saints', but the "Committee of Plundered Ministers" conferred the curacy upon Samuel Smith. The selection caused profound disappointment. After a few months, however, Smith exchanged this living for the rectory of Harrietsham, a more valuable preferment. Wilson was then appointed to the incumbency of Maidstone, still retaining that of Otham, for which he obtained a curate.

The life of Wilson had been in some respects a remarkable one. Born at Catterlen, in Cumberland, in 1601, he graduated at Cambridge, and was in succession collated to pastoral charges in Surrey, Hampshire, and Middlesex. From Teddington, in the last-named county, he removed to Otham. George Swinnock, a native of Maidstone, and one of the two thousand ministers who were ejected from the Church in 1662, wrote an account of Wilson's life. When Wilson came to Otham, he says, the Maidstone people were "much troubled and dejected at the deadness and dullness of the ministry under which they lived." Wilson preached "not only twice every Lord's-day, but also every holiday, and at funerals, though the persons interred were poor, and nothing could be expected for his pains." The people employed at the fulling mills used to work on Sunday, but he convinced both masters and servants of the ungodliness of their conduct, and the mills were closed. His severe Puritanism, however, soon gave offence to the ecclesiastical authorities. He refused to read to his congregation the "Book of Sports," decreeing that Sunday afternoon was to be kept as a holiday, with games and amusements, in every parish; whereupon he was suspended by the Court of High Commission, and his "cure was committed to such persons as he could not own or join with, which caused him to remove his congregation to Maidstone," where he was warmly supported by his friends. A letter of his to the parishioners of Otham having been read to them by one Dr. Tuke, both he and Tuke were summoned before the High Commission. They were forced to attend the Court periodically for the space of three years. When the Scotch Covenanters, in resentment of Laud's attempt to introduce the Liturgy into Scotland, crossed the border, sword in hand, the archbishop thawed a little, and restored Wilson to Otham; but the reconcilement was of brief duration, for in 1640, Wilson, having declined to read the prayer against the Scots, was cited to appear at the visitation of the Archdeacon of Canterbury at Faversham. The archdeacon gave him time to reconsider his position, and nothing further was heard of the matter till one day a messenger arrived from London with orders to bring him before the Privy Council. Wilson escaped from Otham and concealed himself in the country. When the storm was over, and Laud was a prisoner in the Tower, he returned to his parish, where his popularity was greater than ever. In 1643 he was chosen by Parliament to represent the diocese of Canterbury in the Assembly of Divines at Westminster.

Coming to Maidstone, Wilson effected a marked change in the habits of the parishioners. The frequent and regular services at All Saints', both on Sundays and week-days, were in striking contrast to the irregularities of Barrell's time. He generally held a meeting in the Free School on Sunday evening, and questioned his audience on the services of the day. "Maidstone," says the pious Swinnock, "was formerly a very profane town, insomuch that I have seen morrice-dancing, cudgel-playing, stool-ball, cricket, and many other sports openly and publicly on the Lord's-day;" but during Wilson's ministry these and other abuses came to an end. "Though the town was full of people, yet you could hardly see one person in the street after the sermons on the Lord's-day, and I have known when the mayor hath searched the inns and alehouses he hath scarce found one of the town there." During the excitement of the civil war, Wilson, without approving of the attitude of Cromwell's party towards the king, took sides with the Parliament, and consequently his ministrations were often very distasteful to the Royalists, who on one occasion, in 1647, locked up the church and would not allow him to preach in it. He appealed to the "Committee of Plundered Ministers," and after some trouble and delay the keys were given up to him. The Corporation in the previous year had conferred upon him the freedom of the borough.

In the report of the Parliamentary Commission appointed early in 1648 to ascertain the value of all benefices within the Church of England, the following survey occurs:—

True and perfect survey taken by Edward Boys and Samuel Chittenden, Esquires, Ralph Watte and George Northcote, Gents., the third day of April, A.D. 1648, of the rectory of Maidstone and titheries of Detlinge and Loose, with all and singular their appurtenances, &c.

Imprimis, we find the said rectory and titheries to be in the possession of Nicholas Crispe, gent.

Item, we find that to the rectory of Maidstone there is neither house, barne, nor glebeland.

Item, we find that to Detlinge there is a barne containing three bayes, timber built, walde [walled] with borde, and covered with thatche.

Item, we find that to Loose there is a barne containing four bayes, timber built, walde with borde, in part tyled, in part thatche.

The rent reserved to the archbishop is yearly	£74	3	0
The improved rent over and above the said reserved rent we value to be worth yearly	200	0	0
The total of the original and improved rent together is	£274	3	0

We are informed that the said rectory and titheries are in lease to Sir John Hendon, Knight.*

Thomas Wilson was twice married, and had eleven children. John Bigge, a jurate of the borough, bequeathed to his eldest daughter † £100, and when Fairfax's soldiers, in June 1648, were searching the town for arms, they found the money concealed in the minister's house; it was taken away, but afterwards restored. A good linguist, and well read in ancient and modern authors, Wilson took great pains in preaching and catechising, but his constant labours at length undermined his naturally robust constitution, and he died in March 1653, aged fifty-two.‡

On his death-bed Wilson had expressed a desire that John Crump, the son of one of his most attached friends, should succeed him in the curacy. This request was complied with, and Crump's ministrations in Maidstone extended over nine years. On the Restoration of the monarchy in 1660, Archbishop Juxon added £37 6s. 8d. per annum to the curate's stipend, and the sequestrators who had managed the affairs of the church since the close of Barrell's career were relieved of their charge, the parish being again placed under the jurisdiction of the See of Canterbury. By the Act of Uniformity, passed in 1662, clergymen of Puritanic sympathies were called upon to choose between the Church and Nonconformity. Crump refused to comply with the provisions of the new law,

---

* Parliamentary Surveys, vol. A., f. 403, Lambeth Palace Library. Written on the margin at the top of the folio are the words, "Rectory of Maidstone, titheries of Detlinge and Loose, and Loddington."

† She was subsequently married to the Rev. William Belcher, who in 1662 was ejected from Ulcombe.

‡ Neal's "History of the Puritans," vol. ii., p. 293.

and was ejected from his preferment. He was not an extreme Puritan, and after his ejectment the conforming minister of Boxley occasionally allowed him to officiate in his pulpit. According to Calamy,* "he was a considerable divine and a useful preacher, blessed with a most agreeable temper, and remarkable for his affable deportment, which much recommended him to those with whom he conversed." He died at Maidstone in 1667.

The next incumbent was John Davis, who was also rector of Otham. He died in 1677, and was succeeded by Humphrey Lynde, vicar of Boxley. Great excitement and alarm at that time pervaded the Protestant party, and Parliament called upon all persons holding any place or position of civil trust, to repair to their parish church and receive the Sacrament according to the form of the Episcopal Church of England, and to send a certificate of the same to the Quarter Sessions. The sacramental certificates, showing the administration of the holy rite at All Saints' Church, and giving the names of many of the leading inhabitants in Charles II.'s reign, are preserved among the borough records. A fragment of the declaration presented to the General Sessions of the Peace, held at Maidstone, on July 20, 1679, which is also extant, ends in the following words :—" I doe declare that I doe believe that there is not any transubstantiation in the Sacrament of the Lord's Supper or in the elements of bread or wine at or after the consecration thereof by any person whatsoever."

At the time of Lynde's settlement the stipend was further augmented. Archbishop Sancroft, in 1677, granted the small tithes of the "boroughs" of Week and Stone—the parish having been anciently divided into four such districts, of which Maidstone and West Borough were the other two—and the commodities of the churchyard, as well as a moiety of the

* "Nonconformists' Memorial."

small tithes within the "borough" of Maidstone, towards the maintenance of the incumbent. Lynde died in 1687. Then followed Edward Roman, who held the curacy until his death in 1692, when Gilbert Innes, M.A., who had formerly been vicar of Chislet, near Canterbury, and of St. John's, Thanet, was collated to the living.

Innes was a man of great energy. Finding that the small tithes of Loddington were detained by the lessee under the appropriation, he claimed them as belonging to the perpetual curate of All Saints'. The claim was resisted, and the case was tried in 1707 at Westminster. During the trial it was suggested that the curacy of Maidstone was worth £300 per annum, to which it was replied that the legal dues did not amount to more than £150. The Court decided in Innes's favour, and for several years he received the small tithes of Loddington, but after his death they were again lost for a time to the perpetual curate. For a long series of years, however, they have been regularly received by the incumbents of All Saints'. Innes, who performed his ministerial duties without any assistant, died in 1711, aged sixty-one, and was buried in the church, near the vestry door.

Josiah Woodward, D.D., was then removed from the chapelry of Poplar to the vacancy at Maidstone, and to enable him to keep an assistant here, Archbishop Tenison at the same time collated him to the rectory of Newchurch in Romney Marsh. A zealous promoter of charity schools, he directed collections to be made in aid of them at the evening lectures which he delivered on the Friday before the monthly Communion, and which were attended by large numbers of the parishioners. He was the author of many tracts and discourses, and one of the last sermons he published was entitled, "The Divine Original of Civil Government: a sermon preached at the parish church of Maidstone, in Kent, at the election of the Mayor for that Corporation, Nov. 2, 1711; published at the request of the Mayor, Jurates, and many gentlemen and other inhabitants of Maidstone." Dr. Woodward died August 6, 1712, about eighteen months after his settlement in the town, and was buried close to the rails of the communion table, where a flat stone, bearing a Latin inscription, records his virtues.

His assistant, Samuel Weller, LL.B., was promoted to the curacy, which he latterly held in conjunction with the rectory of Sundridge. To Weller belongs the merit of having added a valuable collection of books to the Parochial Library, which, there is reason to believe, was founded in Innes's time, when, through the liberality of friends, a number of volumes appear to have been brought together. On the death of the Rev. Dr. Thomas Bray, of St. Botolph's, Aldgate, an advertisement appeared stating that his large and choice collection of books would be sold for £50, on condition of their being used as a parochial library in some corporate town in the south of England. Weller at once started a subscription for the purpose of obtaining the books; and the sum required being ultimately raised, and the purchase effected, the books were deposited in the room over the vestry at All Saints'. Though in 1736 a catalogue of the library was printed, little attention was paid to it previous to 1810. In that year John Finch, the assistant curate, re-arranged the library and made a new catalogue, carefully correcting the inaccuracies of the former one. He "found many valuable books missing, and a still larger number irretrievably damaged by the incursions of worms and damp." The volumes which were missing and decayed, including two copies of Bishop Walton's Polyglot Bible and Calvin's works, amounted to about 100, and the whole number remaining in the library appears to have been 710.* Since the period of Finch's overhaul, several volumes are missing, and a mediæval manuscript copy of the Scriptures, in folio, has suffered by the excision of many of its beautiful initial letters. A number of years ago the library was removed to the Museum.

Weller died in 1753, and a black marble stone was erected to his memory in the north aisle of the chancel.† He was succeeded by John Denne, eldest son of John Denne, Archdeacon of Rochester, who resided at the Palace, there being then no dwelling-house appropriated to the incumbent of All Saints'. The following are the names of the subsequent ministers:—James Reeve, from 1800 to 1842; William Vallance, from 1842 to 1854; David Dale Stewart, from 1854 to 1878; and the Venerable Archdeacon Dealtry, the present incumbent.

Respecting the tithes of Maidstone, a few words remain to be said. The rectorial tithes, as previously stated, were leased out to laymen in the middle of the sixteenth century, the first lessee being Christopher Roper. Levin Bufkin was the lessee in 1595, his devisees in 1619, Sir Edward Hendon in 1643, Sir John Hendon in 1648, Dr. Griffith Hatley in 1681, Thomas Bliss in 1714, Wm. Horsmonden Turner in 1745, Mrs. Eliz. Turner in 1781, and Sir Charles Booth in 1790. The incumbent of the old church received annually £20 from the Archbishop of Canterbury, and £30 from the lessee, but since 1862 these ancient stipends have been paid

---

* "Notes and Queries," 1852. Finch's Catalogue was not printed.

† Newton says that in 1741 the services in the church were as follows:—Prayers and sermon twice every Sunday. Every day in the week, morning prayer; and on Saturdays, holydays, and their eves, both morning and evening prayer; the same all the Lent season, together with catechizing the youth and expounding the catechism to them and the congregation, on Wednesdays and Fridays. Celebration of the Lord's Supper every first Sunday in the month, besides three several Sundays successively at the time of each of the great festivals. Sermons on the State festivals and on Good Friday.

to the vicar of St. Philip's. In 1866, All Saints' ceased to be a perpetual curacy, as appears by a document of which the following is a copy :—

To all to whom these presents shall come, we, the Ecclesiastical Commissioners for England, send greeting: Whereas it has been made to appear to us that certain tithes or rent charges in lieu thereof, arising within the parish of All Saints', Maidstone, in the county of Kent, and in the diocese of Canterbury, belong to the incumbent of the church of such parish, now we, the said Ecclesiastical Commissioners for England, acting in pursuance of the District Church Tithes Act, 1865, do hereby declare that from and after the time of the publication of these presents in the "London Gazette," pursuant to the provisions of the same Act, the said church of the parish of All Saints', Maidstone aforesaid, shall be and be deemed to be a vicarage. In witness whereof we, the Ecclesiastical Commissioners for England, have hereunto affixed our common seal, this 5th day of July 1866.

The last lessee of the rectorial tithes was Mr. W. T. Baldwin, of Stede Hill, Harrietsham. At the expiration of his lease, on the 24th of May 1877, the tithes lapsed to the Ecclesiastical Commissioners, who have augmented out of them, on the principle which they call a "local claim," the stipends of the incumbents in several of the new ecclesiastical parishes. The vicar of All Saints' receives the small tithes of the whole parish, except those of the West Borough, and the Ecclesiastical Commissioners are entitled to the extraordinary tithe rent-charge upon hops and fruit in the whole parish.

CHAPTER V.

ALL SAINTS' AND OTHER MAIDSTONE CHURCHES.

The Fabric of All Saints' Church—Its Architecture—The Organ Loft—Organs, Ancient and Modern—The Original Roof—Restoration of the Building—Destruction of the Spire—Bells and Bell Ringing—Monuments in the Church—Funeral Regulations—The Chapel of St. Faith—Ancient Chapels—Recently-erected Churches.

THERE are two questions which an examination of the fabric of All Saints' Church naturally suggests. The first turns upon the point as to whether the building occupies the site of the former church of St. Mary. There is unfortunately no direct evidence which might enable us to give a positive answer to the question. Richard II.'s license to Archbishop Courtenay empowers him "to *convert* the parish church of St. Mary into a collegiate church," as if the new structure was intended to be a re-edification of the old one, or, at any rate, to be erected on the same site. It should also be noted that the churchyard and adjoining ground formerly contained many ancient foundations. The chamberlains' accounts for the year 1574 mention a certain payment for "fetching a load of stone from the churchyard;" and in 1792 upwards of a hundred tons of stone were taken up at a spot about forty yards to the east of the church, and sold for £14 18s. 9d. It may therefore be supposed that All Saints' occupies pretty nearly the site of St. Mary's, the only difference perhaps being that it stands a little more to the westward than did the building which it superseded.

Then the question has been asked, Was the whole of the church built at the same time? Here we are in no difficulty, as an inspection of the building can lead to but one conclusion, that both the nave and the chancel date from the end of the fourteenth century. "No architect," says Mr. Whichcord, "would have any hesitation in attributing the complete re-edification to the same period. The form of this building presents none of those variations in arrangement that one finds in churches whose parts are of various dates, and where modifications were required to meet the newly introduced customs of successive generations. Perhaps few single buildings possess more completeness and uniformity than this church exhibited in its original state. One general idea is prevalent throughout, with a correspondence of parts, proportions, and details very uncommon in middle age structures; and which is interfered with only by such deviations from the original design as may reasonably be supposed to have occurred during the period of its erection." Mr. Whichcord thinks that the building may have been in a condition for use when the king's licence for the College was obtained; but this, we think, is improbable, as Courtenay, in his will, expressly directed that the residue of his property, after certain legacies were paid, should be expended in the construction of the church, showing that at the time of his death the edifice was yet incomplete.

The interior of All Saints' is surpassed by few parish churches in England. Its great and striking characteristic is its size and symmetry. From end to end it measures

227ft., the nave being 91ft. wide, and the chancel 64ft. Looking through that noble vista, with its arcades that for five hundred years have resounded with voices in holy worship, one is disposed to wonder why a church of such large dimensions should have been erected at a time when it might have held within its walls the entire population of the parish. This, however, may be explained. Mediæval churches were not built merely for use in ordinary worship, but were also designed in order to afford accommodation for the spectacular displays and processions that distinguished the old ceremonial worship. Separate altars also, each with its fitting environment, were provided for the chantry and mass priests, and there was an endless succession of services. We have also to remember that All Saints' was originally a collegiate church, and that the chancel was regularly made use of by the master and canons of the College.

The church, like the College, belongs to the Perpendicular period. The nave and chancel are divided from the aisles by nine spans of arches, over each of which is a small mullioned window lighting the roof. Within the communion rails the space is parted from the aisles on the the north side by an oak screen, now filled with glass, and on south by a range of sedilia, the five canopied seats occupied by the master and fellows of the College when they celebrated high-mass. At the back of these is the fine but shamefully-defaced monument to Wotton, the first master of the College. The great east window has six lights, with plain mullions, and a head of beautful tracery. It is filled with painted glass, the subject being very effectively depicted, and bears the inscription, "This window is erected to the glory of God and in affectionate remembrance of Alexander Randall, of this town, banker, by his nephews, Samuel and Richard Mercer; he was born January 6, 1797, and died

April 5, 1870." The two smaller east windows, looking into the chancel aisles, have each three lights, and are likewise filled with stained glass. In the pavement immediately under the main east window was buried the ancient altar, a slab of Kentish ragstone, 7ft. in length and 3ft. 3in. in width; but on the erection of the reredos a few years ago it was removed.

From the communion rails three levels or steps lead down to the western portion of the chancel, which is occupied by the massive oak seats that were used by the clergy of the College at ordinary services. These seats are twenty-eight in number, and have the usual provision for turning up. On their under sides are good specimens of antique carving, the objects represented being Courtenay's arms, foliage, heads and half-length figures. In front of the seats are solidly-constructed desks of oak, serving as shelves for books to those occupying the seats. The panels of the desks have cinquefoil headings, and were originally painted with small yellow flowers disposed in the form of a cross. In the north wall of the chancel there are three five-light windows, the lower two having during the past twenty years been filled with coloured glass; and the south wall has two five-light windows, of which the west one contains painted glass, the space corresponding to that filled by the centre window on the opposite side being occupied by the vestry-room and organ-loft. Nicholas Barham, who resided at Chillington House in the early part of Elizabeth's reign, entered into an agreement with the Corporation to keep in repair one of the windows in the south aisle, in consideration of liberty granted him to build five pews for the use of himself and his household.

To what use the organ-loft was originally devoted we cannot be sure; but as the church possessed a store of vestments and other valuable accessories to divine service, it may have been a strong treasure-room, rather than a temporary lodging for a priest. In the first half of the last century this upper room was used as a library, but on the books being removed, it had been closed up; and it was not until the year 1840, on the occasion of building a new chimney for the vestry, that it was again entered. It contained two banners which had formed part of the pageantry of the funeral in 1748 of Colonel Richardson, of Week Street, who married a sister of William Dixon, for many years Recorder of Maidstone. On one of the banners were blazoned the arms of the family of Stydolfe, of Stydolfe's Place, Seal, now called the Wilderness.

The apartment was heightened, and made a receptacle for the organ, in 1851. There had been an organ in the church as early as the reign of Henry VIII. William Powell was the organist in 1556, and received a salary of £5 6s. 8d. During the civil war in the following century, the instrument disappeared; and the next organ of which we have any account was built by Thomas Jordan, in 1747, the cost being met by public subscription. In October of that year, George Launder was elected organist for seven years, at a salary of £30. He was a man of means, and in 1792 had spent more than £100 in adding new stops to the organ. He died in April 1795 There were two candidates for the vacant office, and an election took place on the 8th of May, when the voting was 203 against 178, the successful candidate being Bartholomew Davis. The organ then stood in the centre of the west gallery, whence it was removed about 1840 to the south-west angle of the nave, where it remained till 1851. A new and more powerful organ was erected in 1880, at a cost of £1,600, the heavy part of the instrument filling the loft over the vestry, whilst the lighter portion is placed in the arch opposite the vestry door, 'and the pneumatic tubes being subterranean, the vista of the aisle is unimpeded.

A descent of three steps conducts to the nave, the aisles of which are more than double the width of those of the chancel, into which they open by a remarkably light and beautiful arch. There are six windows, of four lights, on the north side of the nave, and on the south side there are three four-light windows, each filled with painted glass. At the east end of each aisle there is a stained-glass window of three lights. The tower abuts on the south-west angle, and in the south wall, at either side of it, there is a two-light window. The great west window is in design an exact counterpart of that at the east end, and the two smaller west windows are each of five lights. There were formerly three galleries—one over each aisle, and another along the west end of the nave. The south gallery was erected at the expense of the parish in 1667, and that over the north aisle in 1714, at the cost of Sir Robert Marsham, then one of the members of Parliament for Maidstone. The end gallery was removed about 1840, and the two side galleries in 1849, the panelled front of the pews which belonged to Lord Romney, in the centre of the north gallery, being now in the chapel of the Museum.

Until 1823, the pulpit—an ancient oak structure—stood at the west end of the church; it was then removed to the north-east end of the nave, near to the second pier from the chancel. The date of its first erection in All Saints' is uncertain, but the vestry book shows that on July 5, 1692, an order was given to provide a new pulpit and sounding-board. During the work of restoration in 1848-9, a new pulpit, in the Perpendicular style, was erected; this was superseded twelve years later by the present pulpit, a handsome piece of stone work, which stands on the north side, near to the pier which separates the nave from the chancel. The font is a plain octagonal bowl, on a large stem; and on its faces are the borough arms, the arms of the Astley family, and those of Scotland, Ireland, and France, besides other devices.

The "restoration" of the church, so far as at present proceeded with, cannot be regarded as a success, and one has only to glance over the interior to see that it has, by the incongruous plaster ceiling and cornices, and the universal application of whitewash, been shorn of much of its original beauty.*
"The ancient oak roof," says Beale Poste, "was divided into oblong compartments by a framework of beams, which were fluted and moulded. Intersections divided off the four angles of these, so that a series of lozenge-shaped compartments was formed, in which carved ornament was introduced. Wall pieces, a common appendage to the roofs of ancient buildings, descending in the usual way several feet down the sides below the wall plates, were supported by stone corbels inserted at intervals into the walls, carved with armorial bearings or otherwise." At a vestry meeting held on the 6th of June 1788, a committee was appointed to obtain a survey of the roof with a view to repairing the same. On the 2nd of July, the committee having reported that the roof was too much decayed to be repaired at a reasonable cost, the vestry unanimously resolved to "put on a new roof;" and on January 23, 1789, it was decided that the roof should be "built with fir timber, except the plates, which were to be of oak, and to be covered with the best Westmoreland slate, and ceiled flat and plain, with a plastered cornice and ornament round the branch." A month later it was found necessary to appoint a new committee, the old committee having declined

---

* In the hope of redeeming the interior of the church from these unsightly innovations, Mr. William Vaughan, of Maidstone, who died in 1880, bequeathed £250 as the nucleus of a fund for the erection of an oak roof, conditionally on the accomplishment of the work within ten years from the date of his death. Up to the time of writing, however, this laudable challenge has called forth no response.

to act under certain rules laid down by the vestry. Between March 1790 and March 1792 there appears to have been considerable disagreement among the parishioners as regards the contemplated alterations in the interior of the building, and resolutions which were passed at one meeting and rescinded at the next were sometimes carried again at a subsequent meeting; but in April 1792 it was agreed that while the church was being re-roofed, the side galleries should also be lengthened, and the organ removed from the end gallery.* By the summer of 1794 the roof seems to have been completed, as in November of that year the total cost was reported to amount to nearly £3,300. Towards the payment of this sum, £2,500 was borrowed at interest, and the sale of the old lead realised £526, the old timber £45, and the old copper £33.

In the year 1700 the church was re-pewed at the expense of the parish, the number of sittings being 1682, of which 387 were declared to be free for the use of the poor. But pews lined with baize of various colours, then in accordance with fashion, became repugnant to judgment and taste a hundred and forty years later; and accordingly, at a vestry meeting held in September 1845, a resolution was passed that the church should be re-seated, and that the floor should be repaired, and the galleries taken away. But some delay occurred before these alterations were carried out, and the original plans underwent many modifications. It was foreseen that by the removal of the north gallery Lord Romney would be deprived of certain pews which for generations had belonged to his family. His lordship also had a right to two pews in the body of the church, as being annexed to his property, the Palace; in all, sixty-seven sittings. The

---

* These alterations were not carried out.

vestry fully admitted his claim, and when, in January 1847, a subscription was opened to defray the cost of the work, he contributed £500, on the understanding that his rights should be preserved. In compliance with ancient usage, the vestry likewise agreed that a certain number of seats should be alloted for the use of the Corporation and of the Grammar School. At a meeting of the parishioners, in February 1848, a final resolution on the subject was passed, and the alterations were forthwith carried out. The outlay amounted to upwards of £2,000, £300 being allowed for the old fittings. By these improvements additional accommodation for 340 persons was obtained, and towards the total cost the Incorporated Society for Promoting the Enlargement, Building, and Repairing of Churches, subscribed £160, on condition that 770 sittings should be declared to be free for ever for the use of the poor. The church was re-opened on the 7th of September 1849.*

There are five entrances to the church. Two lead into the chancel aisles, that on the south side opening immediately in front of Wotton's tomb. The doorway conducting through the basement of the tower is not now in use. There was formerly an approach to it from the College, a flight of steps having ascended the southern bank of the churchyard in that direction. A porch which sheltered the corresponding entrance on the north side was removed in 1794. It was embattled, and had the exterior doorway square-headed, with escutcheons on either side. The great door in the west end, during the existence of the College, was no doubt the main public entrance.

Within a few feet of the east angle of the north aisle,

---

* During the alterations a taper-stand, or sconce, used in the Middle Ages for placing lights before images, or in lighting up the church for night funerals, was found under the pavement of the nave. Six years after these improvements, the church was lighted with gas for the first time.

there is a small octagonal turret. It leads to the roof of the church, which has a battlemented parapet. Against the exterior of the walls buttresses are placed, in positions almost corresponding to the pillars of the interior arcades. The tower also is surrounded by battlements, and the buttresses, which are of great thickness at the base, run up nearly to the summit of the structure. It was formerly surmounted by a spire, rising 172½ feet from the ground, but during a thunderstorm, on the morning of November 2nd, 1731, the spire was struck by lightning at two o'clock. Fire broke out at the top and began to burn downwards. An alarm was raised that the church was ablaze, and notwithstanding the early hour, a large crowd soon gathered from all parts of the town. The spire was built of oak timbers, bound with supports of the same material and of iron, and covered with lead. There was plenty of water at hand, but very little of it could be brought within reach of the flames, as they flared and flapped in the darkness, high overhead. Down upon the roof of the church the lead poured in molten masses, and an aperture being made therein, a large quantity of the liquefied material rushed into the nave below, doing, however, little damage. By ten o'clock the fire was subdued without having reached the stone work of the tower. The old lead was collected, and sold for £41 15s. 6d. In the churchwardens' accounts the following items have reference to the catastrophe:—

Paid to several persons that assisted in extinguishing the fire	£1 11 0
Colonel Gage's man, for bringing the engine	0 6 0
Cleaning the church after the fire	0 8 0
Shoulder of mutton for the men that watched	0 2 4
To men and women for cleaning and carrying home the tubs	0 10 0
Mr Green, for goods at the church when the fire was	0 12 0
Mills for cleaning the steeple and putting up the lead ashes	0 3 6
Expenses of playing the engine	0 7 0

The flat roof of the tower was afterwards covered with lead, in which is cut in large letters the inscription, "The spire was bvrnt down by lightning, Nov. the 2, 1731." To the north-east angle of the tower a mast was affixed; but the stair-turret has since been heightened, and a flag-staff having been placed thereon, the national colours are hoisted on particular occasions.*

In the tower, which is 78 feet high, there was a peal of bells early in the fifteenth century. We find Archbishop Arundel blessing bells here; and in 1494, when John Lee, master of the College, died, the "fourth bell" was rung for a quarter of an hour. In one of the Corporation books, under date of 30th July 1604, it is stated that, the "great bell" being imperfect, and the second one broken, a committee, consisting of three jurates and the churchwardens, was appointed to have the two bells exchanged or re-cast, the expense not to exceed £30. There were in 1667 "Six bells with ropes well hanged in the steeple." They were re-hung in 1678, and the great bell was re-cast by a founder named Hodgson. In April 1708 the vestry agreed to pay the sexton £6 per annum for ringing the curfew bell and looking after the clock and chimes. The "seventh bell" was repaired in 1719; and two years after, several of the bells were re-cast by Philps, of London. There were in 1741 eight bells, and the great bell was repaired in 1762, at a cost of ten guineas. In January 1784 the bells were found to be no longer fit for use, and an order was given to the firm of Chapman and Mears, of Whitechapel, to supply "eight new and musical bells, the tenor to weigh thirty cwt., and the rest in progressive proportion, the whole to weigh six tons, at £6 per cwt." A contract was entered into whereby the founders were to furnish eight new clappers, and complete the work for £806 5s.; but the sum of £552 was to be allowed for the old bells, which

---

* The only view of the spire which has been preserved is given in Buck's drawing of the town, taken in 1722, which is reproduced in this volume.

also weighed about six tons, besides £8 2s. 6d. for their carriage to London, and the total balance to be paid by the parish was therefore £240 2s. 6d. The new bells were hung, and "opened" by the Leeds ringers, in the same year. On August 16, 1784, the vestry ordered that "whereas the ringing of what is commonly called the curfew bell in winter is useless, and an unnecessary expense to the parish, the same be discontinued for the future." In the minutes of the same meeting, we read that "whereas much damage hath frequently arisen from an indiscriminate permission of all persons, whether ringers or not, at their pleasure to enter the belfry, and there to pull about and ring the bells in such manner and for as long a time as they shall choose, whereby the parish hath in times past been put to great expense, it is ordered that no persons whatever, except known and acknowledged ringers, be permitted to enter the belfry without the unanimous consent of the minister and churchwardens."

There is now in the tower a peal of ten bells, as well as a clock and chimes. A new clock was purchased, and the chimes were repaired, in 1721. Some years ago the latter again got out of order, and their pleasant music ceased; but in 1880, through the public spirit of several townsmen, they were restored. The bells are hung on very strong oak beams, with a large grooved wheel to each bell. Over the belfry the beams in the roof are of enormous thickness; and above these is placed transversely another set of squared beams, not quite so massive, their charred and blackened edges being the only remaining evidence of the fire in 1731. Frequent payments for ringing the bells, and for other matters in connection with them, occur in the churchwardens' accounts, and a few of them are here noted:—

Year	Entry	£	s	d
1604	For wine at the Star, bestowed on ye bellfounders	0	15	2
1643	Paid the ringers at Mr. Maior's election	0	2	4
1660	Ringers at the King's proclaiming	1	0	0

1660	Ringers at the coronation of the King	£1	2 0
	Ringers on the 29th of May	0	10 0
1661	Ringers at the Queen's arrival	0	10 2
1666	Ringers at the last Dutch fight	0	10 0
	Ringers when the Duke of Monmouth came to town	0	10 0
	Ringers for a thanksgiving against the Dutch	0	5 0
1683	Goodman Clupper, for going to Hollingbourne about the bell	0	1 0
1743	Ringing for the victory of Dettingen	0	10 0
1746	Ringing ye bells at ye Rebels' defeat	0	10 0
1747	Ringing at taking the French man-of-war	0	10 0

The following may be given as other curious items in the same accounts:—

1681	Mrs. Davies, for ye Bishop's lodgings	1	10 0
	Gervase Scott, for painting the King's arms	1	14 0
1683	Mending the cushion of Mr. Major's pew	0	2 6
1692	Reading prayers, christenings, and burials, for three days	0	13 0
1698	Mending the Judges' cushion	0	1 0
1717	Will Wyden, for mending the midwives' pen	0	1 6
1719	Spent at meeting Mr. Weller at the Star	0	3 0
	54 bullfinches' heads, for Mr. Major's dinner	0	4 6
	Paid at the Star, for myself and Mr. Dawson, at consulting about the church clock	0	4 0
1737	For pipes and tobacco, at meeting ye Archbishop	0	9 6
1762	For killing ye rats in ye church	0	5 9

Of the many monumental brasses formerly in the church, two only remain. A slab in the floor of the north aisle of the chancel had originally two brass plates—one square, the other oblong—affixed to it; that which is still extant is ensculptured with the figures of the Rev. Richard Beeston, M.A., who died December 26, 1640, and of his wife, with those of their four sons and three daughters.* The other brass is let into the south side of the south-west pillar of the chancel, and is more ancient. It is in memory of the Beale family, and contains numerous figures and mottoes, as well as a Latin geneological inscription of some length.

There are many excellent mural monuments in all parts

---

* In the parish of Warbleton, in East Sussex, is an ancient abode known as Beeston's, and on a stone in the pavement of the north aisle of the church is this inscription:—"Here lyeth ye body of Paul Beeston, gent., who dyed Sep. the 2, 1681, aged 45 years and 5 months. He gave two pieces of land lying in the parish of Maidstone, in Kent, containing about 5 acres, to ye poor of this parish of Warbleton for ever." The land mentioned lies at the verge of the parish, in the south-east angle of the four vents just above Barming Vicarage, and the rent still goes to Warbleton.

of the church, whilst the floor of the chancel and of the passages in the nave is literally covered with stones bearing inscriptions to the memory of deceased inhabitants. Between 1820 and 1830 many of the tombstones at the west end of the nave were taken up, and their inscriptions having been chiselled out, they were used for various purposes at the workhouse in Knightrider Street and elsewhere. On the north side of the chancel there was formerly an ancient altar-tomb with an inscription, only a small part of which was legible in 1630, when it was commonly stated to be in memory of one of the Woodville family, who resided at the Mote in the fifteenth century. The stone was removed on the representation of the archbishop in 1784, as from its position within the communion rails it was inconvenient during the Sacrament; it was then inserted level with the floor. The mural monument to the Astley family, on the south side of the great east window, has two tiers of four figures placed in pairs, the lower two the full size of life, the upper two somewhat smaller. These last represent John Astley, master of the jewel office in Queen Elizabeth's time, and Margaret, his wife. The lower pair of figures are those of Sir John Astley, only son of John Astley, and Catherine Bridges, his spouse. Underneath them, on a marble slab, supported by pillars, are deposited the escutcheon and crest of the deceased couple, sculptured in marble. Four of the compartments of the sedilia are filled with monuments. That nearest the east wall of the chancel contains a memorial to Major-General Lord Astley, Baron, of Reading, who died at the Palace in 1651. In the next compartment is a monument to Sir Jacob Astley, of Melton Constable, in Norfolk, who died in 1719; and two other divisions of the sedilia are filled with a blue marble slab to the memory of the Knatchbull family, of Mersham Hatch, in East Kent.

The inscription on a mural monument on the north side of the east window states that Lawrence Washington died on the 21st of December 1619. Washington resided at Jordan's Hall in Stone Street, and had been for twenty-seven years registrar of the High Court of Chancery; he was an ancestor of the great American General. There is a tablet in the south-west angle of the chancel to the Tufton family, of the Mote. A mural monument in the south chancel aisle to John Davy, a physician of this town, who died in 1649, has the sculptured busts of himself and his wife, and below the heads of his son and three daughters. A Latin inscription on a tablet against one of the pillars of the chancel records the death of Dr. Robert Stapley in 1675, at the age of fifty-seven. There is a flat stone in the south chancel aisle, near the north-west pillar, to Richard Stapleius, M.A., a promising student in medicine and science, who died November 29, 1679, in his twenty-sixth year. Newton, in his account of the tomb-stones in All Saints', gives an inscription to a member of the Maplesden family as belonging to a monument within the church. The monument is not now to be found, but it probably stood on the south side of the building. That several members of the Maplesden family were buried in some part of the church cannot be doubted, as George Maplesden, son of Peter Maplesden, who was concerned in Wyatt's rebellion, expressed a desire in his will, dated 1596, to be buried in "the parish church of Maidstone." But another branch of the family had apparently a place of burial in the churchyard, for John Maplesden, in his will, dated 1575, left directions for his interment in the churchyard, "on the south side thereof, nigh unto the burial of his ancestors." The inscription given by Newton relates to Susan, wife of Gervase Maplesden, who was for many years a member of the Corporation. She was buried October

18, 1603, and left "five sons and six daughters, whereof three sons and four daughters were married and had issue, so that they and their children were four score and ten souls before her death."

In the north chancel aisle there is a tablet to the memory of John Cripps, a member of a family of some influence in the town in the seventeenth century, who died in 1699. A marble slab in the north-east angle of the south aisle records the death of Dorothy Lawrence, grand-daughter of Sir John Lawrence, Lord Mayor of London "in the memorable year 1665." An inscription on a tablet of white marble, affixed to the south-east pillar of the chancel, reminds us of the death, on the 26th of April, 1795, of Sir Charles Booth, of Harrietsham Place, who bequeathed £2,000 for the education of children of poor parishioners. The tomb of the Marsham family is within the communion rails, where three stones inserted in the pavement record the death of various members of the family, the earliest inscription referring to the infant son of the "Right Hon. Robert, Lord Romney, and Priscilla, Lady Romney, who was born August 26, 1748, and died February 14, 1749."

None of the existing tombstones in the churchyard are ancient. There are no inscriptions dating from the sixteenth century, and those referring to the first half of the seventeenth century are very few.* In olden times bodies were interred in the churchyard, and death-knells were rung, at all times of the day and night. The practice eventually became odious and annoying to many of the townspeople, and at a vestry meeting on June 20, 1722, it was resolved "That whereas an unreasonable custom has prevailed of deferring funerals till

---

* The "Gentleman's Magazine," for August 1794, contains an illustration of a shrine in Maidstone churchyard, bearing the fragment of an epitaph, in old Roman capitals, "Therefore, prepare to follow me."

very late in the night, to the damage of the trade of the town and to the great inconvenience of the inhabitants, therefore, for the time to come, any person or persons having the care of funerals shall be obliged to bring their dead to the church or churchyard before the hour of ten of ye clock from Ladyday to Michaelmas, and before the hour of seven of ye clock from Michaelmas to Ladyday," failing which the minister "shall and is hereby desired to refuse to read the Burial Service after the said hours." In August 1784 a resolution in the following terms was passed:—" Whereas it has been customary at all hours of the night to ring out the bell for a person just then dead, to the great disturbance of the inhabitants, now the continuing such custom being totally unnecessary, and as it may one time or other be attended with disagreeable if not fatal consequences to some of the relations or friends of the deceased, it is therefore agreed and ordered that from Michaelmas to Ladyday no bell should be rung out for a dead person between the hours of ten o'clock in the night and seven o'clock in the morning; and that from Ladyday till Michaelmas no bell shall be rung out between the hours of eleven o'clock in the night and six o'clock in the morning; and it is further ordered that no knell for a burial shall be rung longer than fifteen minutes, neither shall any bell be tolled longer than one hour preceding any burial, for which the sexton may charge two shillings for the great bell, and one shilling for any lesser bell." * At a vestry meeting on September 24, 1787, it was agreed that the latest hour for funerals, according to the season of the year, should be as follows:—In the months of May, June, and

---

* Occasionally the offices of sexton and parish clerk were held by one person. The first clerk was appointed in 1559, when he assisted the incumbent in reading part of the service in the church. In 1711 this parochial officer received a salary of £14 per annum, and in April 1800 the salary was raised to £45.

July, half-past eight o'clock; April and August, seven; March, September, and October, half-past five; November, December, January, and February, half-past four.

There are three schools in connection with All Saints' Church. The Blue Coat School, which has been for many years located in the old workhouse in Knightrider Street, was founded by the Rev. Dr. Woodward in 1711, and has since been supported by legacies and subscriptions. The National School in College Road was instituted in 1814, out of a smaller school which had been formed in 1787. In 1872 a third school was established in Padsole Lane.

Having thus sketched the leading events connected with All Saints', and endeavoured to impress the character of the building upon the mind of the reader, as well as to notify a few of the more interesting of its numerous memorials of past generations, we will now gather up the threads of ecclesiastical history which have been dropped in the course of our narrative of what must always be regarded as emphatically the mother church of Maidstone.

The ancient chapel of St. Faith was built in the thirteenth century, probably for the convenience of the inhabitants who lived in the eastern parts of the parish. Early in the sixteenth century it was annexed to the College, and when that house was dissolved, it was purchased by the Corporation, the property being described in the first Charter as "one chapel and one churchyard or piece of land commonly called St. Faith's churchyard." The property was afterwards sold by the town to Peter Maplesden, of Digons, with a reserve to the parishioners of liberty to hold divine service in a part of the chapel, and to use the yard for burials. It passed in 1561 into the hands of Nicholas Barham, of Chillington House; and in 1572 the Corporation granted the use of the chapel and yard to the Dutch refugees who had settled in the town. Barham's son Arthur sold the property in 1609 to Henry Hall, and the latter devised it to his grandson George, who in 1624 disputed the rights of the Corporation. The Mayor and Jurates thereupon resolved that if burials were not permitted in the yard, according to a deed of agreement that had been entered into with Arthur Barham, legal proceedings should be taken against Hall. The following year they made an order that " householders and their families who for their poverty be not assessed to the poor" were to be buried in St. Faith's yard. The order, however, was not carried out; and Hall would appear to have relinquished his contention as far at least as regards the Dutch people, who continued to hold their services in the chapel until 1634, when it was closed by order of Archbishop Laud. It was opened again in 1646, and was for the next ninety years, with one considerable interval, made use of by different bodies of Nonconformists. Used for some years as a public hall, the remaining part of the chapel became a ladies' boarding school about the beginning of the present century, and latterly it was converted into a storehouse for the West Kent Militia. The building—a view of a portion of which is given on the left of the annexed sketch—was pulled down in 1858.*

There were anciently in the town one or two other chapels. An allusion to the chapel of St. Anne was made by Hasted in the folio edition of his History,† though he omitted it in his octavo edition. Certain lands, called Caring and Perryfield, in Maidstone, situated " beside and near to the chapel of St. Anne," are referred to; but as no reference to

---

* After its demolition, two pillars, with capitals and bases, belonging to the ancient edifice, were uncovered; they are now set up in the garden at the back of the Museum.

† Vol. ii., p. 106.

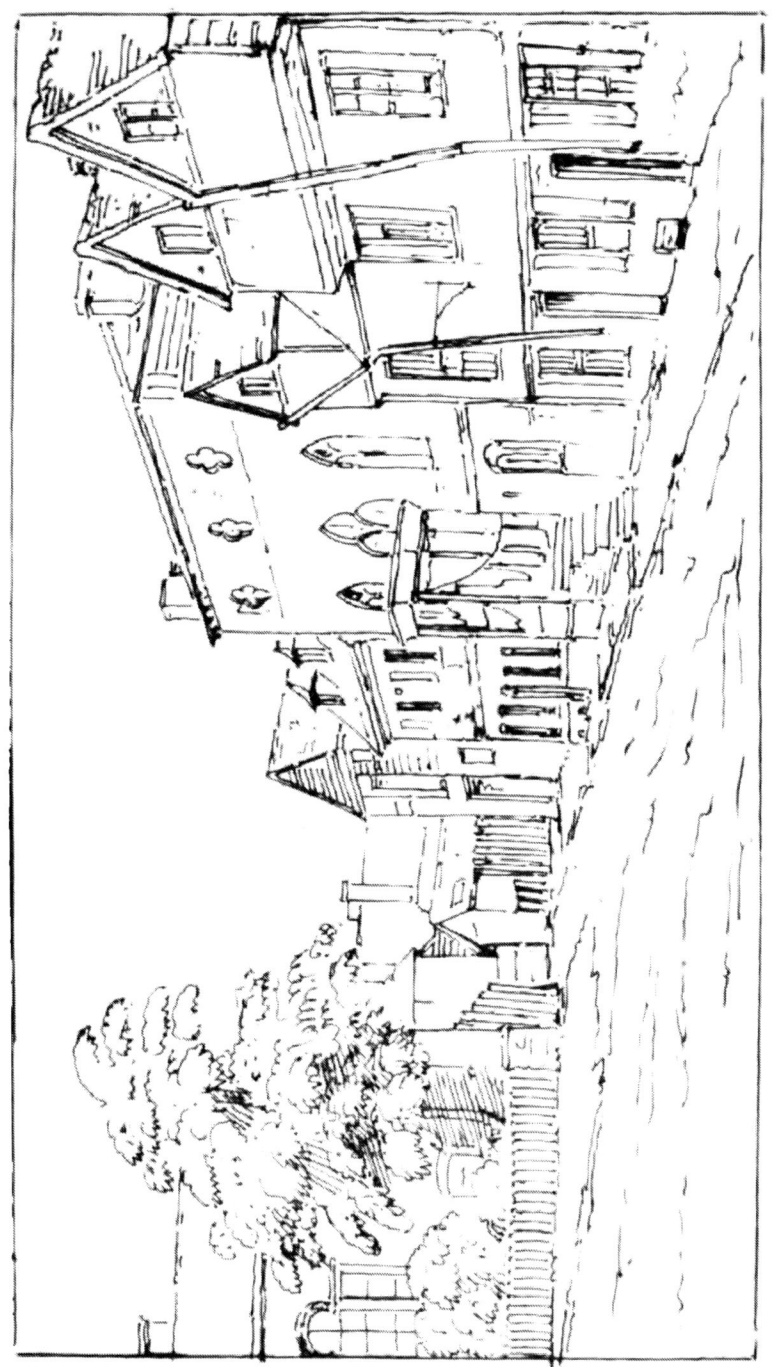

East side of St. Faith's Green.

such a place of worship has been found elsewhere, Hasted may have been mistaken. Of the chapel which was dedicated to St. John, and which existed as early as 1457, we have authentic details. It stood on the east side of Lower Stone Street, where there was anciently a piece of land called "Chapel Croft." Reference is made to it in the re-grant of lands enumerated in a deed of exchange between Henry VIII. and Sir Thomas Wyatt the elder. It is again mentioned in the collector's book for the manor of Pimpe's Court in 1547, wherein a garden is stated to be situated in the parish of Maidstone, near the chapel of St. John. There is likewise mention of it in a deed relating to Shales Court and other property conveyed by Mrs. Elizabeth Fane to Walter Hendley, in October 1575.

The parish of Maidstone is now divided for ecclesiastical purposes into nine parishes, eight of which have been formed during the past forty-five years. On September 26, 1826, the foundation-stone of Holy Trinity Church was laid, and the building—which is surmounted by a cross, 135ft. from the ground—was completed by the 29th of October 1828, when it was consecrated by the archbishop. The total cost amounted to £13,079, of which £5,221 was raised by subscription. A parish was assigned to the church in 1841,[*] and by an order in council, three years later, the patronage was transferred from the incumbent of All Saints' to the archbishop, the stipend being at the same time augmented to the extent of £100 per annum out of the rectorial tithes of Cliffe, in the Hundred of Hoo.

St. Peter's Church is a modern adaptation of an ancient chapel believed to have originally been connected with the Hospital for poor travellers which Archbishop Boniface

---

[*] In this year the deaneries of Sittingbourne, Charing, and Sutton, were transferred from the archdeaconry of Canterbury to Maidstone.

founded at Maidstone in the middle of the thirteenth century. Fifty years ago the chapel was in a dilapidated state, having for many years been used by a brewing firm for storage purposes. In 1836 the building was restored, and enlarged by the addition of a transept, at an outlay of about £3,000. The ancient part, with its handsome lancet windows, is a fine specimen of the Early Pointed style. It measured before the alterations, 59ft. 6in. long by 25ft 1in. wide, and was 33ft. high from floor to ceiling. In the south wall, close to the east end, are four deeply recessed niches, with trefoiled hoods, three of them sedilia, and the most eastern a piscina or drain which received the water with which the chalice was rinsed. Further down, about midway between these sedilia and the old entrance-door, is another piscina of plain design. During the excavations forty-five years ago, large quantities of human bones and skulls were found, leading to the belief that the chapel was originally surrounded by a burial-ground. The church was opened for public worship in July 1837, and a year or two after, the first parish or district separated from the perpetual curacy of Maidstone was assigned to it.

With regard to the other Maidstone Churches, it may be stated that St. Stephen's, Tovil, was consecrated in 1841, and was assigned a parish in February 1843. St. Philip's was built in 1857, and in 1861 the district in which it is situated was constituted a parish. St. John's, Mote Park, was erected in 1860. In 1861, St. Paul's was consecrated, and had a parish alloted to it in the same year. The Church of St. Faith was erected in 1871, on the site of the ancient chapel, and in the same year a parish was assigned to it. Consecrated in 1876, the church of St. Michael and All Angels has a tower 74ft. high, containing a peal of bells.

An enumeration was made in 1880 of the persons above

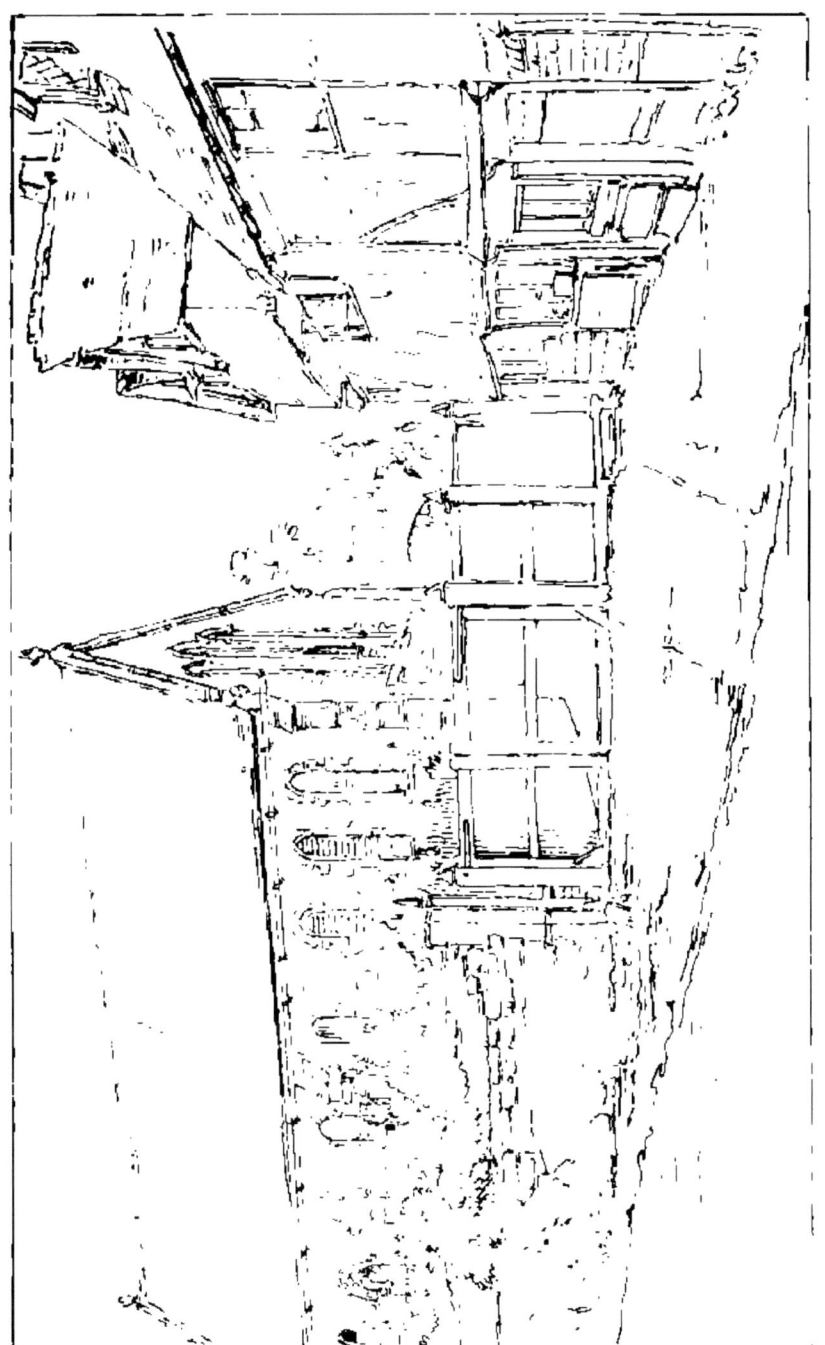

St. Peter's Chapel, and Entrance to Newark House.

twelve or fourteen years of age who attended seven of the Maidstone churches on the morning of January 18, and on the evening of January 25 in that year, and as the figures thereby obtained will show to readers in the future, more or less accurately, the relative positons occupied by the different churches in the town at the present time, they may here be given. The people were counted as they entered the church-doors, and the result was as follows, the third column showing the number of sittings (allowing 20in. to each sitting) provided at each place of worship :—

	Morning Attendance.	Evening Attendance.	Number of Sittings.
All Saints'	390	504	1714
Holy Trinity	652	901	1423
St. Peter's	100	64	417
St. Paul's	189	334	802
St. Philip's	110	250	637
St. Faith's	160	237	620
St. Michael's	183	362	584

CHAPTER VI.

NONCONFORMITY IN MAIDSTONE.

The Dutch Refugees—John Gifford, the Baptist—Prosecutions under the Conventicle Act—Ministers Ejected in 1662—The Early Baptists at Tovil and Maidstone—Simon Pine—Joseph Wright as Medical Man, Prisoner, Mayor, and Baptist Minister—The Old Presbyterian Congregation—George Swinnock, the Preacher and Author—The Week Street Congregation—Other Dissenting Chapels.

SO great were the hardships to which the Walloons or French-speaking Flemings of the Low Countries were exposed in the middle of the sixteenth century, that many of them emigrated to England to seek liberty and peace in the midst of the politico-religious crisis through which the nation was then passing. A small body of these Dutch refugees settled in Maidstone, under the protection of Queen Elizabeth, in the year 1573. At a time when toleration was scarcely understood, they were allowed to retain their own ecclesiastical discipline, and the Corporation granted them the use of St. Faith's chapel and burial-ground. They were in all probability the first Nonconformists who worshipped in Maidstone as a distinct congregation apart from the Established Church. Nicasius Van der Schuere was their first minister, and allusion is made to him in a tract which was published in London under this curious title—"A Very Wonderful and Strange Miracle of God, shewed upon a Dutchman of the age of 23 years, who was possessed of Ten Devils, and was by God's mighty Providence dispossessed of them again, the 27th of Januarie last past, 1573." (N.S.) Reginald Scott, in his "Discovery of Witchcraft," refers to the tract, and says that the mayor of Maidstone (John Staylett), and several of his brethren, were induced by the Dutch minister to lend some countenance to the affair. The person by whom the pseudo-miracle was chiefly wrought bore the excellently congenial name of John Stickelbow; a Divine power made him "the instrument to cast out devils, with four other credible persons of the Dutch church. The deception," adds Scott, "was so strange and so cunningly performed that had not his knavery afterwards brought him into suspicion, he should have gone away unsuspected of this fraud."

With the exception of this incident, the religious services of the refugees do not seem to have attracted any public attention until the year 1634, when Archbishop Laud endeavoured to restrain their privileges by introducing among them a Dutch translation of the English Liturgy, and requiring those of the first and second descent from the original settlers to attend All Saints' Church. John Millar, their minister, refused to read the Liturgy, and was summoned before Laud, with the result that he and his congregation were debarred from holding a service of their own in Maidstone. The immediate effect of this policy was the dispersion of several of the Dutch families. Those who remained, however, had their religious liberties restored to them during the Commonwealth, and Kilburne, the Kentish topographer, who wrote in 1658, states that St. Faith's chapel was then used by the Dutch people. When Episcopacy was resuscitated, on the accession of Charles II., they were specially exempted from the penalties of the Act of Uniformity; but their services were occasionally viewed with some degree of suspicion, and Daniel Poyntel, a learned minister of Staplehurst, for delivering "A Discourse against the Hierarchy" in St. Faith's chapel, was warned to beware lest his conduct gave offence to the bishop. How long the Dutch families continued to worship in the town as a separate sect does not appear; but in course of time they lost their individuality, and were absorbed in the general population.

Though the meetings of the "strangers" were permitted, little consideration was shown to other Nonconformists in the town. Archbishop Laud and his Consistory held it to be their duty to force men to attend the Episcopal Church, and in this severe exercise of ecclesiastical power they were supported by the civil authority. Every year Laud drew up a report to the king on the state of the dioceses of Canterbury and Rochester. In 1634 he stated that he found at Maidstone "divers professed separatists," and that "much Nonconformity had of late years spread" in the neighbourhood. The next year he reported that there were still many refractory persons in the parish. During the Civil War and the period of the Commonwealth those inhabitants who had felt that they could not conscientiously conform to the system of public worship which the law required, received a considerable acquisition to their number, and when Thomas Wilson, a firm Puritan, was appointed to the perpetual curacy of All Saints' they secured a temporary triumph.

The Kentish rising of 1648 was the signal for a slight oscillation of public feeling in favour of the Church. But the defeat of the Royalist forces at Maidstone once more dashed the hopes of the Episcopalians. One of the impetuous persons whose inopportune action led to that disastrous event was John Gifford, a native of this county. A major in the king's army, he was taken prisoner, with eleven other Royalists, and sentenced to death; but he managed to escape, and ensconced himself in London, where for several years he led a very dissolute life. Being subsequently brought under the influence of religion, he abandoned his former scenes of dissipation, and became a preacher. He founded a Baptist congregation at Bedford, and baptised John Bunyan on the 21st of September 1656.* Bunyan was also admitted a member of his congregation, and on Gifford's death in 1671, he was chosen to succeed him in the pastorate.

During Cromwell's ascendancy, Protestants were free to declare their opinions on church government, but attendance at a place of worship was strictly enjoined. At the Quarter Sessions at Maidstone in 1652, a fine was imposed upon Robert Foster for "not sanctifying of the Lord's-day in exercising of himself in the duties of piety and true religion, publiquely and privately, one Lord's-day within a month last past." When Episcopacy was restored in 1660, harsh measures were adopted against the Dissenters. With special severity did the rod of persecution fall upon the people called the Quakers. In 1660 William Watcher, a grocer, and fifteen other members of that sect, were committed to Maidstone gaol for holding a meeting at Cranbrook, and refusing—in accordance with their peculiar doctrines—to take the oath of allegiance to the Government. Soon after this Watcher again got into trouble, and for declining to give sureties "for his good behaviour," was marched to Maidstone, where, after ten weeks' confinement, he died in prison. George Fox, the founder of Quakerism, had visited Cranbrook in 1655, and made many converts. John Stubbs, William Caton, and several other pioneers of the Society of Friends, had also

---

* Brooke's "Lives of the Puritans," vol. iii., p. 257.

travelled into Kent, and "the priests and professors stirred up the magistrates at Maidstone to whip them for declaring God's truth unto them."* John Collins and nineteen other Quakers were in prison at Maidstone in 1663 for assembling together and refusing to take the oath.†

By the passing of the Conventicle Act in 1664, a meeting of more than five persons for religious worship not consistent with the Prayer Book was declared a seditious assembly. Under that statute many Nonconformists were ruined by heavy fines, and left to die in crowded prisons. Samuel Fox, a Quaker, for praying at a conventicle in Maidstone in 1681, was mulcted in the sum of £30, which would be equal to £100 at the present day; and John Gregson, Benjamin Chambers, Henry Roberts, and Henry Green, for being present at this and other meetings, each suffered distress of goods to the amount of £32. In the following year three of these persons, Gregson, Green, and Roberts, were again taken before a magistrate and fined £21 19s. for holding conventicles in the town.‡

When the Act of Uniformity came into operation in 1662, decreeing that the Book of Common Prayer should be used in every parish church and other place of public worship in England, many of the ministers in Kent, as elsewhere, declining to conform to its provisions, were deprived of their preferments. John Crump, the incumbent of All Saints', was ejected from his living. Other clergymen connected with Maidstone, who left the Church of England in consequence of their inability to comply with the terms of the Act, were the following:—Joseph Whiston, who had held religious services in the Grammar School during the Com-

---

* "Journal of George Fox," vol. i., p. 198.
† "Calendar of State Papers."
‡ Besse's "Sufferings of the Quakers," vol. i., pp. 296-7.

monwealth. He undertook the pastoral charge of a congregation at Lewes, in Sussex, and died there in 1690, at the age of sixty-three. Calamy writes of him as "a man of large wisdom, who did much to promote unanimity among Christians of different denominations." Edward Newton, son of Lawrence Newton, a zealous Puritan of Maidstone, had been rector of Lewes. After his ejection, he was invited to become the minister of a Dissenting congregation at Maidstone, but he remained at Lewes, where he exercised his ministry as a Nonconformist for nearly fifty years, dying on the 23rd of January 1712, aged eighty-five. Henry Symons, M.A., and Samuel French were also ejected ministers, the former of whom delivered a sermon before the judges at the Maidstone Assizes in March 1657. French had been the incumbent of Malling. In 1684, for preaching within five miles of Malling, contrary to the statute of 1665, his goods were distrained, and he was imprisoned for six months in Maidstone gaol. While in prison he was treated, according to Calamy, with unusual severity, and was allowed neither fire nor candle, no one being permitted to visit him except his wife, who persisted in sharing his sufferings. He afterwards became minister of a congregation at Staplehurst, where he died August 20, 1694.

Two small but distinct bodies of Nonconformists, each with its own Scriptural doctrines and views of church polity, had in the meantime preserved a clandestine existence in the town. These were Presbyterians and Anabaptists. Since the close of the Commonwealth they may be said to have existed in spite of the law, and their condition during the greater part of Charles II.'s reign was very deplorable. They were insulted with impunity in daylight, and sent to prison for holding a meeting. To impugn the Prayer Book was a crime. Hired spies watched their conduct, and every imprudent word dropped in the street came to the ears of the magistrates. When the monarchy was restored in 1660, many of the Anabaptists living in Maidstone and the neighbourhood were thrown into prison for refusing to take the oath of supremacy. They drew up a memorial to King Charles, setting forth the grounds of their grievance. It was entitled, "The Petition and Representation of the Sufferings of several peaceable and innocent Subjects called the Anabaptists, now Prisoners in the Gaol at Maidstone, giving their Acknowledgment of the King's Authority and Dignity in Civil Things, over all manner of persons within his Majesty's dominions." After a lengthy statement of the reasons of their belief, the memorialists concluded with the remark, "From all this that we have said, thou the king mayest see that not without grounds do we deny the taking the oath of supremacy, which calls for obedience as well in spiritual and ecclesiastical things and causes as in temporal," and referred his majesty to Matthew v. 33, and James v. 12. The petition was signed, in name of the imprisoned Anabaptists, by William Jeffery, who had been a preacher at Sevenoaks, John Reve, one of his elders, George Hammon and James Blackmore, both of Biddenden.

The members of this sect afterwards rejected the name of Anabaptists, as associating them with the scandals of the German Anabaptists of the sixteenth century, and designated themselves General Baptists. Where they assembled for worship in Maidstone does not appear, but in all probability they met by stealth in their private houses. Availing themselves of the "Declaration of Indulgence" in 1672, they obtained licenses for two meeting-houses, one at Tovil, the other at Maidstone. Their most influential member at this time was Simon Pine. In the early part of Charles II.'s reign, he gave them the little burial-ground which still exists on the south side of Tovil. But his services to the cause of local Nonconformity were not to be of long duration. He died in 1681, at the age of forty-seven, and his headstone, near the south wall, is the oldest in the ground.*

Joseph Wright, a man of ability and great force of character, who was deeply imbued with religious convictions, was the first pastor of the congregation. Born in 1623, he was educated at one of the universities,† and became fully qualified as a medical practitioner. At a comparatively early age he espoused the cause of the General Baptists, and soon occupied a prominent position among them. In 1661 he signed the famous "Petition" which was owned and approved by twenty thousand Baptists. This petition he was selected, with the distinguished Lincolnshire Nonconformist, Thomas Grantham, to present to Charles II. The king admitted the two delegates to his presence, and not only appeared to receive the document very graciously, but promised them his protection. Charles, however, on this as on other occasions, made no attempt to fulfil his pledge, and soon after Grantham and Wright were apprehended and carried before a magistrate. Wright was called a Jesuit and a Papist, and lodged in Maidstone gaol. Here he penned an address to the king and the nation, entitled, "Sion's groans for her Distressed, or sober endeavours to to prevent the shedding of innocent blood." The appeal was without effect, and his imprisonment continued. When at length liberated, he was harassed with other prosecutions under the Conventicle Act and the Act of Uniformity, and altogether he lay in Maidstone gaol for twenty years.

* The Pine family resided at Tovil House—not the present building of that name - till 1712. The house was originally the property of William Grocyn, master of Maidstone College.

† Ivimey's "English Baptists," vol. ii., p. 237.

Remaining, during that long period, firm and unshaken in his religious profession, he watched diligently over the interests of the Baptists, and practised medicine while in prison for the support of himself and his family.*

When eventually restored to liberty, Wright at once undertook the pastorate of the Tovil and Maidstone congregation of Baptists. James II. was now on the throne, and with a view to aid his endeavours in favour of the Roman Catholics, he attempted to conciliate the Noncomformists by announcing, in April 1687, his intention of protecting them in the free exercise of their religion. At the same time his Court used its influence to promote the election of Nonconformists to positions of trust in the country. Several Dissenters became members of the Maidstone Corporation, and on December 2, 1687, a communication was sent from Whitehall to the Mayor and Jurates, requiring them to confer the office of chief magistrate upon Joseph Wright "without administeringe to him any oath but the vsual oath for the due execucon of that office, wee being gratiously pleased to dispence, as wee do hereby dispence, with his takinge any other oath whatsoever; and for so doinge this shall be your sufficient warrant; and so wee bid you ffarewell." The third day after this letter was written the Corporation met, when "Alexander Osborne and Joseph Wright being put in nominacon by the Maior and Aldermen for the comons to choose one of them to be maior for the ensuinge yeare, the comons vnanimously elected the said Joseph Wright, accordinge to his Majestie's mandamus or letter mandatory directed to his trustie and well-beloved the Maior, Aldermen, and Corporacon of his Majestie's towne of Maidstone." The distinction had not been solicited by Dr. Wright, as he was generally called, and when it was

---

* Taylor's "History of the Baptists," vol. i., p. 288.

seen that the king was about to be deposed he retired with the sanction of the Burghmote, having occupied the mayor's chair for eleven months.

The following year saw the passing of the Act of Toleration, and a foundation laid for the complete emancipation of religion from prelatical oppression. Wright thereafter devoted himself exclusively to the cause of the Baptists. He preached every Sunday to the local congregation, whose meetings were held alternately at Tovil and Maidstone until the year 1701. One of the members was Mr. Bedwell, who then resided at Bydews, and he allowed them the use of one of the rooms in his house at a fixed rent. The room, an oblong though not large apartment on the ground floor, is still in existence, and here they continued to meet for the next forty-five years. Wright kept a minute-book of the proceedings of the congregation, and all the entries are in his handwriting down to the time of his decease in 1703.* He had attained his eighty-first year at the time of his death. His remains were interred in the little burial-ground at Tovil, where a stone, with inscriptions in Greek and Latin, was raised to his memory.

The next minister of the congregation was not Robert Knight, as Ivimey supposes,† but Joseph Smith. He preached at least once a week at Bydews for nearly thirty years, and died in 1733. The members being few, some difficulty was occasionally experienced in maintaining a minister, and in 1739, as appears by the minute-book, six of the members agreed to give quarterly the following sums towards the support of the ministry, viz., Thomas Pine, sen., 10s.; Thomas Elgar, 8s.; Thomas Mercer, 10s. 6d.; Thomas Pine, jun., 5s.; John Pine, 5s.; and John Blieth, 5s. In 1746 they

---

* For these notes respecting the Tovil congregation the writer is indebted to a volume of MSS. left by the late Rev. Beale Poste, and now in the possession of his family at Bydews.

† "History of the Baptists," vol. ii., p. 241.

removed from Bydews to a meeting-house in Rose Yard, Maidstone. At the beginning of the present century they united themselves with the old Presbyterian congregation in Market Street, and ceased to exist as a separate body.

This Presbyterian congregation had been formed about the time of the Restoration, being chiefly composed of those who had renounced Episcopacy during the Civil War and the Commonwealth. The Presbyterians were in 1672 allowed to hold their meetings in St. Faith's chapel, having secured as their minister George Swinnock, the friend of Thomas Wilson, of All Saints' Church. Swinnock was a man of good abilities, a warm and practical preacher. The son of Thomas Swinnock, of Maidstone, he was baptised at All Saints' on the 17th of February 1627. He studied partly at Cambridge and partly at Oxford, and was elected a Fellow of Baliol College. Having been curate at Rickmansworth, in Herts, he became in 1651 vicar of Great Kemble, in Buckinghamshire. But he refused to comply with the Act of Uniformity, and his last sermon was preached at Great Kemble on Sunday, August 17, 1662. In this discourse he makes the following reference to the occasion:—

> Beloved friends, I esteem it my duty and privilege that I may write after the Apostle's pious copy, ye are the people to which I was first called to be a pastor. Though opportunity hath sometimes been offered for greater preferment, yet I still waived all thoughts of leaving my first love, and removal to any other parish. I have been amongst you these eleven years, and cannot wholly complain that I have spent my strength in vain. I have enjoyed more of God in His ordinances amongst you than ever I have enjoyed in all my life; I cannot but acknowledge that many of you have had much kindness and respect for me, not only above my deserts, but much above what any parish that I have known or heard of in the county, have had for their minister.

Swinnock was ejected in the following week. He afterwards became chaplain to Richard Hampden, of Great Hampden, thus escaping many of the privations which others of the "Two Thousand" had to endure. In this family he remained till his removal to his native town in 1672. But his pastoral labours in Maidstone were brought to an early termination. He died on the 10th of November 1673, and was buried in the parish churchyard.

A fertile and animated writer, Swinnock published several works. In 1662 he printed a treatise entitled, "The Fading of the Flesh," and in the dedication to the Corporation and inhabitants of Maidstone, he says:—"The occasion of this discourse, as is well known to you, was the death of your neighbour and my dear relation, Master Caleb Swinnock (who was interred May 21, 1662), whose father and grandfather had three or four times enjoyed the highest honour, and exercised the highest office, in your Corporation." Swinnock's mother died in 1634, and his father a few years later. Several of his early years were consequently passed under the roof of his uncle, Robert Swinnock, who, as stated in a former chapter, was the means of bringing Thomas Wilson to this neighbourhood. In another of his dedications he alludes with evident gratitude to the religious training he received while under his uncle's care. The following passage, taken from one of his sermons, and addressed to the Corporation of Maidstone, may be given as a fair specimen of the seriousness of Swinnock's manner :—

Sirs, I beseech you, give me leave to be faithful unto you. Will it not be a dreadful time with you, when you are tumbling on your dying beds and near your eternity, if conscience should fly in your faces for your falseness and unfaithfulness in your places, and make you cry out, "Oh that I had never been Mayor of Maidstone! oh that I had never been Jurat! for then I should not have now to answer before the dreadful tribunal of a righteous God for all the oaths, fornication, profanation on the Lord's Day, and other evils which I might have hindered and did not, and for all the good which I might, by my holy pattern, and encouraging others in piety, have done, and would not!" Alas! ye cannot imagine the dreadfulness of such a man's condition on such a day.*

The next three ministers of the Presbyterian congregation had also, like Swinnock, been ejected from the Established

---

* In 1868, Swinnock's writings were edited by a Council of seven ministers of the Free Church of Scotland, and published in five large volumes. With regard to his principal work, "The Christian Man's Calling," the editors say :—" It is one of the fullest and, we venture to think, one of the best exhibitions of the Gospel in its application to the ordinary affairs of life; there are few better works of practical religion in our language."

Church. Samuel Borfet was vicar of High Laver, in Essex, and after settling in Maidstone, the spirit of persecution in the neighbourhood waxed so fierce and intolerable, that he retired to London. Robert Perrott was ejected from Dean, in Bedfordshire, and after experiencing many viscissitudes, he came to Maidstone, where, besides practising as a medical man, he preached twice on Sunday, and gave a weekly lecture. He died at the age of eighty-seven, and his funeral sermon was preached by John Durant, his successor. Between the years 1692 and 1707 Perrott and Durant baptised twenty-two persons at St. Faith's chapel.

A few of the more prominent among the succeeding ministers may here be noticed. Benjamin Mills was appointed in 1736, and in the same year the present chapel in Market Street was erected on ground given by Mr. Wickars, one of the members. At the Quarter Sessions for the county, held at Maidstone on January 13, 1737, Mills certified that the new building was "a fit and proper place for the exercise of religious worship." In 1740, some rather strong remarks on the Dissenters having been made by Samuel Weller, the incumbent of All Saints', the minister of the new chapel entered into a warm controversy with that gentleman, and before the matter ended several pamphlets were published on both sides. Mills left Maidstone for Uxbridge in 1745. The choice of his successor led to a serious dispute in the congregation. The members were still generally known as Presbyterians, but the name had become a misnomer, as Arianism had long since crept in amongst them. Not only the trustees of the chapel but most of the leading members were Arians; they accordingly selected a pastor after their own views. A few of the members disapproved of the choice, and seceding from Market Street Chapel, they founded what has since become the Week Street Independent Congregation. The new minister was Israel Lewis, a Welshman. He died in 1770, aged fifty-three, and was buried in All Saints' churchyard. His successor was William Hazlitt, M.A., the father of the celebrated critic and essayist. Hazlitt remained in Maidstone about ten years, having removed to Ireland, of which he was a native, in 1780. He went to America in 1783, and four years later returned to this country, dying at Crediton, in Devonshire, in 1820, aged eighty-four. In July of that year his successor in Maidstone, Abraham Harris, also died, having officiated in the pulpit of Market Street Chapel for the long period of forty years. The law which made it blasphemy to speak against the Trinity was repealed in 1813, and the members of the congregation then declared themselves of the Unitarian persuasion, which is now their tenet.

Reverting to the origin of the Week Street Congregation, we find the cause of the secession of 1745 categorically stated as follows:—

The main and determining reasons of our separating from the Presbyterian congregation were these that follow, viz., I. Our not having the liberty of proposing a third candidate upon the non-election of the two that had been offered. II. Our having a minister arbitrarily imposed upon us, without so much as giving us notice of the intended election. III. Chiefly, that we had sufficient grounds to believe that the minister who has been chosen for a pastor was not sound in such doctrines as we esteem to be the fundamentals of Christianity, and upon which we desire to build our hopes of pardon and salvation.*

The seceders hired a house in St. Faith's Street, called the Rookery—now tenanted by the curator of the Museum—and had it certified for public worship. John Colville, a preacher from Goudhurst, conducted the opening services. His sermon, which was afterwards printed, is stated to have been "preached to the separated congregation at Maidstone, on July 21, 1745, being the first Sabbath after the opening of their meeting-house." In the spring of 1747 the freehold of two houses in Week Street was pur-

* "Church History of Kent," by the Rev. Thos. Timpson, p. 335.

chased, and in the following year a chapel, 40ft. long by 33ft. wide, was erected on the site, at an outlay of about £400.

Herbert Jenkins was ordained as minister of the new congregation in May 1749, and he continued his labours here till his death in 1772. During the next ten years the pulpit was occupied by various ministers, and in 1782 the members, who at that time numbered only nineteen, invited Edward Ralph to become their pastor.* Those were not the days of hasty ministerial settlements, and at Week Street Chapel Ralph preached on probation for nearly twelve months. He carried on an extensive business in Cheapside, London, and had been a convert of George Whitefield. He then determined to enter the ministry, and with this view underwent a course of preparatory instruction. In 1783, believing that his ministrations were likely to prove acceptable in Maidstone, he disposed of his business, and was ordained in Week Street Chapel. The congregation increased under his pastorate, and in 1812 additional accommodation was provided by the erection of side galleries. He preached three times every Sunday, and held services during the week in the surrounding villages. At length, however, his health began to give way, and in the spring of 1817 he found it necessary to resign his charge. He died in London on the 9th of June 1818, in his seventy-fourth year, and was buried in Bunhill Fields Cemetery.† His successor in Maidstone was Edmund Jinkings, who died here in 1856. A larger chapel was built in 1822, and this again was superseded in 1864, when the present place of worship was erected.

* The number of Dissenters in the town in 1782 was stated by Gilbert Innes, incumbent of All Saints' (who took a census of the population,) to be "very nearly" as follows:—Presbyterians, 209; Baptists, 44; Independents, 42; Methodists, 138; Quakers, 2; total, 435.
† "Bunhill Memorials," p. 223.

Of other Dissenting congregations in the town it is unnecessary to write at length. A number of Methodists held services in the Old National School, on the east side of St. Faith's Green, in 1774. The Wesleyan Methodists built a chapel in Union Street in 1805, and a more commodious building was erected near the same site in 1823. A congregation of particular Baptists was founded about the year 1811 by Messrs. Bentliff and Harris, and in 1823 they erected a meeting-house in King Street; this chapel was rebuilt in 1862. The King Street congregation has since become undenominational. Another section of Baptists, having no connection with the old Tovil congregation, built a meeting-house in the town in 1807, and removed in 1834 to Bethel Chapel, Union Street. A second Independent Chapel was erected on the south side of Tunbridge Road in 1875, and in 1880 a place of worship for the Roman Catholics was built at the north end of Week Street.

The following table shows how many people above twelve or fourteen years of age attended the principal chapels in Maidstone on Sunday morning, January 18, and on Sunday evening, January 25, 1880, and also the number of persons each place of worship can accommodate :—

	Morning Attendance.	Evening Attendance.	Number of Sittings.
King Street (Undenominational)	203	248	591
Wesleyan (Union Street)	230	347	866
Week Street (Independent)	124	179	687
West Borough (Independent)	74	100	423
Bethel (Baptist)	105	171	300
Presbyterian (Brewer Street)	56	77	388
Providence (Mote Road)	60	84	256
Primitive Methodist (Brewer Street)	31	46	179
Unitarian (Market Street)	52	85	303

CHAPTER VII.

THE FRATERNITY OF CORPUS CHRISTI.

Gift of the Hall in Earl Street—The Fraternity sanctioned by the Crown—The Brotherhood Hall—Number of Brethren and Sisters at various times: their Annual Contributions—Rent-roll of the Fraternity—The Annual Accounts—Chantry in All Saints' Church—Feasts on Corpus Christi Day—List of Wardens—The Fraternity Dissolved—Hall and Lands Purchased by the Town.

ONE of the characteristics of the Middle Ages was the formation of fraternities or guilds having for their object the regular observance of certain religious services, and the relief of their members in sickness and old age. Through the munificence of individuals, these associations amassed great wealth, and usually exercised an important influence over the affairs of the towns in which they were situated. A religious guild was established in Maidstone by a number of the townspeople, who described themselves as the "Guardians, Brethren, and Sisters of the Fraternity of the Body of Jesu Christ." Their design was to uphold the doctrine of the Real Presence, and in some respects they appear to have followed the rule of St. Benedict.

The brotherhood existed at first without any direct authority from the Crown. By a deed bearing date of 1422, we learn that the old Hall at the bottom of Earl Street, in which the meetings of the fraternity were held, originally belonged to John Hyssenden, who is described as a noble and venerable man. In reverence of the Holy Sacrament of the Body of Jesus Christ, he enfeoffed twenty-five inhabitants of Maidstone, elderly and discreet men, in "a certain edifice, to be called the Brethren Halle," with its cloisters and outbuildings, adjoining Earl Street. He directed that the property was to descend to their heirs and successors, and that a part of the deed was to be kept by the wardens of the fraternity, and another part by the guardians (wardens) of Maidstone Church.[*] There is a further reference to the origin of the society in the report of the commissioners appointed by Henry VIII. to inquire into the value of colleges, chantries, guilds, and monasteries, with a view to their suppression. The report says:—"The Fraternity or Guild of Corpus Christi in Maidstone, the first founder whereof is not known, seemeth to have taken its beginning by an honest congregation of the inhabitants there, and was after, in the time of Henry VI., made and established a perpetual guild, to the intent that one priest should celebrate and pray within the church of Maidstone, as well for the prosperous estate of the kings of England and the brothers and sisters of the said guild, as also for their souls after their departure from this life." It may be doubted whether the fraternity dates from beyond the year 1422, as it may have been called into existence solely on account of Hyssenden's gift. Having existed in an orderly and virtuous manner for a number of years, Henry VI., in 1441, confirmed it by letters patent under the Great Seal, made it perpetual, and granted to it certain

---

[*] Clement Taylor Smythe Coll., vol. ii., fol. 6.

privileges and immunities. Robert Est* and Richard Barbour were named as wardens, and they were authorised to purchase and hold lands to the annual value of £20, and to found a chantry in All Saints' Church.

Built in the Perpendicular style, the Hall in Earl Street consisted of a refectory, a chapel, three cloisters, and other apartments. In a Corporation record, dated 1597, the property is described as "a fair hall, a kitchen, divers other rooms, cloisters, yard, and two gardens." Notwithstanding that it was occupied by the fraternity for upwards of a century, and as a Free School for 320 years, the building, its four walls, doorways, and much of its roof, yet remains in a good state of preservation. Each of the side walls is penetrated by three two-light windows, with cinquefoil-headed divisions, the mullion being crossed by a horizontal bar. The other windows are modern. On the first floor, which extends over rather more than half the length of the building, there are several rooms, also of modern construction, which were formerly used as bedrooms.

At the close of the fifteenth century there were a hundred and fifty to two hundred brethren and sisters connected with the guild. The female members formed but a small proportion of the whole, seldom numbering more than twenty. In the year 1474 the numbers were—brethren 105, sisters 19; in 1478, brethren 113, sisters 18; in 1487, brethren 136, sisters 15. Each member paid an annual contribution, 2d. being the lowest payment and the highest 6s. 8d. Members apparently belonging to the middle class paid 1s. or 1s. 6d. each, while those of higher position gave more liberally. Thus Lady Elizabeth Culpeper paid 2s., the Prior of Leeds and the Abbot of Boxley 3s. 4d. each, the Master of All Saints' College 4s., and Sir Henry Ferrers,

---

* Est, nine years later, took part in Jack Cade's rebellion.

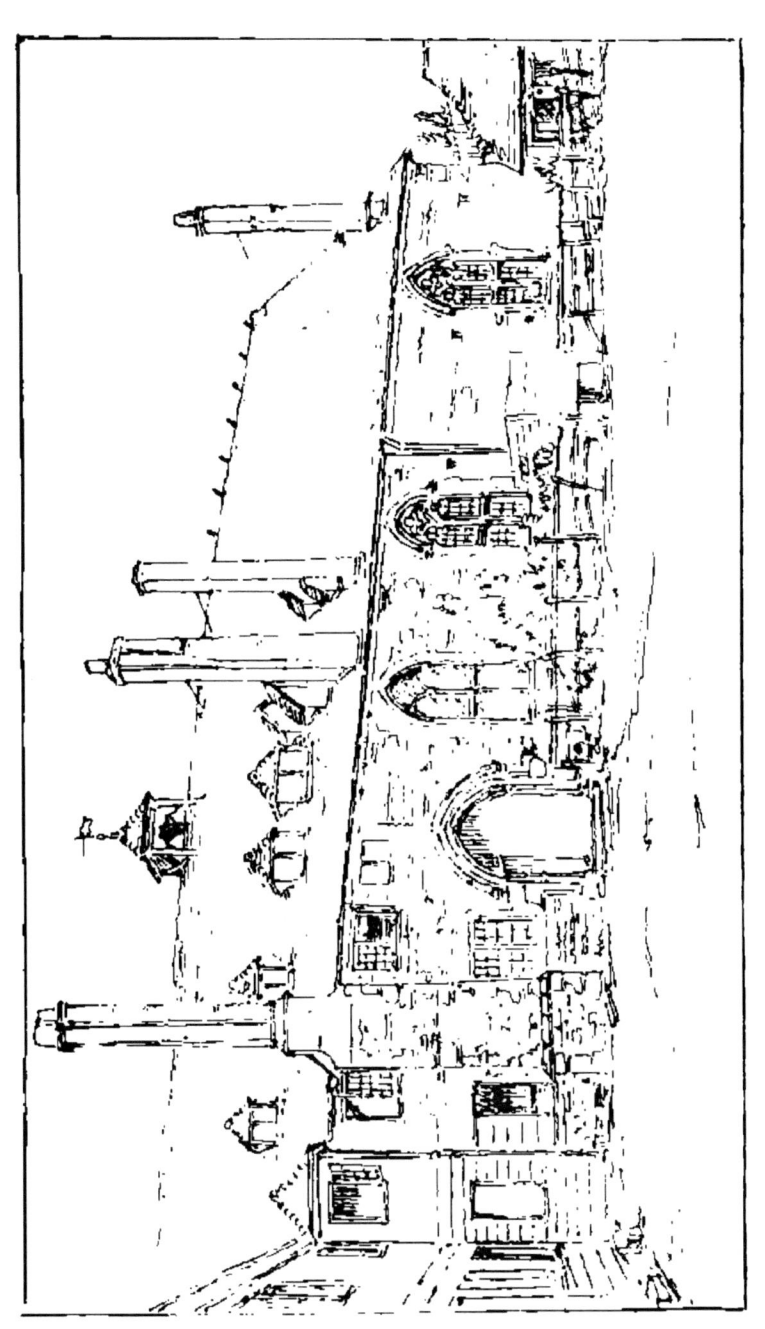

who was on several occasions high sheriff of Kent, 6s. 8d. Among other persons of influence who were members at various times, we find the names of Richard Lee, who was twice Lord Mayor of London; John Pimpe, of Pimpe's Court; Richard Culpeper, of East Farleigh; Thomas Jordan, who resided at his seat in Stone Street; Sir Thomas Bourchier, of Leeds; John Gunsley, of Maidstone; the rector of Otham, and the vicars of Boxley and Thurnham. For the benefit of the sick, the infirm, and the unfortunate, small almshouses were maintained, three in Pudding Lane, and six on the south side of Maidstone bridge, each consisting of a room on the ground floor and a garret above.

Besides the members' contributions, which amounted in 1478 to £12 11s. 2d., gifts and legacies were made to the fraternity, and from time to time lands and houses were purchased. Who the principal donors were does not appear, but one Richard William, whose will was proved in 1438, bequeathed 10s. to the brethren and sisters. The rent-roll of the guild for the year 1475 is as follows:—

				s.	d.
A farm, with house				30	0
Land at the Bower, occupied by Robert Reve				30	0
,, Bordongate, West Borough				6	8
,, St. Mary's, Hoo, in occupation of John Horsted				30	0
,, Maidstone, occupied by John Piper				16	0
Land and house at Maidstone, occupied by John Egremond				26	8
,, ,, occupied by William Page				20	0
,, ,, ,, John Clay				6	8
,, ,, ,, Richard Sawyer				12	0
,, ,, ,, John Coke				3	4
,, ,, ,, Nicholas Joce				26	8
,, ,, ,, Andrew Vydyan				3	4
,, ,, ,, Hugo Tunbridge, in Lytelpeckmd, Maidstone				3	4
,, ,, ,, William Eme, at Dodyngton				3	4
Land at Maidstone, occupied by John Carter				3	4
Orchard and garden adjoining Hall, occupied by Robert Cole				6	8

At a later period of its existence the fraternity owned land at East Peckham, and let out many tenements on lease at Maidstone—one in Knightrider Street, one at the south-east corner of Pudding Lane, and one at the west corner of

Gabriel's Hill, called "The Forge," which in 1544 was let to William Green for a term of ninety-nine years, at a yearly rent of 28s. There is still preserved a lease, dated 30th November 1459, according to which the wardens granted to Stephen Tolle for fifty-one years, a messuage, with appurtenances, situated in Maidstone, at a rent of 3s. 4d. per quarter, and a payment of twopence per annum to the lord of the manor. One of the rent-rolls shows that ten acres of land were let at a rent of 50s., and in another case a rent of 5s. was paid for two acres.

An inventory of the goods of the fraternity was made in 1476, from which it appears that there were at the Hall in Earl Street, among other articles, a mass book, a challis, a pair of silver cruets, a pair of pewter cruets, a pax of copper gilt, a pax of lead, an altar cloth stained of the Resurrection, "a corporas with gripe, a corporas with an hair, a vestment of purple, with all the apparel," besides fourteen tables, fifteen forms, thirty-three trestles, three brass pots, two great pans, upwards of thirty pots, nine table cloths, and more than thirty dozen pewter vessels. The uses to which some of these articles were put will be presently seen.

Most of the annual accounts of the fraternity from 1474 to 1497 are preserved among the muniments of the Corporation. They are written on rolls of parchment, and attached to each roll is a small book of paper containing each item of income and expenditure. The accounts for 1481, 1492, and 1493 are missing, and they are more or less incomplete down to 1497, when they are again lost till 1510.[*] One or two extracts from these ancient parchments may be interesting, as showing the comparative value of money four hundred years ago. Here are a few items of expenditure for 1474:—

---

[*] Gilbert's "Antiquities of Maidstone," 1865.

		s.	d.
A load of sand		0	5
Two bushels of lime		0	5
Four gallons of lamp oil		4	0
Tapers for the altar		0	3
A key for William West's gate		0	2
Binding of two tubs		0	2
Two men for five days' work in the garden, each at 2½d. per day		2	1
For their meat and drink		1	6
John Elmer and his wife, for two days in the garden		0	10
Their meat and drink		0	6
John Tyler and his child, for four days in tyling the Hall		1	8
Their meat and drink		1	0
One hundred tiles		2	0
A dozen dishes of pewter		4	0
A deed for a piece of land called Westbine, lying at Half Yoke		0	3

The total disbursements for a single year sometimes amounted to £30. A few items, culled from the accounts at random, include £1 12s. 4½d. paid for a hogshead of wine, 2d. for mending a lock at the Hall, 1d. for a lamp, 11d. to a carpenter for repairing a house in Pudding Lane, and 4d. to Robert Cole for drawing up an indenture.

At the chantry in All Saints' Church prayers were daily offered up by the priest for the souls of the deceased members. The priest in 1476 was William Downe, who received a yearly stipend of £6 13s. 4d. He resided at "Town House," which, with an acre of ground attached to it as a garden, was afterwards let at 13s. 4d. per annum. The chantry was situated at the east end of the north aisle of the church; the altar steps remain, but the altar itself was removed at the Reformation. On the eve of dirges and masses the church bells were rung, the ringers being paid by the guild. In connection with these celebrations other expenses were also incurred, as will be seen by the following extract from the accounts for 1475, under the head of "Dirge":—

	s.	d.		s.	d.
The priest and clerks	3	4	Three pints of Romney	0	5
Sexton for ringing, and keep of lamp	1	4	Crost, for bread	0	1
			Two pots of ale	1	3½
Bedeman	0	1	For small ale	0	2½
Saffron, for cakes	0	3	More ale	0	9
Eggs and milk	0	6			

But the great event in the life of the fraternity was the sumptuous feast held on Corpus Christi Day, for which it was customary to make preparations on a vast scale. Tables were placed in the centre of the Hall, the floor was covered with new rushes, and in the large garden adjoining, trestles and forms were also arranged in rows for the further accommodation of guests. At the festival in 1474 fifteen cooks and nine spit-turners were employed, and they were obviously not too many for the work they had to do. The fare for that year consisted of 128 geese, 52 chickens, 43 pairs of pigeons, 10 or 12 pigs, large quantities of oats, 10 gallons of milk, more than three quarts of honey, to say nothing of bread—potatoes were not yet introduced into this country, for America had not been discovered—butter, fish, malt, cream, eggs, garlic, salt, and spices. The cooks were paid 1d. to 1s. 2d. each. Part of the festival expenditure for another year is as follows:—

	s.	d.		s.	d.
Three pigs	1	0	Eighteen rabbits	2	3
Five pigs	1	10	Twelve bushels of oats	3	0
Three capons	1	6	Reward for the venison	1	4
Peck of white salt	0	3½	Twenty bushels of malt	11	5
Five chickens	0	5	A lamb	1	2
Twelve chickens	1	6	A quarter of mutton	0	6
Twenty chickens	1	8	A rib of veal	0	7
A leg of veal	0	4½	Half a lamb	0	7
Eight bushels of wheat	5	8	Two hundred eggs	1	0
Two capons	1	2			

Every year geese in large numbers were procured for the feast, and under this head the chief cost of the celebration was incurred. In 1475, 109 geese were purchased; in 1476, 114. The number was increased in 1478 to 123, for which the sum of 29s. 7d. was paid. In this year a man received 4d. to buy the geese, and another received 2d. for "cleaning" them. Four years later a still greater number of these birds were secured for the feast, 134 having been purchased in 1482, at an outlay of 31s. 8d. The expenditure of the fraternity for this year amounted to £27 5s., and the receipts to £31 1s. 1½d.

The wardens were elected or appointed annually. Many of their names have been lost, but those which have survived, with the year of office, are here given:—

William Beale	1430	Andrew Tilden and Stephen Dunmowe	1483
Robert Est and Richard Barbour	1441	Stephen Dunmowe and Wm. Bedell	1484
John Bell and John Mudlee	14—	Wm. Bedell and Wm. King	1485
Wm. Beale and Thomas Walter	1459	Wm. King and Richard Cawnt	1486
Bartholomew Everden and William Pocock	1461	Richard Cawnt and Wm. Gusing	1487
Robert Reve and Richard Afforde	1469	Wm. Gusing and John Wood	1488-9
Robert Raynold	1474	Robert Raynold and Philip King	1490-1
Robert Raynold and William Beale	1475-6	John Wingham and Wm. Lily	1494
Robert Raynold and John Frere	1477-8	John Pierson and Richard Thilman	1496
Richard Arnet and Walter Hoyges	1479-80	John Pierson	1497
Richard Arnet and John Philpot	1481	Walter Herenden and Thomas Goar*	1544
John Philpot and Andrew Tilden	1482		

This fraternity, with other religious guilds, was suppressed about the year 1547, and its property seized and vested in the Crown. It was then of the annual value of £40. The property, however, did not long remain in the king's hands. A suitable building for a grammar school was much wanted by the inhabitants of the town, and a desire was expressed to secure the Brotherhood Hall for the purpose. But the means for doing so not being obtainable, they received permission from the Duke of Somerset, who was Protector for a few months in 1548, during the minority of Edward VI., to sell the plate and vestments of All Saints' Church, and by this transaction the town was enabled, on payment of £205 4s., to purchase the Hall in Earl Street as well as the Corpus Christi estates. The Charter by which Maidstone was first incorporated in the same year, states that for the sum mentioned "all the late Fraternity or Guild of the Body of Christ, now dissolved," was granted to the town, including "our one messuage, commonly called the Brotherhood Hall, and our

---

* Thomas Goar was mayor in 1559. Herenden tenanted a part of the College lands, after the dissolution of that house.

one garden to the same messuage adjoining; and our one messuage, our one garden, and all those our lands, containing by estimation twenty-eight acres, situated in the parish of Maidstone, and now or late in the possession of Thomas Brook." Twelve other pieces of land with cottages attached are also mentioned in the Charter as becoming the property of the town. With the accession of Queen Mary, and the consequent revival of Romanism, these arrangements were partially suspended, and several of the estates of the late fraternity came again into the hands of those who had previously held them. But when Elizabeth came to the throne the privileges and liberties of the Corporation, which had been revoked, were restored, and the right of the town to the Brotherhood Hall and the Corpus Christi lands was confirmed.

Much of the subsequent history of these estates has been lost, but a few particulars have been gathered from various sources. One of the tenants under the Corporation in 1597 was John Fremlyn,[*] and another was William Beale, who was one of the borough chamberlains in 1568. Other tenants at this time were John Romney, who was mayor in 1593, chamberlain in 1603, and a jurate in 1604, and John Green, who was mayor in 1596, jurate in 1604, and chamberlain in 1605. Towards the close of the sixteenth century a piece of land at East Peckham, formerly the property of the fraternity, was sold by the Corporation. The almshouses in Pudding Lane were sold in 1599; those on the bridge were retained, and, as we learn from the chamberlains' accounts, they were

---

[*] John Fremlyn appears as mayor in 1588. An indenture in the Close Rolls, No. 605, states that on February 2, 1561, John Fremlyn ("ffremlsyn"), of Newington, Sittingbourne, purchased of John Culpeper, gentleman, of Gray's Inn, Middlesex, for the sum of £280 10s., "all that messuage and eighty acres of ground called the Bower, in Maidstone, now or late in the tenure of Edith Gosling." A farm at the Bower, thirty acres in extent, had formerly belonged to the Corpus Christi Fraternity.

repaired in 1595, several corner tiles and four bushels of lime for that purpose having cost 2s. Four acres of land in the West Borough were in 1607 leased to William Fremlyn at a rent of 22s. In order to enable the Corporation to meet sundry law expenses incurred in the Star Chamber and the Court of King's Bench, the farm previously in the occupation of Thomas Brook was in 1628 disposed of to Robert Swinnock, who held the office of mayor in 1630. Thus as one municipal exigency after another arose, the lands which had been purchased by the fraternity or bequeathed to it by pious men and women, were broken up and sold, and they have since been incorporated with other property, or so altered and transformed that it would now be difficult to identify them.

all the scholars. The school was intended for boys who received elsewhere the first rudiments of education; but at the outset children were entered who were not sufficiently advanced to follow the course of instruction required by the school orders. The Corporation in 1559 determined to put an end to this, and an order was made that no youth should be admitted unless he was "able to reade perfectlie upon a Latyn booke, and wryte his owne name." At the same time each scholar was to pay one shilling a year, the subjects of instruction being "grammar, humanity, poetry, rhetoric, and the Greek grammar." On March 12, 1567, the Corporation decided that "from henceforth the scolemaster of the Gramer Scole should have for his stipende and wage £10 by the yeare, of good and laweful money of England, quart'ly payable; and when the scolemaster should have in his scole above the number of fourteen scolers of such as were not children of the inhabitants within this towne and parishe, that the scolemaster so longe should be charged with a sufficient learned usher." Rowland Stubbersfield became master in 1575, and his appointment afforded an opportunity for making several new regulations, according to which prayers were to be said at seven in the morning, and teaching was to continue till eleven; the scholars were to meet again at one, and be dismissed for the day at five or six o'clock. Scholars residing in the town were to pay 4d. each per quarter, and those living in the country 1s. each, towards the "maintenance of comon bookes neadefull to the scole, as a dictionary and the like;" and in addition every scholar was to pay 4d. per annum for "firinge, woode, and matts."* The Corporation resolved to visit the school once a year, and the mayor was expected to give ten shillings in silver to three of the best scholars.

* Clement Taylor Smythe Coll., vol. ii., fol. 284.

The chamberlains' accounts show that the old Brotherhood Hall, which rang no longer with the hilarity of the festive board, was from time to time repaired at the charge of the borough. In 1567 the sum of £1 14s. 6d. was paid for tiling the roof; an oak board for the master's study cost 3s., and a carpenter received 8s. for repairing the cloisters and making a new clerestory. William Crosweeke, of Snodland, supplied bricks for building a chimney, and his charge was £1 1s. 6d.

At the close of Elizabeth's reign the usher received a salary of £6 13s. 4d.; but, owing apparently to a want of funds, his services were soon after dispensed with. In 1613 the Corporation again agreed to engage an usher, his salary to be raised by an assessment not exceeding twopence in the pound, upon every inhabitant rated at not less than two shillings for the poor.

Another benefaction to the school in 1618 was doubtless appreciated with the hearty gratitude that springs from a deep sense of the utility of the gift. Robert Gunsley,[*] rector of Titsey, in Surrey, dying on the 11th of November in that year, left by will the tithes of the rectory of Flamstead, in Hertfordshire, to University College, Oxford, for the purpose of maintaining at that University four scholars, natives of Kent, two to be chosen from this school, and two from the Grammar School at Rochester. He also bequeathed to the Fellows of the same college the appointment of the curate of Flamstead, with a stipend of £60, and directed that "whensoever the said curate's place should be void," one of his own scholars should "have the refusing of it before any other." The testator likewise specified that scholars of his own name and kindred should have the preference for the

---

[*] A person of the same name was baptised at All Saints' Church in 1543.

exhibitions. Accordingly the first boy chosen from the Maidstone school was Thomas Ayerst,* a relative of Gunsley, and during the next hundred and twenty years seven of the youths sent from this school to Oxford were also his kinsmen. These scholars have chambers, and £15 per annum each.

A third benefactor to the school was Dr. John Davy, of Maidstone, who died on May 11, 1649, and was buried in All Saints' Church. He bequeathed sixteen acres of land in the parish of Newchurch, in Romney Marsh, then let at £18 per annum, towards the support of the master and usher. Davy was the third son of Robert Davy, of Norwich.

Thomas Elmstone was master at the close of the reign of Charles I. He was a hot-headed Royalist, and gave so much offence to the Town Council that he was dismissed. The next two masters having given no better satisfaction, a committee, consisting of the perpetual curate and others, was formed in 1651 to examine the candidates and report to the Corporation. One Hassard, having been examined in religion, grammar, rhetoric, poetry, Latin, and Greek, was recommended and eventually appointed. The Corporation had agreed in the previous year that the master should have twenty marks,† and the usher twenty nobles‡ yearly, the said payments to be made by the borough chamberlains out of the £10 per annum settled upon the school by the Corporation, and the £10 given by Lamb; also that the master should have two-thirds of the rent of the land bequeathed by Davy, and that every scholar who was the son of "a freeman and inhabitant of the town and parish," should pay quarterly in advance one shilling to the master, and sixpence to the usher.

---

* Perhaps related to Thomas Aierste, mentioned at p. 111.
† A mark, 13s. 4d. ‡ A noble, 6s. 8d.

A few weeks after his appointment Hassard died. John Turner, of Malling, then became a candidate, and having satisfactorily passed the scrutiny of the committee, the office was conferred upon him. He was allowed to employ a person to teach the younger scholars to write, "on condition that the children of poor parents should be taught." Frequently, however, orders made by the municipal authorities were evaded, and the Mayor and Jurates were themselves not very punctual in their annual visit to the school, nor did they often take the trouble to ascertain whether their regulations were being complied with. They then became their own accusers, and directed an entry to be made in the minute-book that a yearly visit should be paid to the school on the first Wednesday in June, failing which the following penalties to be imposed, namely, the mayor, 20s.; jurates, 10s. each; common councilmen, 5s. each. In 1668 the day was altered to the second Wednesday in July.

A person named Law, who was master in the opening years of William and Mary's reign, proved a dishonour to his profession and to the town. A Corporation minute, dated February 1692, states that he was "liable for the murder of Mr. Thomas Wyatt, and had fled for the same."* Thomas Wyatt was the eldest son of Edwin Wyatt, serjeant-at-law, who resided at Chillington House. Law was afterwards apprehended, but admitted to bail; and in the interval preceding his trial, though suspended by the Corporation, he continued to preach in the town, much to the annoyance of the Mayor and Jurates. He was tried at the Kent Assizes in the same year, and being convicted of the manslaughter of Wyatt, he was ordered to "remain in prison without bail."

* "21 February 1692.—On Saturday night last, or rather Sunday morning, one Mr. Lawes, schoolmaster of Maidstone, being at an inn, and drinking with Serjeant Wyatt's son, upon some quarrel, Lawes killed Wyatt and fled for it."—Historical MSS. Commission, Fifth Report.

One of the boys who attended the school during the years 1743 and 1744 was George Horne. His previous education had been conducted by his father, Samuel Horne, who was rector of Otham, where young Horne was born on the 1st of November 1730. Under the tuition of Deodatus Bye, the master of the Maidstone School, he made rapid progress, and at the age of fifteen was elected to the Gunsley exhibition at University College, where he graduated M.A. in 1752, and B.D. in 1759. Five years later the degree of D.D. was conferred upon him, and in 1781 he became Dean of Canterbury. In 1790 he was consecrated Bishop of Norwich. He died at Bath on the 17th of January 1792, and was buried at Eltham. During his last illness he had a presentiment of the time of his death, and it is related that about three days before that event occurred, he said to those who were with him, "Have you made a note of the 17th day of this month?" Upon their answering in the negative, as not knowing what the question meant, "Then," he replied, "I will; so bring me a book," and he noted it down accordingly, with the day of the week on which it was to fall. Dr. Horne was the author of many published discourses, and also a "Commentary on the Psalms." Boswell, in his "Life of Dr. Johnson," says that Horne once entertained thoughts of reprinting Walton's "Lives," with notes and illustrations, but abandoned the intention on being informed by Johnson, though erroneously, that Lord Hales was engaged on a similar work.

Deodatus Bye resigned the mastership in 1746. Another of his pupils had been Christopher Smart, who was born in 1722, at Shipbourne, near Tunbridge. His father, Peter Smart, came to reside at Hall Place, Barming, in 1726; he died in 1732, in his forty-fifth year, and was buried in Barming churchyard, where an altar-tomb near the church door —the inscription being now obliterated—was erected to his memory. After his father's death, Christopher Smart was sent to the Grammar School in Earl Street, where he remained for several years. Admitted in 1739 to Pembroke Hall, Cambridge, he soon brought himself into notice by the excellence of his Tripos verses.* Four times successively the Seatonian prize was adjudged to him, and in 1745 he was elected a fellow of the Hall. He had early began to cultivate a taste for poetry, and intending to devote himself to literature, he settled in London in 1753. In the previous year he had published a quarto volume of verse entitled "Poems on General Occasions." This handsome volume included "The Hop Garden," a poem in three cantos, which, abounding in passages of striking and picturesque description, at once became popular, and created in literary circles an impression that with more mature years some still greater effort might be expected from him. But the budding promise of his early manhood was never realized. He continued to write, and in 1765 published a "Poetical Translation of the Fables of Phædrus," and subsequently a "Translation of the Psalms;" but both works were of very unequal merit, and the critics were almost unanimous in condemning them. Eventually he fell into reduced circumstances, and his mind became deranged. Johnson had before now befriended him, and during his protracted illness the doctor wrote several papers for a periodical in which the poet was concerned, with the object of securing his claim to a share in the profits of the publication. Whether the great lexicographer's generous interposition was of any avail, we have not been able to learn. Smart lingered in a half-demented state for several years, and at length expired on the 18th of May 1770. His collected poems were in 1791 published in two volumes.

This seems the most appropriate place wherein to notice the

---

* Cunningham's "Lives of Eminent Englishmen."

career of another Maidstone scholar who afterwards rose to eminence. John Pond was born in 1767, and educated first at the Grammar School, and then at Trinity College, Cambridge. In 1811 he was appointed astronomer-royal, an office which he held with distinction till 1835, when he retired upon a pension. He died at Blackheath, September 7, 1836, and was buried at Lee. The branch of astronomy to which he latterly turned his attention was the determination of the places of the fixed stars; and in knowledge of the instruments and methods of observation which the study required, as well as sagacity in avoiding and detecting error, he had, in his day, no superior. In 1833 he finished his standard catalogue of 1,113 stars.

On the 3rd of November 1818, the Rev. E. M. Allfree, the master, was examined before the Commissioners of Education as to the state of the school and its endowments. An abridgment of his evidence is as follows:—

I receive £20 per annum from the Corporation, £10 from Lamb's benefaction, and £10 settled on the school by the Corporation at the original foundation. I have also the rent of sixteen acres of marsh land in the parish of Newchurch, Romney Marsh, left under Davy's will, and now let at £17. I, like my predecessors, have had the management of this land. When I was elected in 1805, the land was let on lease for seven years at £42 per annum; and when the lease expired, I re-let the land at £50. But my tenant failed, owing a year and a half's rent, and leaving the land in so bad a state that it lay useless for two years; I then let it at the present rent. I also receive £6 per annum from the purchase of the land-tax chargeable on the vicarial tithes and glebe lands of Hoo, near Rochester; this was given to the school in 1806 by Mrs. Christina Rice, widow of the Rev. John Rice, of Wartling, in Sussex. I have now ten sons of freemen, who pay a guinea a quarter; and the sons of non-freemen pay six guineas a year. Freemen's sons are entitled to be taught the classics gratis, the payment being for whatever else they are taught. I consider I can refuse non-freeman's sons or not. I have fifteen boarders. My whole number of scholars is now about twenty-eight. I have no usher, but a writing master in the house, who also teaches arithmetic.

The foundation-stone of the present school premises was laid on October 19, 1870, by Sir John Lubbock, the eminent banker and man of science, then one of the members of Parliament for Maidstone. The building stands on the south side of Tunbridge Road, on a fine elevation. It was opened by the mayor on the 10th of October 1871, having cost about £3,500, of which the greater part was raised by subscription. The old Hall in Earl Street, having served as a school-house for upwards of three hundred and twenty years, was then sold, and it has since been converted by a brewing firm into a cooperage.

In 1871 the endowments were further augmented by gifts of four free scholarships, tenable at this school. The bank officers of the United Kingdom in that year raised, by shilling subscriptions, a sum of nearly £700 as a testimonial to Sir John Lubbock, in appreciation of the boon conferred by his Bank Holiday Act. At Sir John's request, the money was equally divided, for the promotion of education, between Maidstone Grammar School and the City of London College. With the interest of the portion of the fund given to this school a free scholarship was forthwith instituted, Lady Lubbock supplementing the gift by a contribution of £100. The three other scholarships were founded by several friends of the late Alexander Randall, in memory of that gentleman's distinguished services to the town.

When the new premises were erected, the building was placed under trustees, though the Corporation still retained its authority over the school. The Charity Commissioners drew up a new scheme for the administration of the institution in 1881, according to which the governing body was to consist of thirteen persons—the mayor of Maidstone, as *ex-officio* governor; nine representative governors, to be appointed for three years, one by the School Board, two by the county Justices, and six by the Corporation, conditionally on that body paying for the purposes of the school a yearly sum of not less than £100; and three co-optative governors, to be elected for eight years by the general body of the governors. The master had hitherto been a clergyman of the Church of England, but under the new scheme he was not required to be in holy orders. So long, however, as the master then in charge held office, the scheme was not to come into full operation.

CHAPTER IX.

MUNICIPAL AND PARLIAMENTARY HISTORY.

The Portreve and his Brethren—Incorporation of the Town—
The first Charter revoked—The second Charter—Representative Burgesses in Parliament—Curious By-Laws—
Early Creation of Freemen—The third Charter—How
Corporation Meetings are announced—Andrew Broughton:
his share in the Death of Charles I.—The fourth Charter—
The Kentish Petition of 1701—Five Justices Imprisoned by
the House of Commons—Thomas Bliss—Disputes between
the Corporation and the Inhabitants—The Corporation
Dissolved—The fifth Charter—Corporation Feasts—The
sixth Charter—New Town Hall—The Corporation Rentroll in 1822—Non-Resident Freemen—Parliamentary and
Municipal Reform.

PREVIOUS to the incorporation of Maidstone in the reign of Edward VI., the townsman who had the honour of acting in the capacity of mayor or chief magistrate was called the Portreve. Associated with the Portreve were twelve of the leading inhabitants; they were assisted in the exercise of their civic functions by a number of persons, sometimes as many as twenty-four, who, acting probably as special constables, took an oath at the Portmote—the Portreve's court—to maintain good order in the town. A retrospective breviat drawn up by the Mayor and Jurates in March 1597-8, states that from "time out of mind" Maidstone had been governed in this manner. The first Portreve of whom we have any record is William Beale, who filled the office in 1422; and the next is Richard Dene, who discharged the duties pertaining thereto in 1459, and who was one of the many Kentishmen who, nine years before, had been pardoned by the king for their share in Cade's rebellion. In 1496, as we learn by a lease executed on behalf of the Corpus Christi Fraternity, to which his signature is attached, John Wood was Portreve. Robert Reeve held the post in 1475, and William Beale in 1534.

The Portreve and his brethren were eventually found "insufficient in law" to conduct the government of the town. For that reason, and perhaps also with a view to compensate the inhabitants for any loss of prestige that may have been sustained by the suppression of the college and the Corpus Christi Guild, a Charter of Incorporation was granted by Edward VI. It is dated July 4, 1548, and the preamble states that "for many years past the rule and government of the town was esteemed to belong to certain of the inhabitants, commonly called the Portreve and Brethren of the town of Maidstone," which was then "the chief port of the river Medway." The Charter provided that the corporate body was to bear the title of the Mayor, Jurates, and Commonalty,* and that the first mayor was to be Richard Heeley, with the following twelve jurates, viz., Richard Basse, John Ippinbury, Robert Gosselyn, William Reve, James Beret, Richard Almon, Richard Hooker, William Green, Thomas Gore, William Tilden, Peter Maplesden, and John Dendley. Power was given to the Corporation to make by-laws, and the mayor was appointed clerk of the weekly market, four fairs to be

---

* "Commonalty," the general body of the freemen.

held yearly. With the Charter was given a small mace, which was borne by a Corporation officer on high occasions.

No notice of the creation of freemen appears in the borough records for two years after the incorporation of the town. The freedom of the borough, carrying with it the parliamentary and municipal franchise, was acquired by birth, purchase, apprenticeship in one of the guilds or companies into which the trading portion of the community was divided, or by gift of the Mayor and Jurates. Unless a man obtained his freedom by one or other of these methods, he was not allowed to carry on any kind of business in the town, and in case of default he was heavily fined. In 1551 "William Beale, freeholder, was sworn and entered to be a freeman of the company of drapers of this town, before the mayor, chamberlain, and other of the jurates, and hath agreed with the chamber for his freedom"—so runs an entry in one of the Corporation books. Altogether, a hundred and forty-four inhabitants were made freemen during Edward's reign.

But the outbreak of Wyatt's rebellion in 1554 was fraught with evil consequences to the borough. Newton observes that when Mary came to the throne, Maidstone was one of the towns which had petitioned her to retain the Protestant religion as established by Henry and Edward, thereby incurring the animosity of the Queen and her court. When the knight of Allington proclaimed his intention of preventing the Queen from wedding a Spanish Prince, the inhabitants therefore willingly rallied to his standard, the mayor and many of the principal townsmen taking part in the rising. For this breach of loyalty, as well as their zeal for the Reformation, the Charter was forfeited, and they were deprived of their municipal and parliamentary privileges.

The town remained unincorporated till December 1559, when a second Charter was granted by Queen Elizabeth, conferring additional liberties. The first mayor appointed under this Charter was William Green, and the jurates were Thomas Gore, William Mowseherste, William Collett, William Tilden, James Catlet, Richard Hooker, James Busbridge, Clement Lutwick, William Smyth, Ambrose Ippenbury, Nicholas Austen, and Thomas Beale. The mayor was to be a justice of the peace, and the liberties of the Corporation were to extend over the Medway from East Farleigh bridge to Hawkwood, in the parish of Burham, near Rochester. A serjeant-at-mace was to be appointed, and the inhabitants were exempted from serving on juries empanelled out of Maidstone.

Authority was also given to the freemen to return two burgesses to Parliament. There is no reason to suppose that this right had previously been enjoyed by the freemen, or that Maidstone was a parliamentary borough by prescription, possessing the privilege, in virtue of its population and commerce, of sending two representatives to the Legislature. It is true that in 1553 William Wotton and John Salwyne had been elected to represent the town in Parliament, but the election was disputed, and Edward's Charter was ordered to be examined to determine the question. The result of the inquiry does not appear, but as no mention is made of such authority in the first Charter, it is probable that the freemen, presuming on other liberties granted to them, had decided, on insufficient grounds, to return Salwyne and Wotton. We have also, in support of this view, the statement of Lambarde, who lived in those times, that the right of sending representatives to Parliament was given to Maidstone by Elizabeth; and it may be remarked that in the passage in the Charter granted by that sovereign, which conferred power to return two burgesses to Parliament, no expression is used which would justify the supposition that the privilege had been formerly enjoyed by the inhabitants. The first members elected under the second Charter were Henry Fisher and Nicholas Barham, townsmen, who took their seats in the House in 1563.*

The duties of recorder and town clerk were for many years performed by one person, the dual office having been held by Henry Fisher in 1560, and by Nicholas Barham in 1562. In 1607 the duties were separated, the person who first held the office of town clerk apart from that of recorder being Henry Dixon.† Richard Hasker was appointed chamberlain of the borough in 1561, his duties being to keep the accounts of municipal property, receive rents and other payments, and discharge Corporation bills.‡ From the year 1567 the office was held by two individuals, one being chosen by the Mayor and Jurates, and the other by the Mayor, Jurates, and Commonalty.

Some of the by-laws passed by the Town Council in Elizabeth's reign are amusing. The observance of Sunday was strictly enjoined, and any tradesman who from the year 1562 was found with his shop open on that day was to be fined one shilling. In those days the authorities depended largely upon the kindly efforts of nature to circumscribe the boundaries of fields and gardens in and around the town, and it is not therefore surprising that in 1565 an order was issued, according to which those who broke down hedges were to be mulcted in the sum of one shilling, or in default whipped at

---

* See Appendix, No. 1, for list of members of Parliament.
† See Appendix, No. 3.
‡ The Chamberlains' Accounts are in the strong-room at the Museum. They begin in 1561, but are very irregular till 1586, from which date to 1614 they are complete, with the exception of those belonging to the years 1694, 1692, and 1608. The accounts are missing from 1647 to 1659.

the cart's tail. There being evidently abundance of work for willing hands, stringent measures were taken by the Corporation to prevent idleness and street lounging. A by-law passed in 1568, decreed that every young man "that liveth idly in the town" was to pay sixpence to the chamber for every day "he should be found idle and not using his art," and if, on conviction, the money were not forthcoming, he was "to be imprisoned by the mayor until he should reform himself." The same law applied to unmarried women, under forty years of age, who were out of service. There was no Licensing Act at that time, but in 1574 the Corporation anticipated the enactments passed three hundred years later, and issued a notice warning tavern-keepers that they were to be fined for aiding in drunkenness.

There are numerous entries in the borough records referring to the admission of freemen during, as well as subsequent to, Elizabeth's reign. Indeed, the earlier minutes of the Corporation proceedings, which date from September 9, 1563, almost entirely consist of lists of persons who, by payment of a specified sum, compounded for their freedom. Often from twenty to thirty apprentices belonging to different guilds were made freemen in one year. On the 27th of October 1579, "Thomas Ford, draper, late citizen and alderman of Canterbury, was admitted by general consent to be one of the body corporate, and his contribution was set down at £8, and he was sworn as a freeman." The presentation of the freedom of the borough was a compliment occasionally paid to persons of distinction, and to this class of freemen belonged Sir John Scott, Sir Walter Covert, of Leeds Abbey, Sir Francis Barnham, Sir Humphrey Tufton, and Sir Francis Fane, of whom the three last-named afterwards represented Maidstone in Parliament.

A third Charter was granted to the town by King James,

on the 31st of December 1604. It bestowed several new privileges of a minor character, and named Edward Maplesden as the first mayor, and James Franklyn, Gabriel and John Green, John Fremlyn, John Romney, Stephen Heeley, William Plomer, Richard Highwood, Walter Fisher, Thomas Grenville, Richard Maplesden, and Thomas Swinnock as the first jurates. The Charter, however, did not give satisfaction, and a few years afterwards a fund amounting to £160 was raised to defray the expense of obtaining one which should be more in accordance with "the wishes and expectations" of the Corporation. This fourth Charter was granted on July 12, 1619. It directed that the mayor, recorder, and two of the senior jurates were to be justices of the peace, the mayor also to act as coroner. Power was given to levy tolls on all moveable goods coming into the town by road and river; and the jurisdiction of the fortnightly court then held for the determination of actions and replevins was defined as extending to the parishes and hamlets of East Farleigh, Loose, Barming, Boxley, Allington, Millhall, Linton, Offham, and Newhithe. The mayor named in the Charter was Walter Fisher, and the jurates were Gabriel Green, Edward Maplesden, Stephen Heeley, John Crump, Thomas Swinnock, Ambrose Beale, John Banks, Thomas Knatchbull, William Horsepool, and Richard Duke.

Occasionally the services rendered by the commonalty under the new Charter were not such as to commend them to the Mayor and Jurates. Thus the Town Council or Burghmote, as it was called, expressed an opinion "that the commonalty, or whole body of the freemen, used to assemble in too great numbers, and they not always of the most sufficient sort, for the transacting any public business, thereby occasioning great disorder and confusion;" and it was resolved that they "should be hereafter represented by twenty-four or thirty men at the most, who were to be freemen and freeholders within the Corporation, and to be called the Common Council." By-laws touching a variety of matters affecting the condition and morality of the town were passed by the Mayor and Jurates. In order to give effect to one of these, the borough was divided into wards, and "wardens" in the respective districts were enjoined to take notice of all "rogues, vagabonds, idle persons, unthrifts, malefactors, unlicensed houses, tippling houses, unlawful games and sports, victuallers entertaining guests after nine of the clock at night (not being lodgers) in an unlawful manner; inhabitants who received in their houses sojourners or lodgers who were suspected persons, or of evil fame, or likely to prove or bring a charge to the town; what apprentices or other servants were from time to time received and retained by inhabitants, that an account might be taken of them and of their behaviour, and for what time and upon what terms they were retained; young fellows and wenches living out of service; Sabbath-breaking by travelling, or worldly labours, sports, or pastimes, tippling, drinking, or other disorders upon that day; poor people not employing their children to school or work; the neglects and abuses of officers of all sorts; common nuisances and annoyances of the streets by hogs, rubbish, filth, or otherwise." This by-law was printed and circulated, and the wardens were required to report the result of their observations to the mayor.

After 1613 unlicensed beggars were to be fined one shilling, or failing payment, to be carried to a house of correction. The penalty for keeping shops open or selling goods on Sunday was 2s. 6d. Elaborate precautions were taken against outbreaks of fire. Ladders and buckets were provided for that purpose, and "two discreet inhabitants" were appointed to see that certain houses in which flax was wrought were not in danger of ignition, and to keep a watchful eye over defective chimneys. At another time the ladders and buckets were ordered to be renewed, and in 1624 the Corporation provided two long ladders and twelve leather buckets for the general use of the town, but in order that the leading tradesmen should not wholly depend upon these in cases of emergency, brewers, innkeepers, and maltmen were requested to keep upon their premises a ladder of a "prudent length." Every inhabitant assessed at from 4s. to 12s. a-year was to provide one leather bucket, and each inhabitant rated at more than 12s., two buckets.

The Corporation occasionally interposed in the management of All Saints' Church, but its interference did not invariably meet with the approbation of the minister, and between the Rev. Robert Barrell and the Mayor and Jurates there was often a conflict of authority. In the Council Chamber, though the influence of the Parliament was predominant, there were many who warmly supported the cause of King Charles. Barrell, who was a hot-brained Royalist, on one occasion remarked to a parishioner that he "wished God would put it into the heart of the king to set the City of London on fire, and burn up the Puritans."* The meetings of the Corporation were usually announced from the pulpit of All Saints', but in 1634 Barrell, desirous of finally excluding the mayor and his colleagues from the management of the church, refused to read the notices on Sunday. The offended mayor remonstrated with him, but to no purpose, and at length he arranged to convene his court independently of the minister. A bass-horn was purchased, and with this the crier went round the town on the morning of the day on which the Corporation was

* Affidavit of Jane Ellis, widow, Historical MSS. Commission, Fifth Report.

to meet. He first took his stand at the corner of East Lane and Gabriel's Hill, and blew upon his horn three times in three successive minutes. Proceeding down the High Street, he again blew thrice at the Conduit, opposite the Star Hotel. Then he went to the upper end of Bullock Lane and sounded thrice more; and finally he blew again his triple trumpeting at Wren's Cross. During spring and summer the crier went his rounds at five in the morning, and in autumn and winter at seven o'clock.

One of the persons admitted to the freedom of the borough in 1645 was Ann Halsnod. At a Court of Burghmote held on January 15 in that year, " her fine being assessed at 40s., whereof she paid 20s. in hand, and promised to pay 20s. more at Michaelmas twelve months, she was made free, being the eldest daughter of a freeman, and having no brother to be made free." * Very jealously were the rights of the freemen guarded. Strangers coming to the town were popularly known as "foreigners," and persons who harboured them were liable to a penalty of 3s. 4d. per week. No child under twelve years of age, being a foreigner, was allowed to be apprenticed to trade. A foreigner wishing to obtain his freedom, in order to carry on business in the town, had to pay a fine of £10, and in the early part of the eighteenth century the fine was £20. Any attempt to evade the restriction so imposed was visited by a severe penalty.

Of the members of the Corporation who sympathised with the Parliament in its resistance to Charles I., none exhibited more vehemence in detestation of the king's conduct than did Andrew Broughton. This conspicuous Roundhead was born in 1603, but it is not certain that

---

* Vol. i., f. 264, C. T. Smythe Coll., contains a complete list of freemen from 1598 to 1838.

Maidstone was his birthplace.* He set up in the town as an attorney, and appears to have acquired a lucrative practice. An examination of the parish register enables us to throw some light upon his family. Dorothy, his daughter-in-law, was buried in the churchyard of All Saints' on the 7th of March 1634. He had a daughter Sarah, who was interred April 15, 1635, and at least two sons—Thomas, who died in May 1637, and Andrew, who was baptized in January 1637. Broughton became a common councilman in April 1636, and on the 22nd of October 1647 he was elected a jurat.† In January 1648 a distinction of a different kind was conferred upon him, and by the party whose exploits in the field and in Parliament he had watched with growing admiration—he was appointed to one of the clerkships in the High Court of Justice.‡ Before many months had elapsed the Royalists in the county rose in arms against the Parliament, and on the 1st of June their small force was shattered by Fairfax at Maidstone. On the 2nd of November in the same year the Corporation almost unanimously elected Broughton to the post of chief magistrate of the borough for the ensuing twelve months.§

* In the panelling on the walls of the old Grammar School in Earl Street the name of "Andrew Broughton" was rudely cut. When the panelling was removed many years ago, the piece containing the name was rescued from destruction, and framed and preserved by John Newington Hughes. After the death of Mr. Hughes at Winchester, whither he had removed from Maidstone, the panel found its way to the museum at Taunton, where it was recognized among other curiosities in 1865. The name was supposed to have been cut by Andrew Broughton, or his son.

† He was one of the borough chamberlains in the years 1638 and 1639, and again in 1650. His name also appears as one of the seven sequestrators, who in 1643 were entrusted with the management of All Saints' Church.

‡ The orders referring to this appointment are as follows:—"January 10, 1648.—Andrew Broughton was named and appointed one of the clerks of the Court, with John Phelps; and a messenger of the Court was sent to summons the said Mr. Broughton. January 12, 1648.—Mr. Andrew Broughton attended according to former order; and it was thereupon again ordered that Andrew Broughton and John Phelps, gentlemen, be, and they are hereby appointed and constituted, clerks of the said Court, and enjoined to give their attendance from time to time accordingly."

§ He had been nominated for the same office in the previous November, but James Ruse was chosen.

The time was thick with startling events. Cromwell had humbled every foe, and Charles was a close prisoner. The 20th of January saw the now submissive but dignified king placed upon his trial, and Broughton, in virtue of his judicial position, became one of the clerks of the Court. On the eighth day the trial terminated, and that tremendous sentence which shook every despotic throne in Europe was read by the mayor of Maidstone.* Twelve days later, for attempting to govern without the consent of the people, Charles was beheaded at Whitehall.†

Broughton, on his return from London after the king's execution, attended All Saints' Church on Sunday as usual, when Thomas Wilson, the minister—whose discourse sometimes extended to forty-six printed quarto pages—preached one of his impassioned and outspoken sermons, in which he remarked that "David's heart smote him when he only cut off the skirt of Saul's garment, but men dare nowadays to cut off the head of a king without remorse." Hearing this, Broughton rose from his seat and left the church, whereupon Wilson observed that "when the Word of God comes home to a man, it makes him fly for it!" Broughton, it is said, never attended the church again, but procured Joseph Whiston, another minister, to officiate in the Grammar School.

The emoluments he received for his services to the Parliaments enabled him to erect a large house, which is still standing, on the south side of Earl Street. In June 1649 he was appointed clerk, and afterwards coroner, to the Upper

---

* Newton, quoting from the "Trials of the Regicides," states that Broughton read the charge or impeachment as well as the sentence, after the reading of which latter the whole Court stood up to express its assent thereto.

† Among the Clarendon State Papers is a printed list of the persons who tried the king, with manuscript notes by "Mr. Broughton, of Maidstone," as one of the "counsellors-assistant to the Court."

Bench, but he continued to reside in his mansion at Maidstone. At the expiration of his term of office as chief magistrate of the borough in November of that year, he retained his position as one of the jurates and was made a justice of the peace.* He regularly attended the meetings of the Corporation, and at the sitting in July 1650 he appears in the list of those present as "Andrew Broughton, Esq.," the names of the other jurates having the simple prefix of "Mr." After the spring of 1652, however, he was continuously absent for several years, some portions of the interval having been spent at Westminster, where he represented Maidstone in the later Parliaments of the Commonwealth. In November 1658, during his absence, he was proposed as a candidate for the mayoralty, but Gervase Maplesden was elected. The next Court of Burghmote he attended was held on October 30, 1659, when the sitting appears to have been a protracted one. On the 2nd of the following month Broughton once more became mayor of the borough.

But another great national crisis was approaching. The last Court of Burghmote over which Broughton presided met on the 18th of January 1660. In the last week of May Charles II. landed at Dover, and the monarchy was restored. Newton says he had been told that Broughton, in his capacity of chief magistrate, was present at the proclamation of the king at the Town Hall, on the 29th of May, and that he had a horse in waiting, which he immediately mounted, and rode off, no one knew whither. There can be little doubt, however, that Broughton did not attempt the daring act which is

* During his mayoralty the little mace (a large one, towards the cost of which Ambrose Beale paid £30, had been procured a few years previously) was sold for £3 18s. 4½d., and a mace, without the king's arms, was bought for £48 3s. 5d., of which £10 had been bequeathed by John Bigg, an ardent Roundhead.

here attributed to him, and that several months before the Restoration he had prudently anticipated the fate in store for the persons remaining in England who were immediately concerned in the death of Charles I. At the Corporation meeting on the 5th of June, complaints were made of the "long absence" of the mayor, and the mace-bearer was sent to Broughton's house in Earl Street to inquire after him. The answer brought back was that Mr. Broughton's servants said their master was not at home, nor did they know where he was, or when he would return. It was then resolved to give "notice to Andrew Broughton, maior, that if he did not return and take upon him the execution of the said office of maior, he would be removed from the said office." The day after this meeting he was included in the king's proclamation against the Regicides.

Within ten days two other meetings of the Town Council were held, Broughton's flight forming the chief subject for consideration. At the meeting on the 15th of June it was reported that the mayor, "amongst others in the country, hath fled, and doth absent himself from being brought to tryal according to law for treason, wherewith he and others stand respectively charged, by information of the Lords and Commons in Parliament assembled, touching the death of his late Majesty, King Charles the First, late king of these realms." A crowded meeting of the jurates, freemen, and freeholders was convened at the Grammar School on the 18th. The king's proclamation was then read, and Broughton was "discharged from the office of maior." Moreover, he was required to appear before the jurates and freemen to answer for matters "closely connected with the murder of his late majesty." At the same time Richard Bills was elected to serve as mayor for the remainder of the term.*

---

* See Appendix, No. 2, for list of mayors.

Broughton, however, had quitted Maidstone for ever. He retired, with others who were implicated in the death of Charles, to Vevay, on the Lake of Geneva. There he lived for twenty-eight years, and there, on the 23rd of February 1688, he died. In the church of St. Martin wherein his remains were interred a stone was raised to his memory on which was engraved a Latin inscription, recording that "having been banished from his country for delivering the sentence of the King of Kings, he was content to end his pilgrimage among strangers, and in his eighty-fifth year, suffering from old age alone, he rested from his labours and slept in the Lord."

On the accession of Charles II. the Mayor and Jurates lost no time in evincing their loyalty, and a crown was affixed to the large mace at a cost of £24 4s. 5d. Municipal affairs thereafter presented no feature of special interest until 1682, when, in the words of a Corporation minute, the "Charters were foolishly surrendered by a letter of attorney to Mr. Wyatt, recorder." A fifth Charter, dated October 26, 1682, was then obtained, the corporate title of Mayor, Aldermen, and Common Council being therein applied, for the first time, to Maidstone. Robert Saunders was named as mayor, and the aldermen were Samuel Wood, Garret Callant, John Dunning, John Lawes, George Walker, William Weldish, Francis Curtis, Thomas Bliss, George Peirce, Robert Salmon, John Fowle, and Thomas Marshall. There were to be twenty-four common councilmen, viz., John Viney, Richard Wattell, William Russell, Richard Heeley, John Newington, John Carey, John Peirce, John Greenell, Robert Panghorne, Thomas Hope, Stephen Fowle, Thomas Harris, George Hodges, Alex. Osborne, John Tonge, Robert Brook, sen., Richard Mussery, Walter Weeks, Geo. Webb, Stephen Osborne, George Manby, Matthew Chaundler, John

Howe, and Daniel Hope. Newton, writing in 1741, states that "it being supposed that the former Charters were not legally surrendered, and that this new one was rather designed to serve a party interest than the common good of the Corporation (to which it seemed to be of no real advantage), they had declined acting by it ever since" the compulsory retirement of King James in 1688.

But before James happily left the throne vacant by his pusillanimous flight, he attempted to aid the Roman Catholics on the plea of relieving the Dissenters from disabilities, and promoting their election to positions of trust in the kingdom. In 1687 he forced the Corporation to elect as mayor of the borough Joseph Wright, a Baptist minister. A few weeks after, we read in a Corporation minute, that an order was received "from a Popish king, namely, James the Second, to discharge seven aldermen and twelve councilmen at once." On the 30th of January 1688 another order came from Whitehall to discharge four other aldermen and eleven common councillors. At the same time Edwin Wyatt, the recorder, and Robert Saunders, sen., the town clerk, were summarily dismissed, the office of town clerk being conferred on Mr. Lamb, a Dissenter. But the order concerning Wyatt being forthwith revoked, he was allowed to retain his position. A fortnight previous to the landing of the Prince of Orange at Torbay, Wright retired from the mayoralty, and on the 20th of October Robert Saunders, jun., was chosen to serve during the remainder of the term.

There was great excitement in Maidstone in the spring of 1701. The death of Charles II. of Spain, and the succession of Philip Duke of Anjou, grandson of Louis XIV., to the Spanish throne, raised serious apprehensions as to the growing power of France, and the feeling prevalent in Kent was that the united forces of the two countries would become the tyrannisers over Europe. A draft petition to the House of Commons was accordingly sent down from London to Maidstone with a view of getting the Justices of the county to adopt it. The petition implored the House "to have regard to the voice of the people, that our religion and safety may be effectually provided for; that your loyal addresses may be turned into bills of supply, and that his most sacred majesty (William III.) may be enabled powerfully to assist his allies before it be too late." At the General Quarter Sessions held at Maidstone on the 29th of April, the petition was submitted by William Culpeper, of Hollingbourne, and in a few hours it received the signatures of all the deputy-lieutenants present, more than twenty justices of the peace, the members of the grand jury, and many freeholders. William Culpeper, his younger brother Thomas Culpeper, who was married to Lady Taylor, of Park House, Sandling Road, David Polhill, of Otford, Justinian Champneys, of Vinters, and William Hamilton, of Chilston, were appointed to carry the petition to London.

When they arrived on the 8th of May at Westminster, Sir Thos. Hales, one of the members for Kent, requested them not to present it, as it was nothing less than an impertinent piece of advice to the House. Other members also advised a similar course. Not to be daunted, however, William Culpeper, parodying a famous remark of Luther, replied, with an air of defiance, "If every tile upon St. Stephen's chapel were a devil, I would still present the petition." After waiting half an hour in the lobby, the five Justices stepped forward to the bar of the House, and delivered the document to the Speaker. "Gentlemen," said the Speaker, "is this your petition?" "Yes, Mr. Speaker," was the reply. "And, gentlemen, your hands are to this petition?" "Yes, Mr. Speaker." "Carry it to them and see if they will own their hands." A clerk having taken the petition across the floor of the House, the Justices avowed their signatures, and were then requested to withdraw.

They retired to the lobby, and were there waited upon by several members, who told them that they had incurred the risk of imprisonment, and ought to offer an apology. Their answer was given in writing as follows:—"We are humbly of opinion that it is our right to petition this honourable House according to the statute 13 Car. 2. As to the matter of the petition, we intend nothing offensive to this honourable House." A debate ensued which lasted five hours, and a majority of the House voted that the petition was "scandalous, insolent, and seditious, tending to destroy the constitution of Parliament, and to subvert the established government of the realm."

The five Justices were committed to the custody of the Serjeant-at-arms, who conducted them to the Castle Tavern in Fleet Street. Here they remained for three days, being visited by many of the citizens and several influential members of the Whig party. The news of their imprisonment created great sensation in Maidstone, and Lady Taylor was much agitated at the detention of her husband. Wishing to see her ladyship, Thomas Culpeper was permitted by an under officer to return to Maidstone for two days on parole. When the Serjeant-at-arms heard of his liberation he was highly indignant, and ordered the four other prisoners to be kept in close confinement. They were removed under cover of the night to a house in Fox Court, Holborn, Champneys and William Culpeper being placed in the garret, and Hamilton and Polhill in the cellar. The next morning they were visited by the Serjeant, and on the prisoners complaining of their harsh treatment, he flourished his sword and used such overbearing language that William Culpeper ventured to tell him that he hoped he should "live to see him hanged."

Thomas Culpeper did not surrender himself on the 12th of May, at the end of his two day's parole. On the 15th, however, the Serjeant-at-arms informed the House that he held a letter from him promising to give himself up that day. The Serjeant also stated that although the prisoners had voluntarily delivered their swords to him, he feared an effort would be made to rescue them. They were then lodged in the Gatehouse Prison, Westminster, whither they had been conveyed under a warrant from the Speaker. By order of the House their imprisonment was to continue till the end of the Session, but a conviction began to dawn upon the Government that their detention was illegal, and the excitement throughout the country was so great that Ministers became somewhat alarmed for the consequences. It was therefore deemed expedient to prorogue Parliament on the 23rd of June, about a month earlier than usual, and the prisoners were forthwith released.

The five Justices were the heroes of the hour. Wherever they went in London ringing cheers greeted them, and a banquet in their honour was held at Mercers' Hall, Cheapside. They set out for Kent on Thursday, the 2nd of July. Crowds awaited them all along the route. The citizens of Rochester huzzaed them through the city, and the Maidstone people went by hundreds, both horse and foot, to meet them at Blue Bell Hill. At Sandling, about eight o'clock in the evening, they were met by the gentlemen of the neighbourhood with their coaches, and as they proceeded, amid deafening cheers, along the streets, the way was strewed with flowers and evergreens. It was market day at Maidstone, and the town was full of country people. At Park House the Culpepers were welcomed by Lady Taylor, Lady

Culpeper, their mother, and by other ladies of quality. The day concluded with an immense bonfire, round which the healths of the five gentlemen were drunk with enthusiasm. At Bearsted the church bells were rung, and hundreds of people continued together all night there, ready to welcome William Culpeper on his way to Hollingbourne. But the reception at Maidstone had detained him too long, and he remained over night at Park House.*

Political feeling appears to have then been running very high in the town. The local Whigs were represeented by Sir Robert Marsham, and the Tories by Thomas Bliss, the proprietor of the brewery in Stone Street. Whichever party happened to be in the ascendant generally took advantage of the special power it possessed by admitting only its own partizans to the freedom of the borough, and the favour was sometimes conferred upon paupers and such as were inmates of the workhouse. The latter at election times were particularly susceptible to treating and bribery; and the votes of these impecunious persons seem to have been much resorted to during the polling for members of Parliament in January 1701. The election was followed by a petition, which was heard at some length before a parliamentary committee. It was then declared that freemen in receipt of alms or charity had no right to exercise the electoral franchise. An old leaflet, dated November 20, 1701, evidently written by a Whig, animadverts in strong terms upon the conduct of Thomas Bliss. That gentleman, it is stated, influenced poor freemen by lending them money, which they were seldom asked to return. Other voters, we are told, were governed by "pot and pipe." Immediately after the disso-

---

* These particulars are gathered from two lengthy treatises printed in 1701, and entitled "The History of the Kentish Petition," and "Jura Populi Anglicani; or the Subject's Right of Petitioning set forth," the latter said to be from the pen of Daniel Defoe.

lution of Parliament, the taps of the publichouses which belonged to him were "running day and night," and plenty of good flip and punch could be had, with nothing to pay. The election in 1702 called forth another petition which, *inter alia*, charged the Corporation with having used unlawful means to influence the electors. A similar decision was given as in the previous year, and not only was the election declared void, but as a punishment upon the constituency, it was ordered that no writ should be issued for Maidstone during the rest of the Session.

These proceedings, as well as other petitions which were founded upon contested elections during the next few years, tended only to fan the violent spirit of the rival parties. But a question of a different kind was soon to be forced upon the attention of the freemen—the right of electing jurates. The Mayor and Jurates were popularly known as the upper bench, and the common councilmen as the lower bench, of the Corporation. The two benches were at loggerheads. According to the contention of the upper bench, the common councilmen had no voice in the election of jurates, and at a special meeting of the Corporation in 1715 a by-law to this effect was, in spite of much opposition, passed by the upper bench.* The by-law continued in force till 1730, the jurates, as vacancies occurred, being elected by the Mayor and Jurates only. But in that year informations of *quo warranto* were, on behalf of the commonalty, filed against seven of the jurates who had been thus elected. Two of the cases were argued on demurrer, and judgment being given

---

* It was during this stormy period, in the year 1723, that the following ominous entry as to the borough records appears in one of the Corporation books:—" Examined and looked over all the writings of that old chest without a lid in the comens rome, and those papers that do remain there are only fitt for fire; and in the other chest of the same rome which is locked with one lock those papers are of no value now, but only for tobacco paper."

against the defendants, the five other jurates disclaimed. There remained in the Corporation only three jurates, and these were chosen by the Mayor, Jurates, and Common Council previous to 1715.

A Court of Burghmote was held on the 10th of January 1738, at which the three jurates, one of them presiding as mayor, three common councilmen, and fifty-four freeholders were present, when fifteen inhabitants were elected to the common council. Six common councilmen were then elevated to the upper bench. Soon after, the persons who had been ousted as jurates challenged the right of the three jurates who were elected previous to 1715, on the ground that they were not chosen by the mayor, jurates, and commonalty at large, as directed by the Charter of 1619. One of the cases was tried at bar, and a verdict was obtained against the defendant. The two other jurates thereupon disclaimed. The six new jurates were now the only occupants of the upper bench, and in November 1740 one of their number, Daniel Kirby, was appointed chief magistrate for the ensuing year. But their reign only lasted a few months, for in 1740 informations were filed against them, and as it was shown that the three jurates by whom they had been chosen were themselves not legally elected, they also were ousted. The Corporation, being thus left without a jurat, was dissolved. Add to this the forfeiture of the Charter, and the fact that for the next six years there was neither mayor nor town clerk, and it will be seen that, by the folly of the Corporation, the town was placed in a humiliating position.

Efforts were not wanting to retrieve the lost privileges, but without immediate success. The Tory party was headed by Lord Guernsey, son of the Earl of Aylesford, and the Whig party by William Horsmonden Turner, who was born in 1678, being the son of Anthony Horsmonden, of Maidstone, by his second wife Jane, daughter of Sir William Turner, of Richmond. Turner had recently purchased the estate of Harrietsham Place, where he resided. Two petitions were in 1743 sent to Westminster from Maidstone praying the Crown to grant a new Charter. One was from the Aylesford party, suggesting that the Mayor and Jurates only, or at most the common council, as distinct from the general body of the freemen, should have the right of electing jurates; and the other, from the Turner party, advised that the whole body of the freemen should possess the right, and stated that from 1619 to 1715 the jurates were invariably elected by the Mayor, Jurates, and Common Council. Both petitions were referred to the Solicitor-General, who ultimately recommended a new Charter, but made certain recommendations which displeased both parties in the town, and against which fresh petitions were lodged.

At length, after the lapse of six years, it became evident that the Crown intended to incorporate the town anew. Towards midsummer 1747, the subject was warmly discussed in Privy Council, where the opposing parties used all their interest to have the Charter framed in accordance with their particular views. After discussions lasting, it is said, three nights, a Charter, modelled generally on the recommendations of the Solicitor-General, was granted on the 17th of June. A pamphleteer, writing some years later, says that a parliamentary election being then impending, Turner brought the Charter in triumph to Maidstone, where, being read to the freemen, it was received with acclamation. He was thereupon appointed recorder, and elected to represent the borough at Westminster in conjunction with the Hon. Robert Fairfax.*

---

* Turner was twice married—first, on May 25, 1725, to Elizabeth, widow of Thomas Bliss; and secondly, in 1745, to Elizabeth Read, of Gravesend. He died in 1753, and was buried at Maidstone.

This, the sixth and last Charter granted to Maidstone, restored certain privileges formerly enjoyed by the freemen, and named Edward Hunter as the first mayor, with twelve jurates, viz., Joseph Smalwell, John Mason, Thomas Nightingale, Thomas Argles, John Harris, Richard Mussery, Stephen Page, George Curteis, John Rogers, Thomas Pope, jun., Jonathan Weldish, and Samuel Stevenson, jun. With the jurates were to be associated forty common councilmen, consisting of Roger Harris, Edward Argles, Thomas Hassell, David Polhill, James Baxter, William Russell, Thomas Baytop, Richard Wottall, jun., Nicholas and John Rawlings, William Manser, Robert Pine, William Purlis, William Borman, John Pope, Shadrack Illden, Stephen Prentis, Samuel Stevenson, sen., William Davis, Richard Shepherd, Samuel Ellis, sen., William Foster, Edward Ellis, John Alexander, Thomas Wildes, sen., Henry Jefferys, William Stacey, George May, John Barnes, John Rudkin, Thomas Rhode, John Hammond, Stephen Goffe, Thomas Bensted, Simon Goldwell, John Adams, Thomas Broomfield, John Reader, Thomas Wildes, jun., and Josiah Lane. The mayor was to be elected annually on the 2nd of November, while the jurates and common councilmen were to "continue in office during their several natural lives, unless they, or any of them, should in the meantime be removed for misgovernment or misdemeanour, or for any other reasonable cause." With regard to the mode of their election, it was provided that "as often as any of the jurates should happen to die, or be removed for any reasonable cause from office," it should " be lawful for the said Mayor, Jurates, and Common Council henceforth to nominate and elect any person or persons out of the common councilmen to be a jurate or jurates." The common councilmen were to be chosen by the Corporation "out of the remaining principal inhabitants" of the borough.

The new Corporation met on the 3rd of July 1747, being the first meeting since November 2, 1740. The various officers were then appointed, and attention was at once directed to the state of the property belonging to the town, much of which had been sold to defray the expenses incurred in the prolonged litigation which preceded the granting of the Charter. A committee was appointed to report as to the several rents and other monies due to the Corporation, and at a subsequent meeting the chamberlains were instructed to take legal proceedings, if necessary, to recover the amounts still outstanding. The affairs of the borough were now to be conducted with every appearance of legality and order. Courts of Burghmote were held regularly, and every jurate or common councilman who appeared at Corporation or other public meetings without his gown was to be fined 10s. This fine was afterwards increased to one guinea.

It was agreed in 1758 that the mayor should receive a salary of £50 "towards defraying the charges of keeping a decent table, and entertaining at breakfast and dinner such of the jurates and common councilmen as should from time to time attend and accompany the said mayor in their gowns to and from divine service, and other expenses incident to the office of mayor." It was thought that by accompanying the mayor in their gowns to All Saints' Church on Sundays the jurates and councilmen would "greatly contribute to the dignity of the Corporation." But Thomas Pope, who was then chief magistrate, refused the proffered remuneration; and in August 1759 the motion relating thereto was rescinded.

The meetings of the Corporation had hitherto been held in a low-pitched, old-fashioned room in the Lower Court House. This room was called the "court hall" and also the "common hall," and its capabilities were in no respect equal to the growing requirements of the Corporation. In May 1758 it was decided to erect more suitable premises, but some delay occurred before the work was carried out. The "common hall, with the prison, bridewell, and appurtenances thereunto adjoining," was pulled down in 1763, and on the same site the foundation-stone of the present Town Hall was laid. Towards the cost of the building Lord Aylesford and Lord Romney each gave £100, and another donor £300; while the justices of the western half of the county contributed £500, in consideration of which they were to have the use of the Hall for the Kent Assizes and for transacting county business. The lower part of the eastern end of the Town Hall, comprising the present entrance and the space now filled by the three windows at each side of it, was originally open arches, connected by iron rails, and enclosing a pavement leading to what was called the lower court, where the civil cases at the Assizes were tried. The space was taken into the lower court in 1847.

Our forefathers did not share our ideas of municipal economy and abstemiousness. They could indulge with an easy conscience in feasting at the public expense. Many feasts, some of them on a sumptuous scale, were held every year, and they often formed no inconsiderable portion of the Corporation expenditure. The cost under this head had in 1704 assumed such formidable proportions that a resolution was carried in the council chamber stating that "it appeareth unto this court absolutely necessary that we resolve upon some rule to guide us in our public expenses." It was then decided to limit the annual expenditure as follows:— For the mayor's dinner, £18; Fifth of November, £3; the king's birthday, £4; King Charles's restoration, £3; King George's accession, £4; Easter sessions, £3; Michaelmas sessions, £3 10s.; the court-leet,* £6 10s.; original Court of Burghmote, £6 16s.; at each Court of Burghmote held by adjournment, £2 19s; Court of Survey of the river,† £10; the Prince of Wales's birthday, £3.; King George's coronation, £4. At a Corporation meeting in 1727 it was reported that the above resolution had not produced the "desired effect," and the order as to allowances was thereupon renewed.

Further limitations, generally in the direction of increased economy, were from time to time made. In 1732 it was ordered that for the future £15 should be allowed for the mayor's dinner, £2 for the Fifth of November, 25s. for each of the sessions at Easter and Michaelmas, £4 for the original Court of Burghmote, £2 for the king's coronation, £5 for the court-leet, £2 for the king's birthday, and £5 for the mayor's fishing. If the sum expended at any of the celebrations should exceed the stipulated amount, the extra was "not to be paid out of the borough fund." At a subsequent meeting of the Corporation in the same year it was agreed that "no more than £5" should be allowed at the Kent Assizes "towards the charges of the judges' lodgings,‡ besides the usual presents of a calf and lamb, and two dozen of wine, and one barrel of strong and one barrel of small beer." But this rate of progress was too rapid to last. With the

---

* The court-leet was held by the Mayor and Jurates, with the recorder as steward. At this court the peace officers of the parish were chosen, consisting of a high constable and four inhabitants, usually tradesmen, whose duty it was to see that no illegal games or other unlawful practices were carried on. When the latter were appointed a baton on which the borough arms were blazoned, was sent to each of them, and they were called borsholders. In 1612 the high constable and borsholders, with their staves of office, were ordered to walk the streets every market day and two other days in the week.

† This was familiarly called the "mayor's fishing." The chief magistrate was conservator of the Medway from East Farleigh bridge to Hawkwood, and he called a court once a year to inspect the condition of the river.

‡ In 1723, £10 had been allowed for this purpose.

P

year 1749 a reaction set in, and the scale was "revised" as follows:—For the original Court of Burghmote, £10; the court-leet, £8; the king's birthday, £3; the mayor's fishing, £15, and every person present at such fishing was to pay 2s. 6d. The allowance for the mayor's dinner was in 1758 raised to £17, £5 being voted for the quarter sessions, and £5 only for the mayor's fishing.

A few years after, another unfortunate dispute arose between the Corporation and the inhabitants. There was a contested municipal election on April 9, 1764, when the freemen returned four inhabitants who were opposed to the malfeasance and extravagance which characterized the proceedings of the Burghmote. By way of retaliation, the majority in the council chamber then passed a by-law depriving the commonalty of the right of voting for common councilmen, and vesting it in the Mayor, Jurates, and Common Council, with such of the freemen as had served the office of churchwarden and overseer of the poor. This decision the freemen disputed, and in 1766 it was overruled by judgment of the Court of King's Bench. With a view to evade the edict of the Court, the Corporation met in February of that year, and carried another by-law, by which the right of electing common councilmen was vested in the Mayor, Jurates, and Common Council, and forty of the senior freemen. The freemen again appealed to a higher court, but in January 1767, the leaders of the ruling party thought proper to let judgment go against them.

Yet they had not altogether relinquished their claim. On March 14 the Corporation met and resolved to increase the number of privileged freemen from forty to sixty, intending thereby to create an impression that as the Town Council consisted of fifty-three members, the freemen would have a preponderance of votes. This concession, however, did not satisfy the freemen, as it was maintained that nearly one-half of the sixty senior freemen were non-resident, and therefore seldom able to record their votes, while others were paupers or too old and enfeebled to take part in an election. A vacancy presently occurred in the common council, and offered an opportunity for testing the question. Of the sixty senior freemen, only seven went to the poll, and several of these, there seems no reason to doubt, came from the workhouse. The obnoxious by-law was afterwards set aside by the Court of King's Bench, and a mandamus was issued by the Court for filling up the vacancy in accordance with the spirit of the Charter. Lord Mansfield, who tried the case, remarked that the Mayor and Jurates of Maidstone "would overturn the Constitution itself, if it were in their power." *

The effect of these law-suits was to still further impoverish the town, the Corporation, in prosecuting its case, having made liberal use of the public funds. Large sums of money also continued to be spent in municipal feasting. It appears to have been chiefly for long-standing accumulations under this head that in 1780 a bill, amounting to £163 16s. 8d., was presented to the Corporation for payment. The account was not disputed, and it was ordered that "no part of the Corporation revenues should be expended at the election of mayor, at any Court of Burghmote, or court-leet, till such money was paid."

At the general election in September 1780, Clement Taylor, of this town, offered himself as an Independent candidate for

---

* The following paragraph, relating to an election for common councilmen, appears in the *Kentish Gazette*, December 12, 1772:—"Mr. G. Prentis and some other friends have done a service to the town of Maidstone by preserving the freemen their right of voting for their common council, of which they would certainly have been deprived had not the above gentleman and his friends, at the expense of £900, secured to them that privilege."

Maidstone, in opposition to the Hon. Charles Finch, brother to the Earl of Aylesford. Sir Horace Mann, the late Whig member, offered himself for re-election, being strongly supported by the Marsham family; and after an exciting contest, Taylor and Mann were returned by considerable majorities. Prior to this election, the representation of the borough had, during a number of years, been struggled for and divided by the Finch or Tory party and the Marsham or Whig party, and the leaderships of those two aristocratic families, by whom the constituents were held in very light estimation, thenceforth disappeared.*

Much of the property belonging to the borough was at various times disposed of to meet the extraordinary expenses of the Corporation. The rent-roll in 1714 amounted to upwards of £180 per annum. In 1727 it was decided that as in times past lands and tenements had been sold in a "clandestine manner," no lease should in future be given, or any property sold, without the consent of a majority of the Corporation. A committee appointed in 1822 to examine the borough rent-roll, reported in December 1823 that the Corporation possessed the following lands, tenements, tolls, and fee farm rents:—

1. The Town Hall.
2. The Corn, Fish, Butcher's, Butter, and Cattle Markets, the tolls for the same being leased at the annual rent of £120.
3. The Vaults under the Town Hall, let at £25 per annum.
4. Two Houses next the Town Hall, let at a rent of £50.
5. Shop in the passage-way between the Marquis of Granby and the Sun alehouses, let at £7 per annum.
6. The Fair Meadow.
7. Wharf adjoining the same, let at £45.
8. Wharf and warehouses adjoining the last-mentioned, let also at £45.
9. Wharf and warehouses adjoining the last-mentioned, let at £15.

* A Canterbury paper, dated September 13, 1780, observes that "by the virtue and spirit of the independent freemen," the Finch interest was "completely overthrown." Clement Taylor, in his address of thanks to the freemen, assures them that the "noble stand" they had made "must convince" the Finch party that "when they were determined, they would be *free*."

10. Seven and a half acres of Land adjoining the turnpike road in West Borough, let at £18.*
11. Two acres of ground, called Pest-house Land, in West Borough, let at £3.
12. Two Cottages at the upper end of Stone Street, let at £7.†
13. Rent-charge of 40s. per annum issuing from a small piece of meadow land in Stone Street.
14. Rent-charge of £6 issuing from premises on the west side of Gabriel's Hill.
15. Rent-charge of 20s. issuing from premises in High Street at the south-east corner of Pudding Lane.‡
16. Rent-charge of 10s. issuing from part of a tenement in Middle Row which was built over a passage-way granted by the Corporation.

Reference has already been made to the admission of non-residents to the freedom of the borough. As the poll-books prove, these strangers formed an important element at parliamentary as well as municipal elections. A few figures will illustrate this. At the election for members of Parliament in June 1723, 844 freemen recorded their votes, and of these 215 were non-resident. Of the 744 who polled in March 1768, 256 were non-resident, living at Yarmouth, Norwich, Maidenhead, London, Bristol, and in various parts of Kent, Essex, Berks, Dorset, and Sussex. The number of non-residents who voted in October 1806 was 229, against 409 residents; and in March 1820, 210 non-resident and 258 resident voters went to the poll. In 1825 there were 813 freemen, of whom 490 were resident in Maidstone. Of the 795 householders who paid rates in that year, only 172 were freemen, and the number of freemen among the 1,578 householders whose rates were paid by their landlords was 174.

A contemporary writer,§ anticipating the reforms enforced by Parliament a few years later, observes that a serious objection to the state of things in 1825 was that the influence exercised by the 323 non-resident freemen was often

---

* Let at £15 in 1749.
† In 1658 the Corporation sold four cottages in Stone Street for £60, and two cottages on St. Faith's Green for £50.
‡ This house, which had previously belonged to the Corpus Christi Fraternity, was in 1597 tenanted by John Romney.
§ James's "Charters, and Documents of the King's Town and Port of Maidstone," 1825.

prejudicial to the interests of the town, and that many of the resident voters were in absolute pauperism, some of them actually "living in the workhouse." That the latter class of freemen were in a special degree exposed to pecuniary allurements was notorious; yet in those pre-reform days electoral venality was not the monoply of pauper voters. At one of the parliamentary elections twenty-one freemen agreed not to accept less than a certain sum of money for their votes. They hid themselves in a hay-loft, and from time to time had notice of how things were going. Towards the close of the poll the voting had left the candidates so nearly equal that the election was completely in the hands of these men. One of the candidates was then acquainted with their whereabouts, but the ladder to the loft having been adroitly drawn up, he was kept at a convenient distance. After much pleading and gesticulating, he promised to come to their terms. The ladder was let down, and finding it the true way to success, he passed upwards into the loft, where matters were arranged to their mutual satisfaction. The twenty-one voters thereupon proceeded in a body to the poll, and carried the election.

The last parliamentary election prior to the passing of the Reform Bill was in May 1831. 891 freemen, of whom 247 were non-resident, recorded their votes, and the two Liberal candidates were returned. Public opinion in favour of the great measure was making itself felt. The poll for the county was then taken on Penenden Heath, and thinking that a Tory would contest the seat, and also with a view to save the expenses of their candidate, a large number of East Kent reformers had arranged to march to Maidstone, and to bivouac in a barn on the road. But no Tory candidate appeared. The Bill passed in June 1832, and the effect of its operation was speedily realized. On December 12 in that year Maidstone was called upon to choose two representatives for the first reformed Parliament, and as the poll-book shows, the non-resident voters, who figured so prominently at previous contests, had almost entirely disappeared. Of the 945 electors, 873 went to the poll, and again returned the Liberal candidates. The borough was then for the first time divided into four " compartments " or wards. Formerly the polling had extended over more than one day. It lasted three days in 1807, and two days in 1806, 1812, and 1830.

In the autumn of 1821 three vacancies occurred in the common council of the Corporation, where the Tories were at that time in a majority. The polling for the vacant seats being, as the Whigs thought, unduly delayed, they obtained a mandamus from the King's Bench, on November 10, directing the filling up of the vacancies within fifteen days; but on the representation of the recorder, the term was prolonged to the 23rd of January following. In the meantime the election was fixed for Friday, January 11. The Whigs nominated Thomas Durrant, William Jury, and Robert Mason, and the Tory candidates were Thomas Tassell, Benjamin Ruck, and George Poolly. Each party put forth its whole strength. A sudden appeal to the freemen living in London resulted in about a hundred of them being brought up to the poll in six four-horse stage coaches. The polling lasted seven days, and at the end of that time the successful candidates were Ruck, Poolly, and Tassell. Of the 738 electors who recorded their votes, 294 polled on the first day, 140 on the second, 180 on the third, 66 on the fourth, 32 on the fifth, 17 on the sixth, and 9 on the seventh. This was pronounced by one of the local papers to be " the severest contest ever known in the annals of Maidstone." It had cost one side alone upwards of £1,600.

But the Municipal Corporations Act brought about great

changes. It reduced the Corporation from fifty-three members, to a mayor, five aldermen, and twelve common councillors, the number of the latter being subsequently, as the population increased, raised to eighteen. It further enacted the practice of annual elections, a fourth of the Town Council retiring every year. The first municipal election after the Bill received the royal assent, was held on the 27th of December 1835, when the Tory candidates were defeated. It only remains to be added that in 1864 the Commissioners of Pavement were superseded by the formation of a Local Board of Health. The sanitary condition of the town has since been much improved, and many beneficial though costly improvements in other directions have also been effected.

CHAPTER X.

ANCIENT STATE OF THE TOWN.

Leland's Visit—The Manor of Maidstone—Manors of East Lane and Wyke—Population in 1572—Sanitary Condition of the Town—The Plague—The Bear Ringle—The Queen's Players—Conduits in the High Street—Benefactions to the Poor—Fearful Ravages of the Plague—Letter-carrying in the Seventeenth Century—The King's Mead—Visit of Samuel Pepys—Population in 1695—The Poor-Rate—Smallpox—Population in 1782—The Streets Paved and Lighted—Street Nomenclature—Old Inns and Taverns.

JOHN LELAND, in his travels through England, visited Maidstone about the year 1538, and in his quaint language, thus describes the town:—"The ruler of the place is cawled Port-Ryve. Ther is in the towne a fair Colledge of prestes. Courtenay was the fownder of the Colledge, where the master is a Prebendarie; the residue are ministers to synge devyne service. The Castel standeth about the myddes of the town, being well maynteyned by the Archbishop of Canterbury. Ther is the commune gayle, or prison of Kent, as in the shyre town. Maidstone is a market towne, of one long streete, well builded, and full of innes."* It has been suggested that

---

* Leland's "Itinerary," vol. vi., f. 2.

the building to which Leland refers as the Castle, is the old county prison, with flat roof and embattled parapet, which stood near the top of the High Street; but as the prison belonging to the county was never maintained by the archbishops, and seeing that Leland, in his next sentence, expressly alludes to it as a separate building, the conjecture is somewhat wide of the mark. Evidently the Castle, in the traveller's mind, was no other than the archiepiscopal Palace, and his mistake in describing it as standing near the middle of the town may be attributed to the fact of his being a stranger to the locality. In the time of Henry VIII., though there were dwelling-houses in Upper Stone Street and in Knightrider Street, the town chiefly lay, as at present, in a north-easterly direction from the Palace.

The "one long streete" mentioned by Leland was no doubt the line of streets running north and south, comprising Week Street, Gabriel's Hill, and Stone Street. Other streets or lanes, branching off at right angles to the main street, had been formed, but they were not then of sufficient importance to require notice. The names of the principal streets were derived from the districts or "boroughs" into which the parish was divided. These districts were of very ancient origin. The "Borgha de Wyke,"* the borough of Stone, and Stone Street, are frequently mentioned in the rent-rolls of the fourteenth century which are deposited at the Lambeth Palace Library. There were also the boroughs of Maidstone and Westree, the latter known to this day as the West Borough. But these parochial distinctions, when Leland saw the town, were probably losing their significance.

---

* The name may owe its origin to an ancient Maidstone family; among a number of youths who were ordained in St. Mary's Church, Maidstone, in the year 1268 was one Thomas Wyke.

It was about the time of Leland's visit that the manor of Maidstone was transferred from the See of Canterbury to the Crown. The archbishop, as lord of the manor, had previously received the rents paid by the tenants in occupation of the land. A letter written by Archbishop Morton in the last decade of the fifteenth century shows that several of the tenants at that time refused to pay their rents on the plea that they were being overcharged. The collector had appealed to the Primate, and the latter wrote to him stating that, until the tenants who complained could show in writing that the land in their occupation had been divided or had passed into other hands, he was to demand payment of the amounts due as they were entered in the rent-roll. Part of the roll for the year 1510 is in the Lambeth Palace Library. It enumerates twenty-two tenants, one of whom lived at "Padsholemill." The rents ranged from a penny and upwards per annum, the largest sum, £8 13s., being paid by the master of the College. There is a second roll, evidently complete, but without date, containing the names of two hundred and fifty tenants. In this roll the names are grouped under separate districts, thus :—Maidstone, eighteen tenants, paying £2 16s. 2d.; Stone, thirty-two tenants, paying £8 16s.; Wyke, sixty-five tenants, paying £10 5s. 4d.; East Lane, twenty-nine tenants, paying £4 1s. 8½d.; Stone Street, eighteen tenants, paying £2; Wyke Street, twenty-five tenants, paying £8 19s. 6d.; Weald, twenty-one tenants, paying £4 0s. 9d; Lodyngton, thirty tenants, paying £20 8s. 5d. The total rent-roll thus amounts to £61 7s. 10½d.; but in addition to the above there are the names of twelve tenants, standing apart, as not coming under any particular district.

A survey of the manor was made in 1650. In this survey

we read as follows:—"The manor of Maidstone did of ancient time belong to the Archbishop of Canterbury, and continued so till the reign of Henry VIII., and then it was annexed to the Crown. It so remained till the reign of King James, who granted the same to the city of London. It was then conveyed to the Countess of Winchelsea, and by descent came to Heneage, now Earl of Winchelsea. To the manor belongeth the court-leet for the whole Hundred, excepting the town and parish of Maidstone, whose inhabitants Queen Elizabeth did incorporate, and among many other privileges, did grant unto them view of frankpledge within that town and parish. The manor-house and site thereof, which is called the Palace, the said queen didst grant in fee farm (in her 26th year) to John Astley, Esq., and it is now in the possession of Jacob Astley. More to the said manor belongeth court-baron and other privileges; and it doth principally lie within the said town and parish of Maidstone, but doth extend unto the town and parish of Goudhurst, Marden, Horsmonden, East Farleigh, Boxley, and Detling, and all the tenants hold by fealty suit of court and rent, and by no other service."

Portions of the manor were granted by Queen Elizabeth, some in fee and others for terms of years, to various persons. When James I., in 1623, conferred upon Lady Elizabeth Finch, widow of Sir Moile Finch, of Eastwell, the title of Viscountess Maidstone, he granted to her, out of the rents of this manor, the sum of £13 6s. 8d. per annum. Five years after, when the same lady was created Countess of Winchelsea, Charles I. granted to her and her heirs, for the better support of the new dignity, a further sum of £20 out of the manorial rents of Maidstone. A few months later, September 9, 1628, the king granted the manor, among other premises, to trustees for the use of the said lady and her heirs, in fee, at a yearly rent of £57 16s. 2d. The Countess of Winchelsea died in March 1633, and was succeeded by her eldest son, Thomas Earl of Winchelsea.

The manor of Maidstone originally contained several smaller manors, held under the archbishops, of which the more important were those of Wyke, East Lane, and Stone. Of the last-named we know little. The manor of East Lane was part of the possessions of the Priory of Leeds, and after the dissolution of the monasteries, it was granted by Henry VIII. to the newly created Dean and Chapter of Rochester in 1541. Under the Act passed during the Commonwealth for abolishing Deans, Chapters, &c., this manor, with other premises in the neighbourhood of Maidstone, was sold to Philip Viscount Lisle;* but in the time of Charles II. it was restored to the Dean and Chapter of Rochester. According to a memorandum left by the late Beale Poste, the manor-house stood on the north side of East Lane. It was a large building, and in the windows and over the mantelpiece were coats of arms.

The lands of the manor of Wyke appear to have extended in one direction from Week Street to beyond Penenden Heath. A survey of this manor, undated, but obviously referring to the first half of the sixteenth century, is preserved among the Harleian MSS. in the British Museum. It may be abridged as follows:—

The site of the manor-house called the Weeke, alias Fisher's House, with yard, garden, malthouse, and other buildings, all which are walled about, and contain 1r. 37p.

Two fair barns belonging to the same, with stable and house, yards, orchards, dovehouse, and a tenement thereto adjoining, containing 2a. 2r. 30p.

One close of pasture or upland meadow thereunto adjoining, called Butcher's Mead, 5a.

One other close of pasture called Pound Field, with a tenement adjoining against the pound, 5a. 2r.

Nine fields, containing upwards of eighty-two acres; and one piece of coppice wood within the same, 1a. 3r. 4p.

One other close of pasture, called Loampitts, 10a. 2r. 36p.

One field called Town Land, 15a. 1r. 7p.; and coppice wood within the same, 1a.

---

* Close Rolls, 3497, No. 33.

One field of arable land called Gallows Close, 4a. 2r.; and one parcel of coppice wood next to the Gallows, 2a.

Two other pieces of arable land, containing about seventeen acres; and one other close of arable land called Fulling-pit Field, 7a. 0r. 28p.

Three other closes of arable land, one called Thornelie Hills, containing above twenty-seven acres; and one piece of coppice wood adjoining, called Hookewood, 11a. 3r.

One parcel of common called Pickenden Leyes, lying in Pickenden Haugh, 50a.

These, with other lands enumerated, make a total of 245a. 2r. 31p.

Clement Taylor Smythe believed that an ancient building which stood, fifty years ago, on the north side of Union Street, opposite the entrance to Church Street, was the manor-house of Wyke. But his friend Beale Poste arrived at a different conclusion. The latter held that the gable-headed building which still exists at the south-west corner of Union Street and Week Street, with the ancient wall on the north side of the garden, was the old manor-house; and the evidence, so far as it goes, tends to confirm his theory. William Fisher, he states,[*] occupied the house in 1511, and his lands were charged with the manorial rent of 46s. 2d. The Fisher family in 1617 conveyed the estate to the Merchant Taylors' Company. In the Maidstone Manor Survey of 1650 the house is described as having lately been the property of the Merchant Taylors, but it was then in occupation of John Beale, gentleman, and about two hundred acres of land are mentioned as being attached to it.

During the greater part of Queen Elizabeth's reign the sanitary condition of the town was not such as to conduce to the good health of the inhabitants. The population was not large. In the eight years beginning with 1565 and ending with 1572 the average death-rate was sixty-two per annum.[†] It is probable the annual mortality was little less than twenty-five per thousand inhabitants, and the population of the whole parish would therefore not exceed 2,500 persons. The number of inhabited houses in the town in 1565,

---

[*] "Archæologia Cantiana," vol. i., p. 162.
[†] See Appendix, No. 4, for statistics from the register of All Saints'.

according to a return made to the Crown in that year, was two hundred and ninety-four; but two or three families sometimes lived under one roof. At one time a surgeon with his family occupied the ground floor of a moderate-sized house, another family the second floor, while a tailor and his wife lived in the upper storey. The poor inhabitants, to eke out a subsistance, kept pigs, which were allowed to roam at large in the daytime. In the High Street, and in Week Street, Gabriel's Hill, and Bullock Lane, there were deep, foul gutters, into which the pigs turned with avidity, and among the garbage and other refuse deposited therein found a ready means of appeasing their hunger.

Under such a condition of things the inhabitants were exposed in an aggravated degree to the ravages of the worst forms of contagious disease. That scourge of our ancestors, the plague, frequently visited Maidstone. The first visitation of this malignant fever of which we have any details was in 1544, when five members of one household—Joan, Alice, Gervase, and John Nash, and Alice the mother—died and were buried within a fortnight. Many of the indigent inhabitants, living in over-crowded dwellings and under circumstances which rendered them peculiarly liable to the epidemic, were swept away. The poor were very numerous in proportion to the population, and when the town was first incorporated, the Mayor and Jurates experienced much difficulty in finding employment for them. The sick and the aged were occasionally maintained out of the municipal funds, and aid was also given by private residents. In 1558 Mildred Philips left by will to John Beare, her executor, a tenement in Stone Street, to be used as an almshouse by poor men and women, who were to be nominated for the same by the said John Beare or his heirs, "with the advice and consent of the churchwardens for the time being." A garden adjoined the tenement, and "fixed and standing in it" was a quern, a mill for grinding corn, which consisted of two circular flat stones, the upper one pierced in the centre with a narrow funnel, and revolving on a wooden pin inserted in the lower. The grain was dropped into the central opening, and the upper stone was revolved by means of a stick inserted in an opening near the edge.

The plague again broke out with fearful virulence in the autumn of 1562. The crier went round the town and announced that the Michaelmas Fair, which was then being held, could not be continued because of the pestilence. Communication with London was immediately suspended, and strangers fled to their homes. Meetings of the people were prohibited, lest they should contaminate each other. For a time All Saints' Church was closed, and marriages were postponed, while infants were taken to Otham and Loose for baptism. The fear of the terrible contagion was in everybody's mind, and no one cared to nurse the sick. In July 1563 the Corporation issued the following ignoble order:—

It shall be lawful for the Mayor and Jurates from henceforth for evermore to command and appoint any person or persons now dwelling, or that shall at any time hereafter dwell, in any house or houses commonly called an almshouse, to serve with any person or persons dwelling within the same town and parish in the time or times of the plague or pestilence, or any other sickness, and that they do their best endeavours, diligence, and service for the comfort, help, and succour of the sick; and for such of those as shall refuse to do the same it shall be lawful unto the said Mayor and Jurates immediately upon the said refusal to displace, turn out, and put forth any person so refusing; and that they and every of them forthwith and for evermore forfeit and loose all such his or their rights, estates, or possessions as they or any of them had in the same house or houses.

In the following year about a hundred and fifty inhabitants died from the plague; seven were buried in one day. Many persons died from the same cause in 1574, and also in 1578, when seven members of one household were, within six days, interred in All Saints' churchyard. The disease reached a climax in 1579, when upwards of forty persons succumbed to its ravages. There were partial outbreaks in 1589-90-1, and in the latter year, so scandalous had the sanitary state of the town become, that the Mayor and Jurates at length attempted measures of relief. They issued an order warning the people living in the almshouses in Stone Street, Pudding Lane, and on the bridge, that if they continued to "keep hogs or swine in the rooms or houses where they lived," they would each be fined, at the discretion of the mayor and four of the jurates, 3s. 4d., "to be levied by the sale of the said hogs or swine." About thirty deaths from the plague occurred in 1592, and in October of that year a by-law, in these terms, was passed by the Corporation :—

Forasmuch as this town, being of itself placed in a sweet and wholesome air, hath greatly been festered with divers infections and dangerous savors and noisome airs by occasions of the common and usual going and coming of hogs and swine in the streets and lanes of the said town ; and forasmuch as it is found by experience that divers great annoyances, hurts, and harms have been committed and done by suffering of the said hogs and swine to go and roam in the streets without a driver, and the same is likely more and more to increase unless some good order be therein taken by reason of the common keeping of swine by divers of the poorer sort who are not able to keep, feed, and maintain them with their own provision, by occasion whereof the said swine are forced to seek their feeding and sustenance abroad, to the great annoyance of the inhabitants of the said town.

This by-law concluded by imposing fines on the owners of the pigs found wandering in the streets. The plague, notwithstanding these restrictions, visited the town at short intervals. In 1595 the borough chamberlains paid 6s. 8d. "for burying of William Ellis and his wife, of the plage," and 4d. for Kate Durrant, "when it was thought shee had the plage in vittells." Fifty persons died from the disease in 1594, forty in 1596, and sixty-five in 1597.

Camden, writing about this time, describes Maidstone as a "neat and populous town, stretched out into a great length," and, like Leland, by whose statement he was probably misled, erroneously alludes to the Palace by name as standing in the middle of the town. Notwithstanding frequent visitations of the plague, the sports, pageants, and pastimes of the age were not forgotten. An enclosed space in the High Street, a few yards below the top of Mill Lane, was called the Bear Ringle, and here the coarse amusement of baiting bears was indulged in. An area of a hundred and forty-eight yards in this Bear Ringle was in 1574-5 paved with six cartloads of stone brought from the Palace. The King's Mead, or Fair Meadow, was a common sporting place. Several walnut trees, a piece of the maypole, and a wooden house which stood in it, were blown down during a great storm in 1586. In a Corporation breviat, dated 1597, it is stated that "the inhabitants, from time whereof there is no memory of man to the contrary, have had, used, and wholly enjoyed the Mead for a place to shoot in, and for other disport pastimes and recreations, as well as for the mustering and training of soldiers."

The King's Mead was no doubt made use of for some of the merry doings with which the town annually celebrated Queen Elizabeth's coronation. On the Queen's Day, as it was called, a number of children, dressed in fanciful costumes, were placed upon a wooden framework which was covered with tinsel and coloured paper and paint, and carried about the town. Wax candles, torches, fireworks, and all the paraphernalia of a pageant were provided, and the ringers made music with the church bells. On one occasion John Hayward received 6s. 8d. out of the Corporation funds for torches and wax candles, while 3s. 4d. was paid for ringing the bells, and 6s. for fireworks. Occasionally professional actors, licensed by the Government, were employed at this and other celebrations. The players generally performed in the open air, and a stage was sometimes dispensed with. In "Midsummer Night's Dream" Quince points out to Bottom, his brother actor, where the company of which they were members were to dress and play—"This green plot shall be our stage, this hawthorn brake our tiring house." Before the performance commenced a notice somewhat after this manner was delivered:—" Here begins the proclamation of the 'Two Merry Men' in the playground, in the month of August, the year of God 1588; made in Maidstone." In winter time the Grammar School was sometimes given up for the use of the players, and at Christmas 1588 they played at the Star Inn. The chamberlains' accounts for 1586 show that 20s. was "given to the Queen's players, and in wyne bestowed by appointment of Mr. Maior;" and smaller sums, as 6s. 8d. and 13s. 4d., were in other years paid to them.

In Elizabeth's reign the inhabitants obtained their chief supply of water from an excellent and copious spring at Rockyhill. The reservoir was surrounded by four walls and covered with tiles, and the water was conveyed in pipes across the Medway to conduits in the High Street. The principal conduit—an illustration of which is given on the title-page of this work—was erected about the beginning of the sixteenth century. It stood nearly opposite the Star Inn, and was an octagonal tower, 24ft. high and 8ft. in diameter, constructed of well squared masonry. At the top was a clock and dial, as well as a lantern and bell, the latter being rung when fish was brought to the town. The ascent to the clock-work in the cupola was by a winding flight of stone steps occupying the whole interior of the building, and opening to the street under a small pointed arch on the north side. In 1562 a new frame was made for the cistern, and the lead-work was renovated at an outlay of 8s. 7d. Various repairs were again made in 1588, and in 1599 new glass was inserted in the lantern, the clock being also repaired and the woodwork repainted.

In the last decade of the sixteenth century several benefactions were made to the poor. George Langlie died in 1592, and bequeathed the value of a house and garden in

East Lane, amounting to £22, in order to establish a fund "to set the poor of the parish of Maidstone on work." Three other residents also gave by will the sum of £5 each for the benefit of the aged and the needy. In September 1595 John Amye, merchant, of Maidstone, made a bequest of a somewhat unusual character, "knowing that there were and by all former time had been an exceeding number of very aged, lame, and poor people who, through their great wants, had not wherewithal to set them nor their children in work, but were by that means forced to become beggars from door to door, in which they, being a little accustomed, did never fall to labour again, but to robberies, and all other profanities." He directed that a certain portion of his property should be sold, and out of the money arising therefrom he bequeathed the sum of £130, to be held in trust by two of the jurates, who were to pay out of the estate £10 yearly to Joan, his wife, and within five months after her death they were to repay to his executors, "at or in the south porch of the church of Maidstone," the said £130, of which £30, and also £15 in the hands of his executors, were to be distributed among poor and sick parishioners. The remaining £100 was then to be held in trust by the Mayor and Jurates, who, within seven years, were to employ the same "in buying of hemp, flax, wool, or such other wares, to the end that the poor people of the town might be set on work by dressing, spinning, or repairing of the said wares or stuff, and have competent recompense out of the increase and profits thereof for their several labours and pains, that thereby their children might be kept from idleness and loitering tending to beggary."

In February 1596 the Mayor and Jurates accordingly entered into an arrangement with Robert Dann, weaver, whereby he agreed, on payment of £100 by way of loan for six years, to "set on work in the dressing and working of wool, flax, tow, or hemp," ten poor persons, not under seven years of age. Amye's money was made use of in this way for sometime, and in 1602 a portion of it was employed in teaching poor children to make "cauls, buttons, button moulds, thread, or the winding thereof, or the like honest easy arts, whereby they might in a very short space get towards their living, at the least, ten pence or twelve pence weekly." When the poor-rate came in vogue, the money was thrown into the Corporation fund, and lost in the litigation which followed.

The plague was once more prevalent in the town in the autumn of 1602, and in the summer and autumn of 1603. In the former year, four children of a widower named Hammond died within five weeks, and in the sixth week the father was cut off, a whole family being thus annihilated. In the latter year the death-roll increased to one hundred and twelve. Great difficulty was experienced in obtaining nurses for the sick, and as the inmates of the almshouses were living on charity, and without occupation, the Corporation again ordered them, under pain of expulsion, to admit into their rooms, and to wait upon, the more desperate cases. At the same time the owners of pigsties which had long existed on St. Faith's Green were ordered to have them at once removed.

These precautions, however, produced no immediate abatement of the excessive mortality. Twenty-five persons died from the plague in 1604, and sixty-two in 1609. The disease was again very fatal in 1614, when the number of deaths was ninety-one. It prevailed also in the years 1615-6, and in 1625 the Mayor and Jurates issued an order that "no hoyman, foot or horse post, should, during the infection in the Metropolis, carry or receive any goods from Maidstone to London, under a fine of £5; and no inhabitant was to take or lodge any stranger from London or other places." By the month of August in the same year the pestilence had so far subsided that a public fast was observed; but in 1626-7 the deaths were again very numerous. More than forty persons died from this cause in 1634. In 1636, when the plague was raging in London, the Corporation posted seven watchmen at the chief entrances to the town, with orders " to keep all suppositious persons " from coming into the streets, the cost of this supervision being defrayed by an assessment collected weekly.

On the 18th of October 1665 Sir John Banks, of the Friars, Aylesford, wrote to Samuel Pepys, of the Admiralty, entreating his interest with the Duke of York on behalf of a letter from gentlemen of Maidstone, praying that sick men might not be sent there from the Fleet, as Maidstone was the only town in Kent which was free from the plague. He stated that the militia and one of the duke's troops were already quartered in the town, and pointed out that to remove disabled men thither would be a "great inconvenience."* On August 27, in the following year, the plague was reported in London to be "very hot in Maidstone." It had broken out in the month of July. Fearful havoc was wrought among the prisoners in the County Gaol, High Street, and it was found expedient to use the George Inn, East Lane, as a temporary prison, where three of the prisoners died. A pest-house for the reception of the sick was opened, and within its walls a mother and her two daughters, and many other inhabitants, perished. What added to the horrors of the time was that the two principal surgeons in the town, William Cox and Nicholas Bennett, died during the visitation, though not of the plague. In the

---

* "Calendar of State Papers," 1665.

last week of August nineteen victims were buried in one day, the mortality during the month amounting to seventy. The number of deaths rose in September to one hundred and six, and in October to one hundred and ten. It decreased in November to twenty-four, but in December it rose to thirty-two; and the "Black List" for the year reached the fearful total of three hundred and forty-seven, the deaths from other causes being a hundred and thirty-six.

Although the infection was generally supposed to be conveyed from London, yet the means of communication with the Metropolis and with other distant parts of the country, in ordinary circumstances, were very limited. At a time when the conveyance of a letter from Maidstone to London cost 1s. 6d., and from Maidstone to Rye 3s., correspondence, save upon matters of business, seldom passed between friends. The postal service was liable to innumerable mishaps. Letters were carried by unauthorised persons, and were not only frequently delivered long after date, but sometimes never reached their destination. The grievances arising from this state of things were brought under the notice of the Corporation in August 1641. An order was then made naming certain persons who were to act as postmen, and stating that for the future there were to be three authorised posts to London weekly, on Mondays, Wednesdays, and Fridays; any postman who disobeyed the new regulations, or who chose to perform his journey on any other than the days stipulated, was to forfeit 5s., while persons found carrying letters without the sanction of the mayor were to be fined 10s. each. William Goteer was in 1667 appointed postmaster for Maidstone. The country being then much agitated by the disastrous continental wars of Charles II., he petitioned Lord Arlington, a member of the Government, for a passport through Kent for himself and three servants to secure them from being impressed into the service of the Fleet.

The borough records acquaint us with improvements from time to time made to meet the growing requirements of the inhabitants. In response to a memorial from a number of the residents, the Corporation in 1625 erected a conduit at the lower end of the High Street. An order was given for the erection of another conduit at the upper end of the same thoroughfare in 1645, the cost not to exceed £40. This, the third conduit in the High Street, consisted of a rude mass of stone-work, with a flat top and without ornament, except two small shields of the town arms. Nor were the more superficial wants of the inhabitants forgotten. In 1640 the King's Mead was closed at both ends; trees had previously been planted along its sides at a cost of 6s. 8d. The Corporation in 1642 resolved to convert a part of it into a bowling green. The Mead, then a greensward, was let on lease to Benjamin Poole for eleven years, at a rent of 50s. per annum; and the lessee was bound to make a handsome green for the players, for which he was to be allowed the sum of 10s., to be deducted from his rent.

During the Commonwealth the Mayor and Jurates prohibited strolling actors from performing in the town. Nor did the Puritan section of the Corporation induce them to tolerate street preachers any more than itinerant players. On the 23rd of July 1656, they published the following order:—

Whereas it is found by dayly and frequent experience that divers heady and turbulent persons doe wander up and downe and sometimes intrude into pulpits and publique meeting-places, by law designed and appointed for the due, orderly, and peaceable publique preachinge of the Word and dispensinge of the ordinances of God by persons lawfully authorised and orderly and approved and allowed thereunto, and sometimes in a confused tumultuous manner gather together greate assemblies and concourses of people in open streets and market-places upon pretence of preachinge and publique teachinge; whereas they have noe lawful authoritie, approbacon, or allowance to be publique preachers or teachers, and in truth their intent and ayme is to vent their own giddy fancies sometimes in raylings and revellings against ministers and ordinances of God, they are hereby warned that for every such offence they shall be proceeded against by action and suite at the common law as intruders and trespassers.

The plague last attacked Maidstone in the summer of 1667, when the deaths were, in June, thirty-three; in July, forty-two; in August, thirty; in September, twelve; in October, fourteen; in November, two; in December, three; or a total for the whole year of one hundred and fifty-four. There was great distress in the town, and the Archbishop of Canterbury sent £20 to John Davis, incumbent of All Saints', for "the poor and afflicted of Maidstone," the donation being thankfully acknowledged by John Beale, the mayor.

Samuel Pepys, being on a visit to Chatham, drove thence to Maidstone on the 24th of March 1669, and spent several hours in the town, closely observing everything coming under his notice. He tells how he stepped into a barn and saw the process of flax-beating. There were several such barns to be seen, and a century later they were numerous. Pepys records at some length in his "Diary" the impressions of his visit.

"I went to Hill House," he says, "and there did give order for a coach to be made ready, and got Mr. Gibson, whom I carried with me, to go with me and Mr. Coney, the surgeon, towards Maidstone, which I had a mighty mind to see. A mighty cold and windy, but clear day; and had the pleasure of seeing the Medway running winding up and down mightily, and a very fine country. And I went a little out of the way to have visited Sir John Bankes, but he at London; but here I had a sight of his seat and house, the outside, which is an old abbey just like Hinchingbroke, and as good at least, and mightily finely placed by the river; and he keeps the grounds about it, and walls and the house, very handsome. I was mightily pleased with the sight of it. Thence to Maydstone, which I had a mighty mind to see, having never been there; and walked all up and down the town, and up to the top of the steeple and had a noble view, and then down again. In the town did see an old man beating of flax, and did step into the barn and give him money, and saw that piece of husbandry, which I never saw; and it is very pretty. In the street also I did buy and send to our inne, the Bell, a dish of fresh fish. And so having walked all round the town and found it very pretty as most towns I ever saw, though not very big, and people of good fashion in it, we to our inne and had a good dinner; and a barber came to me and there trimmed me, that I might be clean against night to go to Mrs. Allen [at Chatham.] And so staying till four o'clock we set out, I alone in the coach going and coming."

It is probable that the population of the parish at the time of Pepys' visit was about 3,200. Four hundred and ninety householders were in 1669 assessed to the poor-rate, but the number, as given in the rate books,* varies considerably, and not always in an increasing ratio, in different years. From the rate books we learn how in that year the population was distributed. The parts of the borough most thickly populated were the High Street or High Town, and the line of Week Street, Gabriel's Hill, and Stone Street. There were a hundred and ten houses in the High Street, sixty in Week Street, twenty-five on Gabriel's Hill, and a hundred in Stone Street and uplands. The exact number of houses cannot, as a matter of fact, be ascertained from the rate books, but eleven are indicated as standing in Middle Row, seven in Pudding Lane, thirteen in Mill Lane, sixteen on St. Faith's Green and Waterside, thirteen in Bullock Lane, thirty-three in East Lane, and forty-four in the West Borough.

The assessment to the poor, as the rate books testify, was the heaviest impost borne by our ancestors. In the third quarter of the seventeenth century, the rate was imposed " by the churchwardens and overseers upon the inhabitants and occupiers of lands and tenements within the town and parish, according to their several abilities, to be confirmed by the mayor." There were several calls in the course of a year, and in 1668, for instance, one was made in April, and also in June, August, October, and December. The call in April produced £59 7s. 4½d., and each of the four other calls yielded a similar amount. In 1678 calls were made on June 17, July 13, September 23, and on December 13, and in 1679 on June 6, July 18, September 5, and October 31. The churchwardens' and overseers' accounts show how some

---

* These are complete from the year 1668, with the exception of a gap of seventeen years between 1746 and 1763.

of the money thus obtained was expended. Among the disbursements for 1678 are the following:—

	s.	d.
March 26.—Payd for a poore man	3	0
„ 29.—To Goodman Darnoll, for making David Carlor a coate and payre of britches	4	0
April 25.—For mendying and nayleing Raynoor's shooes	0	10
October 3.—To Goodman Wall for mayntayneing a hopper	6	0
„ 10.—For a coate and wastcoate for Burgisse's child	1	6

The receipts for the same year include 5s. received from "Elias Gregson for working on Sunday morning with his mill," apparently as a penalty for Sabbath desecration.

Through the praiseworthy exertions of Gilbert Innes, the perpetual curate of All Saints', a census of the population was obtained in 1695. That indefatigable gentleman made a house-to-house visitation of the parish, and the number of inhabitants was ascertained to be 3,676. The town then began to increase more rapidly than at any previous period of its history. In 1720 the Earl of Winchelsea alienated to Lord Romney his interest in the manor of Maidstone. A court-leet and court-baron for the manor was held annually, at which a constable was chosen, and also a borsholder for each of the parishes of Barming, Boxley, Detling, Linton, and one for the conjoined parishes of Loose and East Farleigh. A court-baron is now held once in six or seven years, and about two hundred owners of property still pay quit-rents to the lord of the manor. A number of owners of property in King Street, Middle Row, Mill Lane, and Earl Street, pay quit-rents, under the manor of East Lane, to the Dean and Chapter of Rochester.

Owing to outbreaks of smallpox, the mortality of the parish was often augmented to an alarming extent in the eighteenth century. The parishioners in vestry assembled boldly grappled with the difficulty. In May 1746 they instructed the church-wardens and overseers to prosecute at the assizes certain parties who were responsible for the presence in Maidstone of persons suffering from this loathsome disease. They in June of the same year passed an order for "suppressing disorderly public houses, and punishing or removing out of the parish lewd and disorderly persons." The deaths from smallpox in 1753 were seventy, and the number increased to upwards of a hundred in 1760. The vestry, in July 1766, engaged a surgeon from Essex to innoculate poor people at the workhouse, the charge for each person not to exceed 5s. 3d. In that year fifty-four persons died from smallpox.

Towards the close of George II.'s reign a soldier of the 50th Regiment was shot in the Fair Meadow for desertion. In Buck's view of the town, as it appeared in 1722, the Meadow is shown with a picturesque row of trees along its eastern and western sides. These trees were so damaged by a thunderstorm in August 1763 that the Corporation ordered them to be cut down and the ground grubbed. A considerable sum was realized by the sale of the timber; a portion of it was added to the new Town Hall fund, and the remainder was expended in the purchase of young elm trees, a row of which was planted along each end of the Meadow, and an avenue of three rows along the side next the river. Additional space being required for the stock markets, these trees have at various times been removed. The Meadow was macadamised in 1825.

Following the example set in 1695 by one of his predecessors, John Denne, the incumbent of All Saints', made an enumeration of the inhabitants in September 1782. The result of the census was to show a population of 5,755, being an increase of 2,079 in the course of eighty-seven years. Of the total number of persons, 727 were living in the rural parts of the parish, which comprised the Bower, Loddington, Barming Heath, Tovil, Penenden Heath, Buckland, Half Yoke, Sheppy Court, and Goulds Court. Tovil was credited

ANCIENT STATE OF THE TOWN.

with 167 inhabitants, and Loddington with 63. How the 5,028 persons in the town part of the parish, and the houses in each street or locality, were distributed, will be understood by the appended table.

	Inhabitants.	Houses.
High Street and Middle Row	909	173
Mill Lane	177	35
Pudding Lane	148	31
Gabriel's Hill	247	46
Stone Street	891	192
Knightrider Street	232*	15
East Lane	676	117
Square and Maryland Point	50	14
Week Street	675	136
Fair Meadow	85	20
Earl Street	223	42
Havock Lane	66	15
St. Faith's Green	84	25
Waterside	111	22
Bridge Street and Bridge	108	26
West Borough	346	73

The proportion of persons to a house was $5\frac{6}{13}$, to a family $4\frac{89}{100}$; while the mortality was one in $37\frac{2}{5}$, being rather below the average of other parishes having a similar population.

In the last decade of the eighteenth century the Corporation undertook to repave the town. The streets and lanes had long been exceedingly defective. They were badly lighted, and may be described as consisting of a series of abrupt depressions and elevations. A contemporary writer called their condition "scandalous," and asserted that in winter nights, when the yellow flicker of an oil lamp perched at the corner of the main thoroughfares only rendered the darkness visible, they were a source of inconvenience and even danger, as the depressions were generally either covered with ice or full of water, into which the passenger plunged ankle deep,

---

* This would include the inmates of the workhouse.

or was carried along unceremoniously on some secret "slide" whereon mischievous youths had been disporting themselves.

A committee of the Corporation was in 1790 appointed to obtain an estimate of the cost of the proposed improvement, and on January 17, 1791, the following notice was issued:—"The Mayor requests a meeting of the inhabitants at the Town Hall on Saturday morning to hear and take into consideration the report of the committee appointed to estimate the expense of paving, lighting, watching, and cleansing the public streets and lanes of this town." The cost of paving the principal streets with Kentish rag and Yorkshire and Moor stones, carrying drains through them, and fixing up lamps, was estimated at £9,000; and the interest thereon, together with the outlay for watchmen, the lighting of the lamps, and the repair of the pavements, would, it was reported, amount to £750 a year. To meet this expenditure it was proposed to levy a rate of 1s. 6d. in the pound on all householders, half to be paid by the landlord and half by the tenant, and to erect tollgates at the four main entrances to the town. These propositions were embodied in the Maidstone Paving Bill which was introduced into Parliament in the same year.

As the greater portion of the country produce was regularly brought into Maidstone for sale, or for conveyance by river to London, the people living in the district surrounding the town were strongly opposed to the proposal to erect turnpike gates. Nor was the opposition unprecedented in its character. Previous to 1772 a turnpike gate was for some time fixed at the west end of the bridge, but in that year the vestry urged Mr. Punnett, the deputy recorder, to use his influence to have it removed therefrom, and, if necessary, to have it set up at some point not nearer to the town than "a house known by the name of the Seven Stars," which stood where now is Somerfield House, on the west side of London Road. Now that an attempt was being made to again exact tolls on cattle, horses, and vehicles entering Maidstone, the country gentlemen and farmers held meetings in opposition to the Paving Bill. They contended that the requisite money could be raised by other means; and so far did their views meet with approval that a subscription list, for the purpose of obtaining funds to oppose the Bill in Parliament, was opened, and subscriptions to a large amount were promised.

Owing to subsequent disagreement, however, the subscription list fell through. Encouraged by this circumstance, the Corporation still clung to the turnpike gates. But the idea of imposing tolls on live stock and vehicles found no more favour at Westminster than in Mid Kent, and at a meeting, in May 1791, of the Corporation and freemen, it was announced that the clause relative to the turnpike gates had been struck out of the Bill. Nevertheless the measure was approved, and in June it received the royal assent. It was entitled an Act for "widening, improving, regulating, paving, cleansing, and lighting the streets, lanes, and other public passages and places in Maidstone; for removing and preventing encroachments, obstructions, nuisances, and annoyances therein; for the better supplying the said town with water; and for repaving and maintaining the highways within the parish." Commissioners of Pavements were appointed to carry out the provisions of the Act, and in 1792-3 the town was paved, drained, and lighted, the expenditure being met by rates in the ordinary way. The conduit, which stood in the centre of the High Street, was then destroyed, when the dates 1567 and 1669 were discovered upon the leads of the roof, indicating no doubt the periods of different repairs, though the latter date was supposed to mark the age of the clock.

It may be well to conclude this chapter with some remarks on the street nomenclature and the old inns of Maidstone. First as to the streets. High Street, as previously pointed out, was anciently called High Town; it is mentioned as such in a Corporation minute of 1597, and in the poor-rate books it is first styled High Street in 1707. Middle Row occurs in a deed bearing the date of 1446. The earliest mention of Gabriel's Hill is in a document of the fifteenth century. Thomas Charles conjectured that the convent of Franciscans which was founded here in the fourteenth century, and which, it is supposed, stood in this part of the town, was dedicated to St. Gabriel, hence the name of the hill. The junction of the four roads at the bottom of Upper Stone Street was known as Wren's Cross in the reign of Henry IV. We first meet with Knightrider Street in 1602; the name, according to Clement Taylor Smythe, is derived from the processions which used to pass that way when the archbishops kept state at the Palace. East Lane is coeval with the manor of that designation; it was changed to King Street after the visit of George III. to the Mote in August 1799.

The name of Pudding Lane appears in a deed dated 1485. Waterside was anciently called the Hythe, or landing-place. Earl Street was known as Earls Lane in 1599; it was afterwards, when live-stock were penned there on fair days, designated Bullock Lane, and the present name was adopted previous to 1735. Whether the suggestive title of Havock Lane was intended to perpetuate the recollection of the ravages of the plague, or of the havoc created among the Royalists by Fairfax's soldiers in 1648, is uncertain; it is not noticed in the poor-rate books until 1704. The Bower takes its name from a field called Bower Down, referred to in deeds of the time of Henry VIII. A mansion known by the appellation of

Kingsley House.

Rockyhill existed in Elizabeth's reign. From the year 1680 "Westree" or "West Tree" appears in the poor-rate books as West Borough. Union Street and Brewer Street date from the first quarter of the nineteenth century. The former was originally a by-way called Tyler's Lane, from a tradition that Wat Tyler and the rebels entered the town from that direction; and the latter derives its name from the large brewery, once owned by the Cripps family, which previously occupied the lower part of the site. Kingsley estate belonged to a family of that ilk which flourished there in the eighteenth century; and Sandling Road was so named from the sand-pits which formerly existed in that locality.

Hardly less ancient than many of the streets are the signs of some of the inns and taverns of old Maidstone. A few of these signs have been shown continuously for centuries. Leland's visit in 1538 left an impression in the traveller's mind that the town was "full of inns." If he entered Maidstone by Stone Street, he would find the Ship, as at present, on the east side of Gabriel's Hill, and the George Inn and the Bull a few yards higher up on the same side. The Bell stood at the east corner of the hill, and at the opposite corner was the Chequers. A step or two along the High Street would bring him to the Queen's Arms, and, close by, the Swan; so that within a short distance Leland would find no less than seven inns or alehouses. The Bell was still at the top of Gabriel's Hill in 1650, and the landlord about that date was John Watson, who may have been the host of Pepys when he visited Maidstone. The existing house in Week Street, which bears the sign, is very ancient; there is a pleasant flavour of grave old fashion and cosiness about the place, and little has, as yet, been touched or pulled down. It was new fronted in 1711, probably at the time when the inn was removed from Gabriel's Hill. The Swan was of unfathomed antiquity; it is mentioned as "Le Swan" in 1476, and Edward Pretty, F.S.A.—now, with Clement Taylor Smythe, passed into the domain of the antiquities which both explored so well—surmised that the sign was meant as a compliment to the Lancastrians, a swan having been one of the supporters of the arms of Henry IV. The last house which inherited the appellation, a curious old building in which our forefathers delighted to assemble for refreshment, stood on the south side of the High Street, and was pulled down in 1852.

A few more signs may be noted. We find mention of the Star in the sixteenth century; it was the leading hostelry in the town in the time of Charles I., and here it was that the Royalists met, on the eve of the Civil War, to discuss the Kentish petition. The present building, even in its modern shape, retains much that is quaint and old-fashioned, and recalls one of those scenes in old inn parlours which Dickens was so fond of describing. A house bearing the sign of the Rose and Crown stood on the north side of the High Street in 1608, and other taverns in the same street in the middle of the seventeenth century were the White Horse and the Rose, the latter having extensive premises. Up the Rose Yard, curiously retired, was the Turk's Head. This inn was an evening resort of the Corporation. It was once kept by Woollett, the father of the engraver; the passage is as it was in young Woollett's day, and his eyes must have been often raised to the old carvings on the roof. Pretty supposed that the Mitre was the ancient hostelry for the people visiting the episcopal court; but the manor survey of 1650 shows that the Mitre did not then exist. The building which the present Mitre premises superseded was believed to date from about the year 1630, and its only points of antiquarian interest consisted in a flight of stone steps and two small Gothic windows.

At the lower end of High Street, on the south side, was an ancient house which displayed the sign of the Crown in 1610; it had a stone window with iron bars, and above an antique corbel for the support of the timbers in the upper part of the roof. On the opposite side of the street was a lodging-house, vulgarly called "Louse Tavern," a sort of dark den, with grimed windows, whose dissipated frequenters, on Sunday forenoons, and particularly about the hollow and hungry hours of night, used to hang round the entrance or carouse within its dingy walls. During the Commonwealth the Red Lion stood at the corner of High Street and Week Street; the house was demolished in 1857, having latterly become a little shaken and awry, queerly shaped about the roof, but snug and compact. The Castle was situated on the opposite side of Week Street in 1650, though the title deeds of the present building go no further back than 1746; it was here, during the stirring years of the French Revolution, that the Jacobins met, and harrangued on universal suffrage and annual Parliaments.* Higher up the street, on the same side as the Castle, were, in the middle of the seventeenth century, the Nag's Head and the Anchor of Hope, and, on the west side of the street, the Woolpack.

A few yards along East Lane in 1650 was the sign of the Cock, the effigy of this tutelary bird strutting with becoming gallantry over the tavern door.† On the north side of the

---

* John Gale Jones, in his "Sketch of a Poetical Tour," 1796, says:—"The Castle Inn was reputed to be a house for Jacobins, and the Star Coffeehouse was, I believe, the rendezvous of the aristocracy," p. 79. He states that on the 24th of February 1798, a meeting was held at the Castle "to consider the best means of obtaining universal suffrage and annual Parliaments."

† That the sign was not a misnomer is indicated by the following advertisement:—"At Edward Williams's, at the sign of the Cock, in East Lane, Maidstone, on Monday, May 23, 1774, a match of cocking, between the gentlemen of Little Chart and the gentlemen of Maidstone; to show eleven cocks, for two guineas a battle, and five the odd battle. To weigh and fight one battle before dinner. There will be a close pit; and a good ordinary on table at one o'clock."

street was established, some years later, the Three Tuns. When several old buildings were subsequently cleared away, the Cock disappeared, and the Three Tuns took his place. In 1650 there were two alehouses in Stone Street called the Dolphin and the Blueboard. An old playbill, announcing a humorous ditty to be sung at the local theatre, entitled "The Maidstone Landlords, or a Song about Signs," gives the following curious list of inns and taverns as existing in the town in 1798:—Coach and Horses, Compasses, Sun, Nag's Head, Anchor of Hope, Union Flag, Bell, Castle, George, Ship, Town's Arms (Stone Street), White Lion, Coachmakers' Arms, Plough, Fortune of War, Roebuck (Mote Road), Globe, Golden Lion, Queen's Head, White Hart, King's Head, Prince of Wales, Rodney, Crown and Sceptre, Rose and Crown, Dark Sun, Bull, Star, Mitre, Swan, Turk's Head, Red Lion, Kingsley's Head, Three Tuns, Dog and Bear, Royal Oak, Queen Anne, Coal Barge, Unicorn, Paper Mill, and the Ball. The latter was the sign of a house adjoining the Town Hall, which was in 1714 let on lease by the Corporation at a rent of £12. When the Hall premises were extended about the year 1853, this house was removed, but it had been discontinued as a tavern for many years before.

CHAPTER XI.

MAIDSTONE DURING THE CIVIL WAR.—STORMING OF THE TOWN.

The Kent Assizes in 1642—Petition to the Parliament—A Committee of Members sent down to Maidstone—Petition to the King, and Suggestions to the House of Commons—The King's answer—Agitation in 1643—Cause of the Kentish Rising in 1648—Lord Fairfax commissioned to suppress the Rising—Main body of the Royalists at Rochester—March of Fairfax to the Medway—Maidstone stormed—Fairfax leading his troops to the Attack—No Relief from Rochester—Surrender of the Defenders—Pacification of Kent—Maidstone Men at the Trial and Execution of the King—Old Soldiers—The Fairfax family.

WHEN the commission for the Kent assizes was opened at Maidstone, on the 22nd of March 1642, the breach between King Charles and the Parliament had become irreparable. Maidstone was not without experience of the King's arbitrary system of government. In 1636 the parish had to remit for ship-money £160, which would be equal to at least £500 at the present day; and the Justices of the Peace for the county often voted subsidies for the support of the throne.* But when the assizes commenced in March 1642 Charles had been deprived of the power of collecting his supplies through the Parliament. He had failed in his attempt to arrest the five members in the House of Commons, the Parliament had refused to comply with his demand for a levy of the Militia, then the only military force in the kingdom, and, fearing the threatened violence of the London populace, he had fled to the north.

Sir Thomas Mallet, the judge, arrived in the town on the 20th of March, and Sir Roger Twisden, of East Peckham; Sir George Stroode, of Squerries Court, Westerham; Sir John Sedley, of St. Clere, Ightham; Sir Edward Dering, of Pluckley; the Hon. Richard Spencer, of Orpington, with other Justices of the Peace, put in an appearance on the following day. On the evening of the 21st, Twisden and Stroode had an interview with the judge at his lodgings, and subsequently went to the Star Inn, where they found a number of the justices at supper. A petition against the King, which had just been presented to the House of Commons, in name of the county, formed the subject of an animated conversation. Two or three of the justices expressed approval of the petition, but the majority were of opinion that it conveyed an erroneous impression of the state of public feeling in Kent. One speaker, who held the latter view, suggested that it might not yet be too late to draw up a petition which would acquaint the Parliament with the real feeling of the county. Twisden, Stroode, and Dering—the latter of whom, as one of the members for Kent, had recently been ejected from

---

* Sir Roger Twisden, of Roydon Hall, East Peckham, in his Journal, which is printed in the "Archæologia Cantiana," vol. i. to iv., says that while sitting on the bench at the Maidstone assizes on March 24, 1641 (New Style), a bill of six subsidies from the House of Commons was handed to him, showing that they were to be paid not in the ordinary way into the Exchequer, but at Guildhall. He was startled at this, but being assured on the subject, he did the best that lay in him for assessing the "gift."

the House—accordingly repaired to Spencer's lodgings, and there discussed at length the form which the proposed petition was to take.

The next day Dering was chosen foreman of the grand jury, and towards the evening he mentioned to the judge the course which he and many of the justices intended to pursue. Sir Thomas Mallet replied that he had no authority to interfere in the matter. At Twisden's suggestion, several gentlemen of the bench and of the grand jury then retired to a private house, and agreed upon the heads of the petition. Later in the evening a similar meeting was held, and on the following day the petition was drawn up. Two days after, it was adopted at the assizes, many influential signatures being appended to it.

The petition professed to represent the "gentry, ministers, and commonalty of the county of Kent." It prayed that a law might be framed for regulating the Militia of the kingdom, that the "precious liberty of the subject might be preserved entire," and that "his Majesty's gracious message of the 20th of January last for the present and future establishing of the privileges of Parliament," the liberties of his subjects, "the security of the true religion professed, the maintaining of his Majesty's just and royal authority, and the establishing of his revenue, might be taken into consideration." The petitioners, in conclusion, besought the House to "consider the sad condition that the whole land was in," and pointed out the necessity of "a good understanding" being "speedily renewed between his Majesty and the Houses of Parliament."

The petition, says Twisden in his Journal, "transcendently incensed" the House of Commons. Sir Thomas Mallet, for not opposing it at the assizes, was committed to the Tower. Dering, Twisden, Stroode, and Spencer were arrested and confined in a house in Covent Garden; while Thomas Stanley, the mayor of Maidstone, received a peremptory summons to appear at Westminster.* An attempt was made at the quarter sessions, on April 19, to disown the petition, but according to Twisden, the people continued to sign it. In the same month Stroode, Twisden, and Spencer were released on heavy bail, a surety of £20,000 being demanded from Twisden for his reappearance if called upon. Sir Thomas Mallet was also set at liberty. On April 22, Thomas Stanley complained to the House that he had attended for a whole week, but had failed to learn of what he was accused, and prayed to be discharged or admitted to bail.

One morning at the close of the month, many country gentlemen and others proceeded with the petition to Westminster. London bridge was closed against them, but on giving up their swords, they were allowed to pass into the city, and the petition was subsequently presented to the House. Measures were promptly taken by the Parliament to prevent any disturbance of the peace in the county. A Committee of members was sent down to Maidstone to sit with the judge at the assizes in July. The Committee consisted of seventeen members, including Sir Francis Barnham, of Boughton Monchensey, and Sir Humphrey Tufton, of the Mote, who represented Maidstone. At this early stage of the conflict between Charles and the Parliament, Maidstone, in spite of the attitude assumed by its representatives, was evidently in sympathy with the royal cause. It was not so in the county generally. Of the seventeen members who represented Kentish constituencies, two only were active adherents of the king. The majority of the Kentish gentlemen either remained neutral, or zealously supported the Parliament.

In the afternoon of the 22nd of July, the Committee sent

---

* Historical MSS. Commission, Seventh Report.

a communication to Sir Thomas Mallet, the judge, stating that as "some ill-affected persons in the county were endeavouring to disperse rumours to the scandal of the Parliament, and to censure the proceedings against the promoters of the late dangerous petition," several gentlemen had been appointed as a Committee to attend the court, and "by all lawful ways and means, to preserve the said county not only in peace amongst themselves, but in a right understanding of the proceedings of Parliament." When the assizes opened on the following day, several members of the Committee appeared on the bench, and two days later they again attended the court, and arranged to meet the justices at the judge's lodgings. A conference was held, but without any satisfactory result. The justices thereafter wrote to the Committee, affirming that the communication which the latter had sent to the court was founded on "misinformation," and stating that having their authority committed to them under the Great Seal of England, "they dared not, in the execution of it, join with any not so authorised." The members of the Committee replied to this letter on the 26th of July by issuing a proclamation calling upon the sherriffs, justices, mayors, and other officers in the county to assist them in the discharge of the "orders and commands of Parliament."

These proceedings created extraordinary commotion in the town. In the afternoon of the day on which the proclamation was put forth, several members of the Committee again took their seats on the bench, and through their chairman, Sir Henry Vane, of Fairlawn, Shipbourne, exchanged some angry words with the justices. Sir Thomas Mallet declared that these interruptions were causing great agitation, and if they were continued he should be obliged to adjourn the court. The Committee then retired. Later in the same day

Twisden tells that he went to the court and there found "divers young gentlemen," including Sir John Mainy, of Linton Place; Sir John Tufton, eldest son of Sir Humphrey Tufton; Sir Edward Filmer, eldest son of Sir Robert Filmer, of East Sutton; and William Clark, of Wrotham, who was afterwards killed in the battle of Cropredy Bridge. These ardent Royalists informed the judge that they had brought certain instructions to one of the members for the county to acquaint the Parliament with a petition which was about to be sent to the king at York. One of them proceeded, amid some confusion, to read the following petition, which has not been hitherto printed in any Kentish history:—

<small>Most gracious Soveraigne,—We do, with all thankfulnesse, acknowledge Your great Grace and favour towards us and the whole kingdom, in passing many good Laws for the benefit of Your subjects, in promising to ease us of all our grievances, and graciously inviting us, by Your letter directed to the Judge of our Assize, full of love and care for Your people's Good, to Petition for redress of them, promising a gracious answer; and wee should with all humility have presented them to Your Majestie at this time, did not the present great distractions and apprehentions of a Civill War (which wee earnestly pray God to divert) put us beyond all thoughts of other grievances. For prevention whereof, wee have with all loyaltie of heart to Your Sacred Majestie, with all love and faithfulnesse to our countrey, presented our humble advice in certaine Instructions to one of our Knights of the Shire now here present with a Committee from the House of Commons, to be presented by him to that Honourable House, the copie whereof wee make bold to annex unto this Petition: Most humbly desiring Your most Excellent Majestie, that if it shall please the Houses of Parliament to satisfie Your Majestie's just desires in these particulars, that then Your Majestie would be graciously pleased to lay downe Your extraordinary Guards, and cheerfully meet Your Parliament in such a place where Your Sacred Majestie and each member of both Houses may be free from tumultuary Assemblies. And as in all duty bound, wee shall daily pray for Your Majestie's long Life and prosperous Reigne over us.</small>

The instructions referred to were "from the county of Kent" to "our servant, Master Augustine Skinner," of Tutsham Hall, West Farleigh, who had been elected one of the knights of the shire, in room of Dering. He was required to inform the House of Commons that he had found the county in full peace, and that the county conceived that the "principal means" whereby the distractions of the nation might be settled were these:—1. That his Majesty's magazine might be delivered up to him. 2. That the Militia might be laid aside until a law was framed providing for the liberty of the subject as well as the defence of the kingdom. 3. That the Parliament might be " adjourned to an indifferent place," where his Majesty and the members of the House might meet and confer with honour and safety. 4. That his Majesty's navy might be immediately restored to him.

Though they abstained from any active share in the proceedings, Stroode, Twisden, and Spencer were present during the reading of the petition, which was forthwith carried to York by Mainy, Filmer, and Clark, and presented to the King on the 1st of August. The King's reply, dated August 4, and written by Lord Falkland, was very skilfully worded. Setting out with the remark that he had never made the least promise or profession of redressing the grievances of his people which he had not been and would always be ready to perform, he stated that he required no other reparation for the injuries and indignities he had received than to have his " town, goods, and navy restored to him," and to have a safe place agreed on where he might " be present with his great Council for the composing all misunderstandings and making the kingdom happy." He complained that a general had been made to command his subjects against him, and to march towards him with cannon, while every effort was put forth to cut off all succour and supply from him, as from a foreign enemy. Lest the petitioners might unjustly suffer for presenting their petition, he assured them that he would " with his utmost power and assistance protect and defend them against any power whatsoever which should question them for so doing; " and concluded by requesting that his answer, together with the petition and instructions, should be read in all churches and chapels in the county.*

---

* The petition and instructions, together with the King's reply, form a small eight-page pamphlet, with this imprint—" First printed at Yorke, and now reprinted at London for William Smith, 1642," and the rose, the

These doings gave fresh offence to the Parliament, and the persons immediately concerned in them were ordered to appear before the House. Spencer, Twisden, Stroode and others were apprehended and conveyed to London. Their estates were eventually sequestered, or they were forced to compound for them by ruinous payments. Troops were dispatched into Kent, and on their arrival at Maidstone, the tradesmen closed their shops. No disturbance, however, occurred; and the soldiers made a tour of the county. Returning by way of Faversham, they reached Aylesford on the 27th of August. At the Friars they seized arms and plate, some concealed in the roof of the house, and Sir Peter Rycaut, who resided there, was sent to Upnor Castle. The same day they plundered Barham Court, Teston, the residence of Sir William Butler. In the evening they were well received at Maidstone.* Two men, however, gave them some annoyance. These men they tied back to back and brought to an extemporised gallows, telling them they had but a few moments to live. But at the critical point a soldier rode up with a pretended reprieve, and one of the men was set at liberty; the other they carried away with them.

Charles had meanwhile hoisted the royal standard at Nottingham, and for the first time since the wars of the Roses, English blood, shed in battle by English hands, crimsoned England's soil. The summer and autumn of 1643 were exciting months in Kent. In July of that year the Royalists in the county made an ineffectual attempt at Sevenoaks to create a diversion in favour of the king.

---

thistle, the Prince of Wales plume, and the harp, each surmounted by a crown, representing the four divisions of the kingdom, adorn the top of the page on which the King's answer begins. This rare pamphlet is in the library of Mr. William Tarbutt, of Cranbrook.

* Historical MSS Commission, Fifth Report.

On the 28th of September, Thomas Twisden, the recorder of Maidstone, was summoned before the Parliament, and certain information concerning him was, on the 10th of October, referred to the Committee of Kent for examination. A letter was written from Maidstone, on October 25, ordering "trained soldiers and volunteers, both horse and foot," to assemble on Penenden Heath, so that the county might be "in a better posture for defence." *

But the great Kentish rising did not take place till 1648. The fortunes of the conflict which was waged from one end of the country to the other had in the interval been virtually decided. Charles was a prisoner, and the heavy march of Fairfax and Cromwell had at length overthrown the brilliant array of the Cavaliers. The cause of the Kentish rising may be briefly explained. In June 1647 the Parliament had passed an ordinance against the celebration of religious festivals and fast days, as "vain and superstitious observances;" but in spite of this, the usual service was held on Christmas day at St. Andrew's Church, Canterbury. The mayor of the city endeavoured to enforce the ordinance, and was urging the citizens to open their shops, when a tradesman insulted his worship, who struck the offender in the face. A mob collected, shots were fired, and the mayor was thrown into the kennel. The Royalists saved the magazine, and placed guards at the gates of the city. During the next few days many acts of violence were committed. After the lapse of several weeks, a regiment of infantry, under Colonel Hewson, was sent from London to Canterbury. Having destroyed the city gates and parts of the ancient wall, the colonel ordered Sir William Mann and several other gentlemen to be arrested and conveyed to Leeds Castle, the residence of Sir John Culpeper, a Royalist, but

---

* Camden Miscellany, vol. iii., p. 39.

which was used by the Parliament as a prison. A special commission was opened at Canterbury on May 11, 1648, to try the prisoners. But the grand jury ignored the bill. The jurymen were requested to reconsider their decision, and again the same verdict was returned. Under these circumstances the judges agreed to detain the prisoners until they had heard from Westminster. A clamour was at once raised against the Parliament, and the grand jury adopted a petition to both Houses, praying that the forces under the command of Lord Fairfax might be disbanded, and testifying their loyalty to the King.

The petitioners invited the public to sign the petition, and accompany it to Blackheath—an appeal which in many quarters met with a ready response, among the subsequent signatures being that of Lambard Godfrey, afterwards recorder of Maidstone. At the request of the Speaker of the House of Commons, the standing Committee of Kent met at Maidstone on May 16, and issued an order to all persons in authority to suppress the petition and to prevent the intended meeting at Blackheath, while arrangements were being made to secure the castles, garrisons, and towns of the county. The House passed a vote of thanks to the gentlemen of the Committee, and directed them to "put down all tumultuous meetings upon any pretence of petitioning or otherwise."

By way of answer to the Committee, the petitioners urged their adherents not to be put down by threats, but to persist in carrying the petition to Blackheath. Thinking that further remonstrance was inexpedient, the Committee directed the trained troops to muster at different places appointed in the county. Matthew Carter,* who was subsequently quartermaster-general of the Royalists, states that at Maidstone only

---

* "True Relation of the Expedition of Kent, Essex, and Colchester," 1650.

twenty men responded to the call. The next step was the publication by the petitioners of a manifesto, in which they avowed their determination to present the petition, "not doubting of a fair reception from both Houses of Parliament," and charged the members of the Committee with exasperating the people, and increasing the taxes of the county for the purpose of maintaining "their own luxury and pride."

It was about this time that Roger L'Estrange, the young scion of an ancient Norfolk family, visited Edward Hales, of Tunstall Green, grandson of Sir Edward Hales, a firm supporter of the Parliament. L'Estrange and Hales were warm adherents of the royal cause, and while talking over the fortunes of the Royalists, L'Estrange suggested that his friend, then in his twenty-fifth year, should head a rising in Kent. Hales caught up the idea with enthusiasm, and called a meeting of the Kentish Royalists, who thereupon proclaimed him general, with Sir Thomas Peyton as his chief lieutenant. Warrants to the constables of the Hundreds were issued, inviting the people to adopt measures for the relief of the King, then a prisoner in Carisbrook Castle. The seamen of the fleet in the Downs caught the loyal infection, and putting Vice-Admiral Rainsborough and other officers on shore, they declared for "King and Kent." Alarmed at these unexpected movements, several members of the Committee took refuge at the Friars, Aylesford, but were pursued by Royalists and apprehended. Hales ordered his men to assemble at Rochester, previous to mustering on the 30th of May at Blackheath, for the purpose of carrying the petition to Westminster.

The Parliament, as a last resort, then sent two of its members to Rochester with a promise of indemnity to the "malignants" if they would lay down their arms; but these delegates were placed in confinement. This insult to the

Parliament necessitated the adoption of energetic measures for suppressing the rising. On the 26th of May the reduction of the county was consequently confided, with full discretionary powers, to Lord Fairfax. That skilful general lost no time in placing himself at the head of a picked body of his veteran troops.

A letter published at this time asserted that the men of Kent were "resolved to become the champions of Church and Crown, scorning to be abridged either in the matter or manner of their intended petition, which they meant to present in the same manner to Parliament as the Houses were wont to petition his Majesty, and that was, with a paper in one hand and a sword in the other." According to another letter, they were marching towards London, and some of them were as far as Dartford, though the majority were still in the neighbourhood of Rochester and Maidstone.* By the 29th of May the more advanced body of the Royalists had reached the vicinity of Blackheath. There they found Fairfax and his force. Ten of them, petition in hand, asked to be allowed to pass up to Westminster. Fairfax declined their request, and told them he had no doubt that if they laid down their arms the Parliament would forgive them. Thus checkmated, the Royalists fell back into the interior of the county, this movement being accelerated by a rumour that Fairfax, whose troops were much enraged against them, was upon their track and intended to offer them battle that night. The same day, indeed, the Parliamentary general commenced his rapid march to the Medway. On the 31st, when Fairfax was at Meopham, the Royalists

---

* Among the letters and pamphlets which the Kentish insurrection called forth were some lines in which, after the usual allusions to the White Horse, the Royalist party were thus heroically addressed:—

May you unconquer'd still remain, tread down
The common foe, and help the King to the Crown;
May after ages say thus, Noble Kent
Gave the greatest blow to that curs'd Parliament!

quartered at Rochester drew up a "remonstrance," in which they declared that they had taken up arms to defend themselves, and that they invaded not the Parliament's right, but stood firm to secure their own.

Fairfax had started from Blackheath with seven regiments of horse and foot,* consisting, according to one writer, of 7,000 men, and, according to another, of more than 8,000. Ludlow, in his "Memorials," says the Royalists outnumbered the Parliamentarians by at least one half. We may therefore estimate Fairfax's strength at about 7,000 horse and foot, and as his troops were well disciplined, full of enthusiasm, and thoroughly inured to war, they would form a compact and powerful little force. Carter says that 10,000 Royalists were under arms; while Fairfax, in one of his despatches, computes them at 11,000, and John Rushworth, his secretary, makes a like calculation. The lowest reckoning is 7,000, the highest 14,000.† It is unlikely that Carter would overestimate the strength of his own side, and his statement may probably be taken as the nearest approximation to the truth.

But though in mere numbers the Royalists were superior to their opponents, they were far inferior to them as soldiers. Their discipline was defective, and their arms were somewhat promiscuous, though Carter asserts that seven or eight thousand infantry marched from East Kent in "a very orderly and military manner," and were "all well accoutred." Moreover, their ardour for revenge had undergone a chill. They were disappointed in their expectation of assistance from Essex and other counties, and now that they had to depend entirely upon their own resources, they hesitated to entrust

---

* Rushworth to the Speaker: Tanner MSS., Bodleian Library, vol. lvii., p. 119.
† Letter dated May 30, 1648.

themselves to the unskilled generalship of young Hales. Colonel Washington,* Colonel Culpeper,† and other gentlemen, were suggested for the post, Hales expressing his readiness to acquiesce in the appointment of a more capable leader. But while the Royalists were wasting their time in discussing this matter, the troops of the Parliament were moving steadily upon them.

Detaching a small party of horse and foot to secure a pass near Northfleet, Fairfax left Meopham on the 1st of June, and pressed on towards Maidstone. Most of the villages and hamlets through which he passed were deserted by the men, who had cast in their lot with the Royalists; and their wives and children were in extreme anxiety for their fate, " making sad moan," one correspondent says, " fearing the ill success of their husbands." Fairfax reached Malling without having encountered any resistance. Here a short halt was made, and then the march was resumed, his intention being to cross the Medway and attack Maidstone the same evening.‡ With this view he directed his course towards Barming Heath by lanes that have been altered north of the London road, and descended by Barming rectory to get his guns over East Farleigh Bridge, about two miles south-west of the town. While crossing the heath he descried several thousand troops assembled on the bluff of the hill east of Kit's Coty House, on the other side of the river. The main body of the Royalists, ignorant of the exact whereabouts of their

* This was Sir Henry Washington, who had conducted the defence of Worcester during the siege of that town. He was first cousin of Lawrence Washington, who was grandfather of George Washington, the hero of American independence.

† John Lord Culpeper, of Leeds Castle, who was ennobled in 1644 for his services to the royal cause.

‡ "This day we hope to be over the river at Maidstone or Aylesford, and to force the enemy to fight or swim, for we have left a strong party of horse, foot, and dragoons, to make good the pass at Rochester, whilst we fall on the other side of the river and make good Maidstone and Aylesford."— Letter dated June 1, 1648.

antagonists, had met there to appoint a commander. The choice fell upon the grey-headed George Goring, Earl of Norwich,* a man of little military experience, while Hales became lieutenant-general.† Uncertain where the blow would fall, the Royalist leaders had previously divided their force, about 2,000 men occupying Maidstone, and the rest being encamped between Aylesford and Rochester. They agreed to act strictly upon the defensive, and to content themselves with holding the passes.‡

The early part of the 1st of June 1648, the most memorable Thursday in the history of Maidstone, was clear and warm. The sunshine lighted up the tender green of the meadows, and many a timbered gable cast its brown shadow athwart the principal streets. Bordered for the most part by hedgerows, then gay with primroses and violets, a high road, intersected at intervals by narrow lanes, led to the village of East Farleigh, running almost parallel with the Medway, and separated therefrom by wooded slopes and hop-gardens.

Sir Gamaliel Dudley was governor of Maidstone, with Sir John Mainy as his chief lieutenant. They had taken some pains to make the place defensible. A rude earthwork § was constructed on the south side of the town. Stone Street was barricaded with trees, and across Gabriel's Hill a stockade was hastily raised. There was another earthwork at the top

---

* He married Mary Nevill, daughter of Lord Abergavenny.

† "News from Kent," June 2, 1648, says:—"The Earl of Norwich, who was designed to be their general, made a speech of encouragement to them, saying that he would desire them to go no further than he went himself, and that if they failed now they should be for ever slaves. The foot were ill-armed, and some whole files rode on horseback in a rude and uncouth manner. Squire Hales was to be lieutenant-general, and Sir William Compton their major-general. Sir Bernard Gascoigne, a French monsieur, offered to bring fifty lieutenants for the service."

‡ "The whole," says one of the combatants, "resolved not to fight, but to hold the passes."

§ Newton, writing in 1741, says that "some remains of this were to be seen not many years ago."

of the hill, well supplied with case-shot, and having pieces of ordnance pointing down the four ways of the two lines of street which here intersect each other. The leading families had left the town, and the houses in the main thoroughfares were deserted. Wilson, the incumbent of All Saints', was also preparing to depart. "Where is your God now?" shouted some profane Royalists, as they caught his horse's bridle, and once or twice turned him back. A gentle word or two was the pious man's reply, and as he rode away he thought of the text, "My God is in Heaven, and hath done whatsoever He pleased." *

Late in the afternoon the defenders of the town were still ignorant of Fairfax's movements; but as his force was known to be in the heart of Kent, it was foreseen that the attack might come at any moment. Sir John Mainy, in order to prevent a surprise, consequently sent a troop of horse along the Farleigh road to guard the southern entrance to the town. The weather, so clear and bright only an hour or two before, had now completely changed. Dark clouds obscured the evening sky, and towards sunset rain poured in torrents.

A few minutes past seven o'clock a trooper galloped into Stone Street with the news that Fairfax's men had been encountered about a mile distant, on the Farleigh road. So sudden was the alarm that the town was thrown into confusion; but efforts were quickly made to restore order, musketeers were hurried into the houses, and soon every door and window was in a state of defence. Finding the bridge at Farleigh but slightly guarded, Fairfax had crossed the river,† and sent forward a troop of dragoons to view the town

---

* See Swinnock's Life of Wilson.
† "The Lord Fairfax with his whole body marched down towards Maidstone, and finding the river slightly guarded about Farleigh bridge, easily got over, and with a strong body fell upon the town before those within it were alarmed."—Carter.

and prepare for the advance of his main body. While executing this order, the dragoons came in contact with the Royalist outposts, and in the first skirmish drove them from their ground. Supports, both horse and foot, sallied out of the town, and attacked the dragoons with great fury, recovering part of the lost position. The dragoons fell back upon a detachment of musketeers and pikemen who were being brought up with all speed from Farleigh.

Within the town the excitement was intense. Messengers were despatched to the Earl of Norwich for assistance; and the news of the extreme peril of Maidstone spread like wildfire from village to village, up the vale of the Medway, and round over the hills to Rochester and Chatham. Then, to the great joy of the defenders, Colonel Brockman* rode along Week Street at the head of eight hundred cavaliers, watermen, and London apprentices. The number of the defenders was thus augmented to about three thousand armed men. A reserve of horse was drawn up in the High Town, and men were hurried forward to the scene of action on the Farleigh road, where the fight was waxing hot and furious. Fairfax's pikemen had been repulsed, and Royalists were picking them off from behind the hedges. Just then Colonel Brockman, with a party of foot, came up, and Sergeant Ginder bravely led them on, but was himself seriously wounded in the hand, and otherwise disabled.† His men rushed into the ranks of the Parliamentarians, fighting without order, but resolutely and hand to hand.

Fairfax and his officers were astonished to see their own disciplined troops thrown into confusion. In those days it was necessary for the general not only to direct the movements of his men, but to encourage them by a display of

---

* Sir William Brockman, of Beachborough.
† "Calender of State Papers" (Domestic, 1665.)

personal bravery. Fairfax, seated in his coach, had been impatiently watching the conflict. He was suffering from an acute attack of gout, and his right foot was wrapped in bandages. His staff entreated him not to expose his person to danger; but this hero of a hundred fights, who by one desperate charge had turned the tide of battle at Naseby, and with his own hand seized the royal colours, was not thus to risk the ignominy of defeat. He mounted on horseback, and heedless of danger, led his troops to the charge.* Nothing could withstand that impetuous rush. For a few minutes there was a deadly hand-to-hand struggle, and many a gallant Royalist was laid low as the dark form of Fairfax towered over the storm. The resistance was broken, and amid the rain and flying bullets, the Royalists retreated.

Nine o'clock rung forth from the grey tower of All Saints' as the actual storming of Maidstone commenced; and those of the defenceless inhabitants who remained in the town had endured two hours of the most harrowing suspense. All hope of further relief from Rochester was at an end. Old Goring, in a fever of indecision, was dawdling on the Rochester road, not knowing what to do.† Sir Gamaliel

---

* The general, says one of the combatants, could not be prevailed upon to remain with the body in the field, "but mounted and exposed himself to great danger, being one of the first in this action." So "tedious and desperate" was the resistance, observes Heath, that Fairfax was "forced to light out of his coach, and to lead his men on in person." See also Rushworth's letter, dated June 2, and Markham's Life of Fairfax, p. 307.

† Roger L'Estrange gives a disgraceful account of the old man's conduct. "Towards evening," he says, "we received intelligence that Maidstone was alarmed, and that the enemy was drawn up before it; by and by, they had assaulted it. When advertised, the Earl of Norwich resolved for Maidstone; upon him waited Sir Bernard Gascoigne and myself, in all eight persons. By the way we encountered more fugitives, their messengers all upon the spur, and the word was for relief. At last, two miles from the town, we found that the enemy had passed the river (which we little expected), and possessed all the avenues. Hereupon my lord determined for Rochester again, and to send immediate succour. There arrived, it was consulted what to do. Colonel Culpeper propounded to draw out horse and foot to a man incontinently and fight. Then some cried 'twas too late, and others that the men were weary, and some that their men were lying too

Dudley and Sir John Mainy presented their boldest front to the assailants. Every available man was called up in the final defence. In the fields at the top of Upper Stone Street sixty horsemen of the Parliament, their steel caps and breastplates gleaming through the darkness, fell upon a party of horse carrying the royal standard, and made great slaughter. A few Royalists in the rear rushed to the aid of their comrades, and were met by the remnants of the party galloping down the street. Once within the town, a galling fire from door and window was directed against the Parliamentary troops.* Fairfax then ordered Colonel Hewson's regiment to the front. Throwing himself into the thick of the fight, Hewson was knocked down with a musket, Major Carter wounded, and Captain Price killed. The colonel quickly recovered himself, and pressed the defenders so hard that they wavered, and fell into disorder.† Along the passage thus opened up, he pursued them, and met with little opposition as he crossed the Len bridge.‡ On Gabriel's Hill defenders and assailants closed at push of pike, and the struggle began anew. But Fairfax continued to send up fresh troops, and from point to point the Royalists were forced back. The guns opened upon Fairfax's men as they came up the hill, and for a while the latter were kept in check. Eventually, however, the guns were silenced. Then the fight was transferred to the High Town, where the

---

far apart, that they could not get them together. In a word, they rejected wholesome counsel. It was then demanded what they would do. It was answered, 'what they could.' About midnight we received tidings that the town was forced; that the foot had stood very gallantly and repelled theirs, the horse not so well." Carter endeavours to exonerate Goring, but he was absent, and L'Estrange was on the spot.

* "The Royalists used all those ready engines of death which the houses afforded, to the very great slaughter of the red-coats."—Heath's "Chronicle."

† Ludlow's "Memorials."

‡ Greenwood, in his "County History," incorrectly implies that the bridge was hotly disputed. "At the bridge we found little opposition," is the remark of one who was present.

Parliamentary musketeers rushed furiously on with their broad swords and the butt-ends of their muskets, and the day closed in a deadly struggle.

The Royalists, after five hours' fighting, were at midnight driven into the churchyard, where they surrendered and were made prisoners.* Others, however, had mounted their horses and escaped, every man shifting for himself. Many of them, being ignorant of the roads, fled wildly in all directions. A few were overtaken, and sold their lives dearly; others hid themselves in the hop gardens.

Never was victory more complete. Sir John Mainy and 300 Royalists were slain; and Sir Gamaliel Dudley, Sir William Brockman, Squire Scott, and 1,300 men were captured, besides 500 horse, 3,000 arms, 9 colours, and 8 pieces of canon.† There is no mention of wounded. I have not found any Royalist estimate of Fairfax's losses, but that they also were heavy may, I think, be inferred from the peculiarly difficult nature of the work in which his men were for so many hours engaged. John Rushworth says that only thirty men on their own side were slain, but a pamphlet published three days after the fight states that the town was

---

* "At last they came to the churchyard, and from thence to the church, and were forced to capitulate, none coming to their relief, unless it were a few scattering men, who, hearing they were engaged, left their quarters without orders, and huddled into this crowd of confused destruction which they were overwhelmed in."—Carter.

† These are Fairfax's figures. Rushworth, who wrote on the morning after the storming of the town, perhaps before the returns were complete, states that 200 Royalists were killed, and 400 prisoners taken; but nearly all the foot must have been captured. A letter from Rochester, dated June 5, 1648, says:—"Sir John Mainy slain, with his will in his pocket, 120 slain more, 30 of the army killed, 1,500 prisoners taken: Sir Gamaliel Dudley taken, who said he would advance against London and cause all manner of sins to be committed there, for to pull down God's judgments upon the city. Taken also Sir William Brockman, Colonel Scott, Colonel Price, and several others of note. One of the clerks hanged himself in a bell-rope; 40 barrels of gunpowder taken." In another letter we read:—"The business at Maidstone far greater than at first presented. We took above 1,400 prisoners, 500 horse, 16 barrels of gunpowder, 12 tuns [casks?] of match, and 200 arms."

"stormed and subdued with a loss of 80 men," which is no doubt much nearer the truth. The dead appear to have been buried in old St. Faith's churchyard, where quantities of bones were recently found; and the bodies of those who fell at the commencement of the action were interred in Postley Fields. The soldiers who were slain in the vicinity of East Farleigh bridge were buried in a field close to a lane leading from Barming to Farleigh, where, a hundred and fifty years later, many bones of men and horses, an ancient gold ring, and pieces of decayed leather, armour, and spurs, were discovered.

Three eye-witnesses each wrote an account of the fight at Maidstone—Secretary Rushworth; a "person of credit," signing himself "I. T.;" and Lord Fairfax. Rushworth's account, dated from Maidstone on June 2, at six in the morning, was addressed to Speaker Lenthall, and conveyed to the House of Commons the first intelligence of the victory. It is as follows:—

"The particulars are too many to be related at this time concerning this last night's engagement with the enemy at Maidstone, which, in brief, was such as never was since these wars began; this army struggled with so much difficulty to overcome a stubborn and resolute enemy. The fight began about seven of the clock at night, about a mile from Maidstone, and before we could beat them from hedge to hedge, and get in at the barricades, it was past nine; and after we had entered the town, we disputed every street and turning, they having eight pieces of canon which they discharged above twenty times upon our men in the streets, and by God's mighty help and assistance we overcame them between twelve and one of the clock at night, being every minute in all that time firing upon their horse and foot, and they upon us, it being extreme wet weather during all this time of engagement. We took about 400 prisoners, and near as many horse. Our forlorn hope of horse gave the red standard of horse as gallant a charge as ever was seen, which is said to be General Hales his troop. The reason why the engagement began so soon, the train and the rear of the army being three miles off (and not come up), was, that the forlorn of horse and foot being engaged in viewing the town before it was dark, came off safe, the enemy being with their whole body of horse and foot within two miles on the top of the hill towards Rochester all day long in view of our army, about 8,000 men, who, as they perceived that we did not dispute the pass at Aylesford, which was very difficult for us to have done, sent in a supply of 1,200 horse and foot to those before in the town of Maidstone, who came in just as we engaged, being seamen, apprentices, and most part commanders and cavaliers that have formerly been in arms against the Parliament. There were in all, as we guess, 200 then slain in and about the town; and Captain Price, a very honest and stout gentleman, Colonel Hewson's captain-lieutenant, were also slain, and about 30 more of our men, most falling at the mouth of the canon with case-shot. We took eight pieces, six iron and two brass, and abundance of arms. Having been up all night, and want of time, cannot send more particulars at present. Only I desire God to let you see how the old quarrel is revived by the same party with greater violence than at first. You will shortly understand what earls, lords, and other persons of quality appeared in this business. His Excellency [Lord Fairfax] from the first minute of the engagement to the last could not be drawn off from a personal and hazardous attendance on the service, and is much impaired in his health."

"I. T.," in a letter also dated from Maidstone on June 2, gives a good account of the action :—

"In my last letter I acquainted you of our marching to this town, according to the advice of a council of war, which was thought and conceived more facile and better to engage the enemy than at Rochester or Northfleet; and when we drew near Maidstone we found the lanes barricaded with trees and other things which were thrown in the ways, and the hedges lined with musketeers. Yet after some time spent (with great difficulty), we beat them from one place to another, till we had driven them back to the very town; and at the bridge we found little opposition, but the streets were strongest fortified and the stoutest defended of any that I have known in all the late unhappy wars. Their ordnance, loaded with case-shot, did us some mischief before we could get under their shot. The rain was more disadvantage to us than to them; for they shot out of windows and at doors, but in this service the firelocks were of great use to us. From the time we had begun the fight till we had gotten the town, was six or seven hours. In the first action I cannot but observe unto you the gallantry of a party of about sixty of our horse, which charged another party of theirs, where ours gave them a thorough charge; and did such execution upon them that it is thought there is not a man of the enemy's party that was not slain or wounded. In this town were about 2,000 men, amongst which were a few of the Kentish countrymen, but seamen, watermen, and such as came to them from London were the only fighting men they had amongst them. Of these we took about 1,400 prisoners, horse and foot, of which you will have a list by the next; they are for the present put into Maidstone church."

Lord Fairfax's official despatch is dated Rochester, Sunday, June 4, and runs thus:—

"Upon Thursday, in the evening, about seven o'clock, after very long marches, we got near the town, and a troop of dragoons was sent to make good a pass, whilst the town was viewing at what place our men might best enter, it being resolved upon to force our passage in case of resistance, the gaining of that town over the river being of great advantage to our affairs. But before there could be a view taken of the town, the dragoons had engaged the enemy, and forced them from that ground which they kept. The dragoons, being very forward to engage, pursued, and so the enemy drew forth a considerable party of horse and foot to maintain a pass against us, which necessitated the drawing down of the greatest part of the foot, with some horse; and though that part of the town was of the greatest difficulty to enter, yet through the goodness of God, our men made their entrance and became masters of the town, after four or five hours' hot service, the town being very strongly barricaded; and through the darkness of the night, and our ignorance of the town, they disputed the barricades and places of advantage with our men, playing hard with their canon upon them; in which service both horse and foot did exceedingly well; and particularly I cannot but take notice of the valour and resolution of Colonel Hewson, whose regiment had the hardest task (Major Carter, his major, being hurt, and Captain Price, a deserving and faithful officer, slain.) The best of their men were there, whereof many were cavaliers and London apprentices. They looked upon the consequence of that place to be very great, and therefore did resolve to make what resistance they could; the old Lord Goring being that day proclaimed general, at the head of the army, upon a hill near Aylesford, where we saw their body drawn up, which, as their prisoners since do confess, and they themselves gave out, consisted of 8,000, besides those in Maidstone and Aylesford, in both which places there were about 3,000, those of Aylesford coming as a fresh supply to relieve those engaged in Maidstone. There were near 300 slain, and about 1,300 prisoners, many of them being taken next morning early in the woods, hop yards, and fields, whither they fled in the time of the fight, amongst which were gentlemen of good quality, Sir Gamaliel Dudley, Sir William Brockman, Squire Scott, Major Price and others, a list whereof is preparing to be next. There were about 500 horse, 3,000 arms, 9 foot colours, and 8 pieces of cannon, with store of ammunition also, taken in the first charge which our forlorn hope gave the enemy's horse, wherein our horse carried themselves very gallantly (as I since hear). Sir John Mainy and divers others of quality were slain. After it pleased God to give us this great mercy in the gaining of the town, their men received so great discouragement that the greatest part of their army left them and were dispersed, and a great number of officers and gentlemen since fled to shift for themselves. Their word at the engagement was 'King and Kent;' ours, 'Truth.'

"Having thus possessed ourselves of the passes at Aylesford and Maidstone, the enemy being much confused with our success, and their own men deserting them, they at last marched over Rochester bridge towards Blackheath with about 3,000 horse and foot, most of whom were cavaliers, apprentices, and watermen. Our men not being able to make so speedy after them as was necessary, I sent Colonel Whalley with a party of horse and dragoons after them; upon whose approach they have left Kent, and are fled over the water to Essex by Woolwich and Greenwich. Colonel Whalley is in pursuit, and I doubt not but he will give a good account of that service. I have sent Colonel Rich with a party of horse and foot to relieve Dover, where I trust we shall find the same presence of God as hitherto hath been. My prayer to the Lord is that this great mercy may be further improved, to His glory and this kingdom's good. I thought fit to present unto your lordships these papers enclosed, taken from the enemy, whereby you will receive the depth of their plot, and their engagements to pursue what they have undertaken.* I desire you to be pleased to move the House on the behalf of the widow and children of Captain Price, that some provision may be made for them, and the arrears of her husband paid unto them for their present subsistence." †

This despatch, which was addressed to the Earl of Manchester, was by order of the House of Lords communicated to the Lord Mayor and Common Council, and a letter of thanks was directed to be sent to Lord Fairfax. On June 12, the House made an order for payment of £10 to John Williams and £20 to the rest of the messengers who carried the despatch to London. ‡

The Parliament estimated the victory so highly that a thanksgiving was ordered in " the parish churches of London and Westminster." All authorities are unanimous in declaring that no engagement during the civil war was contested on both sides with more stubborn bravery and endurance. Clarendon says the Maidstone fight was " a sharp encounter very powerfully fought with the general's

---

* One of the papers contained these instructions: "To fortify bridges, and to break down those bridges which are not fit to be fortified; stop up the fordes." "The train-hands of Maidstone"—so ran another paper—"have lent two auxileries, &c., 80 arms, who desire to have them again, and that the auxileries be otherwise furnished."

† The House voted that his arrears, and £200 in addition, should be paid to Captain Price's widow.

‡ Historical MSS. Commission, Seventh Report.

whole strength; and the veteran soldiers confessed that they had never met with the like desperate service during the war." Baker states that "Fairfax stormed the town twice, but was both times repulsed; the third time he got entrance, and the fight lasted six hours."* Von Ranke says the storming of Maidstone was "one of the most murderous conflicts of the whole war." †

On Friday, the day after the action, Fairfax's men searched the town, and found quantities of arms concealed in the houses. They remained during the night in Maidstone, and on Saturday afternoon advanced towards Rochester.‡ A halt was made on Penenden Heath, where a council of war was held. Several soldiers were also proceeded against for misdemeanours, and James Pluer, a private in Colonel Barkstead's § regiment, for stealing three shillings from a country woman, was tried by court-martial and ordered to be shot. ‖ The march was then resumed, and on approaching Rochester,

---

* "Chronicles of the Kings of England," p. 560.
† "History of England," vol. ii., p. 522.
‡ "The Weekly Intelligencer, sent abroad to prevent Mis-Information."
§ Barkstead was a regicide; at the Restoration he fled to Germany, and was there betrayed, and in 1662 butchered at Tyburn.
‖ The general had on the 30th of May issued the following proclamation against plundering:—"Whereas I have had several complaints that divers soldiers going into several men's houses under pretence of getting victuals and drink, have searched the rooms in their houses and have taken cloths, linen, and other goods; for the prevention of the like evil for the future I do hereby strictly require all soldiers whatsoever under my command that at their peril they do from henceforth forbear the like violence to the houses or goods of any: And all officers, as they will answer the neglect at their peril, are strictly to look to those under their respective charges, to see that no such things be done, or if they be, that the offenders be brought to punishment, which I do hereby declare shall be severely executed: And for the supplying of the soldiers with victuals and necessaries (while the army shall keep the field) care shall be taken for bringing in and distributing the same in a public way or (if that fail) the commanders of the respective regiments, troops, or companies are to take care that, where there is a necessity of taking victuals for the soldiers' relief, some officers be appointed to see it done orderly and without further damage or prejudice to the inhabitants, and whatever such goods hath been injuriously taken from any as aforesaid, I require that restitution be forthwith made, otherwise the persons with whom such goods shall be found, or those by whom they were taken, shall be immediately proceeded against according to martial law."

it was found that the Royalists had fled, the citizens being "full of discontent, and cursing against Lord Goring and his followers." The mayor of Rochester, whose name was attached to the Royalist commission for raising arms, was made a prisoner, and nearly a thousand pikes and firelocks were discovered in the city.

The Royalists had on Friday abandoned Rochester. Lord Norwich sent a portion of his force into East Kent, and the rest marched to Blackheath. Lord Fairfax despatched a body of men after the Blackheath party, and himself proceeded to Canterbury, where the Royalists surrendered; and in a few days he completed the pacification of Kent. On June 10 he was at Gravesend, and following Norwich and his rabble rout into Essex, he laid siege to Colchester on the 13th. The Parliament passed an ordinance on the 3rd of July for raising £14,000 from the estates of such of the Royalists in Kent and Essex as had joined in the insurrection, and this was followed by another for sequestering the estates of the principal delinquents in Kent, the composition finally paid being one-fourth of the value of the estates. Colchester capitulated on the 28th of August, when 3,471 prisoners were taken, and Sir Charles Lucas and Sir George Lisle, who had broken their parole of honour, were tried by court-martial and shot. Sir Bernard Gascoigne,* also condemned, was pardoned by the general. Lord Norwich and Lord Capel were tried at Westminster Hall, the latter being beheaded, while the life of Norwich was saved by the casting vote of the Speaker.

After the short but decisive campaign in Kent and Essex, the Parliamentary regiments returned to London. Meanwhile measures were being taken for the trial of the King. In December 1648, when more than a hundred members of

---

* He was an Italian adventurer, his real name being Bernardo Guascooni.

the Parliament were driven out by the process known in history as "Pride's Purge," Colonel Rich's regiment of horse occupied New Palace Yard, and the foot regiments of Colonels Hewson and Barkstead lined Westminster Hall and the lobby of the House of Commons. By this act of lawless violence the Council of Officers were enabled to create a High Court of Justice for the trial of Charles. Andrew Broughton, mayor of Maidstone, as mentioned in a previous chapter, was one of the clerks of the court. Thomas Read, of Maidstone, was one of the thirty-four witnesses against the King; he deposed that in the end of August or the beginning of September 1644 he saw Charles at the head of a guard of horse between Loswithiel and Fowy, in Cornwall. Another Maidstone man, Thomas Trapham, who was a surgeon in the Parliamentary army, assisted to embalm the King's corpse, and it is said that, having attached the head to the body, he turned round to the spectators and remarked that he had "sewed on the head of a goose." Trapham died in Buckinghamshire, December 29, 1683.

No one who examines the borough and parochial records of Maidstone for the year 1648 would entertain the slightest suspicion that the town was stormed by Fairfax's troops on the 1st of June. Neither the town clerk nor the incumbent of All Saints' at the time of the fight made any entry on the subject. The Corporation met and elected a chief magistrate on November 2, 1647, and did not meet again until the last week of July 1648, when there was a large attendance, only two jurates and four common councilmen being absent. An order was then given for repairing the Brambles prison in the High Street; and it is probable that the desperate struggle which took place in that part of the town may have necessitated these repairs. There are no burials entered in the parish register for the first four days of June 1648. The register for succeeding years, however, contains some ominous facts. Greenwood, referring to the fight on the 1st of June, says that "the loss on the part of the townsmen was so great that for many years afterwards, of the females marrying at Maidstone, by far the largest number are observed to have been widows." The registers support this statement, for from 1649 to 1654—in which period the number of marriages was considerably below the average—as many as forty-two widows were married at All Saints' Church, while in 1655 no less than fifty-four widows contracted marriage, the total number of marriages in that year being one hundred and thirty-seven.

After the Restoration, several of those who fought and bled in the royal cause at Maidstone took occasion to remind the authorities of their services to Charles I. Thus in 1662 Abraham Reeves, a blacksmith, applied to the Corporation to be made a freeman of the borough; and the Mayor and Jurates, considering that Reeves was a "soldier for his late Majesty in the fight at Maidstone, where he lost one of his fingers," granted his request on payment of the nominal sum of £3. Brave Thomas Ginder in 1665 made a direct appeal for relief to Charles II. He was then in his seventy-first year, and described himself as a yeoman of Eltham. He stated, in his petition to the king, that he was the eldest sergeant in the foot company under Sir William Brockman, and led the van in the engagement at Maidstone, where he was much wounded and lost his right hand, being afterwards imprisoned for twelve months. Richard Hodges, of Maidstone, in 1666 petitioned the king for a letter to the governor of Sutton's Hospital to elect his grandson John, a poor scholar, in room of his brother James, who, contrary to the practice of that institution, was sent out as an apprentice on the breaking up of the school at the visitation of the plague. He said that he lost all his sons in the service of Charles I., and that one of them left a widow and four children. The petition was accompanied by a paper signed by several gentlemen of the town, certifying to the applicant's sincerity and loyalty.

This chapter would perhaps be considered incomplete by some readers unless it showed how the connection of Lord Fairfax's family with this neighbourhood was brought about. The Parliamentary general, who died in 1671, was the third Lord Fairfax. The fifth lord married the daughter and heiress of Thomas Lord Culpeper, on whose death she succeeded to Leeds Castle, near Maidstone. Her only daughter was married to Denny Martin, of the Salts, Loose; and the seventh lord, who died in 1793, bequeathed Leeds Castle to his nephew, the Rev. Denny Martin, who was followed by his brother, General Martin. When General Martin died, he left the Kent estate to Fiennes Wykeham, his second cousin through the Martins. The buff leathern doublet, white embroidered waistcoat, and white kid shoes of the great general, his miniature by Hoskins, and many Fairfax pictures, are still preserved at Leeds Castle.

During some alterations at the Castle in 1822, a quantity of useless furniture, including an old oaken chest filled apparently with Dutch tiles, was set apart for sale. The chest was bought for a few shillings by Gooding, a shoemaker of Lenham. Under the tiles he found a pile of manuscripts. Not recognising their value, he cut several of the parchments into measuring strips, while others found their way to Maidstone, to be used by the milliners as winders for their thread. Several pieces coming under the observation of John Newington Hughes, banker, of Maidstone, he hastened to Lenham, and purchased the whole of the remaining manuscripts. He sold them to Mr. Bentley, the publisher, and from them was compiled the four volumes entitled the " Fairfax

Correspondence," containing Lord Fairfax's official despatch on the storming of Maidstone, and a mass of valuable information relating to the civil war. Most of the original letters were afterwards secured for the British Museum.

CHAPTER XII.

COURTS AND PUNISHMENTS.

Early Courts and Prisons—The Court House—Preparations for the Assizes—Old Legal Punishments—The Upper and Lower Court Houses—The County Prison and the Brambles—Cases at the Quarter Sessions during the Commonwealth—Trial of Witches—Tragedy at Lees Court—Cases at the Assizes in Charles II.'s reign—County Prison and Bridewell in King Street—First person executed for Sheep-stealing—Demolition of the Lower Court House—Riot at the County Prison—Visit of John Howard—State Trial at the Town Hall—Number of Prisoners tried at the Assizes—List of Executions on Penenden Heath—Public and Private Executions.

SIX hundred years ago the Itinerant Justices, when they visited Kent, usually held their Eyre at Canterbury or Rochester; but we know from official records that more than once during the reign of Edward I. they journeyed to Maidstone, and here sat in judgment upon those whose crimes or offences had brought them under the notice of the chief administrators of the law. Petty civil and criminal cases were in mediæval times dealt with by the Portreve, who, with several or all of his brethren, was invested with authority to hold a court for such purposes. This jurisdiction is referred to in the accounts of the Corpus Christi Fraternity for the year

1480: "Item for a playnt in the Portryve's court agayn Thomas Sylvester." A Court of Peculiar, for the proving of wills, existed in Maidstone as early as the fourteenth century. It was originally attached to St. Mary's Church, and probably afterwards to the College of All Saints, the master and fellows having power to grant probates and letters of administration. There are extant at least two wills which were proved in this court—those of John Stoyl in 1367, and of Richard William in 1448, to which latter the seal of the court is appended.

At a very early period there were two prisons in the town —the county gaol and the archbishop's prison. The archbishop had a prison here in the year 1255, in which heretics and excommunicants were confined. The Lambeth Registers state that Thomas Latter was appointed keeper of it in May 1444. In 1538 the prison was given by Archbishop Cranmer to Henry VIII. in exchange for other property. It appears to have then remained for some years in possession of the Crown. The county prison, which stood near the top of the High Town, belonged to the western divison of Kent. Upon the battlements of this building in 1590 the people of Maidstone saw the quarters of some traitors set upon two poles, which, with the staples for fixing them, cost 12s.

In the time of Henry VIII. the Kent assizes were held at Rochester, Canterbury, Maidstone, East Greenwich, Dartford, Sevenoaks, and Milton-next-Gravesend. During Elizabeth's reign they were held at Rochester more frequently than at any other town in the county. The house in which the judges opened their commission at Maidstone stood on the site of the present Town Hall. It was built in the latter half of the sixteenth century, at the joint expense of the borough and the western division of the county, and was called the Court House. Raised above ground on square wooden pillars, it looked a compact structure, with high lattice windows, and many gables. It is described as "the shire house" in the will of John Amye, written in 1595. The following reference is made to it in a Corporation breviat, dated 1597, viz., "The town at their charge, with the aid of the county, did build a session house for the sessions and assizes, and a court house and other rooms for themselves, whereunto adjoin these messuages, purchased by the town of John Mors, gent., of which the one is called the high cage, now in the occupation of Richard Tanner, by lease for a yearly rent of 40s., quarterly payable, and the two other messuages Robert Hall holdeth by lease from the town for a yearly rent of 30s., of all which the Mayor and Jurates of Maidstone are seized in the fee simple; and they stand at the upper end of the Middle Row." The cage referred to, in which rogues and vagabonds were confined, stood by the Court House stairs.

When the assizes were held at Maidstone, prisoners were tried at the Court House, and Kilburne states that a shed was erected in the High Town for the court of Nisi Prius. Posts were driven into the ground, and carpenters were employed to set up the woodwork. Gravel and paving were laid down, and rushes and herbs were placed as a carpet beneath the judge's feet. The bench was hung with green cloth, hired from gentlemen in the town, and the "tilt" above the judge's seat was white-limed. Enclosures for counsel, witnesses, and clients were formed by bars of wood and ropes tightly drawn, and guarded by several men. Workmen had in 1587 been engaged for two days in erecting this shed in the High Town, when a sudden order came to remove it to the King's Mead, where it was set up during the night by twenty-one men and boys. The beer supplied to them in the course of the work cost 8d., and their wages amounted to 21s. 4d. The assizes over, the shed was taken down, and the posts and framework were stored in the premises of the Grammar School.

The following curious items occur in the chamberlains' accounts for the year 1588:—

	s.	d.
Paid unto the carpenters, and other workmen to help them, and for digging holes to set up poasts, and settinge up the assize court	11	10
Nayles, great and small	4	11
Taylors to hang up the clothe	0	3
Rushes for the judge	0	2
Flagges for to strew the assize court	1	0
Watchmen for servinge their attendance at the assize tyme, and for goinge with the prisoners, and the daye of execution	12	4
Smythe the carpenter and his men for pullinge down the assize court	1	8
Labourers for takinge awaye the timber and other things of the assize court	0	5
Roger Beale and others for landynge divers yeards of greene clothe	3	8
Thomas Cooke for gravellinge and pavinge the assize court	1	8
Judge's servants at the assize	1	8

Nor were these the only expenses connected with the assizes. The lodging of the judges during their stay in the town cost the borough £2 to £3, and substantial gifts were also made to them by the Corporation. These gifts usually took the form of wine or beer, as much as a hogshead of the latter having been given in 1587. Occasionally also sugar-loaves were sent to the judges' lodgings, and sometimes a sheep or a calf. The town likewise provided two cooks, two butlers, two stewards, two chamberlains, and two criers, besides oats and fodder for thirty or forty horses.

Among the old legal instruments of punishment, descending, many of them, from Saxon times, the chief, or at least the most remarkable in Maidstone, were the stocks, the whipping-post, the cucking-stool, the pillory, and the gallows. Scolding women were placed in the cucking or ducking stool, which was a chair fixed at the end of a long pole, balanced on a pivot, and suspended over a pond of water, into which the offender, tied fast in her seat, was plunged. The poet Gay celebrates this chair of correction in the following lines:—

> I'll speed me to the pond where the high stool,
> On the long plank, hangs o'er the muddy pool—
> That stool the dread of every scolding quean.

It is impossible now to fix the date when this cooling apparatus was first introduced into Maidstone, but that it was in request as early as 1562 may be inferred from an entry in the borough accounts for that year, which runs thus:—" Payd unto Henry Smythe for makynge of the cockynge stole, 21s. 8d." In the same year the sum of 50s. was paid " for tymber for the pound, the cockerstole, and some for the crosse;" while, in 1563, 1s. 10d. was expended on the ironwork for the cucking-stool.

As early as 1577 the practice of publicly flagellating delinquents was resorted to, the chamberlains' accounts for that year showing that 4d. was paid to William Simmonds for " whyppinge and sendynge away certain rogges out off the towne." The Maidstone pillory was repaired in 1545 at an outlay of 2s. 6d., and 4d. was paid to a man for setting it up. Two backs for the stocks were made in 1588, and the frame was afterwards repaired in the same year at a cost of 8d. Bakers and brewers who " offended the statute " were severely dealt with, and a baker who, in the year 1600, delivered unwholesome bread for the use of the prisoners in the town gaol, must have had cause to remember the offence. He was put in the stocks for one hour, with a sample of his bad bread placed before him, and he was then ordered to pay 3s. 4d. to the Corporation, a like sum to the poor of the town, and to give three and fourpence worth of good bread to the prisoners.

A few yards to the east of the Court House in the High Town a second building, also supported on pillars, was erected at the charge of the borough about the year 1608. In this building the court of Nisi Prius was held, the erection of a shed for the purpose being rendered no longer necessary. The two structures were henceforth known respectively as the Upper Court House, and the Lower or old Court House. A sketch of them, made in 1623, and drawn with a pencil on ass's skin, was found about fifty years ago among the papers left by Sir Henry Bosville, of Eynesford, and was first published in Baverstock's "Account of Maidstone." A copy of this sketch is annexed.

By letters patent in 1604, Thomas Milward was appointed keeper of the county prison. In February 1631 the office was granted for life to John Collins, who died in 1644, and by will devised his patent, with all the irons, implements, fees, and appurtenances, to his son of the same name. The old archiepiscopal gaol had previously been granted by the Crown to the Corporation, and was known as the Brambles prison. Attached to this prison was a dwelling house, with a shop, and the Corporation used to let the whole premises on lease for terms of about thirty years. At the close of Elizabeth's reign, Richard Willard, the tenant, paid a rent of £2 per annum; and later, in the reigns of James I. and Charles I., he paid £2 13s. 4d. He was bound to keep the building wind-tight, and was personally responsible for the safe custody of the prisoners.

From the beginning of the seventeenth century the Kent assizes began to be generally held at Maidstone, which, from its central position in the county, was recognised as being more accessible to the public than any other town in Kent. In the reign of James I. the assizes were held thirty-two times at Maidstone, and twelve times at other towns; and during the time of Charles I. and the Commonwealth they were held here fifty-four times, and only seven times elsewhere. There were two gaol deliveries in the course of the year, and after the judges opened their commission at Maidstone, they repaired to All Saints' Church, where a sermon was preached. The sermons delivered on these occasions were frequently ordered to be printed, and many of them are still to be found in private and public collections. The two

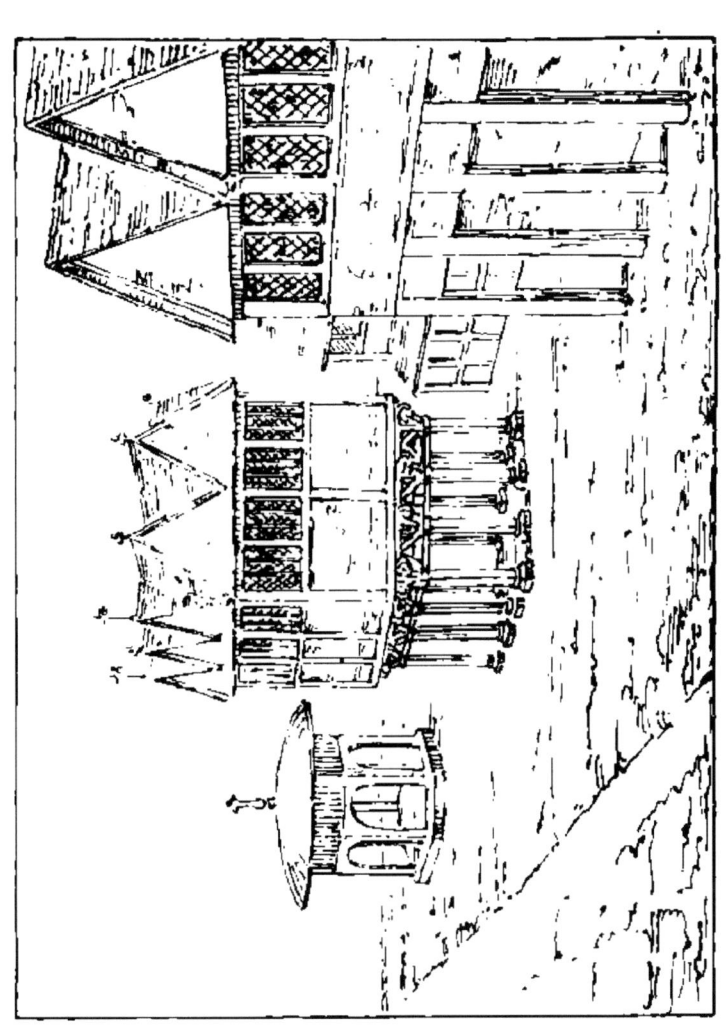

assize sermons for 1638 were preached at Maidstone by Robert Abbot, vicar of Cranbrook. Owing to the agitated state of the county during the civil war, no assizes were held from July 1642 to July 1646, but there were gaol deliveries at Maidstone in 1644 and again in August 1645.

During the seventeenth century the quarter sessions for the western division of Kent were, with few exceptions, also held at Maidstone, in the Lower Court House. At the quarter sessions in May 1650 Thomas Cattel was indicted for setting up in Week Street a "birchen tree, called a Maypole, the same being an unlawful sport." In former times the Maypole had been permanently fixed in the King's Mead, and on May-day merry youths and maidens, with wreaths of flowers suspended from the pole, sang and danced round it in rings. But the Puritans caused the Maypole to be uprooted, and a stop put to these and other festive customs. In 1652 Robert Story, the town watchman, was prosecuted for neglect of duty. Story afterwards showed his contempt for the authorities by destroying the stocks. William French, one of the borsholders, was in the same year fined 6s. 8d., and discharged from his office, for not taking into custody a countryman who was heard to swear. Four men were in 1653 proceeded against at the quarter sessions for "unlawfully playing at and exercising an unlawful, forbidden game called football." Several other persons were included in the indictment, and the presiding justices fined the constables for not taking them into custody.

Quaint Elias Ashmole, in his "Diary," under date of 1652, notes that he went to Maidstone assizes to hear the witches tried, and took Mr. Tradescant with him. Witchcraft was then a capital crime, and the case excited great interest. The prisoners were arraigned before Sir Peter Warburton at the Lower Court House on the 30th of July.

A pamphlet printed at Smithfield in the same year states that two of them confessed to the judge that they had been in communication with the devil, whereupon Anne Ashby, one of the accused, "fell into an extasie before the bench, and swell'd into a monstrous and vast bigness, screeching and crying out very dolefully; and being recovered, and demanded if the devil at that time had possessed her, she replyed she knew not that, but she said that the Spirit Rug came out of her mouth like a mouse." A piece of flesh, which Ashby confessed had been given to them by an evil spirit, was shown to the public at the Swan Inn. It was supposed that nine children, a man and a woman, were bewitched by the prisoners or their associates, besides "£500 worth of cattle lost, and much corn at sea wrecked." Eight or ten of the accused were found guilty, and the "chief actresses," Anne Ashby, alias Cobler, Anne Martyn, Mary Browne, Mildred Wright, and Anne Wilson, all of Cranbrook, and Mary Read, of Lenham, received sentence of death. Sir Robert Filmer, of East Sutton, printed in 1652 a quarto tract, entitled "An Advertisement to the Jurymen of England touching Witches, together with a difference between an English and an Hebrew Witch," in the preface of which he states that "the late execution of witches at the summer assizes in Kent occasioned this brief exercitation, which addresses itselfe to such as have not deliberately thought upon the great difficulty in discovering *what*, or *who* a witch is."

While the summer assizes were being held in 1655, Lees Court, in Kent, the seat of Sir George Sondes, who had been high sheriff of the county in 1637, was the scene of a remarkable tragedy. Sir George had two sons by his first wife. Freeman, the youngest, aged about nineteen, was of a morose disposition, and being envious of his elder brother, whom he regarded as an obstacle to the consummation of his wishes with a young lady to whom he was paying his addresses, he entered his brother's bed-chamber on the night of the 7th of August, and murdered him. He struck him with a cleaver on the head and then stabbed him with a dagger. Next day he was conveyed to Maidstone, and on the 10th he was capitally convicted at the assizes. The execution, at the culprit's request, was postponed to August 21, on which day, attired in mourning, he was carried on horseback to Penenden Heath, two clergymen and many gentlemen attending him. Having dismounted, he stood for more than half an hour while a discourse on the heinousness of his crime was delivered by one of the clergymen; after which a prayer was added, and he then ascended the ladder to the scaffold, and died penitent. The body, after hanging for some time, was put in a coach and conveyed to Bearsted, where it was interred in the church.*

The cage for rogues and vagabonds was in 1654 removed from the Lower Court House to the east end of the bridge. In 1659 the borough chamberlains paid 14s. to a mason for work done in the Brambles, and in 1663 the gaoler was ordered to repair the prison, for which he was allowed half a year's rent. The sum of 83s. was in that year realised from the sale of felons' goods. Every person who was confined in the Brambles had to pay a fee to the keeper on the day of his release. Prisoners, however, were not always able to comply with the gailor's demand, and this was the case with John Stubbs, a Quaker, who, failing to pay the fee on being discharged by the magistrates in 1656, was marched off to a

---

* Sir George Sondes, for his loyalty during the civil war, was in 1676 created Earl of Faversham. By his second wife he had two daughters, one of whom by marriage carried the estate to the Watson family of Northamptonshire.

house of correction in another part of the town.* In August 1666 the stocks were again repaired, for which a carpenter was paid 2s. 4d.

At the assizes in March 1677-8 a poor woman was indicted for witchcraft. Witnesses deposed that she bewitched a young woman who had offended her, and "to make this pretence good there was produced a pint of blood full of nails and crooked pins bow'd into strange forms, all which the witnesses attested the maid had brought up by a vomit." The judge remanded the accused until further inquiries were made. At the same court eight persons were sentenced to death, five for burglary, two for murder, and one for house-burning. The assizes in March 1679-80 lasted four days. James Wattle, grocer, of Maidstone, was acquitted of a charge of murdering his apprentice, a youth of eighteen years; and a man named Bridges was placed before the judge "on suspicion of taking the life of a female child three years of age by tying her in a thin sack and hanging her up in the chimney, and then making a fire of wet straw and other combustible matter, which made a noisome smoke and so smothered her." The prisoner's maid servant, while on a sick-bed, had confessed that this atrocity was perpetrated by her master eighteen years before; and the jury, considering that she was "light headed" at the time of her confession, gave a verdict of manslaughter. Mary Willis and Thomas Ward were ordered to be whipped for stealing several pieces of linen from a hedge near Maidstone; while five men were convicted of felony, and sentenced to be burned in the hand. A man named Field, for stealing two horses, was condemned.

As the population of the town increased, the county

---

* "Robert Marsh, master of Bridewell, buried 3rd March 1691" (Old Style.)—Parish Register.

prison was felt to be a source of annoyance to the inhabitants, and in February 1735 a petition was presented to Parliament stating that the gaol was too small and could not, from its situation, be enlarged, and praying that the justices of the western division might be empowered to purchase a site for the erection of more suitable premises for debtors as well as felons. The prison was a small building, with a flat, battlemented roof, on which the prisoners used to walk and call down to the people in the street. There was no yard in which they could take exercise, and a damp, capacious dungeon occupied the space beneath the ground floor. The father of the late John Newington Hughes remembered when rooms were hired at the corner of Gabriel's Hill to put felons in when the gaol was overflowing. The uppermost of the two houses which then, and for many years after, stood near the top of the High Street, on the west side of the prison, was the residence of the gaoler.*

The sanction of Parliament for the erection of a county prison was obtained in May 1736. A long delay, however, occurred, owing to a difference of opinion between the justices of the eastern and western divisions of Kent, first as to the necessity, and then as to the cost, of a new building, and it was not until 1744 that a site was purchased on the south side of East Lane, and plans were prepared by Mr. C. Sloane, for a felons' and debtors' prison, with yards and keeper's house. The work was completed in 1746, and, much to the satisfaction of the inhabitants, the prisoners in the old gaol were transferred to it in the same year. Being no longer required, the prison in the High Town was then demolished.

* William Shipley, long an inhabitant of the town, who died in 1803, had a thick octavo volume of local MSS. and sketches, including a drawing of the old county prison. It would be interesting to know what became of this volume.

The new prison is shown in the accompanying sketch, the debtors' gaol being the more distant and the felons' gaol the nearer wing, with the keeper's house in the centre; but in order to understand its internal arrangement, a few words of description are necessary. The whole building occupied a space 160ft. long by 156ft. deep, and the front wall was three feet thick, the windows being strengthened, and the light also obstructed, by wooden bars three and a half inches broad. On the first floor of the debtors' gaol there were eight spacious rooms, opening into a lobby 6ft. 2in. wide. Two rooms, each 26ft. by 19ft., were known as the "penniless wards," because each poor debtor who slept therein was charged a penny per week; and two other rooms were used as an infirmary. For male debtors there were two court-yards, one 43ft. by 38ft., and the other 96ft. by 38ft. The female debtors had no court-yard, but only a day room, 13ft. by 10ft. One half of the felons' gaol was reserved for the better class of prisoners, the other for common felons. The former had a day room 16ft. by 13ft., and eight sleeping rooms, two of which fronted the street; besides a court-yard, 42ft. by 18ft. The court-yard for the use of the common felons was 47ft. by 29ft. They had a day room, 15ft. by 12ft., and six sleeping rooms on the ground floor of the average size of 14ft. by 12ft. For the female prisoners there was a court-yard, 18ft. by 12ft., besides a day room 20ft. by 16ft., and two sleeping rooms. There were two dungeons for condemned felons, each 12ft. square, and totally dark, the descent to which was by eleven steps.

By an Act passed in 1741 sheep-stealing was added to the long list of capital crimes. The first person convicted at Maidstone of sheep-stealing was a Cranbrook man by the name of William Pullen; he was executed on Penenden

The County Prisons, King Street.

Heath on the 1st of April 1742. His body was claimed by friends, and conveyed on the back of a horse to Cranbrook, where it was buried in the churchyard within a few feet of the prosecutor's parlour window. This affront to the prosecutor, who had taken a prominent part in parochial affairs, created a great impression in the parish, and he afterwards retired into private life.*

In 1741 the assizes were again removed from Maidstone. They were in that year held for the last time at Canterbury, and then they were taken to Rochester. But after the erection of the commodious prison in East Lane, with all necessary conveniences for the prisoners of the western division, they appear to have been invariably held at Maidstone. Eighteen years later the Lower Court House, and the Brambles prison in the High Street, were pulled down, and the present Town Hall was built, thereby providing better accommodation than had hitherto been afforded for the holding of the assizes. An upper room at the western end of the Town Hall, the walls of which are still marked with the names of prisoners, was thereafter used as the town prison.

Although in that age the new county prison was considered a very creditable institution to the justices of west Kent, yet there was no proper provision for enforcing an effective system of discipline among the prisoners, and the whole management was disfigured by the glaring abuses which then characterised the gaols of England, and which John Howard afterwards did so much to reform. The means were wanting for effectually separating the prisoners, and in consequence scarcely any discrimination of turpitude was observed. Many men were often shut up together. When a stranger was introduced among them he had to pay "garnish," a sort of

---

* Tarbutt's "Annals of Cranbrook Church," pp. 55, 56.

fee to his fellow prisoners, generally fixed at 1s. 6d. to 3s., and if unable to produce the money, he was obliged to part with a portion of his wearing apparel. Prisoners frequently robbed each other, and it is stated that a man once lost ten pounds, while another had a pair of new shoes taken from him. Again, there were no regulations as to the quantity of liquors which debtors might receive, and the proximity of the prison windows to the street afforded a facility of introduction which vigilance often failed to prevent. A sermon was preached to the debtors and felons on alternate Sundays, but for several weeks together there was sometimes no religious service. In the debtors' gaol divine service was performed in a room off the lobby, and in the felons' gaol the chaplain spoke from the landing of the staircase, where few of the male prisoners could either see or hear him. The women prisoners, though some of them were confined here for years at a time, had no religious attention of any kind paid to them.

Under such a loose system of discipline, daring and unscrupulous prisoners found little difficulty in laying secret plans for escape; and this they did, with more or less success, on several occasions. The first and most determined attempt to break out of the felons' gaol was made on the 7th of August 1765. At three o'clock in the afternoon Simon Pingano, Andrew Benevenuto, Samuel Matthews, John Knight, and Thomas Rogers, five prisoners, three of them under sentence of death,[*] were going through the parlour of the gailor, unhandcuffed, to divine service, attended by Stephens, the gailor, with a hanger, a short broad-sword, in his hand, when Pingano, a Genoese, seized the hanger and stabbed Stephens in the stomach. The chaplain, John Denne, incumbent of All Saints', was knocked

---

[*] Knight and Matthews had been condemned for felony, but reprieved.

down and rendered insensible. Possessing themselves of the firearms and cutlasses hanging in the hall, the felons then liberated all the prisoners, knocked off their irons, and forced Holden, the turnkey, to bring them liquors. The town being alarmed, they were fired on from the street, and the fire was returned from the gaol. Fletcher, a publican and breeches maker, was shot through the head as he stood at his own door. At eight o'clock they sallied forth into the town and fired on those who assembled to prevent their escape, wounding several persons. They made way towards Plaxtol, and later in the evening a party of soldiers arrived at Maidstone, and set out in pursuit. Ten of the felons were in a few days retaken in Rove Wood, after a smart engagement, in which Pingano and Benevenuto, the ringleaders, were killed, their dead bodies being brought to the gaol. These two were most desperate fellows, and determined not to be taken alive; and if provided with suitable ammunition, they would probably have sold their lives dearly, but having only slugs cut from an alehouse pot and from an old leaden pump, their fire did little execution.

When the gaol was entered after the escape of the felons, Mr. Denne was found lying under a heap of rubbish in an unconscious condition. Stephens died on the following day. A free pardon was granted to three prisoners who declined to join in the riot, and the remainder of the rioters were tried at a special assize and executed on Penenden Heath in November. During the firing in East Lane, a well-known town character, Tom the Drover, received a wound in the head which permanently deranged his senses, and in the same year he hanged himself in the chimney corner of his lodgings. The shock which Mr. Denne sustained brought on what his brother, Samuel Denne, termed "an intermitting fever of the mind," in which state he continued throughout the last thirty-five years of his life.*

A remarkable instance of the contempt of life often to be found among criminals was exhibited in 1766 by Robert Webber, a prisoner in the felons' gaol. He had been sentenced to death for robbery on board a government ship, but was reprieved. This leniency he did not appreciate, and adopted the novel course of petitioning the Crown that he might be executed. In this petition, which is preserved among the State Papers of the period, he expressed a hope that the laws would not be broken by transporting him, as he neither asked for nor desired a commutation of his sentence. He promised that if his request were granted, he would discover something that would be of great service to his Majesty's subjects. The strong hand of the law was not, however, to be forced, and Webber's life was spared.

At the spring assizes in 1769, Susannah Lott and Benjamin Buss, from East Kent, were convicted of poisoning John Lott, the husband of the first-named prisoner, and condemned. Buss was executed. As the murder of a husband by his wife at that time constituted petty treason, the young woman Lott, on July 22, was drawn on a hurdle to Penenden Heath, and hanged from a peg affixed to a stake; the body was then secured to the stake by a chain, and two hundred faggots were piled round it and set fire to, burning the body to ashes.

John Howard, the philanthropist, in 1776 visited the county prison in East Lane, and the results of his inspection were afterwards published in his general account of the state of prisons in Great Britain and Ireland.† His report states

---

* "Gentleman's Magazine," April 1800.

† Mr. Thomas Pearne, of Loose, has directed my attention to this and several other matters of interest bearing upon the history of Maidstone.

that religious services were held in the prison every Sunday and Wednesday, the chaplain receiving a salary of £50. The debtors had no allowance from the county, and they paid a fee of 12s. 4d. to the gaoler,* and 3s. in "garnish." † The felons were allowed ten chaldrons of coals yearly; each received a loaf weighing 2lb. 4oz. every alternate day, and every day a quart of small beer. They paid 15s. 4d. to the gaoler, and 1s. 6d. in "garnish." ‡ Prisoners about to be transported, in addition to the usual fee, paid 15s., but till their removal they received from the Crown an allowance of 2s. 6d. per week. "The county," says Howard, "has for years past been so considerate as to pay the fees of poor prisoners acquitted." He then gives a table of fees, which may here be condensed as follows:—

	s.	d.
To the gaoler on the discharge of every prisoner for a criminal offence	13	4
To the turnkey on the commitment of every such prisoner	1	0
,, ,, discharge ,, ,,	1	0
To the gaoler on the commitment of every prisoner in a civil action	3	0
,, ,, discharge ,, ,,	7	10
To the turnkey	1	6
For the use of the bedding by the last mentioned prisoners, for the first night	0	6
For every night after the first	0	3
When two such prisoners slept together	0	2

A bridewell, or house of correction, was built on the south side of East Lane, at the expense of the western division of the county, in 1776, several private houses separating it from the felons' gaol. It had a frontage of 60ft., and the eastern boundary wall, which was contiguous to Padsole Lane, was 148ft. in length. There was a day room for male prisoners, 12ft. by 8ft., and also two sleeping rooms, one 22ft. by 16ft.,

---

* The gaoler's salary from the county was £60.

† In 1809 the debtors were allowed three chaldrons of coals yearly; each paid 1s. 2d. per week. There was one room "handsomely furnished for gentlemen debtors," who paid 5s. per week.

‡ Felons on the master's side of the house paid, in 1809, 2s. 6d. per week, and when a prisoner had a room to himself 5s. per week. The female felons who were provided with feather beds paid 2s. 6d. per week; and women who were unable to pay had straw beds in sacking, with two blankets and a rug. The felons were allowed thirteen chaldrons of coals yearly.

and the other 19ft. by 16ft. Their court-yard measured 54ft. by 42ft. An apartment, 15ft. by 12ft., was used as an infirmary. The female prisoners had a day room 8ft. by 7ft., a sleeping room 21ft. by 16ft., an infirmary, and a court-yard 42ft. by 36ft.* A descent of seven steps in this court-yard led to two dungeons, 15ft. by 10ft., and 6ft. 6in. high, in which refractory prisoners were confined. A room above, extending the whole length of the prison, and a lower room, 26ft. by 16ft, were usually let by the keeper to a weaver in the town; and the prisoners, who seldom numbered more than thirty, were occasionally employed in making sacks, beating hemp, and picking oakum.

In the last quarter of the eighteenth century attempts were again made by prisoners to break out of the felons' gaol. Giles, a highwayman, and several other felons, while taking exercise in the court-yard, in January 1776, locked up the keeper and his turnkey in the gaol, and before order could be restored, the keeper was obliged to fire upon them, wounding Giles in the leg. Giles was afterwards convicted before Justice Blackstone of highway robbery, and executed. A plot formed by twelve felons, to effect their escape in July 1786, was timely frustrated by the turnkey. One night in September 1788, James Tyler, assisted by other prisoners, attempted to regain his liberty by cutting away part of a jamb from an upper window in the bridewell. When about to effect his purpose, he was assailed by a furious dog belonging to an adjoining house, which so terrified him that he shrunk from his premeditated descent into the street.

* In 1809 the county allowed fifteen chaldrons of coals yearly for the keeper's house and prison. Fees:—Felons, 13s. 4d.; misdemeanours, 6s. 8d.; faulty servants, 4s. 6d.; garnish, 2s. Prisoners who worked were each supplied with five quartern loaves per week, and those who did not work each received a half-quartern loaf every alternate day. When the women's infirmary was not occupied by the sick, the barrack beds with which it was provided were furnished with bedding for those who could pay 2s. 4d. per week.

Eventually the barking alarmed the keeper, who entered the room and secured Tyler.*

In those days there were few newspapers to waft the news of passing events to every town, hamlet, and cottage; and no newspaper was printed in Maidstone until 1786, if we except a small sheet, of four quarto pages, called the *Maidstone Mercury*, which was published for a short time in 1725. Accounts of the more sensational criminal trials at the Kent Assizes were generally issued from the press as pamphlets, which were hawked about the country by chapmen or pedlars, and sold to a class who unfortunately were unable to obtain a healthier description of mental sustenance. The titles of a few of these chap-books will sufficiently indicate their contents :—

"A Genuine Narrative of the Life and Surprising Adventures of William Page, who was Executed on Penenden Heath, near Maidstone, on the 6th April, 1758, for Robbing Capt. Farrington near Blackheath," with a portrait and a folding plate of the execution.

"Authentick Memoirs of the Wicked Life and Dying Words of the late John Collington, of Throwleigh, who was executed on Saturday, April 7, 1750, at Maidstone, for maliciously hiring John Stone and William Luckhurst to set fire to the barn and ricks of John Clarke."

"The Trial at large of Joseph Stackpoole, Esq., William Gapper, attorney at law, and James Lagier, for shooting John Parker, Esq., at the Assizes held at Maidstone, March 30, 1777; taken in Shorthand Notes by John Gurney."

"The trial of Arthur O'Connor, Esq., John Binns, John Allen, Jeremiah Leary, and James Coigley, for High Treason, under a Special Commission at Maidstone, April 11, 1798."

"Observations on the Trial of James O'Coigley for High Treason, together with an Account of his Death, including his Address to the spectators, and other documents connected with the Trial."

"Life of James O'Coigley, Observations upon his Trial, an Address to the people of Ireland, and several Interesting Letters written by himself during his confinement in Maidstone Gaol."

"Elegaic Stanzas on the Death of James O'Coigley, an Invaluable Patriot, executed on Penenden Heath, on Thursday, June 7, 1798, for High Treason."

---

* See also "Annual Register." vol. xxxiv., p. 41.

The trial in 1798 of O'Connor and O'Coigley, with their companions, attracted the attention of the country to Maidstone. O'Connor, who was nephew to Viscount Longueville, was the proprietor of a Dublin newspaper, and had for some time been a marked man among the Irish disaffected. It was known in the early spring of 1798 that he and O'Coigley, who was called the priest of Dundalk, were proceeding to the south-east coast of Kent, evidently with the intention of crossing the Channel, and as they were suspected of seeking to convey to the French revolutionary government treasonable communications from the notorious London Corresponding Society, an urgent order for their apprehension was secretly issued by the government at Westminster. It was expedient that the constables should be under the supervision of some one of experience, resolution, and keenness to preclude tampering. Lord Romney, the lord lieutenant, was appealed to, and recommended Mr. William Twopeny, of Rochester, a solicitor of high standing, who accepted the commission. It is said that with the warrant for the arrest of the party in his pocket, he attended a meet of foxhounds, and thence rode off on his errand, and that a portrait of O'Coigley, who alone was known, had been supplied for identification. The Irishmen had reached Whitstable by water, incurred suspicion there, and shifted their quarters to Margate, where they, and their three companions above-named, were captured. This well-executed and honorary duty performed by Mr. Twopeny aroused among a certain class a feeling of violent animosity, and there was so much fear of an attempt to assassinate him that for many weeks after he carried a loaded pistol in his pocket.

The prisoners were conveyed to London on the 1st of March. On the 6th they were examined before the Privy Council, and lodged in the Tower on a charge of high treason, a special commission being issued for their trial at Maidstone. The next day they were conveyed in five postchaises to the county prison in East Lane, a party of Light Dragoons escorting them to Farningham, whence they were accompanied during the remainder of the journey by a corps of Yeomanry Cavalry. On the afternoon of April 10, the commission was opened at the Town Hall by Justices Buller, Heath, and Lawrence, the recorder of London, and four serjeants-at-law. The court met again on the 11th and 12th, when Justice Buller announced that the grand jury had found a true bill against the prisoners, and that in order to give them time to bring their witnesses from Ireland, the court would be adjourned to the end of the month. A few days later the guard at the prison was strengthened owing to one of the prisoners having offered an under-turnkey a bribe of a thousand pounds to permit his escape to France. The witnesses from Ireland not having arrived by the 30th of April, the court was further adjourned to the 21st of May.

On that day, at seven o'clock, the trial opened. It had roused general attention throughout the country. The entrance to the court and its approaches were thronged with jurymen, witnesses, and spectators, and the leading Whigs—peers and commoners—were present from London as the friends of O'Connor. The Town Hall had never before, and has never since, held within its walls at one time such a muster of eminent men. With the Duke of Bedford and the Duke of Norfolk sat Charles James Fox and Richard Brinsley Sheridan, "the English Demosthenes and the English Hyperides." Charles Grey, afterwards head of the government which carried the Reform Bill, was there; the impetuous Erskine, the future Lord Chancellor; Sir Francis Burdett, the most popular politician of his time. Side by side with Whitbread, the opulent and voluble, stood the caustic Tierney, who a few days later fought a duel with Pitt. There too was Grattan, the most eloquent member of the Irish Parliament—

With all that Demosthenes wanted, endowed,
And his rival and master in all he possessed.

Among men of lesser eminence were Lord John Russell and Lord Moira, afterwards Minister of War; Roger O'Connor, brother to the accused, and the Earls of Lauderdale, Thanet, Oxford, Suffolk, Egremont, and Guilford. Many of these distinguished visitors had rooms at Mr. Hyde's, formerly the Rose Inn, which became, as it were, the head-quarters of O'Connor's friends, while others were lodged in Stone Street by James Smyth, father of Clement Taylor Smythe.

Three hours and a half elapsed before the jury was chosen, as the Crown challenged twenty-five names, and the prisoners the full number allowed by law. Mr. Abbott stated the case on behalf of the Crown, and the Attorney-General* detailed the whole of the circumstances. Mr. Plomer, counsel for O'Connor and O'Coigley, opened the defence in a speech which lasted four hours and a half. The court adjourned at midnight, and met again at eight next morning, when the examination of witnesses, which had commenced on the previous day, was continued. The entrance to the Town Hall was guarded by a company of the Maidstone Volunteers, in command of Thomas Robert and Finch Hollingworth, and excited crowds again surrounded the approaches. Fox, Sheridan, Grattan, Whitbread, the Duke of Norfolk, Lord Russell, and the Earls of Thanet, Suffolk, and Oxford successively went into the witness-box and bore testimony to the high character of O'Connor, Erskine speaking of him as a man of the "strictest honour and integrity." It was long past midnight when the addresses of counsel and judge were

---

* Sir J. Scott, afterwards Lord Eldon.

concluded. The jurymen were then conducted to a house in the High Street (now No. 28), where they were locked up for forty minutes, at the end of which time they returned to the court and declared that they had found O'Coigley guilty and the other four prisoners not guilty. Justice Buller had anticipated the excitement of the closing scene by preparing beforehand a short address, and this having been read to O'Coigley, sentence of death was passed.

Scarcely had the last words of the judge been spoken, when many of the candles were extinguished, and O'Connor leaped over the bar where he had been standing, and darted towards the door. The Metropolitan constables present rushed after him, but were impeded by several of O'Connor's friends, who purposely stood in their way. Two swords which were lying on the table—part of the prisoners' luggage—were seized and drawn from their scabbards, and in the scramble several persons were struck by the constables. Lord Thanet exclaimed, " 'Tis but fair to let him have a run for it," and pursued and struck one of the constables, who returned the blow with his staff. Robert Fergusson, one of the barristers, in his wig and gown, brandished a stick; and Sheridan got upon the table and asked the bench if O'Connor was not to be discharged. Meanwhile O'Connor had reached the door of the court, which was twice closed against him. At the street door stood Captain T. R. Hollingworth, who threatened to run his sword through the first man who should try to force his way out. By this time O'Connor had been secured, and was dragged back to the bar. When silence was restored, he appealed to the bench for protection, and wished to know why, having been acquitted, he was not allowed to leave the court. To the surprise of many of the spectators, a warrant was then produced by the London constables for the arrest of O'Connor on a further charge of high treason. His counsel, with much warmth, objected to his being tried a second time on the same charge. Justice Buller replied that the bench had no power in the matter. O'Connor begged to speak. "Will the officers," he cried, "take their hands off. My lords, I am surrounded with drawn swords. I am prepared to die. It would be better for the court to doom me to death at once than that I should linger out my life in a gaol." To this the bench made no reply, but ordered the gaoler to take back all the prisoners to East Lane. To keep off the crowd in conveying them to the prison, the Volunteers moved in square, faces outwards, and on Captain T. R. Hollingworth exclaiming to one of the leaders of the mob that he should want him on the morrow, resistance ceased and the excitement gradually subsided.

If O'Connor had succeeded in his attempt to escape from the court, he would have found the means at hand to facilitate his subsequent movements. A postchaise and four was in waiting near the Town Hall to carry him off; there was also a relay of horses to Dover, and a boat there in readiness to cross the Channel. This plan, however, was frustrated. On the third day after the trial, O'Connor was conveyed to London under a guard of Light Dragoons, and afterwards removed to Ireland.* His ill-starred companion, O'Coigley, was, in the forenoon of the 7th of June, placed on a hurdle drawn by two horses, and escorted to Penenden Heath by a company of the Maidstone Volunteers. At the gallows he was brave as a patriot. Taking an orange and a penknife from his pocket, he handed them to an onlooker, and asked

* He was subsequently tried and sent to Fort George, in Scotland. After his liberation in 1802, he withdrew to Hamburg. He married a daughter of Condorcet, the French republican, and took that name, with, however, the aristocratic *de*. Persistent in his political opinions to the last, he appeared in 1847 presiding over a meeting to further electoral reform in the ferment which preceded the expulsion of Louis Philippe. He held the rank of general in the French army, and died near Montargis, April 25, 1852.

him to cut the fruit in order to publicly disprove certain rumours which attributed to him an intention to commit suicide. "I would not," he added, "deprive myself of dying in this manner for my country." He then stepped upon the drop, and in a few minutes all was over. The head was severed from the body by Coleman, a Maidstone surgeon, and the executioner held it up to the spectators, saying, "This is the head of a traitor."

Lord Thanet, Robert Fergusson, Dennis O'Brien, Thomas Thompson, formerly a member of Parliament, and Thomas Carter Brown were, on April 25, 1799, tried at the Court of King's Bench for taking part in the attempted rescue of O'Connor. Thanet and Fergusson were found guilty, and on the 10th of June were each sentenced to a year's imprisonment in the Tower, his lordship being also fined £1,000, and Fergusson £100. They were released on the 10th of June 1800, and the next day, while proceeding to his seat at Hothfield, Lord Thanet was met by his admirers near Maidstone, and drawn through the town in his carriage, accompanied by a band of music, and upwards of a hundred gentlemen on horseback.

Penenden Heath then occupied about thirty acres of ground, on the south side of which stood the gallows. Not a year passed but malefactors were brought to the heath to expiate their crimes with their lives. The criminal code was savage and ruthless in its operation. It appears to have been moulded on the dictum of Justice Heath, who held that there was no hope of regenerating a felon in this life, and as his continued existence would merely diffuse a corrupting influence, it was better for his own sake as well as for society that he should be executed.

At the spring assizes in 1786 twenty-four prisoners were sentenced to death, but in the exercise of a privilege which at that time belonged to him, the judge respited thirteen before leaving the town. In March 1801 as many as thirty-seven prisoners were condemned, for the following crimes:—Two for murder, six for burglaries, eleven for highway robberies, six for felonies, eight for horse-stealing, one for stealing a cow, one for returning from transporation, and two for sheep-stealing. Eighteen were reprieved, and the remaining nineteen were executed, fifteen on Penenden Heath, and four at Shooter's Hill. Culprits were executed on the second day after their conviction, and in the brief interval they were fed on bread and water, no one being allowed to visit them except the gaoler, the chaplain, or the surgeon. They were often conveyed in batches at a time to the heath. Heavily ironed, they were placed in a two-wheeled cart at the gaol, and the vehicle proceeded along the streets guarded by men armed with blunderbusses and halberds, and attended by the gaoler, the chaplain, and the under-sheriff and his officers carrying black wands. The following table shows the number of prisoners who were sentenced to death at the Kent assizes, and how many of such sentences were actually carried out, between the years 1791 and 1810:—

Year.	Spring Assizes.		Summer Assizes.	
	Prisoners Sentenced to Death.	Prisoners Executed.	Prisoners Sentenced to Death.	Prisoners Executed.
1791	4	1	7	3
1792	6	1	9	5
1793	17	5	7	3
1794	8	0	4	2
1795	4	1	1	0
1796	6	1	4	2
1797	15	3	6	2
1798	17	6	5	1
1799	9	3	10	3
1800	18	4	8	5
1801	37	19	10	3
1802	23	6	18	3
1803	13	4	4	2

	Spring Assizes.		Summer Assizes.	
Year.	Prisoners Sentenced to Death.	Prisoners Executed.	Prisoners Sentenced to Death.	Prisoners Executed.
1804	8	3	2	0
1805	20	8	12	7
1806	5	4	6	0
1807	11	5	7	0
1808	12	4	6	3
1809	19	4	8	0
1810	13	4	6	0

One of the persons executed in 1805 was "John Carpenter, alias Hell-Fire Jack, the noted horse stealer," who was a native of Tunbridge Wells. The smugglers had no better friend than Jack, and for a glass of gin or a small gratuity he was always ready to retake, on the highway or in the stable, any horse which the Excise officers might have seized. Knowing every by-road in Kent, he could generally elude the vigilance of the constables; but in 1788 he was captured, and sent for seven years to Botany Bay. At the end of that time he returned to his native county, and renewed his favourite pastime. In the autumn of 1804 he was apprehended for stealing two horses, and condemned at the next spring assizes. He was executed on April 4, 1805. On his way to Penenden Heath he had a flower in his coat, and when passing a butcher's shop he called to the butcher to save a joint for him. Jack confessed while in prison that he had stolen altogether about seventy horses.

Other methods of public punishment were still in vogue at the beginning of the present century. The pillory formerly stood at the top of the High Street, near the Market Cross, but in 1771 the Corporation ordered it to be taken down. It was afterwards set up in the High Street when wanted, at first near the top of the street, and latterly at a spot a few yards to the north-east of the Town Hall. The person whose misfortune it was to undergo this very public form of chastisement was brought from the gaol at noon, and exposed in the pillory usually for one hour at a time, during which, he was often freely pelted with offal and rotten eggs. The last persons who are remembered to have stood in the pillory were two men who, in the first decade of the present century, had assisted French prisoners of war to escape while on parole.

A whipping-post for the flagellation of thieves and vagrants was to be seen in the High Street, about eighty years ago; this was removed probably when the old butter market was erected at the lower end of the Middle Row. Until about the year 1812 the punishment of whipping was often inflicted. Thirteen prisoners were ordered to be whipped at the spring assizes in 1800; ten, five publicly and five privately, in 1804; nine in 1810, and three at the summer assizes in 1811. The punishment was generally administered at the place where the offence was committed. When this happened at Maidstone, the delinquent was tied to one of the pillars of the old corn market, and the lashes were applied by a turnkey from the felons' gaol in King Street. At the assizes in 1811 a man was ordered to be "whipped fifty yards at Maidstone" for entering a house and stealing a tea-kettle, and a like sentence was passed upon a prisoner at the quarter sessions in 1812. In these cases the offender was stripped from the waist and tied to the tailboard of a cart, which was drawn slowly along the High Street, from Diprose's Passage to the Rose Yard, while the stripes were being firmly laid on by the turnkey. An old inhabitant once saw as many as four prisoners whipped together at the cart's-tail, and on another occasion he saw a woman and a man with a wooden leg put through the ordeal. The whipping of female prisoners, whose offences merited this shameful degradation, was, however, usually conducted in private. The stocks,

Hunter's House.

which had stood in various parts of the town, were done away with about sixty years ago.

At the spring assizes in 1801 there were 137 prisoners for trial, the largest number that had ever been tried, up to that time, at one assize. This number has since been greatly exceeded. In 1803 it was found necessary to hold a third court at the Unitarian chapel in Market Street. The gaol calendar at the assizes in March 1817 contained the names of 162 prisoners; and in March 1818 there were 180 prisoners for trial. On the latter occasion two judges sat, as usual, at the Town Hall; they were relieved on several evenings by two serjeants-at-law, and a third court was held at the Baptist meeting-house in the Rose Yard. At the spring assizes in 1822 there were 185 prisoners for trial, and fifty-two of them were sentenced to death, but only five were executed. On that occasion, as well as in March of the previous year, a third court was again held at the Baptist chapel. The first winter assizes for Kent were held in December 1822, when 123 prisoners were tried, the total number of prisoners tried at the three assizes in that year being 366. In 1824 there were 328 prisoners for trial. The summer assizes in 1823 lasted thirteen days, and in 1826 ten days, owing in each instance to a press of civil business. About the year 1850 upwards of 220 prisoners were tried at one assize.

The Town Hall premises did not afford sufficient accommodation for the judges and the grand jury at assize times. From one of the upper windows a temporary bridge or covered way was shot out across Bank Street to the drawing-room window of an adjacent building—called, in the illustrations to this work, "Hunter's House"—whither the judge of the Nisi Prius court retired, and the judge of the Crown court had a retiring room in the old house, formerly the Ball tavern, which adjoined the west end of the Town Hall. The grand jury met at the Bell Hotel, their bills being carried to the Crown court by messengers. The street was littered with straw to deaden the noise of traffic; and the prisoners, chained together for security, were brought from the gaol in King Street and lodged in a temporary timber building which was put up at the entrance to the lower court.

The steady pressure of assize business had forced upon the attention of the county and borough authorities the subject of the amount of prison accommodation in Maidstone. This accommodation had become quite inadequate to the wants of the time. The Corporation found that an upper room at the Town Hall was unsuited for a prison. Through two round windows in this room prisoners could shout to their friends in the street; and in 1798 a woman who was confined here had a singular adventure. At two o'clock in the morning of the 12th of August in that year she endeavoured to escape by getting out on to the roof of the prison. She dropped down upon the roof of the adjoining house, and thence on to the pavement, a distance of about sixty feet; but the crash led to her capture, when it was found that, though much bruised, none of her bones were broken.* In 1807 the Corporation erected a small building at the back of the old workhouse for the reception of the town prisoners, and some years later a watch-house for the confinement of vagrants and petty offenders was built at the east end of the bridge.

In October 1810 the county justices purchased fifteen acres of land at the north end of Week Street for the erection of a county prison, to accommodate about four hundred prisoners. Estimates were obtained for the same, amounting to £150,000, and the building was commenced in 1812. The work proceeded slowly, and the actual cost exceeded the

---
* "Annual Register," vol. xl.

estimate by nearly £20,000, in addition to £11,000 paid for the land. On the 8th of March 1819 the prisoners, to the number of 141, were removed from the felons' and debtors' gaols in King Street to the new prison; and in October of that year the old gaols were sold by auction for £2,300, and the bridewell from which the prisoners were removed in November for £800. The Corporation soon after entered into an arrangement with the county whereby the prisoners belonging to the borough were also committed to the new prison. The court house, with its spacious facade, was erected in front of the prison in 1826-7, at an outlay of £40,000, and in December 1827 the assizes were held in the new building.

In the last quarter of the eighteenth century the sheriff's monthly county court—the relic of the mediæval shiremote—continued to be held in "a poor low shed," as Hasted describes it, on the north side of Penenden Heath. Here the poll at the election of coroners and members of Parliament for the county was also taken. Towards the end of the last century, however, it became customary, after polling a few votes on the heath, to allow the remainder to be recorded at Maidstone; and at length the polling on the heath was done away with entirely, the nominations only taking place there. In 1830 the old shed was taken down, and a small stone house of one room was built. The greater part of the heath, consisting of twenty-seven acres, was enclosed in 1816, and granted, by the lord of the manor's permission, to Maidstone for the employment of the poor.* It proved, however, not to answer the purpose of the Trustees of the Poor to cultivate the heath at the parish expense, and in 1824 the land was sold, the money it produced—£1,700—being voted

---

* About the same time forty-eight acres of Barming Hoath were granted for the same purpose.

by vestry towards the building of Holy Trinity Church. The whole aspect of the heath was subsequently altered by the planting of trees, and by the removal of quantities of sand for the building of the county prison and court house. During the latter operation upwards of three hundred human skeletons were found. Having been disused for many years, the small stone building, euphemistically called the "shire house," was taken away in 1877. The remaining portion of the heath had previously become a common resort of gipsies; and in 1881 the Local Board obtained permission to enclose it as a recreation ground for the town.

The last execution on Penenden Heath was in December 1830, when three young men were hanged for setting fire to some farm property. In August 1831 a poor ignorant boy named John Any Bird Bell, aged fifteen, was executed at Maidstone for the murder of Richard Taylor, aged thirteen, in a wood near Rochester. This was the first execution in front of the county prison, the gallows being erected at the side of the porter's lodge. It had been customary, in the case of soldiers who were capitally convicted, to execute them at the head-quarters of their regiment as a warning to their comrades. The last person thus executed was Benjamin Gardiner, a private in the 50th Regiment, who, in July 1834, was hanged on Chatham Lines for the murder of a sergeant in the same regiment. Altogether, two women and twenty-six men forfeited their lives in front of the county prison, six of them for robbery and similar crimes, and the others for murder. The first execution within the walls of the prison was in August 1868, and up to August 1881 twelve criminals had been privately executed at Maidstone.

CHAPTER XIII.

TRADE OF THE TOWN.

Kentish Ragstone—The Walloon Settlers in Maidstone—Manufacture of Cloth and Linen Thread—Early Cultivation of Hops—The Medway Traffic—Municipal Survey of the River—Issue of Tokens—Wages in 1698—General Trade of the Town—Hop-growing and Hop-picking—Fruit Cultivation—Brewing and Distilling—Paper-making—Fairs and Markets—Market Buildings.

LIKE the town itself, the trade of Maidstone is not a thing of recent growth. In mediæval times Maidstone was famous for its valuable deposits of ragstone. The stone quarried in the neighbourhood was sought after not only for building purposes, but for conversion into terrible missiles of war. With the shot formed from the rough slabs unearthed in the valley of the Medway the walls of many a hostile fortress were doubtless razed, and the gallant Prince Hal was enabled to gain his triumphs in the fields of France. Long despised as an "unwholesome" and "wicked" weed, the hop at length fairly established itself in the good opinion of our forefathers, and while cherry and apple orchards were shedding their blossoms in the light winds of spring, the hop-poles were bristling on the rolling uplands which environ the town. Contemporary probably with the general cultivation of hops, malt-houses were built, and thus was founded that remunerative and expansive brewing trade which has since constituted one of the leading local industries. In Elizabeth's reign the Walloons, flying from the persecution of Philip of Spain, settled in Maidstone, and commenced the linen and woollen manufactures which for many years flourished here. When that textile industry began to decline, another straightway rose up to occupy its place, and the Len and the Loose streams were skilfully turned to account in the making of paper. The Medway too had been rendered navigable, and hoys and barges glided through its glittering windings, freighted with stone, hops, linen thread, paper, and beer for the London market.

In the middle of the thirteenth century a market was granted to Maidstone, and in 1495 the standard of weights and measures for Kent was ordered to be kept here. The stone quarries no doubt gave employment to a large number of the labouring class. Kentish ragstone was extensively used. Newgate gaol was in 1282 repaired with stone from the Maidstone quarries. John Louth and John Bennett owned quarries here in the beginning of the fifteenth century; and in 1418 they received an order from the Crown for seven thousand cannon balls, for which there was stated to be a sufficient supply of stone at Maidstone and elsewhere. Stone from this neighbourhood was largely employed in the fortification of Calais in 1541, the quantity conveyed from Maidstone each month during the progress of the works, costing £42.[*] Its enduring qualities then obtained for it the name of "hardstone;" it is called "freestone" by Kilburne and other old writers, but from its breaking in a ragged or rough manner, it has long been universally known as ragstone.

---

[*] "Chronicle of Calais," published by the Camden Society.

The cruel measures which Philip II. adopted towards the Walloons, or trading people of the Low Countries, had an important effect upon the trade of Maidstone. At different times parties of the Walloons had emigrated to England; but the great influx was in the year 1567, when Philip's celebrated general, the Duke of Alva, with a large army, invaded the Netherlands, and thousands of the industrial classes, with their money and goods, fled to this country. The Mayor and Jurates of Maidstone, in June 1567, petitioned the Crown to allow them to receive a number of these refugees, or, as they were called, " Dutch artificers with their families," who intended to establish their manufactures in the town ; and on the 21st of July the royal sanction was obtained.

Two hundred years before this time Flemish and other foreign cloth-workers had settled in the Weald of Kent, and soon after Elizabeth came to the throne nearly twelve thousand pieces of broad-cloth were annually manufactured in the county, each piece being about thirty yards long, seven quarters in breadth, and weighing eighty-four pounds. The Walloons, by their plodding habits, conduced materially to the prosperity of Maidstone. They took kindly to English ways and customs, and the Corporation allowed them to worship in St. Faith's chapel. They hired houses for their looms, and gave employment to many of the poor inhabitants. Flax was spun by the common people, and made into thread by skilled workmen, while large quantities of broad-cloth, grogram, sackcloth, and baize were woven, and sold at the fairs held during the year. On all such stuffs manufactured by the aliens a duty was levied. In August 1568 the Corporation directed that "all manner of whole pieces and half pieces of grogredgns, sackcloths, woollen cloth, and such like wares, made and wrought in Maidstone by the

Doche people or other strangers born, not being English people, shall be fetched, and from time to time from henceforth, before the same be put to sale." Each piece of cloth was examined by the town officials and sealed with lead. The duty was fourpence a piece on all cloth, except sackcloth, which paid a penny per piece.

Queen Elizabeth, by a letter of license issued apparently in 1573, solicited a favourable reception for the refugees. It is probable that another party of Walloons intended to settle in the town in that year, or the royal license may have been merely a confirmation of protection previously granted. This document is as follows :—

<small>To all our Justices, Officers, Ministers, and Subjects, greeting. Know ye that, for divers special considerations us moving, as well for the help, repair, and amendment of our town of Maidstone, in our county of Kent, by planting in the same men of knowledge in sundry handicrafts, as also for the relief and convenient placing of certain Dutch men, aliens, now residing within our city of London, and elsewhere within our realm of England, being very skilful in divers occupations, arts, handicrafts, and faculties, we may lend to the commodity of our realm, and, namely, for the relief of our said town of Maidstone.—We of, etc., ELIZABETH.</small>

In 1585 there were in the town about a hundred and twenty of these Dutch settlers who were over twenty-one years of age. Under James I. they were no longer aliens, but had all been born in Maidstone, or in this country. The duty was therefore reduced to twopence on every piece of fustian, grogram, linsey-woolsey, baize, and diaper.

The cloth weavers were no doubt members of the guild of drapers in the town. It was then customary for the workers in each trade to form themselves into a guild or company for the protection of their individual interests. A stranger had to be admitted to membership before he was allowed to practice his craft. In the reign of Elizabeth there were five guilds in Maidstone, viz., the artificers, the victuallers, the drapers, the mercers, and the cordwainers. Stephen Norton, of a family anciently seated at Norton Place, Chart Sutton, belonged to the Maidstone guild of artificers in 1474. It was probably his son, of the same name, who was a noted bell-founder in the time of Henry VII. and Henry VIII., and who was buried in All Saints' Church. A bell, with his name upon it, still hangs in the church tower of Chiselborough, in Somerset. Each guild had its own rules and customs; its wares were exhibited at the markets and fairs, and the fees for the stalls were paid over by its officers to the Corporation. Canon W. A. Scott Robertson states that in the time of James I. the Michaelmas Fair was sometimes called the Runt Fair, and as it was held on St. Faith's Day, October 6, it was likewise called St. Faith's Fair. Candlemas Fair was held on the 2nd of February, May Fair on May-day, and Midsummer or Garlick Fair on the 9th of June.

In Elizabeth's reign lads were indentured for long terms of apprenticeship. Thus in 1594 a boy named Francis Gilman was, by order of the mayor of Maidstone, bound for twelve years to William Butler, weaver, of Malling. In consideration of his being "small of stature," the parents of the youth paid a premium of 30s., and Butler covenanted to "give unto his said apprentice two pence a quarter during five of the last years, and in the end of the said term of twelve years two suits of apparel, whereof the one to be for holydays and the other for working days, meet and convenient for such an apprentice."

The Walloons introduced into Kent the woollen and silk manufactures, and the art of dyeing. There can be little doubt that the earlier settlers in the reign of Henry VIII. also imported the hop into this county, and, in course of time, fairly established its cultivation. Before this result could be accomplished, however, much prejudice had to be overcome. The hop was regarded as a plant unfit, in any form, for human consumption. In 1426 an information was laid against a person for putting into beer "an unwholesome weed called an hopp," and not long after Parliament was petitioned against "that wicked weed called hops." A decree was published about the year 1524 forbidding the use of hops in bittering beer because they tended to "make people melancholy"—a quiet hint at their narcotic effect. Thirty years later their cultivation was sanctioned by the Legislature; but public opinion was still in some measure opposed to them, and in the reign of James I. their use was petitioned against and nominally condemned. Their value, however, was being generally recognised, and within the next few years the public taste appears to have become fully reconciled to the strange innovation. Tradition avers that the hop was first successfully cultivated in the neighbourhood of Maidstone. However that may be, it is certain that hop-farming was extensively carried on here in the first half of the seventeenth century, and frequent allusion is made to the hop gardens of Maidstone in records of Charles the First's reign.

Heavy goods were conveyed from Maidstone to London by river. We get some idea of the slender origin of the Medway carrying trade from a return prepared by order of the Crown in 1565. There were in that year four hoys belonging to the town, one of fifty tons, and the others of forty, thirty, and twenty-two tons respectively, the number of persons employed in connection with them being twenty-two. Of the four wharfs then existing, one was at the bottom of St. Faith's Street, and was known, some years later, as the "Towne Wharf." So considerable had the trade become in the reign of James I. that in the borough Charter granted in 1619 the Corporation was empowered to levy tolls for "wharfage, anchorage, and groundage of all and singular ships and other vessels" coming to the town.

Hoys were in those days navigated under difficulties of

which the present traders on the Medway have little conception. The banks of the river were broken and irregular to a far greater extent than they are now, and in the absence of any scheme for "penning" up the water, the movements of vessels depended entirely upon the state of the tide. The disadvantages obviously accruing to the public from this primitive state of things were brought to the notice of Parliament in 1628, when an Act was passed for improving the condition of the river. A second Act was passed by the Parliament of 1661-4, giving power to erect locks on the Medway, and to deepen it and construct a towing-path or horseway, in order to facilitate the carriage of iron ordnance, balls, timber, wood, corn, stone, hay, hops, wool, leather, &c. Fourteen landed proprietors in Kent and twelve in Sussex were appointed to act as Commissioners to superintend the carrying out of these improvements within seven years from the 1st of June 1668, and to levy rates for the carriage of goods, which rates, it was provided, were not to exceed two-third parts of the rate for land carriage from the beginning of April to the end of October, or one half the rate for land carriage from the 1st of November to the 31st of March. Acts of Parliament for the better navigation of the river were also passed in the reigns of Charles II. and George II.

In his position as "conservator" of the river between East Farleigh bridge and Hawkwood, the mayor of Maidstone held annually a Court of Survey. For this purpose he issued a warrant to the bailiffs of the court, directing them to warn seventeen "good and lawful" parishioners to appear before him, "to make a certain jury to enquire of and upon all and every such articles, matters, and things" as should be "given them in charge touching the conservation of the said river." The court usually met at six in the morning, and forthwith proceeded to survey the river, taking note of all owners and occupiers of land whose neglect caused any obstacle to the navigation. During the excursion the mayor entertained the jurors in good style, and a sum of money was allowed by the Corporation towards the day's expenses. In due time the mayor issued his precept to the constable and borsholders requiring them to give notice to all offenders to remove the obstructions before a fixed day, failing which they were summoned to appear at the quarter sessions.

A meat market was held every Thursday at the Market Cross, which stood at the top of the High Town. The Market Cross was an octagonal structure, with a dome-like roof, surmounted by a leaden cross, and supported upon light arches of woodwork, in the spandrels of which were curious carvings representing the killing of an ox and other characteristics of the butcher's occupation. Between the Market Cross and the county gaol were the shambles, which were in 1626 bought by the Corporation from Ambrose Beale, of London, for 6s. In 1612 the town butchers gave offence to the Corporation by carrying on their business during church hours on Sunday, and it was then ordered that they might "keep their shop doors open till eight in the morning, and after evening prayer on Sundays, and not otherwise." The country butchers in 1629 complained to the Corporation that "by reason of the market being kept so late in winter they were forced to travel the greater part of the night, to their great trouble, and many times in danger of being robbed and spoiled." They desired that the market bell should be rung at four p.m. in winter and in summer at six p.m., and that all meat which was offered for sale after these hours should be forfeited. This request was granted, and the bell was ordered to be rung from Hollandtide to Shrovetide at four o'clock.

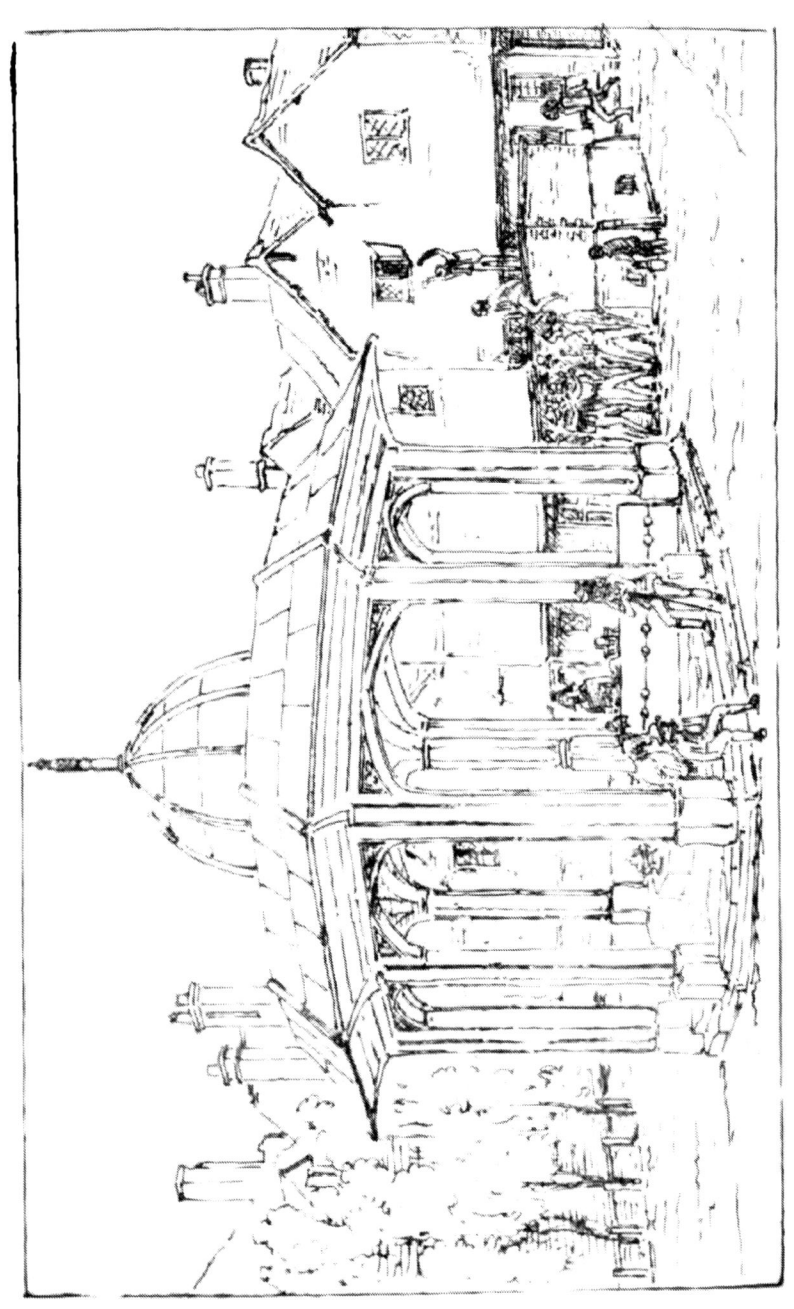

We will now return to the history of the cloth trade. During the reign of James I. many looms were at work in the town. Each loom in which broad-cloth was woven required two men and one quil-winder, and in the course of a week used up ninety pounds of wool, which eighteen women were employed to spin. Several looms for the weaving of narrow cloth were also at work in Maidstone; and in later times, when the trade began to decline, calamancos, camblets, cloth-serges, and cloth for gowns, were manufactured in these looms. But in the first half of the seventeenth century the weavers, who were paid 6s. to 7s. per week, were chiefly employed in the weaving of broadcloth.

When the cloth left the loom it was pressed and cleansed. Toulmin Smith says that this was anciently done by laying the cloth in long troughs filled with water and trampling it with the feet. The line of troughs was called a walk or *walche*, and the person who trampled to and fro was a walker; hence the surname Walker, which, like the familiar names of Smith, Bowyer, and Fisher, had its origin in trade and occupation. A more expeditious process was found through the invention of the fulling mill, which resembled a corn mill, except in what related to the mill stones and hopper. There were several of these mills in the neighbourhood of Maidstone, on the Len and Loose streams, towards the end of Queen Elizabeth's reign. When there was a scarcity of water in the Weald during dry seasons, large quantities of the cloth manufactured there were brought to the fulling mills here by pack-horses.

The process of fulling was simple enough. The cloth to be felted was laid in the troughs of the mill, and a current of water being passed over the wheel, the mallets by their weight and velocity stamped and pressed the cloth, thereby cleansing and rendering it firm and compact. In this operation fuller's earth, with some proportion of soap, was employed to scour the cloth, and remove the oil used in the spinning of the wool and the size added to the warp. Soap alone would have done much better, but it was dearer than fuller's earth, a mineral with a remarkable power of absorbing oil or grease, soft enough to yield readily to the nail, and falling to pieces in water. It was considered so valuable that its exportation from England was prohibited under severe penalties. Fuller's earth was found in this neighbourhood at Leeds and on the Grove estate at Boxley. The vein on the Grove estate was 7ft. thick and 30ft. deep, one portion of which was of a slate-blue colour, while another portion had a dark grey tint.

Towards the close of the seventeenth century the cloth trade of Maidstone began to decline. On the 26th of April 1664 the thread-makers in the town petitioned the House of Commons to remedy the mischief arising to their trade through the exercise thereof by persons who had not served a proper apprenticeship, and through the importation of thread from Holland. The memorial was referred to the Committee of Trade. When George I. came to the throne several of the fulling mills had ceased to exist, or had been converted into corn or paper mills.

With regard to the general trade of the town in the seventeenth century, a few particulars may in this place be given. The town Charter in 1619 gave the Corporation power to levy tolls upon animals and vehicles entering the town, such as a penny upon every laden cart, ox, or horse, and a halfpenny upon every calf or pig. John Mason owned an extensive timber-yard at Maidstone, and on the 1st of January 1666 the government of Charles II. was informed that his timber was "sound and fit for the king's service."

In 1691 Morgan Hall erected a wharf and warehouse at the north end of the King's Mead on a piece of ground which he leased from the Corporation for twenty-one years at a rent of 40s. The rates of wages to be paid in the town and parish were then assessed at the general quarter sessions. Some of the rates thus fixed for 1698 were as follows, meat being given in addition to the wages:—Plumbers. 10d. to 20d. per day in summer, and 9d. to 16d. in winter; bricklayers, 9d. to 18d. in summer, and 8d. to 16d. in winter; glaziers, 8d. to 16d. in summer, and 7d. to 14d. in winter; plasterers, 9d. to 18d. in summer, and 8d. to 16d. in winter; carvers and joiners, 10d. to 20d. in summer, and 7d. to 14d. in winter; labourers, 7d. to 14d. in summer, and 5d. to 10d. in winter; hop-pickers, 6d.; binmen, 15d. Brewers were ordered to sell their ale and beer, free of carriage, at these prices, viz., for every barrel of beer or best ale, 10s.; for every barrel of small beer or small ale, 6s.

When money was scarce in the seventeenth century, copper farthings and halfpennies were issued by the principal traders of Maidstone and freely circulated among the inhabitants. These tokens were payable at the shops or other places of business where they were issued, and more than a score of them have been preserved. Between the years 1648 and 1672 about 570 farthings and halfpennies were struck in Kent; while in the following century only some 30 odd were issued. Every token had a motto and device. One issued by Henry Oliver, of Maidstone, has the borough arms, with two savages as supporters, and the words, "Maidstone halfpenny, 1795;" and for the reverse a figure of Justice, with sword and scales, and the motto, "The spring of freedom, England's blessing, Kent." On another token is a representation of a paper mill and the town arms, with the words, "Payable by J. Smyth at Padsole Paper Mill, 1795."*

---

* See Appendix, No. 5, for list of Maidstone tokens.

After the decline of the local cloth trade, many of the inhabitants continued to be employed in the making of linen thread. Newton, indeed, remarks that as late as 1741 the chief trade of the town was the thread manufacture and the planting of hops. But in the reign of William III. the thread trade had been set up in the West of England, where labour was cheaper than in Kent, and in course of time the Maidstone thread-makers found that they were being undersold. A profitable trade was, however, still carried on here. The thread made in the town was of coarse quality, but being strong and serviceable, and dyed in various colours, it was held in high esteem throughout England, and even in the western counties was "preferred," Newton says, "to most other." It was generally used in Kent for the making of hop-bags. A web of bagging was 4ft. wide and 7½ft. long, five yards being required for a bag. The warp was of thread, and the woof consisted of the same material, or of hay, the threads being nearly as thick as the finger.* The price of bagging in 1770 was 18s. per hundredweight.† Bags, having capacity for two and a half hundredweight of hops, sold in 1791 at 3s. 9d. each. These bags came to be used only for inferior sorts of hops, the best hops being put into "pockets" made of canvass or Hessen, which was imported under the name of "Hambro' rolls." Towards the end of the last century a description of bagging produced at Gainsborough, in Lincolnshire, was used by the hop-growers in preference to that manufactured in Maidstone, and the thread trade here soon after ceased to exist. As late, however, as 1808 there were two small places of business in the town where thread, called, in memory of the Walloon settlers, "Dutch work," was still made.

---

* Marshall's "Rural Economy of the Southern Counties," 1798.
† *Kentish Gazette*, Sept. 1770.

As to the general trade of Maidstone in 1741 Newton says:—

There are on the river very large corn mills which grind for the dock and navy at Chatham, and in a good measure furnish the city of Rochester and town of Chatham with meal and flour, besides great quantities which are sent from hence to London. Here are also several large paper mills and fulling mills*; and from hence are sent to Rochester, Chatham, and other places, great quantities of gardener's ware. By the hoys going from hence is London supplied with corn, fruit, paving stone†, which is exceedingly durable, fuller's earth, and a fine white sand for the glass houses, which is reckoned the best in England for melting into flint-glass and looking-glass plates, and much used for what is called writing sand. From hence also is conveyed to Chatham for the supply of the king's dock and yards there great quantities of the largest oak and elm timber, most of which is brought out of the Weald of Kent, and other places adjacent, by land carriage, and here put on board vessels, which carry it up the river. By these means there is good encouragement for the having here several pretty large hoys, which are constantly passing betwixt this place and London, Rochester, Chatham, &c.

Thirty-three years later, Seymour‡ wrote as follows:—

The country around the town is so plentiful that the Metropolis is supplied with more commodities from hence than from any other market town in England, particularly with great numbers of bullocks, sheep, &c. Timber, wheat, hops, apples, and cherries are also exported in great quantities, with a sort of paving stone, about ten inches square, that is exceedingly durable. Fine white sand is another article of exportation. This is the principal staple for sugar and grocery in this county, and a great part of Sussex is also supplied. Leather is also tanned and curried here. Linen thread, both black and white, and tape, which is made here in great perfection, is another considerable branch of trade; besides twine, cordage, ropes, and bags for hops, which are made here in great quantities.

For nearly two hundred and fifty years the prosperity of Maidstone has largely depended upon the successful cultivation of hops. "Great part of the wealth of Maidstone," wrote Hasted, a hundred years ago, "has arisen from the hop trade, most of the inhabitants having some hop ground, and many estates have been raised by them from this commodity." Though it cannot now be said that most of the townsmen are hop growers, many of the inhabitants, as well as the majority of the people living in the surrounding villages, find employment in the hop gardens. The hop-growing parts of the county are sharply defined by geological boundaries, and the neighbourhood of Maidstone, where the soil consists of the

---

* Only one fulling mill existed here in 1776.
† Many of the streets of London were paved with "Maidstone squares" before stone from Scotland came into use.
‡ "Topographical Survey of Kent," by Charles Seymour, 1774.

loams of the Hythe beds of the Lower Greensand formation, is particularly suitable for the cultivation of hops. The root of the plant in such grounds has been traced to a depth of fourteen feet, penetrating through the undersoil and into the fissures of the ragstone. There are hop gardens here whose first planting no living person can remember. A hundred and fifty years ago Farnham was considered the "first capital town in Britain for hops;"* but Maidstone has long been regarded as the centre of the Kentish hop district.

By the town Charter of 1682 power was given to hold a hop fair in Maidstone. When first planted, hops were sold at 26s. per hundredweight, but Bradley says he had known hop gardens that had yielded a clear profit of £50 per acre.† In the beginning of George the Third's reign considerable quantities of Flemish hops were often smuggled into Kentish ports, and the injury to the trade from this cause became so widely felt that in December 1771 a meeting of hop-planters was held at the Star Hotel, Maidstone, when a resolution was carried asking Parliament to pass an Act preventing the importation of foreign hops. The greater part of the produce in the district surrounding the town was brought to Maidstone for conveyance to London, whither, in 1774, barges sailed from the town wharf three times a week during the picking season.

The cost of hop cultivation has always been heavy. The average outlay upon an acre of ground in full plant was, in 1790, estimated at £20, inclusive of rent and taxes. Labour was then remunerated as follows:—Winter digging, 20s. per acre; polling (including pointing), 10s. per acre; tying, 10s. per acre; stacking poles, 5s. per acre; oast-men, a guinea

---

* "The Riches of the Hop Garden Explained," by R. Bradley, Professor of Botany in the University of Cambridge, 1729.
† Ibid., p. 24.

per week; binmen, 9s. per week; packing, 8d. per bag. The hops were measured in eleven-gallon baskets, and pickers were paid at from a penny to three half-pence per basket. During the ten years ending 1797 the price of hops averaged from £5 to £6 10s. per pocket, containing a hundredweight and a quarter. Plantations around Maidstone have occasionally produced eighteen or twenty hundredweights per acre. "There is," says Mr. Whitehead, "no product of the soil that has made some individuals rich and others poor so quickly as hops."* In the days when foreign competition was unknown, gardens in favoured situations were often mines of gold to the planters. Near the end of the last century a small piece of land in the Maidstone district yielded in one season a ton and a half per acre, and this extraordinary produce sold at £5 per hundredweight, or £150 per acre. In 1787 a grower at East Farleigh, who farmed forty acres at a rent of £40, sold his hops at £10 per hundredweight, and realised the amazing sum of £4,873. A still more remarkable case was that of Mr. E. Selby, who in 1818 sold the hops grown on four and a half acres of ground in East Farleigh parish at the rate of £30 per hundredweight, the whole yield fetching nearly £5,000.†

Farms in a few instances are planted entirely with hops; and the average extent of holdings is about fifty acres, though there is one farm near Maidstone comprising more than three hundred acres. As a rule, on each farm there is a certain proportion of hop land which the tenant is bound by a covenant in his lease to maintain in "full plant." The late Mr. James Ellis, of East Farleigh, possessed £70,000 worth of hop-poles, and sometimes gave employment to 4,000

---

* "Hops: From the Set to the Sky-Lights," by Charles Whitehead, F.L.S., F.G.S., p. 72.

† Each of these cases is mentioned in the contemporary numbers of the *Maidstone Journal*.

persons during the picking season.* Rents range from £5 to £10 per acre, and an average crop of seven hundredweights per acre costs nearly £40 before any profit can be made. The picking begins about the end of August; and at this stage of their growth, when their festooned foliage and clusters of pale-coloured cones are steeped in sunshine, the hops are exceedingly beautiful. The sight of a field of yellow corn, dimpling under an autumn sun, fails to convey the same idea of fertility and beauty. More graceful are the hop gardens than any of those vine-yards of the Rhine or the Gironde that are trimmed and pruned into squat regularity. When parties of pickers invade their long-drawn aisles, a pleasant dash of animation is imparted to the scene. The traveller in the highway hears the merry voices of the "hoppers," shut in by solid walls of greenery, for the tinge of gold on the hops themselves counts for nothing in the mass of green leaves. Three weeks usually suffice for the picking. Each cottage is left for the time with locked doors, and families who would never stoop to other field-work, migrate in a body to the gardens. The home pickers are largely reinforced by contingents from the East End of London, numbering sometimes as many as 25,000 men and women, who are conveyed by special trains into the hop districts. One planter near Maidstone employs upwards of a thousand "strangers" every season, and finds them habitation and firing. Picking is paid for at from three half-pence to six-pence per bushel, and good hands will pick from twenty-five to thirty bushels per day.

"What strikes a stranger the most on entering a hop garden," says an old writer, in allusion to a custom which still prevails, "is the homage with which he is received.

---

* "The Food of London," by George Dodd, 1856.

The fairest or the forwardest of the female pickers, having selected the finest bunch of hops in her view, approaches him with great respect and 'wipes his shoes,' or rather touches them with it, and then offers it to him. This is her way of asking money." The money thus obtained went towards the cost of the supper which was always given on the last day of the hopping, or was expended in another custom, which seems, however, to be now forgotten. This might be termed the "decoration of hats." A few days before the picking on the farm was concluded the pickers decorated the hat of the head binman with ribbons and tinsel ornaments, and the hat of the carter with ribbons only. These hats were publicly exhibited, and then displayed at the hop supper. They were afterwards worn for a day or two in public, the pickers on the different farms vieing with each other in the gaudiness of the decorations.

In the neighbourhood of Maidstone, as elsewhere in Kent, almost every farmer has a certain proportion of fruit-land, as a security against the contingencies of hop-growing.* When hops pay well, fruit trees are grubbed up and hops are planted in their stead, and when hops do not pay, this process is reversed. Three or four centuries ago grapes were largely grown out of doors, wine being regularly made from them; and Hasted states that he "knew two exceedingly fine vineyards in the county, one at Tunbridge Castle, the other at Barming, from which quantities of well-flavoured wine had been produced." In these days it very seldom happens that grapes ripen thoroughly in the open air, even in the warmest summers and in the most sheltered spots. From this it may be inferred that the climate was more genial in former times, and that the mean summer temperature has gradually been lowered, owing in some degree to the clearing

---

* "Fruit-Growing in Kent," by Charles Whitehead, F.L.S., F.G.S.

of the forests which once covered parts of Kent. The loams on the beds of Kentish ragstone are highly suitable for the cultivation of other kinds of fruit. Great quantities of apples, cherries, plums, damsons, pears, currants, and gooseberries are grown and sold annually in the London market. Mr. Webb, in his paper on "Fruit Cultivation,"* states that a farmer near Maidstone realised £100 in one year from an acre of gooseberry bushes.

Filberts, so much appreciated at dessert, are grown exclusively in the neighbourhood of Maidstone. They are often cultivated under apple, pear, and plum trees. A filbert tree has a stem about two feet in height, and the branches are trained to spread out in a saucer-like shape, with a diameter of 7ft. or 8ft., and a height of about 6ft. The average yield is eight hundred-weights per acre, but a single tree has been known to grow forty pounds of nuts. The cob-nut is a heavier cropper than the filbert, an acre of ground generally producing ten hundred-weights, which sell in Covent Garden at £40. There were formerly at Allington Castle several walnut trees of great size. In 1790 the trunks of two of them, at 5ft. from the ground, girted 12ft. each, and weighed upwards of four tons. One of

Pruned Filbert Tree.†

---

* "Transactions of the Institution of Surveyors," vol. viii.

† The above engraving is obtained, by permission, from the "Journal" of the Royal Agricultural Society of England.

these trees was 60ft. in height, and the branches extended nearly 50ft. from the trunk.

Brewing on an extensive scale has long been carried on in the town. The Lower Brewery was owned by John Saunders in the middle of the seventeenth century, and in the manor survey of 1650 it is described as consisting of "one capital messuage with brewhouse, one other house, two malt houses, barns and stables, and one piece of meadow." The Upper Brewery which occupied the lower part of Brewer Street, was once owned by the Cripps family, whose residence, a curious old mansion built in the reign of James I., stood in Week Street, on the east side, almost opposite the top of St. Faith's Street. About sixty years ago the brewery premises were purchased by the proprietors of the Lower Brewery, who sold the ground for building purposes. At the present time there are three large, and several small, breweries in the town. In the first half of the eighteenth century an orchard and osier garden occupied the site of the Medway Brewery.

A distillery for the making of Hollands gin was established in Maidstone by George Bishop, a native of the town. He had for several years conducted a distillery in Holland, and after acquiring the art of distilling the celebrated Schiedam, he returned to England with the intention of setting up a distillery in Maidstone. Finding that there were laws in existence which would interfere materially with the needful operations, he petitioned the Legislature for an Act of Parliament to enable him to carry out his project, the realisation of which, he pointed out, would tend to prevent smuggling by rendering Hollands a home produce. After much opposition in the House of Commons, an Act of Parliament was obtained. A large brick building, with yards and other premises, was erected on the south side of Bank Street, and by the year 1789 the distillery was in full operation. Maidstone Hollands gin was soon in great demand. Walter Rowles, in his historical sketch of the town, says that seven hundred hogs had been kept on the grains from the distillery. When the originator died, the concern was left in the hands of his relatives, Sir William Bishop, George Bishop, and Argles Bishop, whose affairs got into confusion. and in 1818 the distillery was sold. It was then carried on by the purchasers for about a year, when, in consequence of an application made by Argles Bishop to carry on, under the same powers, an opposition distillery which he had set up in premises which have since become the Medway Brewery, the Excise took the opportunity of putting an end to both concerns, on the plea that the original distillery having changed hands, the Act was inoperative. The premises behind Bank Street were afterwards converted into a flour mill. The existing distillery in the West Borough was established about twenty-five years ago.

When the cloth trade had died out, paper-making was commenced in the neighbourhood, and may be said to have since become the leading industry of Maidstone. Paper was first made in this locality on the river Len about the beginning of the eighteenth century. There were in 1719 two paper mills on the Len, within a short distance of the town. They had previously been fulling mills, and were adapted to the requirements of the new manufacture by George Gill, of an old Boxley family. At one of the mills white paper was made, and at the other brown wrapping paper, the river at the former turning three overshot wheels, 8ft. in diameter. The white paper was made from rags, which required thirty-six hours' beating, and which were brought to the mill by hawkers and other persons who found a subsistence by collecting them. Old ropes, sails, &c., which required twelve hours' beating, were converted into brown paper.

The mills became the property of Gill's son William, who sold them in 1731 to James Whatman and William Brooke. Mr. Whatman, who was subsequently the sole proprietor, rebuilt them in 1739 on an enlarged and greatly improved plan. They were then called the Turkey Mills. Mr. Whatman and his son introduced many improvements into the manufacture of paper, and in 1774 these mills were considered "the most complete in the kingdom."* Of Mr. Whatman, the grandfather of the present owner of Vinters, Samuel Ireland wrote in 1793:—"To this gentleman the country is indebted for his great improvements in the art of paper-making, which he has unquestionably carried to a higher degree of perfection and excellence than was before known in this or any other kingdom, and may truly be said to have given additional smoothness to verse and a new face to the literature of this country." † The paper bearing the "J. Whatman" and the "Original Turkey Mill" water-marks is still highly esteemed for its fine quality and superior finish.

There were in 1775 four paper mills in the neighbourhood of Maidstone. A corn mill on the Len at Padsole was in 1650 the property of Sir William Culpeper. It fell into a dilapidated condition towards the end of the last century, and on the site thereof a paper mill was erected by James Smyth in 1796. Carried on for a short time under the firm of Smyth and Hollingworth, it became the property of Thomas Robert and Finch Hollingworth, who in 1799 disposed of it to John Wise and John Hayes, and purchased the Turkey Mills of Mr. Whatman. The Padsole mill, after long remaining unoccupied, was demolished ten years ago, and rebuilt as a flour mill.

* Seymour's "Survey of Kent."   † "Views on the River Medway."

There are at the present time seven paper mills within a circuit of two miles of the town. Springfield Mill was built by William Balston in 1806. At this mill, where handmade paper only is made, 300 operatives were employed in 1840, and the number is now about 400, of whom 280 are females. Hayle Mill, in Loose Valley, was erected in 1808. Upwards of 700 hands found employment at the different mills in 1837, but since the repeal of the paper duty, and the introduction of the penny postage and of cheap newspapers, a great impetus has been given to the paper trade. From four to five thousand tons of drawing, writing, wrapping, and printing paper are now turned out annually at the mills. Upwards of 1,100 hands are employed, and a sum of at least £50,000 is paid yearly in wages.

In 1809 the number of Maidstone barges trading on the Medway was twenty-five, of which seven were employed in the stone trade. There were in 1834 upwards of fifty vessels, of from twenty to ninety tons, belonging to the town. A few years previously the navigation had been much facilitated by the opening of the Thames and Medway canal, which shortened the passage to London by fully thirty miles. The charge for conveying hops to the metropolis was 1s. per pocket, or 2s. per bag. The gross annual tonnage passing through Allington Lock was 120,000 tons, upon which tolls to the amount of £2,600 were collected. The advantages which the canal conferred upon the trades on the river were taken away many years later, when the tunnel was used for the North Kent Railway. Before the extension of the railway to Maidstone in 1844, the town was fed principally through the river. Owing, however, to the general increase of population, and the greater demands of the times, the Medway traffic is still very considerable. Of the barges at present trading on the river, about sixty belong to Maidstone wharfingers. Vessels of a hundred and fifty tons burthen occasionally pass up to Maidstone, but the freights do not, as a rule, exceed a hundred tons. The commercial management of the river is vested by Acts of Parliament in two companies; the Upper Navigation Company has jurisdiction above, and the Lower Navigation Company below, Maidstone.

The dates of the fairs in the seventeenth century have already been given. It may be stated here that in the following century the fair days were altered to February 13, May 12, June 20, and October 17. The October fair was formerly the largest gathering of the year, Bullock Lane being crowded with stock, while the High Street and parts of Week Street were littered with farm produce, wares, and peddlery. Marshall, writing in 1793, says the largest collection of horses which he had seen was at this fair. The market which is held on the second Tuesday in each month for the sale of stock was granted in 1751, and the average number of sheep and cattle offered for sale monthly in 1792 was 1,000 of the former, and 150 of the latter.

It will now be convenient to describe the position of the market premises in the High Street. The corn market was held in the open space under the Upper Court House, and in the room above corn was stored. In 1771 the Corporation ordered that this "corn chamber over the old Court House" should be let to the highest bidder. The room, and a staircase leading thereto, being in a ruinous state, were removed in April 1783, and a new roof, surmounted by a gilt wheat sheaf, was put on, and the columns repaired. Until the year 1608, the corn market had been held under the Market Cross; this afterwards became the butcher's and then the fish market. Shambles were erected on the space where the houses at the lower end of the Middle Row now stand; they consisted of two ranges of low sheds, covered with tiles, and enclosed from the street with pailings and lime trees. Below the shambles, to the west of the weigh-bridge, was the butter market, a small round building with four stone arches, somewhat in the style of the Market Cross; a more commodious octagonal structure, supported by eight wooden pillars, was built on the site in 1806.

The Market Cross, from its position in the centre of the thoroughfare at the top of High Street, was found to be an obstruction to traffic, and in 1771 it was moved aside on rollers to the site of the old county gaol. It was taken down in 1780, and a building for a fish and vegetable market was erected near the same spot, the cost being defrayed by subscription, to which the Corporation contributed £30. This building shared the fate of the former one, and a new market—of which a sketch is annexed, showing also the corn market—was erected on the site in 1805.

In 1823 a committee was appointed by the Corporation to examine into the state of all the markets. The committee forthwith reported that the several buildings were in need of repair, while the corn market was so exposed to the weather that farmers and others complained of injury to their health by attending it in winter. On the 21st of March 1825 the foundation-stone of new market buildings was laid by the mayor, and on March 23, in the following year, they were opened. The old buildings in the High Street were then removed, much to the improvement of the thoroughfare, and at the same time the Corporation ordered that the monthly stock market should thenceforth be held in the Fair Meadow, for which purpose a row of stately elms along the east side of the meadow was cut down. The new market, and the rebuilding of the Mitre hotel and of the King's Arms public-house, cost upwards of

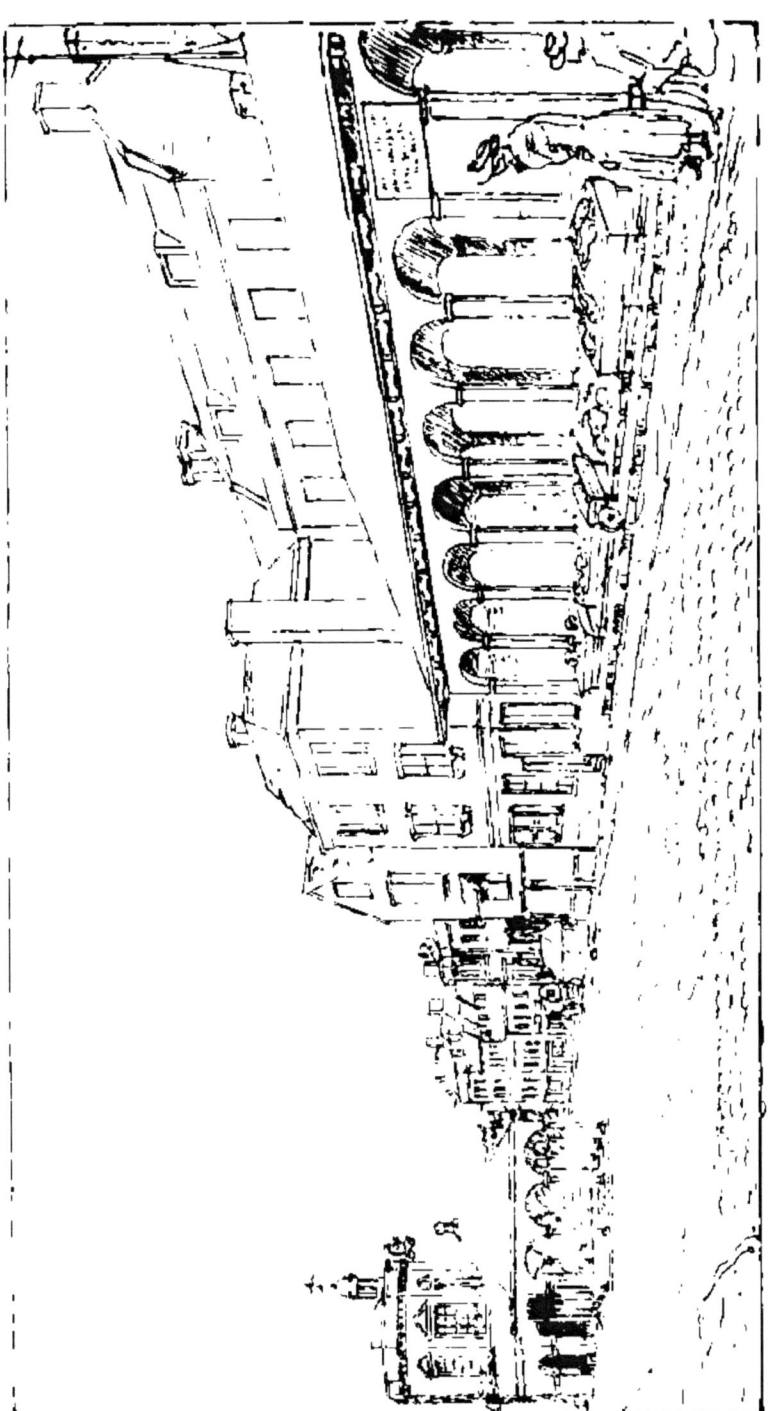

The Market Place....1820.

£13,000, towards which about £2,000 was realised from the sale of old materials and of the timber in the Fair Meadow.

The market requirements had, however, been miscalculated. The sky-lighted end nearest the Mitre, designed as a corn market, was soon found unsatisfactory; while the stalls, beneath parallel slated sheds, carried internally on stone columns, and extending flush into Earl Street—a style of the period still to be seen in Gravesend and other minor markets—were never all occupied. In 1835 the present Corn Exchange was erected. Subsequently, by several years, the colonnades were further shortened, and in 1869 the construction of the Concert Hall and collateral buildings effaced the residue of the 1825 plans. Some of the stone columns may be seen utilised in the new arcading. But even then the mutability of Maidstone market-place arrangements was not over, several of the new stalls having since been converted into offices. Indeed, since the removals from the High Street, stalls have never competed with the shop system.

CHAPTER XIV.

OLD HOUSES AND OLD FAMILIES.

The Mote—Vinters—Park House—Buckland—Shales Court—Kingsley House—Digons—Jordans Hall—Old Houses in the High Town—Hunter's House—The Old Theatres—The Palace—The Astley Family—Sir John Astley's Will—Astley House—Thomas Bliss—Broughton's House—Earls Place—Chillington—The Maplesdens—Nicholas Barham's Will—The Charles Family—Julius Brenchley—The Museum and Public Library.

WE have but to walk along the streets of the town to see that there are still many notable architectural remains of old Maidstone. These ancient buildings are gradually passing away. In the rage for novelty and improvement they are being ruthlessly torn down, and superseded by others that are more in harmony with the wants and tastes of the age. But those that remain are the links which visibly connect bygone times with the present, giving to the chronicles of the past an impress of truth by rendering them in some degree evident to the senses. With the disappearance of one of these dwellings of our ancestors, historic continuity is broken, but if the site can still be pointed out, this apparently trivial fact, bound up, it may be, with the career of those who have left their names in the annals of the town, imparts to the general narrative a more vivid interest. In this chapter we shall take note of some of the older houses, indicate the situation of others that have been demolished, and refer, at such length as their importance may seem to deserve, to some of the families with whom they were associated.

Beginning at the outskirts of the parish, our attention is first directed to the Mote, so called from the Anglo-Saxon word *mót*, signifying a gathering place. The history of this estate reaches back to the first half of the thirteenth century, when it belonged to the wealthy Leybourne family, of Leybourne Castle, in this county. Roger de Leybourne, in the year 1267, obtained from Henry III. the grant of a weekly market to be held at the Mote on Tuesday, and of an annual fair, to continue for three days, at the feast of St. Cross. In the reign of Edward II. the estate appears to have become the property of John de Shoford, " from whom," says Hasted, " it acquired the name of the manor of Shoford." But it may be doubted whether the seat was ever so denominated; as in an indenture in the Public Record Office,* dated 1552, we read of the " manors of Shoford and the Mote," showing that they were then two distinct estates, though they may have subsequently been merged into one.

Bartholomew de Burgersh, who resided at the Mote in the time of Edward III., was present at the battle of Poictiers, and on the order of the Garter being instituted, he was selected as one of the knights-companions. Shortly after his death in 1369, the Mote came into the possession of the Woodville family, who removed thither from Grafton, in Northamptonshire. Of Richard de Woodville it is related that for marrying the widow of John Duke of Bedford without a license, he was fined a thousand pounds. He, however,

---

* Close Rolls, No. 481.

regained the sovereign's favour, and in recognition of his services in the French wars, was created Baron Rivers. By his adroitness and ability he contrived to retain the confidence, during their ascendancy, of the antagonistic houses of Lancaster and York. Elizabeth, his eldest daughter, was married to Sir John Grey, of Groby, and on the death of her husband, she became the consort of Edward IV. Lord Rivers was afterwards created an earl, and promoted to the offices of lord treasurer and high constable of England. While on a visit to Grafton in 1469, he was seized by the adherents of Henry VI., when he was carried to Northampton, and beheaded. Earl Rivers was succeeded by his eldest son Anthony, who was governor of Calais, and held many other lucrative appointments. He was in Shropshire attending the Prince of Wales, a boy of thirteen, when Edward IV. died. Rivers at once set out with the young prince for London, but was entrapped by the Dukes of Buckingham and Gloucester at Northampton. The prince was conveyed to the capital, but Rivers was sent to Pontefract, where he was, like his father, beheaded.

The Mote should have become the property of his brother Richard, but Richard III. granted it to one of his own favourites. On the accession, however, of Henry VII., it was given to Richard Earl Rivers, who died in 1491. The estate was subsequently alienated to Sir Henry Wyatt, of Allington Castle, in whose family it remained until the Kentish rebellion of 1554. After further changes of ownership, it was purchased, in the beginning of Charles the First's reign, by Sir Humphrey Tufton, brother to the first Earl of Thanet, who died at Bobbing Place, Kent, in 1659, and was succeeded by his eldest son, Sir John Tufton, who, dying in 1685, was buried in Maidstone church. Leaving no issue, his will devised the Mote to his niece, one of the daughters of

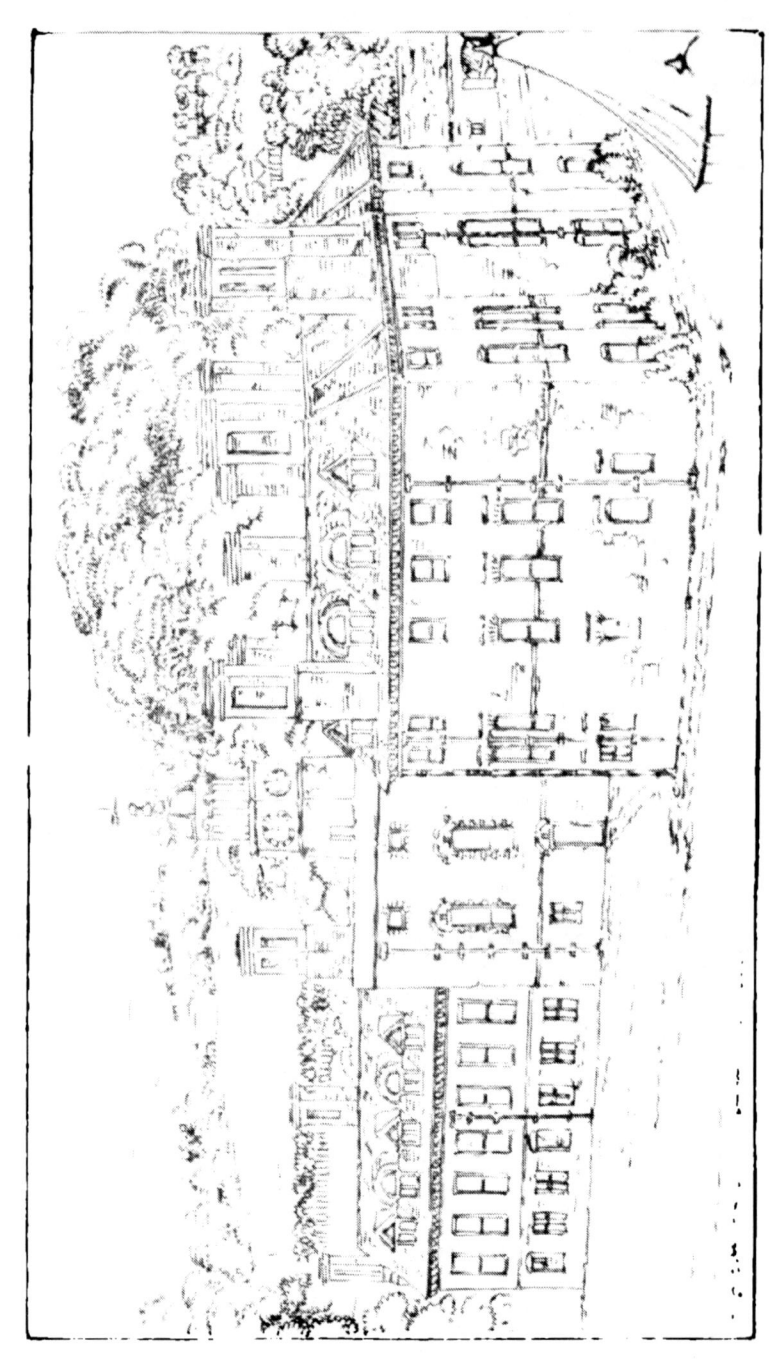

Sir William Wray, of Ashby, in Lincolnshire, who sold it to Sir John Marsham, bart., of Whornes Place, Cuxton, in this county. The Marsham family derives its name from the town of Marsham, in Norfolk, but the above-named Sir John Marsham purchased Whornes Place early in the reign of Charles I. He was high sheriff of Kent in 1692, and died in the same year. His nephew, Sir Robert Marsham, was in 1716 elevated to the peerage by the title of Baron Romney. Charles, the third lord, represented Kent in three successive Parliaments, and was created Earl Romney in 1801.

The former Mote house occupied the most secluded part of the park. It appears to have been built in the seventeenth century, and after it came into the possession of the Marsham family no alterations are believed to have been made in it until it was pulled down in 1799. The accompanying illustration is traced from Alexander's plate of the banquet which was given in 1799 to the Volunteers at the Mote, and part of the royal marquee is shown in order to fix the spot, for where that stood was erected the existing commemorative structure known as the pavilion. The present mansion was commenced in 1794. Standing on a gentle rising ground, it overlooks a fine artificial sheet of water, and the extensive park, of which about 380 acres are in the parish of Maidstone, stretches away in pleasant undulations, the view being diversified by belts and clumps of trees, and enlivened by the glancing forms of deer.

Situated in Boxley parish, though in proximity to Maidstone, is the mansion of Vinters, anciently the residence of a family of that name. John de Vinters in 1408 sold the estate to a son of Sir Ralph de Fremingham, of Loose, who died without issue two years after, and the property descended to Roger Isley, of Sundridge, his nearest relative. On the attainder of Sir Henry Isley for his share in Wyatt's rebellion, Queen Mary granted this seat to Henry Cutt, of Bynbury,* and after several other changes of ownership, it was purchased by Sir William Tufton, governor of Barbadoes, and brother of Sir Humphrey Tufton, of the Mote. His son Sir Charles Tufton, passed it away by sale to Daniel White, who died in 1689, and in the reign of Queen Anne it became the property of Sir Samuel Ongley, of Old Warden, in Bedfordshire, one of the directors of the "South Sea Bubble." After passing through other hands, Vinters was purchased in 1783 by James Whatman, a descendant of an ancient family belonging to the Weald of Kent, the original spelling of the name being Hwatman. He rebuilt the mansion which, by his grandson, the present James Whatman, Esq., was transformed and greatly enlarged about 1849.

Park House, pleasantly embowered amid trees and shrubs, stands on the east side of the road to Rochester, just beyond the boundary of Maidstone parish. In the early part of the sixteenth century this estate was annexed to the See of Canterbury, and at the Reformation it passed to the Crown. In the reign of Charles II. it was in the possession of Thomas Taylor, who married a sister of George Hall, of Digons, and who was mayor of Maidstone in 1649-50. He was created a baronet in December 1664, and died in the following year, being succeeded by his son, of the same name, who married Alicia, sister and heiress of Sir Thomas Culpeper, the last of the Preston Hall branch of the Culpepers, and widow of Herbert Stapley. After his death, Lady Taylor—a title which she retained to the end of her life—married Thomas Culpeper, counsellor-at-law, and subsequently John Milner, M.D., of Yorkshire, whom she survived, and died without issue. Her fourth husband had bequeathed Park House to

---

* Close Rolls, No. 514.

his brother, Charles Milner, who, after her decease, sold it to James Calder, son of Sir James Calder, of Muirtown, in Scotland. In the last decade of the eighteenth century the old house, which stood on the boundary of Maidstone parish, was pulled down by Sir Henry Calder, who, at no great distance, built the present mansion.

In 1828, Park House came into the possession of the Lushington family, and it is now the residence of E. L. Lushington, Esq. Mr. Tennyson, the poet-laureate, who is Mr. Lushington's brother-in-law, spent, in his earlier years, many happy vacations here. It was during one of his visits, about thirty-five years ago, that the Maidstone Mechanics' Institute* held a fête in the grounds of Park House. The prologue to "The Princess" was in a measure founded on this meeting—

>Sir Walter Vivian all a summer's day
>Gave his broad lawns until the set of sun
>Up to the people: thither flock'd at noon
>His tenants, wife and child, and thither half
>The neighbouring borough with their Institute,
>Of which he was the patron. I was there
>From college, visiting the son—the son
>A Walter too—with others of our set,
>Five others: we were seven at Vivian-place.

Again—

>We went
>Down through the park: strange was the sight to me:
>For all the sloping pasture murmur'd, sown
>With happy faces and with holiday.
>There moved the multitude, a thousand heads:
>The patient leaders of their Institute
>Taught them with facts.

A charming description of the sports and amusements of the meeting is then given.

We now cross the Medway, and come to the ancient estate of Buckland, which derives its name from the tenure under which the land was at one time held. Among the Saxons *bocland*, in contradistinction to the *fockland* occupied by the

---

* The Institute was founded in 1836, and ceased to exist in 1881.

common people, was devisible by will, and might be shared in equal portions among the children of the holder. The estate was in the time of King John granted by the Archbishop of Canterbury to Allan de Bocland to hold in frank fee. It was then described as one yoke and ten acres of land, with appurtenances in Maidstone. In the year 1270 it was in the occupation of Walter de Bocland, and a dispute as to its possession arose between him and his brother Allan, who brought the question before the Justices Itinerant, and sought to obtain a moiety of the estate, the tenure of which had been changed by the archbishop without the consent of the Chapter of Canterbury. The plea, however, was overruled, and judgment was entered for the defendant. Buckland, of which four hundred acres were in the parish of Maidstone, was, in Henry the Fourth's reign, merged into the demesne lands of the College of All Saints, and on the dissolution of that house it passed to the Crown. It was granted by Edward VI. to George Brooke, Lord Cobham, whose grandson in 1603 forfeited it for treason. His wife was, however, permitted to enjoy it for her life; and after her death it became the property of Robert, Earl of Salisbury.

William, Earl of Salisbury, about the year 1618, broke up Buckland into three portions and sold them. That portion since called Great Buckland was purchased by William Horsepoole, who married a daughter of Lawrence Washington, of Jordans Hall, and in the reign of Charles II. it was sold to Sir John Banks, bart., from whom it descended to the Earl of Aylesford, in whose family it remains. The old mansion, which stands on a hill overlooking the Medway, is a good specimen of the style of country houses in the beginning of the seventeenth century. South Buckland was in 1720 alienated by Heneage Finch, fourth Earl of Winchelsea, to Lord Romney. Little Buckland, which comprised fifty-two acres, belonged to John Fletcher in the reign of Charles II., and it has since passed through many hands.

At the western extremity of Maidstone parish, near to the northern end of East Farleigh bridge, was the manor of Half Yoke. This estate successively formed part of the possessions of the ancient families of Fremingham, Pimpe, and Isley; and about the end of the seventeenth century it was broken up and sold to different persons.

With these brief notices of the principal seats and estates in the immediate neighbourhood of Maidstone, we shall linger no longer in the rural parts of the parish, but come at once to the town itself. Old houses and old families is our theme, and as we pass from street to street, it will be our aim to recall the form and outline of certain vanished dwellings of our forefathers, and to awaken some of the sleeping memories of olden times. We will start on our perambulation from the south end of Stone Street.*

At the south corner of Tovil Road stood the manor-house of Shales or Sheals Court, some fragments of which still exist. The manor was owned by the Freminghams, and then by the Pimpe family, by whom it was alienated to Sir Thomas Wyatt, who conveyed it to Henry VIII. in exchange for other propety. It was granted by Edward VI. to Sir Walter Hendley, serjeant-at-law, who died in 1552, leaving this manor to Elizabeth, his eldest daughter, widow of William Waller, of Groombridge, whose relative became in 1599 captain of the Maidstone trained band, in which year the borough chamberlains spent 2s. 6d. for wine bestowed upon "Mr. Thomas Waller, our new captain." Sir Walter Waller sold Shales Court in 1574 to Walter Hendley, of Cranbrook. It remained in the Hendley

* I have been considerably assisted in this chapter by a manuscript of Clement Taylor Smythe, written in 1832, and to be found in his Collection, vol. iii., fols. 180-212.

family until alienated to Sir John Banks, at whose death it passed by marriage to the Finch family.

At the north corner of Tovil Road was a mansion which was occupied in 1650 by Richard Duke, for many years a member of the Corporation; and below, on the west side of Stone Street, were several old houses belonging to the town which were demolished in 1836, when the land was sold. Lower down, on the same side, there were to be seen, sixty years ago, the remains of a large house, built of timber and plaster, with arches of the time of Henry VII.; adjoining which was an orchard which has been built upon, and now includes George Street and Orchard Street. On the opposite side of the street stood Kingsley House, which came by marriage into the possession of a family of that name which originally belonged to Herefordshire. Colonel Kingsley fought on the Royalist side in the civil war. General Kingsley distinguished himself at the battle of Minden in 1759; he resided here, and dying on the 9th of October 1769, was buried at Kennington church, near Ashford. The property remained in the family until sold for building sites, and the demolition of the mansion ensued in 1855. Its last occupant was the Rev. William Vallance; it had previously been vacated, after many years' tenancy, by John Brenchley. Below, at the south corner of Mote Road, is a gable-headed house which belonged to John Harris in 1650, and which, more than half a century ago, was converted into three tenements.

Passing along Knightrider Street, we come, on the south side, to the mansion which is supposed to have been known as Digons, apparently from a family so called, A. de Digons having been a member of the Corpus Christi Fraternity. It was long the residence of the Maplesdens, of whom a pedigree is given in the herald's visitation of 1619. Having been forfeited by George Maplesden for joining in Wyatt's rebellion, it was granted by the Crown to Nicholas Barham, serjeant-at-law, who was descended from the Barhams of Teston. His son Arthur, about the end of the sixteenth century, sold the property to Henry Hall, of an old Wye family, whose name was originally spelt Aula, and then it was altered to Haula, and finally to Hall. Henry Hall, who married a daughter of Richard Dering, of Pluckley, lived at Digons, which was sold by his son and heir to Sir Francis Barnham, who greatly improved the building. Barnham's heirs alienated it during the Commonwealth to Walter Franklyn, from whom it passed to a Mr. Beale, of London, who sold it in 1681 to Mr. Griffith Hatley, in whose family it remained till 1815. During preceding years it had been occupied by a Mrs. Jones and her daughter; by them it was styled the Nunnery. Acquired by Dr. John Day, it changed its designation to the Priory, and is still so called, though without the slightest pretence of ever having been a religious house. None of the existing title-deeds are anterior to the year 1730. At the west end of the street, near where the Globe publichouse now stands, was a dwelling-house called Old Court, which belonged in the fifteenth century to the See of Canterbury.

We now return to Stone Street. In Elizabeth's reign the house No. 34, on the west side, was occupied by Robert Balsar, who was twice chief magistrate of the borough. Over the chimney-place in one of the rooms, and also in one of the windows, were the arms of Henry VIII., and Clement T. Smythe conjectured that as it was customary to place the arms of a monarch in the house where he sojourned, Henry may have stayed here on his way to Dover on the eve of the taking of Boulogne. The mansion of Jordans Hall stood on the other side of the street, to the south of Romney Place, and was the residence of the Jordan family, of whom very little is known. From the Jordans it passed by sale to the Roper family, of St. Dunstan's, near Canterbury, and in 1458 John Roper disposed of it to Edward and William Brouch, of Bearsted. Towards the end of Elizabeth's reign it was purchased by Lawrence Washington, a descendant of an old Durham family. In 1643, as appears by the Maidstone manor books, it was in the occupation of Philip Smith and John Godden, and ten acres of land, extending eastward nearly as far as Square Hill, were then attached to it. Jordan's Hall was demolished before 1650, and a moiety of the site was purchased by Daniel Bickman, distiller, who erected thereon two houses in 1656.

On the west side of the street stands Stone House, with its fine old staircase, oak-panelled hall, and carved chimney-pieces. Lady Sackville resided here in the middle of the seventeenth century. A new front was added to the building in 1716, and about sixty years ago the rear was greatly augmented. A large old fashioned house, on the south side of the Lower Brewery, was pulled down about the beginning of the present century; it contained some curious old rooms, and a long gallery lighted by casements. This house was the residence of the Curteis family. Francis and George Curteis, between the years 1679 and 1729, took a prominent part in the municipal affairs of the town.

The river Len which crosses Stone Street has for several centuries been spanned by a bridge, and during the present century, it has also been built over on the west side, where it divides into two streams, the south one having been formed about the beginning of George the Third's reign in order to prevent flooding above the bridge. Crossing the bridge, we pass up Gabriel's Hill, at the west corner of which is an ancient house, facing the High Street. Underneath this house, of anterior date, is a Gothic vault, with ribbed arches. A similar

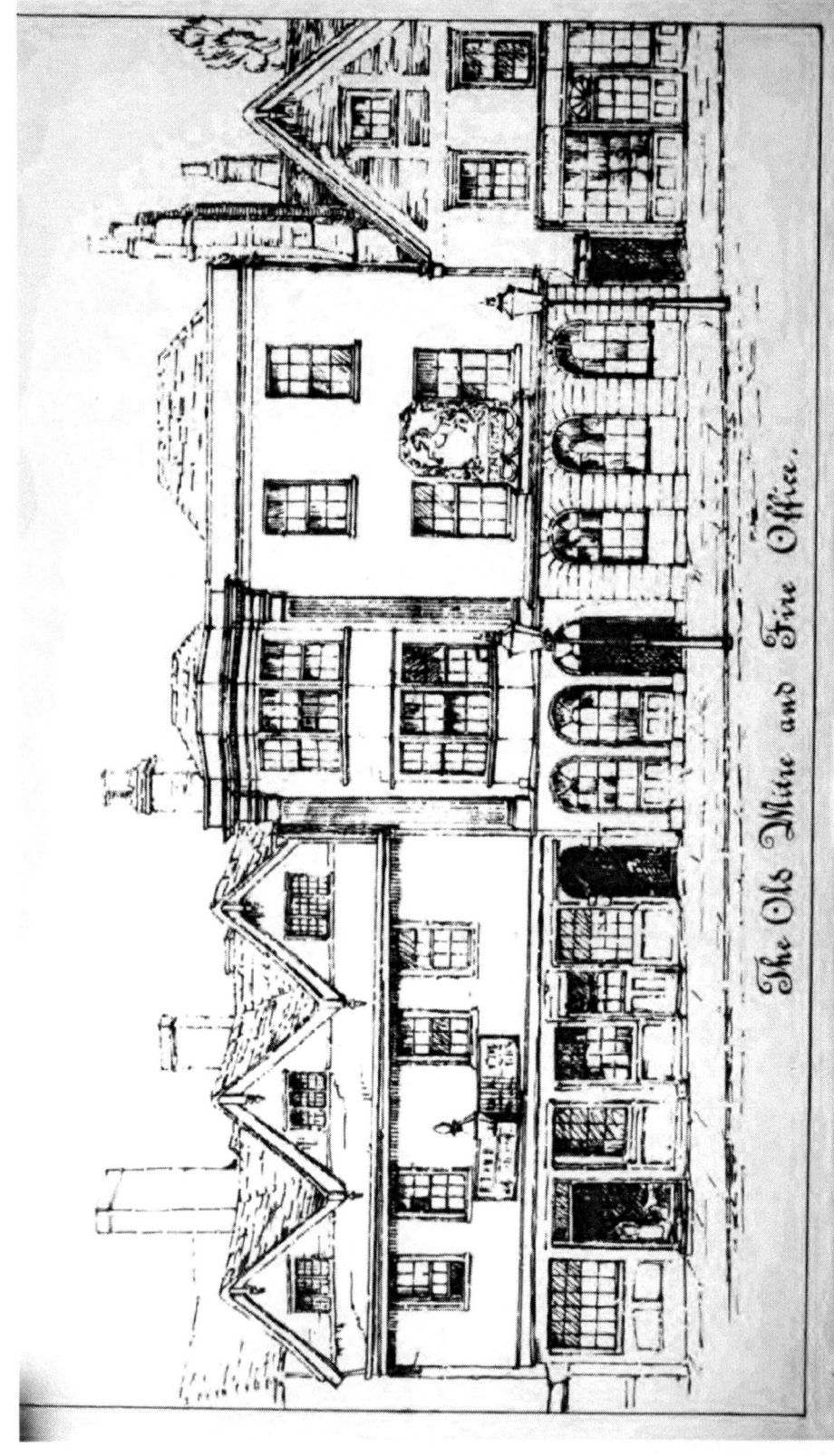

The Old Mitre and Fire Office.

vault exists beneath the house at the opposite corner, but about forty years ago its crown was interfered with for the lowering of the floor.

There are several old gable-headed buildings in King Street, on the north side of which is a large house, now the residence of Mrs. Cutbush, which belonged in the seventeenth century, to the Beale family. One of the Beales, it is said, took an active part in the defence of the town against the Parliamentary troops in 1648; this was probably John Beale, who lived some time here, and died at Farningham. He was knighted at the Restoration. Robert Beale, linen-draper, who was admitted to the freedom of the borough in 1682, is to be distinguished from this family. He was a Scotchman, and died, aged 101 years, in 1755, leaving much landed property at Maidstone and elsewhere. His daughter was married to John Boreman, of Headcorn.

Proceeding along the High Street, an old inhabitant could scarcely fail to notice that many of the low-pitched, timber-and-plaster buildings, with their gables to the street, which were to be seen in this part of the town seventy years ago, have disappeared. The Rose Inn, now Nos. 2 and 3, was in all probability the first brick house erected in the High Street. Opposite the Rose Yard, isolated by the intervening foot pavement, stood two ancient houses which are shown in Mr. Charles's drawing of the Market Place in 1820, a reduced copy of which is given in a previous part of this work. They were in 1839 pulled down by the Commissioners of Pavements. On stripping off the exterior plaster of the lower house, the post-and-pan framing was found braced hollow-diamond wise, and from the central bay windows lateral lights down to the return transom seemed to have existed. Sketches by Mr. Charles, which permit this more positive description than informants' memory would justify, suggest that probably when perfect, although devoid of carving, no half-timber design in the town was finer. A few yards further down the street, on the north side, were several old houses, a sketch of which is here presented, the gabled building on the left being the old Mitre tavern, and the two adjoining buildings the Kent Fire Insurance Office. These houses were rebuilt in 1826. At the back of No. 7 are some architectural remnants which were collected and set up by John Newington Hughes, including a Decorated window of two lights from the old Mitre, a porch from Ashford church, and the Perpendicular east window of Sutton church.

At the east end of Bank Street stood an ancient house in which Edward Hunter, the first mayor under the Charter of 1747, lived. The inscription on his monument in the west wall of All Saints' Church is as follows :—

Near this monument lies interr'd the body of Edward Hunter, gent , jurat, and twice mayor of this town, who died the 15th day of April 1757, aged 72. That his charity to the poor and distress'd, which in his lifetime was very extensive, might after his decease be in some measure continued, he built and endow'd six convenient almshouses in this parish for 3 men and 3 women Also gave by his will to St. Thomas's Hospital £100, to the Foundling Hospital £100, to the poor of this parish £100, to the Charity School in this town £20. He hath dispers'd ; he hath given to the poor ; his righteousness endureth for ever.

This house afterwards became the "Kent Arms" printing office—booksellers and printers formerly used signs for their places of business—and here it was that the first newspaper, the *Maidstone and Kentish Journal*, was established. When Mr. D'Israeli contested the borough in 1837, he called at this house and dictated to the editor (Mr. E. P. Hall, since of the Clarendon Press, Oxford) his address to the electors. On coming to its close, the editor was about to write his signature, when he said, "Leave out the apostrophe; it looks so foreign; write it in one word—Disraeli;" and thus it has ever since been written. The house was pulled down a few years ago on its sale by the trustees of Hunter's Charity, and the space it covered supplied about

House in Bank Street.

two-thirds of the site of Messrs. Wigan and Co.'s new banking house.

Some distance lower down Bank Street is a fine old house which afforded an excellent specimen of the graceful and old-fashioned style of ornamental pargetting, introducing the arms of England at the time of James I. and the badge of the Prince of Wales, with the letters $_I{}^G{}_L$ on a shield. The whole of the front was formerly adorned, like a bride's cake, with garlands and festoons; but about sixty years ago these ornaments, with the pediment, were removed. In the appended photo-lithograph the two upper stories are shown as they appeared previous to the alterations. The house, it has been conjectured, was built by William Gull, or by John Green, who was a member of the Corporation. Gull was descended from an Ightham family, and was for many years recorder of Maidstone.

On the north side of the High Street was a curious old house which, several years since, supplied the site for the new premises of the London and County Banking Company. It had a range of windows in the second story, and on a pane of ancient glass in one of the back windows were the arms of England and France. A view of this house is given in the upper half of the annexed sketch; and in the lower portion is shown a group of buildings at the bottom of the High Street, towards the Fair Meadow. On the right is the lodging house known as "Louse Tavern," and the small building peeping beyond the main warehouse was fitted up as a theatre in the latter half of the last century. This odd-looking erection was advertised as the "New Theatre" in December 1770, when three performances were given hebdomadally for two weeks, the prices of admission being--Boxes, 2s. 6d.; pit, 1s. 6d.; gallery, 1s.; upper gallery, 6d. A story has reached me of actors and audience being caught by a sudden flood and boated round to dry land. A more worthy Thespian shrine was provided, about eighty-five years ago, by Mrs. Sarah Baker, on the site now occupied by Mr. Marsh's shop. It measured 85ft. by 23ft., and had three entrances from the street, over the centre one being a large portrait of Shakespeare painted by William Jefferys, of this town. The undecorated oblong interior contained pit, boxes, and gallery. Edmund Kean, when quite a youth, and yet unknown to fame, made his appearance here, and it is still remembered that during his stay in the town he lodged in a scantily furnished apartment in Dann's Court. Sometimes a star came down from London—Miss Foote, Miss O'Neil, Incledon, and, frequently, Dowton, the comedian, who was Mrs. Baker's son-in-law. But in the end the theatre did not prove a paying concern, and it was accordingly demolished in 1851.

Passing, for a few minutes, out of the High Street, and down what was once called Mill Lane, we come to the Palace, hoary with forgotten summers and, where not ivy-clad, fretted by winter's frost. In 1486 Archbishop Morton, according to Weever, greatly augmented and beautified the Palace, which had fallen into a dilapidated condition. It became, with the manor of Maidstone, the property of the Crown in 1537; and in 1550 Edward VI. granted it to Sir Thomas Wyatt, who forfeited it with his life in 1554. Queen Mary then granted the Palace to Cardinal Pole "for life, and one year after death." * After Pole's decease in 1558, it continued in the Crown till the 10th of July 1562,† when Queen Elizabeth granted to Alexander Parker "all that her old and ruinous house and capital mansion called the Old Palace in Maydstone, and all houses, edifices, buildings, barns, stables, dovehouses, orchards, apple-yards, gardens, ponds, water-

* Close Rolls, No. 1127. † Ibid., No. 848.

1. House in High Street — 2. Lower end of High Street.

courses, and river's banks; and also two pieces of land called Palace mead, and a dovehouse, and Palace pound,* and Palace close, as they were let by Sir Thomas Wyat to Thomas Lucke at 40s. per annum." The premises were subsequently conveyed to William Beynham, gent., of London, who, on July 3, 1569, surrendered them to the Crown. On July 20, 1573, Robert, Earl of Leicester, conveyed them, for some pecuniary sum, to Edward Carye, Esq., and William Dodington, gent.†

The Palace soon after came into the possession of the Astley family. On the 8th of July 1581,‡ Thomas Astley, Esq., of Dartford, a Privy Councillor, for £500 conveyed to his brother John Astley, Esq., of Otterden, also a Privy Councillor, "all that capital messuage or chief mansion-house commonly called or known by the name of the Old Palace, with appurtenances, in Maydestone, and the malt house commonly called the Old Palace stable, and land called old stable close, and Palace mead and dovehouse, and the Palace pound and Palace close." John Astley above mentioned was master of the Queen's jewel house. He at this time held a lease of Allington Castle, but appears to have subsequently resided at the Palace. Dying in August 1596, he was buried in Maidstone church. His son and heir, Sir John Astley, who died January 26, 1640,§ and was also interred in All

---

* The pound, within living memory, was situated about twenty-five paces north of the north-east door of All Saints' Church.
† Close Rolls, No. 941.
‡ Ibid., No. 1127.
§ Sir John Astley by will bequeathed to his wife Katherine Bridges, niece of Lord Edmund Bridges, of Sudley Castle, the furniture of the following rooms in the Palace, viz., "the room commonly used to dine in, and the little red chamber adjoining; the room where my wife now lieth, and the little closet thereto adjoining; the great dining room; the great lodging chamber thereunto adjoining towards the north, and the little chamber within the same; the chamber wherein myself doth now usually lodge; the chamber next adjoining wherein my maid-servants do now usually lie, and the chamber within the same where my cousin, Agnes Bridges, did heretofore usually lie. I bequeath to William Harrison, of Woodnesborough, the

Saints' Church, devised the property to his kinsman, Jacob, first Baron Astley of Reading, of whom a more detailed notice is elsewhere given in this work. Lord Astley died in 1652, and was succeeded by his only son Isaac, who, dying in 1662, left two sons, Jacob, the eldest, and Francis, who died without issue. Jacob, Lord Astley, died in 1688, and was buried with his predecessors in Maidstone church. He left no issue, and the barony became extinct. Lady Astley, his widow, continued to reside at the Palace until her death, July 17, 1692. The property then descended to Sir Jacob Astley, of Melton Constable, in Norfolk, who sold it in 1719 to Lord Romney, in whose family it remained until within a few years ago.

In the front of the existing pile are evidently to be seen portions of Archbishop Morton's work, and a three-light trefoil-headed window at the north end is probably of earlier date; but the greater part of the building appears to belong to the latter part of Elizabeth's reign. A chapel attached to it was pulled down about the year 1730. A fireplace, having on its spandrels the escutcheon of Archbishop Warham, was, a few years since, disclosed near the north end. The Palace has long been occupied as two separate habitations. In the southern portion are the "great dining room" and the "great lodging chamber" mentioned in Sir John Astley's will, the latter being now used as a drawing room. The dais is on the east side of the dining room, which is oak panelled and oak floored, and has the Astley arms carved on the high oak mantel-piece. The kitchen was on

---

. room I now use for my closet, where the most part of my books and papers are, the inner room within the same, and the rooms and places within the said closet and inner room: the little closet going up the gallery, and the whole gallery and little chamber; the chamber over the said closet, sometimes called the schoolhouse, and the inner room thereto; the chamber next the buttery where my sister, Eleanor Knatchbull, usually did lie, with all the inner rooms belonging to the same."

the river side of this portion, where there is an immense fire-place, which has for many years been disused.

Returning to the High Street, and passing several doors to the left, we come to a large old fabric, now No. 60, which is partially hidden behind a modern exterior. During some alterations in 1839, the western part of it was found to have flat Tudor arched doorways, with armorial bearings in the spandrels, and massive carved supports to the roof, with a small screen in six divisions of trefoil-headed arches. This was in the seventeenth century the residence of Gervase Maplesden, and, in more recent times, of the Stone family; the name of Stone occurs several times in the list of chief magistrates between the years 1783 and 1813. Lord Mansfield and other judges, when on circuit, had apartments here. The next building is the Post Office, on the site of which, prior to 1871, stood a spacious mansion known as "Astley House"—a designation which has led to a belief that this was a seat of certain members of the Astley family. That the house never even belonged to the Astley family will be shown by the following facts.

According to an indenture in the Public Record Office,[*] dated December 10, 1584, Allen Barefoot, husbandman, of Ashburnham, in Sussex, for a certain sum of money, conveyed to John Aneston, yeoman, of Catsfield, in the same county, and Thomas Crowcher, husbandman, of Ashburnham, the third part of the property, which had been bequeathed to John Barefoot,[†] his uncle, the then occupant, by Katherine Hopper, his aunt. The existing title-deeds belonging to the house date from 1586.[‡] On the 1st of November in that year the third part above mentioned was conveyed by Aneston

---

[*] Close Rolls, No. 1215.
[†] John Barefoot was one of the borough chamberlains, 1596-7.
[‡] For perusal of these I am indebted to the courtesy of Messrs. King and Hughes, solicitors.

and Crowcher to John Barefoot. A deed of mortgage, between Samuel Barefoot and William Darby, yeoman, of Maidstone, dated October 29, 1631, describes the property as abutting northward to the High Street, eastward to the tenement and garden of Gervase Maplesden, Esq., southward to the "little river," and westward to the tenement and garden previously belonging to John Gosling. On the 5th of July 1634, William Darby and Samuel Barefoot conveyed to Robert Withinbrooke,* yeoman, of Maidstone, "that one tenement lately divided into two habitations," with a malting-house attached; and on the 10th of October 1672 Withinbrooke's kinsman and namesake gave a lease of the premises for nine years to John Pitcher, maltster, of Maidstone. This Robert Withinbrooke's three sons, his heirs in gavelkind, conveyed to Thomas Bliss, May 10, 1681, "all those three messuages heretofore but one;" and in July 1707 Bliss increased the size of the garden by purchasing and adding thereto a strip of ground 57ft. long, north and south, 5½ft. wide at one end, and 9¼ft. wide at the other.

These deeds leave no gap for probable intermediate possession by the Astleys, and not only do not mention an ornate or capital mansion, but indicate that the chief tenement had so far fallen in condition as to have been divided into three dwellings. The augmentation of the garden in 1707 by Thomas Bliss rendered it symmetrical, and the documents quoted above seem to justify the surmise that he erected what, during the last half century of its existence, was called Astley House, working up into it a good deal of old material. To him also may be attributed the summer-house built over the little river at the bottom of the garden, posterior to the date of the house; and the improvement of the garden may indicate its origin. Clement Taylor Smythe, who was

* Withinbrooke was one of the borough chamberlains, 1648-9.

acquainted with this residence as a lodger, says it was called Astley House "for no other reason but to please the fancy of a romantic governess of a ladies' school, who once occupied the mansion, she having previously given the old seat of Digons the name of Nunnery from quite as good authority." Indeed, no occurrence of the appellation is known until Miss Jones, who was the authoress of a romance, transferred hither in 1816 her seminary from Knightrider Street, the lady evidently thinking to enhance with an aristocratic Maidstone name the status of her new location.

Thomas Bliss, who was a native of the town,[*] married Elizabeth, widow of Ambrose Ward, of Yalding. He was churchwarden of All Saints' in 1674. Having obtained a seat in the Corporation, he acted as one of the town chamberlains in 1678 and 1679, and, in November 1682, became mayor of the borough. He was again chamberlain in 1684. He entered Parliament for Maidstone in 1698, and continued to represent the borough until 1708. Dying in 1721, he was buried in the church at Yalding. His widow, then seventy-six, married William Horsmonden Turner, he being about forty-seven.[†] Turner resided at the house in the High Street until his purchase of Stede Hill, Harrietsham, about the year 1747.

The ornate front of Bliss's house, preserved in the annexed photo-lithograph,[‡] was a conspicuous feature of the lower part of the High Street. On a shield in the centre were the

---

[*] An entry in the Allington register refers to his parents—"Mary, daughter of Thomas Bliss, of Maidstone, and Jane, his wife, baptised February 21, 1650" (Old Style).

[†] On a stone in the floor of the chancel aisle in Yalding church is this inscription:—"Here lieth the body of Thomas Bliss, Esq., who died October ye 8th, 1721, aged 74 years. In the same vault, of her owne making, lieth also the body of Elizabeth, the wife of William Turner, Esq., daughter of John Kenward, Esq., of this place, and relict successively of Ambrose Ward, Esq., and of the said Thomas Bliss. She died October 27, 1730, aged 81 years."

[‡] Drawn from a photograph by Messrs. Clarke & Co., of Week Street.

arms of the Barber Surgeons' Company, with the motto, "De Præcipientia Dei." Thomas Bliss was latterly the proprietor of the Lower Brewery, but in the deed of 1681 he is mentioned as being a surgeon. He may therefore have been a member of the Barber Surgeons' Company, and may in compliment have placed the Company's arms on his new mansion. "The whole of the windows in front of the house," wrote Clement Taylor Smythe in 1832, " were formerly casements, but the lower range was many years ago altered to semicircular headed French windows, and a small portico supported by pillars was substituted for the ancient porch. In the roof were six large windows, which were removed some years ago."

Near the bottom of the High Street, on the north side, stood a curious old building, adjoining the lodging-house sketched at a previous page. When demolished about the year 1828, it was found to contain several Tudor arches and fire-places, and in the spandrels of an arched doorway were two carved shields of arms, each charged with three bars. This was the last remaining house in the town with the ancient form of shop-front, which consisted of two wooden flaps, one of which was tilted up, while the other was let down and formed a board for the display of goods and wares. Several cottages situated at the entrance to the footpath under the Cliffe (which was formed by Sir Jacob Astley), were pulled down at the beginning of the present century; the fronts of several of them were painted in fresco with draperies and medallions. The archbishop's park anciently extended from the bridge along the opposite side of the Medway to Fant; it was stocked with deer, and the inhabitants of Maidstone at certain seasons had a privilege of shooting prickets with longbows. Beyond, and extending towards Barming Heath, was an estate called Bower Down, part of which was also known

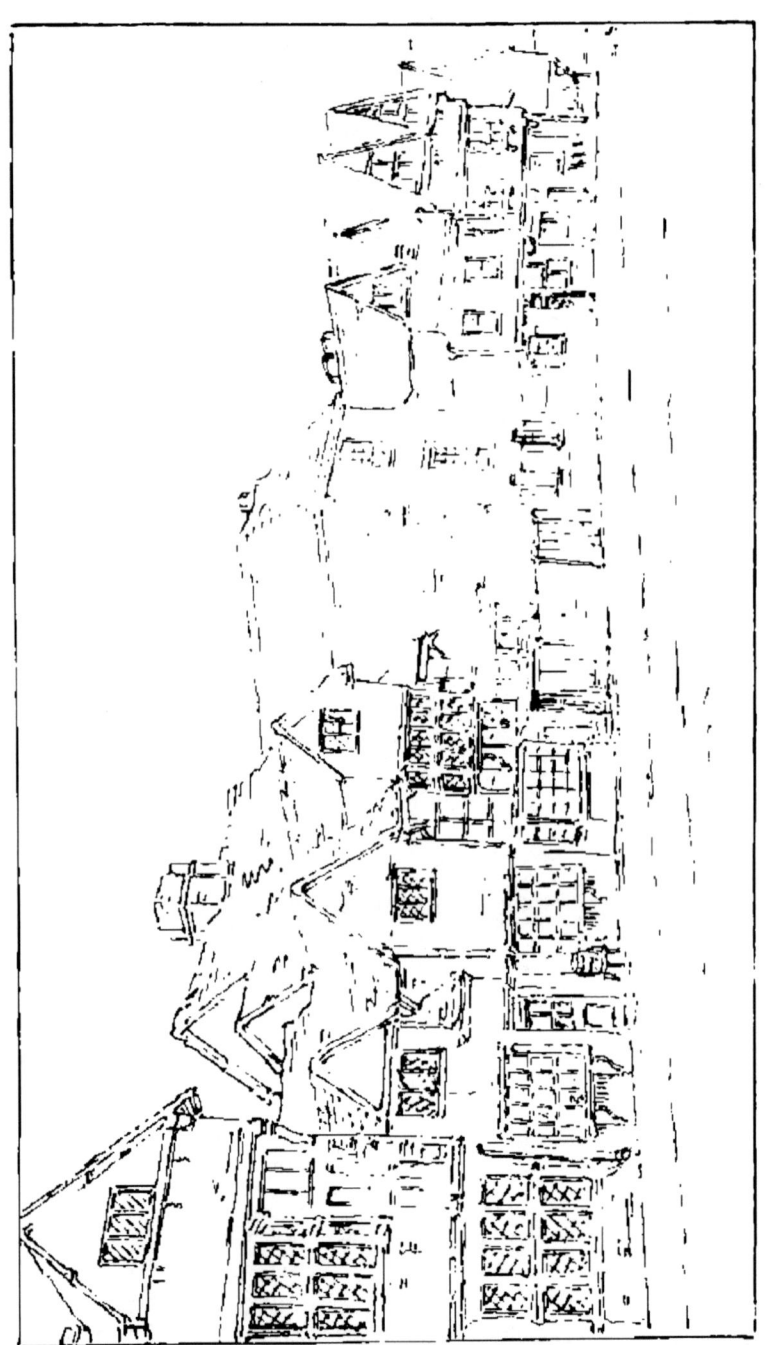

Houses in Keck Street.

as Little Bower. It was purchased by Richard Beale about the beginning of the seventeenth century; he added several other pieces of land to the estate, which then consisted of upwards of two hundred acres. The small estate of Fant belonged to Thomas Bunce in the reign of James I. Fant House, at the southern extremity of Upper Fant Road, was new fronted about seventy years ago.

We will now retrace our steps, and proceed up Week Street. In an old house on the west side of the street, opposite the Bell hotel, there was found, about sixty years ago, the back of a very fine iron stove, having, within the Garter, the arms of the Sackville family in high relief, with the motto of that order. The front of a house further up, on the same side, now converted into two dwellings (Nos. 55 and 57), is decorated with figures and festoons in parget, with the inscription "S. P. 1680" in the centre. The house opposite, on the east side of the street, had originally projecting casement windows, extending from the top to the bottom stories; these were removed about seventy years ago, when a new front was added. It is now a coffee tavern, and during recent alterations a Tudor fire-place and a carved oak ceiling were revealed. The adjoining building, at the corner of Union Street was, it is supposed, the manor-house of Wyke, which was long in the possession of the Fisher family. A pedigree of the Fishers is given in the herald's visitation of 1574. Henry Fisher was one of the borough members from 1563 to 1571, and for the next two generations the name of the family often occurs in the municipal records. The annexed sketch, reduced from a drawing executed by William Alexander, probably about ninety years ago, shows a range of houses on the west side of the street, comprising the site of the Congregational Chapel; some of them still exist in altered aspect.

2 A

There were formerly several very old houses in Earl Street. Half way down this thoroughfare, on the south side, stands the house which was built by Andrew Broughton, the regicide. It was long ago divided into two habitations, both tolerably spacious family residences. The east wing was about eight years ago further altered for the purposes of a club. The only noticeable indications of the original style that remain are two windows of the upper story in the Star-yard side of the house. A shield of arms once existed over the entrance, and the late Thomas Charles could remember Ionic pilasters of plaster on each side of the bay windows. At the Restoration, when Broughton sought refuge in Switzerland, the house, with the orchards, gardens, and stables attached, was forfeited to the Crown, and in September 1661 Charles II. granted it to James, Duke of York, by whom, in December 1663, it was, in consideration of a payment of £247 10s., conveyed to John Greenhill, Esq., of New Sarum, in Wilts, who, in February 1664, reconveyed it to the regicide's son, Andrew Broughton, Esq., of Seaton, in Rutlandshire. An abstract of a deed, dated 1686, shows that the property had been mortgaged to the extent of £1,000, the money being possibly wanted to sustain the elder Broughton in his exile. A price had been set upon his head at the Restoration, and repeated applications were made to the Canton of Berne to deliver him up, but that government refused to accede to them. Broughton the younger held under James II. the appointment of Receiver of Hearth Money.

On the other side of the way, opposite Broughton's house, was a mansion called Earls Place, the grounds of which formed the area between Week Street and Havock Lane, and St. Faith's Street and Earl Street. It was entered by a massive gateway leading into a court-yard, on the west side

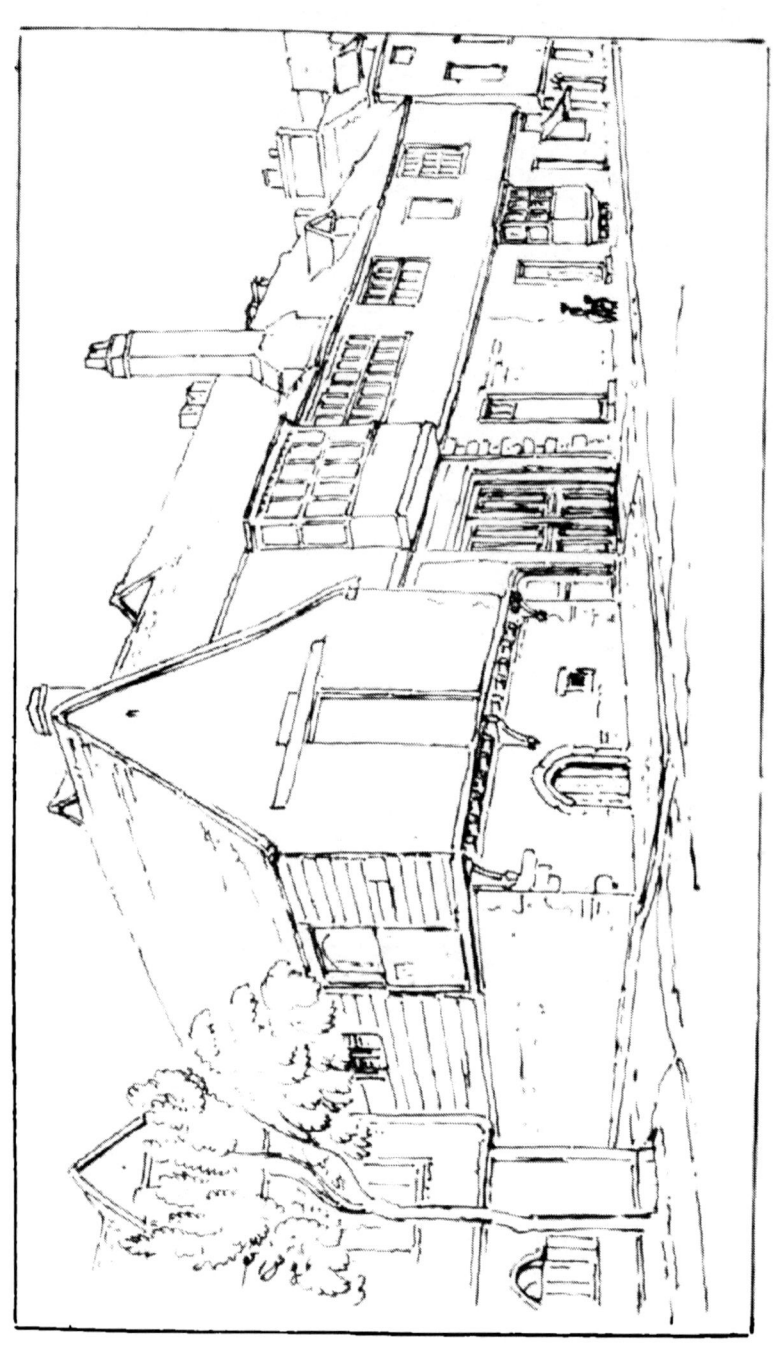

of which was a lofty hall with large windows, filled with glass on which were painted the arms of the Stafford and Lee families, and other devices. The hall gave place about fifty years ago to the house which now occupies the site, but the upper part of the mansion retained much of the aspect shown in the annexed sketch until modernized within the last six or seven years. Earls Place was, in the reign of Henry VI., the residence of the Staffords, and afterwards of the Lee family. Richard Lee was mayor of Maidstone in 1573-4, and died during his term of office.

At the west corner of Havock Lane and Earl Street is an ancient house to which an acre of land was attached. It belonged to William Lilly at the beginning of the sixteenth century, and was in 1650 occupied by Thomas Fletcher, who was mayor in 1663-4. It became a public-house in 1833, and a few years since was converted into two dwellings. An oak pendant, 3½ft. long, with fleur-de-lys and a lozenge-shaped shield, surmounted by a cross, carved upon it, was found, about twenty years ago, affixed to one of the gables of this building. Some distance lower down, on the same side, there was formerly an old house with oriel windows, in which were the arms of Archbishop Warham and other ancient painted glass.

Passing through Havock Lane, we will finish our tour of inspection at Chillington House, in St. Faith's Street. The manor of Chillington or, according to the old spelling, Shillington, was annexed to the College of All Saints, and on the dissolution of that house it was granted to Lord Cobham. The extent of the manorial lands cannot now be ascertained, but, judging from their annual value as given in the College accounts, they do not appear to have been extensive. A piece of land adjoining the entrance to Park House, and once called Chillington Fields, doubtless belonged to the original demesne. In the reign of Henry VIII. the property came into the possession of George Maplesden, of Digons, who forfeited it for his share in Wyatt's rebellion. From a deed among the Corporation muniments, dated 1561, it appears to have been restored to the Maplesdens by Queen Elizabeth. By this deed George, John, and Robert, sons and co-heirs of Peter Maplesden, conveyed Chillington to Nicholas Barham, serjeant-at-law. Barham, who resided at the mansion, died in 1577, and the following curious particulars regarding it are given in his will, which is dated July 23, in that year:—

My will, intent, and meaning is, that if it shall like my sayde wiffe to make her continuance in my house, and to be at her owne flynding, for so long as she shall so live and continue unmaryed, I will she shall have and enjoye all that the ould hall with the butterye or panterye, the chamber hanged with grene, the chamber wherein Nichas Cleke now lyethe, and the two garret lofts over the same chambers, together with the greate chamber over the old hall, and the little closett under the staires for the laying of any thinge she shall be disposed, and together also with the utter seller under the said pantrye, and the room between the brewhouse and the same seller and pantrye: nevertheless my will, meaning, and intent is, that the said Arthur Barham (the testator's son), and his heires, shall have power and authority at all suche times as he shall have brued and is to tun his beare, that for so much beare as he shall lay in the ynner seller to carry the same into the same inner seller, through the said utter seller, and immediately after to redeliver the keys, as well of the dore between the twoe sellers as of the dore of the said bruhouse, which is next unto the utter seller: and my will and meaning is that my said wyffe shall likewise have reasonable use of the said bruhouse when she hath nede to brue, and also of the mast yard for washing as oft as it shall be nedeful, with convenient liberty to dry her clothes in the backside, and to walke in the said backside and orchards for the comfort and recreation of herself and family, and to have the necessary use without interruption or deniall, for her selfe and family, of the necessary houses of office situate in the end of the old orchard, and that at all such times as it shall please God to send his blessinge with reasonable store of fruites, my said wiffe to have of the same, fower bushells of peares, whereof two of somer fruite, and two of winter frute, and twenty bushells of apples, whereof one half of the best sorte. And my mynd and will further is that my wiffe shall have liberty for herselfe and family to resort to the chappell, and for the residue of her family in the said chappell. And my meaning also is that in the winter tyme my said wiffe shall have liberty to dry her clothes in the under gallery adjoining to the walke in the garden at her will and pleasure; and I trust that such loving kindness shall continue between my said wiffe and sonn and daughter-in-law, which I mistrust not between my said wiffe and daughter-in-law, that she may enjoy her pleasure to walke in the upper gallery next the garden when and as often as she shall be mynded so to doe for her reasonable recreation.

Arthur Barham sold Chillington to Henry Hall, of Digons, at some date prior to 1609. Hall's grandson died in 1650 without issue, leaving the property to his sister Elizabeth, wife of Sir Thomas Taylor, who sold it to Sir

John Beale, bart., of Framlingham. After the death of that baronet in 1684, it was conveyed by Elizabeth, his daughter, to her husband, William Emmerton, of Chipstead. Edwin Wyatt, serjeant-at-law, soon after occupied the house, and in 1698 it was sold by John Leche to Robert Southgate. The latter's son, of the same name, became bankrupt as a fruiterer and cider-maker in 1743. David Fuller, an attorney, thereupon purchased the property. He died without issue, and was buried at Northfleet. Mary, his widow, who survived him, died in 1774, and Chillington passed to her relative, William Stacey Coast, of Chartham. The mansion was tenanted in 1779 by Robert Parker, who became a partner in the local banking firm of Brenchley, Parker, Penfold, and Springett. It was conveyed in 1800 to Timewell Bentham, and in the following year was sold to William Charles and Robert Harris.

Mr. Charles was baptised at Bradford, in Wilts, and had been educated for the medical profession, but having married a Miss Arnold, of Maidstone, he settled here, and entered into a business of felting and blanket-cleaning. The business was subsequently carried on in the hall and galleries of Chillington House, and at the fulling mill at Sandling. Mr. Charles died in 1832, leaving two sons, Thomas and William. After the death of the latter in 1840, the business was sold. Mr. Thomas Charles, who, like his brother, remained a bachelor, had been trained to his father's profession of a medical practitioner, but when in middle age he retired into private life, and amused himself by gathering a collection of antiquarian objects. He made drawings of many old buildings in Maidstone and the neighbourhood, and wrote a translation of Boëthius's "Consolations of Philosophy." By his death in 1855 the Charles family became extinct.

Under the advice of the late Mr. Alexander Randall, his

acting executor, Mr. Charles bequeathed to the town his collection of antiquities, and some of his books and pictures, with a request that they might be permanently preserved, and known as the "Charles Museum." The Corporation gratefully received the gift, and at a ratepayers' meeting the Public Libraries Act, 1855, was adopted. Chillington House was purchased by the town for the exhibition of the collection, and the Museum was opened in January 1858. Mr. Edward Pretty, for many years drawing master of Rugby School, and an old friend of Mr. Charles, was the first curator, and the Museum remained under his charge until his death in 1865. His bequest of books, prints, and drawings, formed an important augmentation of the collection.

Except that it had been thoroughly cleansed, Chillington House, the greater part of which was probably rebuilt in Barham's time, continued for some years, as regards structural alterations, pretty much in the state in which Mr. Charles left it. Two doorways, one of them Tudor arched, leading to the east wing, were removed. An upper room in the western part of the building, which had been let to the Mechanics' Institute, was in 1867 assigned to the Kent Archæological Society, and in this room is deposited the society's collection of Roman and Saxon remains, books, and antique furniture.

The old pile was in a dilapidated condition; but through the munificence of townsmen, it has, with excellent taste, been restored. One of the first steps in this direction was was the demolition of the ugly consulting room which William Charles, senior, had erected between the middle and west bays of the front, and the reopening of the window which it had covered, and of other windows that had been built up doubtless in the time of the window duty. As the contributions to the Museum increased, more space was found to be necessary, and this could only be provided by acquiring the premises which formed the wings of the building, and which had not been included in the purchase of 1858. The basement portion of both wings coincided, but the upper stories had at some period been rebuilt. Mr. Randall thereupon purchased the east wing, and made it over to the Corporation for £500. This sum he, with characteristic generosity, refunded as an instalment towards the re-edification, conditionally on the town raising the remainder of the required amount. The wing was rebuilt as nearly as possible in the style of the original fabric, having regard to the altered requirements of the new structure. At the same time the lower gallery was restored, and the garden window of the hall was reopened and filled with painted glass.

Mr. Julius Lucius Brenchley had just then returned from his travels in various parts of the world, having amassed a valuable collection of curiosities illustrative of the manners and customs and the natural history of remote countries. He visited the Museum in company with his fellow-traveller, M. Jules Remy, the French naturalist, and was so gratified with the purpose to which the old manor-house was adapted, that he at once expressed an intention to place a portion of his collection at the disposal of the Corporation. The shells, birds, and insects arrived in 1869, and even with the acquisition of the east wing, the curator was puzzled to find room for them. More space was required, and Mr. Randall was again equal to the emergency. A meeting held at his house in December of that year resulted in a decision to secure the west wing, Mr. Brenchley promising £400 towards the purchase. The property was shortly afterwards conveyed to Mr. Randall, but only a little while before his death. In the course of the demolition, two hidden chimney-pieces were found; and on the spandrels of one of them were the made over to the town his terra cotta figures, and his china, library, bronzes, pictures, and musical instruments, in addition to a handsome sum of money to defray the cost of preserving them. To make room for the entire collection, rearrangement of some of the contents of the Museum was necessary, and the Chillington kitchen and wash-house were converted into the Ethnological Room. In the summer of 1873 the north end of the gallery was restored. Simultaneously the old chapel was rebuilt, the stone and lead lights from the displaced east window of All Saints' being worked up in the new windows, while the little gallery was formed out of Lord Romney's discarded pew in the north gallery of the Old Church. In the following year the eastern portion of the half-timber Court Lodge of East Farleigh was pulled down, and subsequently erected against the east wall of the Museum gallery.

Chillington House, thus restored, is still an excellent example of Jacobean work, and with its antique furniture and fittings, forms one of the most interesting architectural objects in Maidstone. The Museum, of which Mr. Charles's collection was the nucleus, has become a multifarious aggregation of curiosities, gathered from the four quarters of the globe, and is probably not surpassed for local antiquities by any similar institution in the kingdom. Besides a select library of nearly eight thousand volumes, it contains seven illuminated manuscripts and twenty rare books. Among these may be mentioned a large folio manuscript of the Scriptures, twelfth century; a Breviary, English art, of the fourteenth century, embellished with many beautiful initial letters and borders entirely surrounding the page; a Book of Hours, Flemish art, containing several curious paintings; Luther's Bible, 1551; and the copy of Walton's Polygot Bible which was, in July 1658, purchased by the Corporation.

CHAPTER XV.

SOME INCIDENTS OF BYGONE TIMES.

A Monster—Wonderful Crop of Wheat—Visit of Henry VI.—Terrific Storm—Smuggling—Capture of Sturgeons—Military Encampments on Coxheath—The Troops Reviewed by the King—General D'Hilliers at the Bell Hotel—Review of Kentish Volunteers in the Mote Park—Equipment of Maidstone Volunteers in George the Third's Reign—Precautions against Invasion—The last great County Meeting on Penenden Heath.

IN this chapter I purpose to string together a number of isolated incidents, picturesque, grave, or extraordinary, that do not naturally fall within the foregoing divisions of this History. The first of these dates from the time of King John, and partakes of the character of those superstitious wonders which tradition, that old lady who sits chattering on the hearthrug of history, delights to recount. Stow relates that in the year 1206 "about this town was a monster found stricken with lightning, who had a head like an ass, a belly like a man, and all other parts far different from any known creature, but not approachable nigh unto by reason of its stench." No mention is made of this by Lambarde, but it is repeated by Kilburne and Baker almost in Stow's words.*

A wonderful occurrence is related in a letter written on the 4th of August 1694, by a North Devon gentleman, who says:—"One thing may be extraordinary to hint, namely, of a field near Maidstone, in Kent, not tilled these three or four years, which bears this year, without ploughing or sowing, a fair crop of wheat, and Mr. Freke, that came lately from Tonbridge, in my hearing said he saw a crop from one root which bore fifty-eight stalks, I mean ears, and that it hangs up as a monument there." †

In 1437 Henry VI., during his minority, visited Maidstone. Archbishop Chichley was then staying at the Palace, and the youthful king was his guest. Twenty-two years later, several members of the Corporation of Rye, with the mayor and bailiff of Winchelsea, rested at Maidstone on their way to London. An entry in the chamberlains' accounts of Rye states that their dinner here cost them 8d., and a feed for their horses 3d.

On the 8th of September 1692 a shock of earthquake was felt in all parts of England, and Turner, in his "Remarkable

---

* For an account of a remarkable birth at Maidstone on the 24th October, 1568, "at seven of the clocke in the afternoone of the same day, being Sonday," and a number of verses thereon, entitled "A Warning to England," the reader is referred to the "Black Letter Ballads and Broadsides," published by Joseph Lilly, of London, in 1870. The child lived twenty-four hours, and the circumstances, as stated in a broadside printed at Aldergate on the 24th of December 1568, were attested by William Plomer, one of the jurates, and John Sadler, goldsmith, "beside divers other credible person, both men and women."

† Historical MSS. Commission, Fifth Report. Miss Julia H. L. de Vaynes, in the first volume of her interesting "Kentish Garland," states that among the ballads in the Pepys Collection at Magdalen College, Cambridge, is one entitled, "The Maidstone Miracle; or, the Strange Kentish Wonder, being an account of a charitable farmer who, by Divine Providence, had a vast crop of corn which grew in a field which was neither plow'd nor sow'd for several years, it being looked upon to be a reward of his Christian character, &c. Printed for Philip Brooksby at the Golden Ball in Pye Corner."

Providences," observes that at Maidstone "the people generally got out of their houses." A terrific storm of wind and hail, accompanied by thunder and lightning, occurred on the 19th of August 1763, and caused great destruction to property in the parish of Maidstone. Hasted states that it arose at sea, off the coast of Sussex, and entering Kent at Tunbridge Wells, swept across the county to Sheerness, devastating an area forty miles long and from two to four miles in breadth. We are told how hop gardens, orchards, and corn fields were entirely destroyed; how trees were uprooted or stripped of their leaves, and barns and houses blown down; how apples were washed down the gully of Tyler's Lane, in Maidstone; how, on the south side of the High Street, the frames of the windows were broken and driven in by the hailstones, which "beat as loud against the shutters as the strongest blow of a thick club." The hail indeed might rather be called pieces of ice. One piece, picked up at Barming, was in the form of an oyster, and measured nine inches in circumference; and several pieces which measured four and a half inches round, were found ten days after the storm, and sent to London and other places. A subscription was raised by the gentry in the neighbourhood of Maidstone, amounting to nearly £3,000, in aid of poor people who suffered by the calamity.

Smuggling was perhaps at no time so prevalent as in the reign of George III. Traders in contraband goods abounded, and in the third quarter of the last century they imported into Kent large quantities of tea, silk, hops, spirits, and lace. In July 1773 ten hundredweights of tea and many rolls of lace and silk were seized in a barn near Maidstone. While an excise officer and a party of dragoons were scouring the district in February of the following year they fell in with a gang of eighty smugglers within two miles of the town. In the fight which ensued several of the smugglers were wounded. One of the horses threw its rider, and, laden with four bags of tea, ran through Maidstone. The fight resulted in the capture of an enormous quantity of tea and lace.

In July of the same year, 1774, a capture of a different kind was made in the neighbourhood of Maidstone. A sturgeon was caught in the Medway; it was 7ft. 4in. in length, and weighed 160 pounds. Hollingshead remarks that in ancient times the Medway was famous for sturgeon.*

During the wars of the last century, Coxheath, an elevated plain, three miles in length and in some parts nearly a mile in width, and situated about three miles south-east of Maidstone, was frequently used as a camp for troops. In 1756 twelve thousand Hanoverian and Hessian soldiers were for several months encamped on the heath. An incident in connection with this encampment gave rise to some ill-feeling. A Hanoverian, who stole three silk handkerchiefs from a Maidstone tradesman, was brought before the chief magistrate of the town. He might have been charged with the crime of shop-lifting, but in consideration of his being a foreigner in the service of this country, the mayor committed him for trial at the quarter sessions on the mitigated charge of theft. The acting commandant, however, interposed, and alleged that according to a treaty under which the Hanoverians were conveyed to England, a civil court had no power to deal with them; he even threatened violence if the prisoner was not immediately set at liberty. But the mayor declined to accede to the demand, on the ground that if this contention were admitted, the troops might with impunity commit any outrage. At length a peremptory order was received from London, and the prisoner was released. The affair, on

---

* A sturgeon was taken in the river at Maidstone in June 1879, the length of which was 7ft. 9in., and the weight 132 pounds.

becoming known, roused considerable indignation throughout the country, and in the magazines and newspapers of the day the conduct of the Government in -permitting such a treaty to be drawn up was freely denounced.

Coxheath was again the scene of a military encampment in 1778. The reserve forces had been called out, and the government was straining every nerve to reduce the American colonies to submission. Fifteen thousand men were encamped on the heath. On the 18th of September the grenadiers and light infantry, under the Duke of Grafton, with a troop of dragoons, marched to Barming Heath, and engaged in a sham fight, which was witnessed by many of the nobility and gentry of the district. At seven o'clock in the morning of the 6th of October two officers of the Middlesex militia met in a field near Loose and fought a duel, one of the parties being seriously wounded in the thigh. The troops were reviewed by George III. and Queen Charlotte on the 3rd of November. The royal party set out from Montreal, the seat of Lord Amherst, at nine in the morning, and proceeded through Sevenoaks to Coxheath, where the troops were drawn up in line. Their majesties placed themselves in the centre of the force, and subsequently saw the whole line march past in several divisions. They remained in camp till the evening gun-fire, and then drove to Leeds Castle, which was brilliantly illuminated. The king and queen remained at the castle during the night, and the next day they received an address from the Mayor (William Bishop) and Corporation of Maidstone. His majesty conferred on the mayor the honour of knighthood. Before leaving the castle, the king made the following entry in the family copy of Becke's Bible:—

King George the Third and his Queen Charlotte dined and lay at Leeds Castle, in Kent, the seat of the Honourable Robert Fairfax, on Tuesday, the third day of November, in the nineteenth year of his Majesty's reign, and the year of our Lord, one thousand seven hundred and seventy-eight ; their Majesties having that day reviewed his forces encamped on Coxheath, consisting of one regiment of dragoons, six regiments of regular infantry, and twelve regiments of militia, namely, the Hampshire, Middlesex, Surrey, Lincoln, Hertford, Suffolk, Derbyshire, and Yorkshire, and also three companies of Welsh Militia, namely the Montgomery, Radnor, and Pembroke, encamped with a park of artillery.

While the war in America lasted, troops were almost continuously in training on Coxheath, where an assembly room was erected in which concerts were held weekly. In 1779 a militia captain charged a lieutenant with inciting his men to mutiny; this led to a challenge, and early one morning the two officers met in Loose Valley. Shots were exchanged, and the captain, being wounded in the left breast, died before succour arrived. The force on the heath in August 1782 included the 59th Regiment of Foot, a troop of horse, and ten companies of infantry. A Maidstone man, who set up a gambling table near the camp, was, by order of General Conway, the commander-in-chief, drummed through the lines to the tune of the Rogue's March.

A Depôt for the cavalry regiments serving in India was established at Maidstone in 1797, the barracks being erected by John King, one of the magistrates of the borough, who contracted for the work. Horse and foot regiments frequently passed through the town, and their movements were attended with far more bustle than now. Any waggons obtainable, with their owners' horses and men, were engaged at a low mileage remuneration to carry the baggage and the women, children, and invalids—sometimes all the rank and file. On one occasion the Hereford militia started from Canterbury in seventy pressed waggons, each seated to hold twenty men; one division passed through Maidstone, and another over Penenden Heath, on their way to Portsmouth.

Another incident, full of historic reminiscence, may here be noted. At eleven o'clock on the night of the 3rd of August 1798 General D'Hilliers arrived at the Bell hotel, Week

Street. The general was second in command of the secret expedition under Bonaparte, and had been made prisoner on board a French frigate in the Mediterranean, after being present at the capture of Malta, whence he was conveying to the Directory despatches and trophies of the victory. After an embarrassing journey from Portsmouth by Lewes, under limitations of route and time, he slept at the Bell, and set out for Dover on the following morning, accompanied by his two aides-de-camp and three servants. He was described in his passport as of manly and soldier-like appearance, and his bearing was extremely polite to those who surrounded his carriage at the time of his departure.

Our exhausting struggle with France, and the aggressive policy of Bonaparte, gave rise in 1798 to the formation in Kent of volunteer brigades, and elicited from the latter, in the summer of 1799, an imposing demonstration of their loyalty and patriotism. Lord Romney, the lord-lieutenant of the county, invited them to muster in the Mote Park on the 1st of August—fittingly chosen as the anniversary of the battle of the Nile—to be reviewed by the king and entertained by his lordship. The volunteers, with colours flying and bands playing, and wearing oak sprays in their hats, marched into Maidstone on the evening of the 31st of July. At five o'clock next morning the infantry began to move into the park, followed some time later by the cavalry; and by nine the whole force was on the ground. It consisted of 5,319 men—4,305 infantry, under the command of the Hon. Lieutenant-General Fox, and 1,014 cavalry, commanded by Lieutenant-General Sir Robert Lawrie, bart. Forty-two Kentish towns and villages contributed the infantry, and the largest single brigade, that belonging to Maidstone, numbered 267 men.

The striking scene which the park presented is familiar

to us in the large engraving of Alexander's spirited drawing. On the rising part of the lawn at the back of the old Mote house a marquee, festooned and wreathed with flowers and oak boughs, and carpeted with green baize, had been erected for the king and the royal family; and in proximity were several other marquees for the ministers of State and a number of the county nobility. Arranged in two divisions, within sight of the royal tent, were ninety-one tables, which, if placed end to end, would have extended seven miles and a half. Upon these tables cloths were laid, and knives and forks, for nearly six thousand volunteers and other guests. The twenty thousand visitors which the occasion had attracted from all parts of the county, awaited with eagerness the arrival of the royal party. George III. and Queen Charlotte; Princess Elizabeth and Princess Sophia, their two fair-haired daughters; and Prince William of Gloucester, the king's brother, had left Kew Palace at half-past five in the morning. They breakfasted with Earl Camden at the Wildernesse, near Seal, where they were joined by the Prince of Wales, his brother the Duke of Cumberland, and many of the nobility. After some delay, the journey was resumed, and on approaching Maidstone, about half-past eleven, the king mounted his grey charger, and passing across the bridge and under a triumphal arch of hops and fruit, commenced his progress through the town.

The royal standard floated from the Town Hall and the church tower, and the High Street was crowded by a multitude of people in their gayest dresses. Every window was decorated and filled with faces, and overhead festoons of oak boughs, with fluttering streamers of coloured calico, stretched across from the peaked gables of opposite houses. From every window on Gabriel's Hill hung flags or variegated draperies; handkerchiefs were waved, and huzzas broke at intervals to drown the tramp of the horses. On entering Stone Street the royal party passed through another triumphal arch, the loyal tribute of Mr. Flint Stacey. Suspended from the curve of the arch was a large portrait of his majesty, and the whole was surmounted by an immense crown, on which the royal standard was hoisted.

As the park was reached, the roar of guns boomed on the ear, and their majesties were met by the Duke of York; Mr. Pitt, the Prime Minister; Mr. Dundas (afterwards Viscount Melville,) the Secretary of State; Lord Chancellor Loughborough; Mr. Windham, the Secretary for War; and the Earl of Spencer, First Lord of the Admiralty, who had, about an hour before, ridden into the park, each with a spray of oak in his hat. A heavy shower of rain drove the queen and princesses to the shelter of the royal marquee; but the clouds quickly passed away, and the weather remained fine. The volunteers were drawn up in a double line, extending from one end of the park to the other, with the cavalry and a small train of artillery in the background. The different brigades marched past twice, and the review concluded with a sham fight.

Their majesties then repaired to the grand marquee, where they received an address from the Mayor and Corporation, and the honour of knighthood was conferred on Samuel Chambers, the high sheriff of the county. This ceremony over, a sumptuous repast was served out to the royal party; while the ministers of State, with many ladies and county noblemen, were regaled in a separate tent, and the volunteers partook of dinner at the tables in the park. A brief statement of the fare provided for this monster feast will suffice to convey an idea of the splendid hospitality of Lord Romney. The principal dishes were:—60 lambs in quarters, making 240 dishes; 700 fowls, three in a dish; 300 hams, and an equal number of tongues; 220 dishes of boiled beef, 220 dishes of roast beef, 220 meat pies, 220 fruit pies, and 220 joints of roast veal, with seven pipes of wine and sixteen butts of beer. His majesty's health was proposed by Lord Romney; and several other toasts having been given, the royal party left the ground at six o'clock, returning to Kew the same evening. Before leaving the town the king released the insolvent debtors in the county prison. After dusk, the Town Hall was illuminated. On the following day the fragments of the feast were distributed among six hundred poor people living in Maidstone and the neighbourhood, and in the evening there was a display of fireworks in the Fair Meadow.

In admiration of his benevolence, Lord Romney was presented on the 6th of August with the freedom of the City of Canterbury. At a meeting of volunteer officers at Sittingbourne, on the 3rd of September, it was resolved to commemorate the review by the erection of a pavilion in the Mote Park. A circular building, 30ft. high, with a dome supported by nine Doric columns, was subsequently raised, bearing the inscription—"This Pavilion was erected by the Volunteers of Kent, as a tribute of respect to the Earl of Romney, Lord Lieutenant of the County, MDCCCI."

The renewal of war with France, and Napoleon's threatened invasion of this country in 1803, gave a fresh impulse to the volunteer movement in Kent. The county was divided into four districts, each under the charge of a deputy lieutenant, and in every town and village volunteers were enrolled. In the months of July and August a corps of infantry was formed in Maidstone in accordance with the following plan, to which each volunteer appended his signature:—

That we serve without pay (excepting when called out upon actual service), finding our own arms and accoutrements; that we hold ourselves bound at all times to assist the magistrates of this town when called upon; that in the event of actual invasion, we will march to any part of Great Britain it may be judged necessary to order us to, but, unless in that case, our services shall be limited to the district in which we reside; that for the purpose of defraying the incidental charges of the corps, a weekly subscription of one shilling shall be paid by each member thereof, such monies to form a fund, the state of which shall every quarter be made known to the whole corps.

The Maidstone volunteer carried a musket and bayonet; his uniform consisted of a blue jacket with scarlet facings, a white waist belt, and a hat with a crown of black bearskin, a white feather in front, and red feathers round the sides. The blue jacket subsequently gave place to a scarlet coat with Kentish-grey facings. A company of riflemen, comprising the picked men from the main body, was also formed. The rifleman's dress was of green cloth, with black velvet facings and a black belt; his hat was set off with green feathers, and his arms were a sword and a rifle. The wharfingers and bargemen belonging to the town enrolled themselves as a company of river fencibles, which numbered from eighty to a hundred men. They each carried a pike, and wore a blue uniform, with a black waist belt, from which, on the left side, a cutlass was suspended, and in the front was a receptacle for a pistol, such as was used by the cavalry of the day.

Bonaparte's preparations at Calais and Boulogne for an invasion of England gave rise to corresponding exertions on this side of the Channel. Beacons were placed on the highest points along the Kentish coast and in the interior of the county, in order that the whole of the armed forces might, if necessary, be simultaneously alarmed. There was a beacon, well charged with tar and pitch, on Coxheath, and another on Blue Bell Hill. Each beacon was watched day and night by a sergeant, a corporal, and four privates, who had full instructions, in case of emergency, to apply the torch. Troops were again encamped on Coxheath, including the Coldstream, York, East and West Norfolk, and Royal Bucks militia. The Maidstone companies, the cavalry from the Maidstone depôt, and a troop of yeomanry, joined the camp on the 20th of August 1804, when the whole force, mustering 10,000 men, was passed in review before the Duke of York, Lieutenant-General the Earl of Chatham, and Lieutenant-General Sir David Dundas. Mr. Pitt and other ministers of State were also present. This was the last encampment on Coxheath, which was enclosed by Act of Parliament in June 1814.

The country, in 1828, was agitated not by the threat of invasion, but by the question of Roman Catholic emancipation. By a small majority the House of Commons had declared in favour of a measure of relief, and the high sheriff of Kent (Sir Thomas Maryon Wilson) convened a county meeting on Penenden Heath in opposition to the proposed measure. This meeting—the last great popular demonstration on the heath—took place on the 24th of October, when about forty thousand persons assembled, the opponents of emancipation predominating. A resolution in conformity with the object of the gathering was moved by the sheriff, and speeches having been delivered by Mr. Cobbet and other gentlemen, a counter resolution was proposed by Mr. Sheil. He met with incessant interruption, and though encouraged by his friend Dr. Doyle, who had come from France in order to be present, the eloquent Irishman was at length howled into silence. The original proposition was then carried. As showing the enterprize of the press fifty-three years ago, it may be mentioned that a report of the meeting was published the same evening in a London newspaper. But the odd thing was that although Shiel had spoken intermittently for only half an hour, his speech appeared in two of the next morning's papers, occupying from three to four columns of space. Anticipating that Shiel would be the leading orator of the day, the conductors of these journals had induced him to supply his speech beforehand. This mishap elicited from the future author of "Vanity Fair," then in his eighteenth year, the following *jeu d'esprit*, being, it is thought, the first composition which Thackeray published:—

> Mister Sheil into Kent has gone,
>   On Penenden Heath you'll find him;
> Nor think you that he came alone,
>   There's Doctor Doyle behind him.
> "Men of Kent," said this little man,
>   "If you hate emancipation,
> You're a set of fools:" he then began
>   A "cut and dry" oration.
>
> He strove to speak, but the men of Kent
>   Began a grievous shouting,
> When out of his waggon the little man went,
>   And put a stop to his spouting.
> "What though these heretics heard me not,"
>   Quoth he to his friend canonical:
> "My speech is safe in the *Times* I wot,
>   And eke in the *Morning Chronicle*."

CHAPTER XVI.

ENDOWED CHARITIES AND CHARITABLE INSTITUTIONS.

William Hewitt—Sir Henry Cutt—Robert Gunsley—Alexander Fisher—Robert Rowland—Sir John Banks—Thomas Bliss—The Workhouse—Maidstone Union—Mrs. Duke—Edward Hunter—William Gill—John Brenchley—Sir Charles Booth—Mrs. Wright—Mrs. Carter—Thomas Robert Cutbush—Thomas Edmett—The West Kent General Hospital—The Ophthalmic Hospital.

IT is pleasant to reflect that amid the changes of the past the wants of the poor and unfortunate have not been forgotten by those who have had the means of alleviating the sorrows of poverty and misfortune. Scarcely a generation has passed during the last three hundred years but some thoughtful and generous-hearted townsman has bequeathed a portion of his riches to the struggling ones upon whom an adverse fate lays a heavy hand. The fact that at the present time the gross annual income of the endowed charities of Maidstone exceeds £2,000, is a magnificent proof of individual munificence. The earlier of these charities were in ancient times a valuable supplement to the ordinary provision then existing for the relief of the poor and infirm. This provision consisted of a small workhouse, supported by parochial poor-rates, which were also doled out by the overseers and churchwardens, often with scant impartiality and justice, to persons living in other parts of the parish. A workhouse existed in the town as early as 1588, in which year the borough chamberlains disbursed 2d. for rushes to lay on the floor of the house.

One of the first persons to establish a fund for the benefit of the poor of Maidstone was William Hewitt. Nothing is known of him, except that in 1568 he bequeathed a sum of money that should produce four marks a year, or £2 13s. 4d., which amount is still received and distributed annually among poor persons who have not been in receipt of parochial relief.

Sir Henry Cutt, who owned Thurnham Castle and several adjoining lands, died in 1603, leaving in his will directions that a portion of his money, sufficient to yield £3 a year, should be invested for the relief of the poor of this town. The amount derived yearly under the bequest is now £2 12s. Sir Henry's widow erected a monument over his tomb in Thurnham church. She married again, and dying in 1618, was also buried at Thurnham.

In the last-named year the Rev. Robert Gunsley, of Titsey, in Surrey, devised the rents belonging to the rectory of Broadhampton, in Devonshire, to be bestowed in bread and clothing on the poor in the parishes of Maidstone and Rochester. The total income of this charity in 1839 was £154 13s. 8d. It is divided in equal portions between the two parishes, and in 1881 the sum of £98 was distributed in Maidstone.

Alexander Fisher, the fourth and youngest son of Walter Fisher, of Maidstone, died on the 23rd of October 1671, and left by will in trust to the Corporation several houses and upwards of thirty-three acres of land in the parishes of

Boxley and Maidstone, the rents of which to be employed in binding out to trade every year three poor boys born in the town, and in paying annually to four indigent widows £2 each. When the Ashford Road was constructed in 1815, it passed through about four acres of Fisher's land, but these the trustees had previously exchanged with the owner of Vinters for a piece of ground elsewhere in the town. The income was originally £38, but in 1839 the value of the property belonging to the charity was as follows :—Four houses and two gardens, rented at £30; nine acres of land abutting on Sandling Road, £42; thirteen acres at Weavering Street, £40; two other pieces of land, £40; and one acre and a half at the corner of Union Street and Queen Anne Road, £10 10s.; the whole income amounting to £162 10s. A part of the property, being required for building purposes, has since been sold, and the money invested in Government securities. Twelve boys were apprenticed in 1880, with premiums of £20 each and upwards, and a number of poor widows and other deserving parishioners usually receive assistance during the winter.

Further help was in 1707 given to friendless youths by Robert Rowland, armourer, of London, who was a native of Maidstone, having been born in 1633 in a house near the bridge. He by will devised in trust to the Corporation £120, to be lent in sums of £10 each to twelve young men, newly out of their apprenticeship, to assist in setting them up in trade. The testator directed that each of the recipients should pay 6s. 8d. per annum interest, and that the total amount of such interest, £4, should be disposed of as follows, viz., to the minister of the parish for preaching a sermon on the 1st of February in each year " by candle light," £1; to the reader, clerk, and churchwardens, and for candles, £1; and to the poor people living under the Cliffe and upon the bridge, £2.

By the beginning of the present century the money, through failures, &c., had been lost, and in 1805 it was agreed that the £4 which the Corporation had disbursed annually to the minister should be set off against a rent of £5 which the churchwardens, up to that year, had paid to the Corporation for two cottages at the bridge foot.

Sir John Banks, bart., of Aylesford, by will, dated November 22, 1697, bequeathed funds for the erection of six almshouses for six poor parishioners of Maidstone, and endowed them with £63 a year. Each house was to have one ground room with a chimney, a little buttery on the same floor, and an upper room with a chimney, as well as a small garden. The testator died in 1699, and in the following year the houses were built on the south side of St. Faith's Street.

In 1719 Thomas Bliss announced his intention to erect a workhouse at the west end of Knightrider Street, and to present it to the parish. A three-story building, 91ft. by 21ft., was commenced in the same year. It is said to have been finished and fitted up at the charge of the town, but Newton was assured that the benefactor expended upon it upwards of £700. Though capable of accommodating all the paupers in the parish, the house contained, on the 26th of October 1724, only seventeen women, five men, and eighteen children. Of these, three women and eight children were employed in spinning worsted, their earnings, from Easter to October 14, amounting to £18 11s.; while the whole cost on account of the house for the same period was £99 15s. The management of the house was under the superintendence of the churchwardens and overseers, and a contemporary writer states that many of the parishioners were on sufficiently good terms with the last-named officials to obtain weekly relief without entering the house, which they disliked. The same writer says that for many years the poor-rate had amounted to £1,000, but in

1719 it was reduced to £929, and for the year 1724, the time of his writing, it was expected to produce £530.

In January 1765 James Dawbarn was appointed master of the workhouse, with instructions from the vestry to employ the poor in making hop-bagging and spinning wool at a certain rate per head. He had an allowance from the parish of 5s. per week. For the purpose of the manufacture, a storehouse of three floors, 20ft. by 17ft., and a shed, 96ft. by 10ft., were erected in the following year at the back of the workhouse, on ground given by Lord Romney. Dawbarn's allowance was in 1767 raised to £21 per annum; he died in November of the same year, and John Swinnock, of Cranbrook, was forthwith appointed master, and his wife mistress, of the workhouse, the former at £20 a year, and the latter at £10.

At the summer assizes in 1770 the high sheriff of Kent and other gentlemen called attention to the inadequate provision existing for the paupers in the western half of the county, and a committee was appointed to draw up a report on the subject. The committee subsequently recommended the erection at Maidstone of a workhouse for West Kent; but the proposal met with great opposition in the county, and at a meeting held at Maidstone in January 1771, it was abandoned.

Under an Act of Parliament passed in 1805, the Trustees of the Poor—who, by an Act of 1780, had superseded the ancient parochial authority of the churchwardens and overseers—sold eleven almshouses in the town, two being situated in the High Street, two in Week Street, four in King Street, and three in the West Borough. One of the almshouses in the West Borough was erected in 1760 by Edward Waldo Dorrington, of Week Street. By the Poor Law Amendment Act of 1834, the administration of the laws for the relief of the poor was transferred to a Board of Guardians, and the duties of the Trustees of the Poor were thereby confined to the levying of rates to answer, from time to time, the calls of the Guardians. In September 1835 the Coxheath Union was created, comprising all the parishes now constituting the Maidstone Union, excepting only those of Maidstone and West Barming. The parish of Maidstone was added to the Union in May 1836, and West Barming in September 1837, the name of the union area being then changed to the Maidstone Union. The erection of a workhouse at Coxheath, for the accommodation of six hundred paupers, was commenced in 1837, and in March of the following year the new building was opened.* The house has since been greatly enlarged and improved. A proposal to sever the parish of Maidstone from the Union, owing to inconveniences inseparable from the affiliated system, is now under the consideration of the Local Government Board.

In 1787 William Gill, a native of the town, and an alderman of London, gave the interest of £540 four per cent. stock to be divided annually among twenty poor householders in the parish of Maidstone.

John Brenchley, in 1789, built four almshouses in East Lane for aged men and women, and endowed them with £12 each. The same gentleman in 1792 gave a donation of £500 to the Blue Coat School.

In 1795 Sir Charles Booth, of Harrietsham Place, bequeathed £100 to be distributed among the poor of Maidstone within three months after his decease, and £2,000 to be invested in Government securities for the maintenance of a

---

* A workhouse for the parishes of Linton, Loose, East and West Farleigh, existed at Coxheath in 1781, in which year an advertisement appeared for a master to take charge of the poor at a certain sum per head, and to employ them in linen weaving, for which he was to receive payment, according to the amount of work done, every month.

schoolmaster or schoolmistress, or both, to teach poor boys and girls, "inhabitants of or near unto the parish," to read and write. The money was accordingly invested, and a school was opened. In 1817 sixty-five boys and girls attended the school, the master's salary being £50, and that of the mistress £30. Two or three years ago the trustees discontinued the school, and the money, which amounted in 1879 to £99 4s. 6d., is now distributed among the church schools in the town.

Mrs. Ann Wright, of Dulwich, gave in 1805 the interest of £1,100 three per cent. reduced annuities, to be divided annually among thirty poor widows or single women of Maidstone.

Mrs. Mary Duke, at some time anterior to 1736, erected three almshouses on the north side of East Lane, for occupation by three maiden gentlewomen of reduced circumstances, natives of Kent or of London, who were to worship every Sunday at the Unitarian or, as it was then called, Presbyterian meeting-house in Maidstone. Mrs. Duke died in January 1750, and was buried at Aylesford, her native parish. She bequeathed £3 to the poor of Aylesford, and a like sum to the sick and infirm people belonging to the Unitarian congregation. Mrs. Duke also left twenty-nine acres of land in Romney Marsh, as well as other property, for the support of her almshouses, and directed that out of the residue of her personal estate the three gentlewomen living therein should each receive £2 per annum until the money arising therefrom was exhausted. Towards the end of the last century the trustees under the will erected a fourth cottage, and subsequently two other cottages were built with surplus money belonging to the charity, the value of which had, a few years previously, been augmented by a second legacy. Ann Willes, wife of John Willes, of Dulwich, in the parish of St.

Giles, Camberwell, died in 1818, and by will, dated May 13, 1817, devised to the trustees of Duke's charity £1,000 three per cent. reduced annuities, the interest to be divided among the inmates of the almshouses. The land in Romney Marsh was in 1834 let on lease for seven years at a rent of £66, and the whole income of the dual charity amounted to £191 8s.

Through the liberality of Edward Hunter in 1757, six almshouses were erected in Mote Road, in which, during his lifetime, six poor men and women lived rent free. He by will bequeathed, for the maintenance of the houses and their occupants, property which produced £48 a year; and also £2 for the preaching of a sermon on "charity" in Maidstone church, on the 14th of March in each year, viz., 25s. to the minister, 10s. to the reader, and 5s. to the clerk. The income of the charity in 1838 was £183 16s., made up as follows:—Fifty-five acres of land at Willesborough, near Ashford, let at £75 12s.; twenty-one acres at Mersham, let at £18; the testator's house in Bank Street, Maidstone, let at £57 4s.; dividends on investments, £33. In 1851 the trustees erected six additional almshouses, and the twelve cottages are now occupied by poor persons above fifty-five years of age. The present income is about £200, and a sum of £16 is usually given to each inmate.

The late Mrs. Carter, in 1845, erected six almshouses in Orchard Lane, for three male and three female householders in reduced circumstances, and endowed each of them with £15 per annum. This is called the Corrall Charity, after the donor's brother, Philip Corrall, banker.

In 1865 Thomas Robert Cutbush erected six almshouses in Church Street, and endowed them with £52 each, for decayed married tradesmen who have carried on business in the town for not less than twenty years, or for artisans over sixty years of age who have been employed, for a like period, in Maidstone. This gentleman in 1867 founded a second charity for twelve widows and spinsters above fifty years of age who have lived in the town twenty years, and who each receive £26 per annum. He died in January 1871, aged eighty-two.

Thomas Edmett, who died in 1871, bequeathed a sum of money for the endowment of a charity in Maidstone. A scheme, sanctioned by the Court of Chancery in 1875, for the administration of the charity, provides that the income is to be divided into three equal parts, two parts to be applied in payment of annuities not exceeding £20 each to poor persons, aged sixty years and upwards; and the third part to be distributed, on or about the last day in each year, among deserving parishioners in the form of coals, blankets, and warm clothing.

There are, in addition to the above, several bread charities which have been founded at various times, and the funds of which have accumulated during a long series of years. The gross income of such charities amounted to 1879 to £144 1s. 2d.

Previous to 1830 there was no public establishment in Maidstone to which the indigent sick might resort for aid; but early in that year a meeting was called to consider how this much-felt want could best be supplied. A thoroughly earnest and cordial spirit pervaded the meeting, and a resolution was passed to establish a dispensary. A small building was hired for the purpose, and two physicians and two surgeons offered their services gratuitously, while an apothecary was engaged to reside on the premises. Public support was so liberally bestowed that at the end of the year the subscriptions were found to have exceeded the expenditure by £252. The managers were thereby encouraged to persevere in their good work, and in their first report they expressed a hope " at no very distant time to be able to supply three or four beds with the necessary accommodation for the reception of urgent medical cases, or of those patients who might require serious surgical operations." In 1832 plans for a new building were approved at a general meeting of the governors, and a fund was rapidly raised to defray the cost of the same, collections being made in the churches and chapels of the town and neighbourhood. In the autumn of that year a building was commenced at the east end of Marsham Street, and was completed at an outlay of over £1,700. It consisted of a physicians' and surgeons' room, a dispensary, an operating room, and four wards for the accommodation of twenty-four in-patients. Rules and regulations were adopted in April 1833, and in June the West Kent General Hospital was opened. In the death soon after of Dr. Robert Smith, the management sustained a heavy loss. He had been one of the most active of the governors, and to his well-directed exertions the origin of the institution was mainly due.

The generous manner in which the public responded to periodical appeals for support assured the success of the hospital, while the large number of poor people who applied for medical aid in the first years of its existence proved that the boon was thankfully appreciated by the class for which it was intended. From 1830 to the end of 1833, 4,024 persons were medically treated, and in the latter year alone the number of patients was 1,188. The building has since been added to at various times to meet the growing requirements, and the requisite funds have always been forthcoming. Since 1839, legacies have been received amounting in the aggregate to upwards of £16,000, including £10,000 bequeathed by John Brenchley in 1870, and £3,000 by Thomas Edmett in 1871. In 1865 William Peale, of Loose, who died in 1879, by a donation of £2,000, established the Peale Fund, which was increased by subsequent contributions to £5,400. The yearly expenditure of the institution is about £2,800, towards which £1,028 is derived from invested funds, and the remainder is made up by subscriptions, payments by patients, and collections. There is an average of 5,500 patients a year, and altogether 145,000 persons, from a hundred and ninety parishes in Kent, have been treated since the opening of the hospital.

A knowledge of the sufferings inflicted upon large numbers of the working classes in Kent by diseases of the eye induced Mr. John Woolcott, a well known oculist, in 1846 to hire a building in Maidstone where artisans and poor people might gratuitously avail themselves of his skill A public meeting held in April of the same year resolved to obtain subscriptions towards founding an Ophthalmic Hospital for the county. Meanwhile the Earl of Romney purchased the old proprietory school in Church Street, and let it, at a nominal rent, for the reception of patients. Between May 1846 and March 1851 as many as 25,580 persons received treatment at the hospital; and in the latter year funds were raised for the erection of a more suitable building. At a meeting of the working classes it was determined to make a penny subscription throughout the county. The late Jonathan Saunders, a journeyman papermaker, headed this movement, and chiefly through his exertions, a sum of about £500 was realised. On the 5th of October 1852 the new building was opened, at a cost of nearly £3,000. A children's ward was added in March 1861; and eight years later subscriptions were obtained for the erection of a convalescent ward for females. In 1878 there were 265 in-patients and 2,184 out-patients, the whole number of the latter, from 1863 to 1879, being 37,457. Legacies amounting to about £8,000 are invested for the benefit of the institution.

CHAPTER XVII.

MAIDSTONE WORTHIES.

Edward Lee—John Hall—John Jenkins—Sir Jacob Astley—William Shipley—William Woollett—William and James Jefferys—William Alexander—William Hazlitt.

SEVERAL of the persons whose lives are incidentally sketched in the preceding pages might be fairly considered to claim a place under this heading; but by noticing them in immediate connection with the history of the particular events with which they were associated, it is thought that a more intelligible arrangement has been adopted. As the ecclesiastical annals of Maidstone would have been incomplete without Thomas Wilson and George Swinnock, so the story of its municipal history would have been imperfect without the strongly marked personality of Andrew Broughton. In this chapter, therefore, we shall notice chronologically the men of note who were born or who resided in Maidstone, but who were not intimately connected with its civil or ecclesiastical history. The town, it may be observed, has not produced many illustrious names, the most distinguished natives up to the present time being Woollett the engraver, and Hazlitt the critic and essayist.

EDWARD LEE was born at Earls Place, Maidstone, in 1482,

being the second son of Richard Lee and Margaret, daughter of Thomas Darlington.* He was great-grandson of Sir Richard Lee, who was twice Lord Mayor of London. At an early age he was sent to Cambridge, and subsequently to Oxford. By his talents and learning he was admitted to the court of Henry VIII., where he was brought into somewhat intimate relations with Sir Thomas More. He speedily ingratiated himself with the king, and being sent on an embassy to the continent he acquitted himself so dexterously that he rose still higher in the royal favour. In 1529 he was made Chancellor of Sarum, and in the following year he received from Oxford the degree of D.D. On December 10, 1531, the archbishopric of York was conferred on him. He was in 1536 seized by the insurgents concerned in the Pilgrimage of Grace, and, under a threat of death, consented to take an oath of fidelity to them. This gave offence to the court, but he was afterwards pardoned. He died at York on the 13th of September 1544, and was buried in the cathedral. Lee was the author of several works, and in his controversy with Erasmus respecting the great reformer's annotations on the New Testament he exhibited profound learning and polemical abilities of a high order. Though he lived to see the dawn of the Reformation, he firmly adhered to the old faith.

JOHN HALL, a surgeon of considerable promise, was a native of the town, having been born here in 1529. His connection with Wyatt's rebellion has already been noticed. He translated several treatises on pathology, and in 1564 published the "Chirurgia Parva of Lanfranke," containing his portrait, several copies of which have survived the book. Hall was also the author of a volume of hymns, with musical notes. He died at the early age of thirty-nine.

---

* His family continued to reside at Earls Place till the middle of Elizabeth's reign.

JOHN JENKINS, who was born in Maidstone in 1592, became a celebrated composer of music for the violin. His compositions were chiefly fantasias in five or six parts, several of which were much admired both in England and on the continent; but he also published a number of single songs, specimens of which are given in Smith's "Musica Antiqua," and composed twelve sonatas for "two violins and a bass, with a thorough bass for the organ." These latter were printed in London in 1660, and reprinted at Amsterdam in 1664; they were the first compositions of the kind that had appeared in England. Wood, in his "Dictionary of Musicians," says of Jenkins that he was "a little man with a great soul." Though an excellent performer on the viol, he did much by his works to introduce the violin in its place. He died in 1678.

Sir JACOB ASTLEY, to whom in 1640 Sir John Astley, his relative, bequeathed the Palace, Allington Castle, and other estates in this neighbourhood, was the second son of Isaac Astley, of Melton Constable, in Norfolk. Having been early trained for a military life, he served under Maurice and Henry, Princes of Orange, in the Low Countries, and was at the battle of Nieuport and the siege of Ostend. He then accepted commissions under Christian IV. and Gustavus Adolphus, King of Sweden, and distinguished himself by many acts of bravery. Returning to England before the breaking out of the civil war, he entered the service of the king, and in the autumn of 1638, in anticipation of hostilities with the Scots, he was in the Netherlands buying muskets and pikes. In the following January he was in Yorkshire training horse and foot for the Scottish campaign, and a few weeks later, with a small force, he took possession of Berwick. After the king's army had been routed by the Covenanters, he arrived at York, in September 1640, with fifteen thousand men.

During the civil war he was lieutenant-general of the forces in the counties of Worcester, Gloucester, Hereford, and Salop, and governor of Oxford, Reading, and other garrisons. At Edgehill, when both sides were drawn up in order of battle, each hesitating to begin the strife, he uttered this prayer: "Lord, thou knowest that I shall be busy this day; if I forget thee, do not thou forget me." At that moment the first shot was fired from the parliamentary side, whereupon Astley cried to his men, "Up, boys, and at 'em"—the famous expression which was afterwards put into the mouth of Wellington. In 1644 he was created Baron Astley of Reading. The following year, he commanded the Royalist infantry at Naseby, whence he escaped with the loss of his head-piece. Two months later his son, Colonel Sir Bernard Astley, was slain at the siege of Bristol. After the utter defeat of the Royalists at Stow-in-the-Wold, in March 1646, the soldiers brought him a drum to rest upon, and he said bitterly to his conquerors, "Gentlemen, you have done your work now, and may go to play, unless you fall out among yourselves." He was released on parole, and subsequently compounded for his estates.

Clarendon describes Lord Astley as "an honest, brave, plain man, and as fit for the office he exercised of major-general of foot as Christendom yielded. He was generally esteemed; very discerning and prompt in giving orders, and most cheerful and pleasant in any action. In council he used few but very pertinent words." Macaulay, in his stirring ballad on the battle of Naseby, alludes to him—

> And the Man of Blood was there, with his long essenced hair,
> And Astley, and Sir Marmaduke, and Rupert of the Rhine.

At the close of the war he retired to his seat at the Palace, Maidstone, where he quietly passed the rest of his life. He was under an obligation to refrain from again bearing arms against the Parliament, and, unlike Lucas and Lisle, he made no attempt to forfeit his word of honour as a soldier. He accordingly held aloof from the insurrection of the Kentish Royalists in 1648. Lord Astley died at the Palace on the 27th of February 1651-2, and was buried in the chancel of All Saints' Church, where a monument, bearing a clumsy epitaph beginning, "Let th' island voyage in the van speak forth," was raised to his memory. Clarendon, in his History of the Rebellion, published a portrait of Astley, and also one of his son, both copied from paintings at the Palace.

WILLIAM SHIPLEY, long an inhabitant of Maidstone, was originally an artist in London, where he opened a school for the teaching of drawing. Several of his pupils became eminent as painters, and the example of his school contributed, it is said, to the establishment of the Royal Academy. In 1754 he, conjointly with Lord Romney and several other gentlemen, originated the Society of Arts—"one of the noblest designs," says Anderson, "for the improvement of the general commerce of Great Britain which could possibly have been devised."* He for some time acted as secretary, and in 1758 the members presented him with a gold medal, having on one side an emblematical device, and on the other the inscription, "To William Shipley, whose public spirit gave rise to this society." His portrait was published in 1786 as a frontispiece to the fourth volume of the society's "Transactions." Shipley removed from London to Maidstone in 1768, and soon after formed in the town a Kentish Society for the promotion of useful knowledge, of which he held the position of treasurer. The principal object of the society was to assist improvements in agriculture, but its investigations also extended to other subjects, such as mechanics and household economy. A malignant fever broke out in the

---

* "History of Commerce," vol. iii., p. 298.

county prisons in East Lane in 1783, when seventy prisoners were affected, fifteen of whom died within a few days. The society directed its efforts towards improving the ventilation of the buildings, and raised a fund of £350 to enable it to carry out experiments therein. In a short time the disease was rooted out, and at the next Kent assizes the grand jury publicly thanked Shipley and his coadjutors for their humane exertions. Thomas Day, the prison surgeon, published a treatise in 1784, describing the remedial measures which had been so successfully adopted.

The society in 1787 offered a premium of ten guineas " for the best common map, and a corresponding subterraneous map, of any estate in the county of Kent, with a register giving an account of the thickness and contents of the different strata," &c. Shipley died in 1803, at the age of eighty-nine, and there is a handsome monument to his memory in the north-west corner of All Saints' churchyard. He was an ardent student in natural philosophy, and had a happy turn for applying scientific principles to practical purposes. The Kentish Society had at one time nearly a hundred members, among whom were many of the most influential persons in the neighbourhood; but it has long been discontinued.

WILLIAM WOOLLETT was born in a house in East Lane, Maidstone, on the 15th of August 1735. His family originally came from Holland, and had been resident in the town for more than a century. There was a tradition that his great-grandfather escaped from the storming of Maidstone in 1648, and swam over the Medway to his residence at Tovil. The engraver's father was Philip Woollett, who married Ann Banks, of Boughton Monchelsea. Philip was a foreman thread-maker, and was one of a small party or club consisting of twelve members, who met at the Ship public-house, Gabriel's Hill. In 1753 they purchased a ticket for a lottery, and a prize of £5,000 being drawn, the money was equally divided among them. Philip Woollett was asthmatic, and the dust from the flax being prejudicial to his health, this lucky acquisition enabled him to hire the Turk's Head public-house, in the Rose Yard, which was at that time frequented by many of the leading tradesmen and yeomen of the town and neighbourhood.

Young Woollett was educated under Simon Goodwin, whom he surprised by his fine penmanship and skill in drawing. On one occasion he sketched on a slate the likeness of a schoolfellow named Buttonshaw, who had a prominent nose; his master observed the truthfulness of the half-finished sketch, and at his request it was completed and preserved. The graphic talents of the boy also found scope in drawing the portraits of his father's acquaintances. There is in the Maidstone Museum a little book containing fourteen pen drawings of animals and birds; and on the frontispiece are these words, neatly penned: "This was done by me, William Woollett, in the 12th year of my age, March ye 27, 1747." The clear and vigorous execution of these sketches gives them, at first sight, the appearance of old engravings, and, for a lad of twelve years, they are remarkable. It is said that a stranger from London happened one day to be at the Turk's Head, where his attention was attracted to Woollett's handiwork on a pewter pot. This led to his being apprenticed to Timney, a London engraver. Under this obscure practitioner he was taught little or nothing; but by his own industry he was soon able to use the etching needle and graver with facility, and one of his first productions on copper was a portrait, with a pipe in his mouth, of Mr. Scott, father of Nicholas Scott, silversmith, of Maidstone, and commonly called Dippit Scott, from his habit of uttering the euphemism "Dip it" instead of an oath.

Woollett, notwithstanding the apathy of Timney, taught himself a good deal, and developing a manner of his own, soon became known as the most accomplished of English engravers. Engraving in this country was at a low ebb, and those who practised the art in England were chiefly foreigners. Woollett's early productions brought him to the notice of Alderman Boydell, the liberal patron of art in London, who, in competing with the foreign print-sellers, was then spending large sums of money. Boydell engaged Woollett to engrave, for a hundred guineas, Wilson's fine picture of Niobe. He received most of this money before the work was half finished, but finding that he was struggling with a wife and family in an upper lodging in Green's Court, Leicester Fields, Boydell sent him an extra payment of £50. The print, which was published at 5s., sold so well that his patron employed him upon another picture by the same artist. Woollett was ere long appointed engraver to George III. His subsequent works, more especially the "Death of General Wolfe" and the "Battle of La Hogue," are familiar at this day to almost every one, and are still much prized by connoisseurs.

He died at his residence in Upper Charlotte Street, Rathbone Place, on the 23rd of May 1785, and was buried in the churchyard of St. Pancras. One who knew him well thus wrote of him not long after his death: "To say that he was the first man in his profession would be giving him his least praise, for he was a good man; natural, modest, and amiable in his disposition, he never censured the works of others or omitted pointing out their merits. His patience under the continual trial of a dreadful disorder for upwards of nine months was most exemplary, and he died, as he had lived, at peace with all the world. He never had an enemy, and left his family inconsolable for his death, and the public to lament the loss of a man whose works are an honour to his country." An anecdote told of him is interesting as showing that he spared neither time nor labour to ensure the success of his works. Having been for some time engaged upon West's picture, the "Battle of La Hogue," he at length submitted a proof for inspection by the great Anglo-American painter. At first West expressed himself as satisfied with the plate, but upon closer examination he observed that it might be improved by a few alterations, and he showed with a port-crayon the effect he wished to be produced. Woollett immediately consented to make the suggested alterations. "But how long will it take you?" asked the painter. "Oh, about three or four months," replied Woollett; and the patient creature, said West, in relating the circumstance, actually went through the additional labour without a murmur.

On the tombstone—a plain square slab—at St. Pancras is the following inscription:—" William Woollett, engraver to his Majesty, was born at Maidstone, in Kent, upon the 15th of August 1735. He died on the 23rd, and was interred in this place on the 28th of May 1785. Elizabeth Woollett, widow of the above, died December the 15th, 1819, aged 73 years." A visitor wrote with a pencil on the stone this epitaph—

> Here Woollett rests, expecting to be sav'd;
> He graved well, but is not well engrav'd.

These lines gave expression to a general feeling that the talents of the great engraver deserved more adequate recognition by his country. A subscription was accordingly raised for erecting a monument to his memory in the cloisters of Westminster Abbey, to which West and Boydell were liberal contributors. The curiously inaccurate inscription on the cenotaph there is as follows:—" William Woollett, born

August 22, 1735; died, May 22nd, 1785. The genius of engraving handing down to posterity the works of painting, sculpture, and architecture, whilst fame is distributing them over the four quarters of the globe." *

WILLIAM JEFFERYS, a native of Maidstone, was an artist of some local reputation. His best known picture is that of the "Last Supper," which for many years formed the alterpiece in All Saints' Church. Jefferys, says Lamprey, "was in business in the town as a general painter, and consequently had but little time or opportunity to cultivate his talent for the more refined pursuits of the art. He, however, acquired some celebrity by his fruit and flower pieces, which were exhibited in the rooms of the Royal Academy. He died in 1805." †

JAMES JEFFERYS, son of the above, was born in Maidstone on the 8th of May 1751. He was educated at the Grammar School, and, when quite a youth, surprised his friends by his fine talent for drawing and colouring. When little more than twenty-three years of age, he obtained the gold palette of the Society of Arts for the best historical drawing, and subsequently won the gold medal of the Royal Academy with a picture entitled "Roman Charity," which was purchased

---

* No Life of Woollett has been written, and the existing notices of him are, without exception, meagre and inaccurate. The above account – the longest, it may be added, that has yet been published—may be supplemented by the following facts. Woollett left unfinished at his death an engraving, 20in. by 19½in., of James Jefferys's picture, representing the bombardment of Gibralter on the memorable 14th of September 1782. Elizabeth Woollett, the engraver's widow, sold the plate for £80 to John Emes, engraver of St. Pancras; and on January 9, 1788, articles of agreement were drawn up whereby Emes covenanted to finish it, after which it was to be considered of the value of £630; and the said Elizabeth, and Ann, her daughter, agreed to pay to Emes 150 guineas for a one-fourth share of the profits accruing from the publication of the plate, and William Jefferys, the painter's father, also undertook to purchase a one-fourth share for a like sum. The engraving was afterwards published. These articles of agreement are in the Maidstone Museum.

† "A Brief Historical and Descriptive Account of Maidstone and its Environs, by S. C. L.," p. 40.

by Lord Bessborough. In October 1775 he went to Rome to prosecute his studies by the aid of a temporary grant of £60 per annum from the Royal Academy. He remained abroad four years, and on his return settled in Meard Street, Soho. His effective picture of the famous scene before Gibralter immediately after the blowing up of the Spanish batteries, in September 1782, is in the Maidstone Museum, and is known to the public by Woollett and Emes's spirited engraving. Jefferys also enhanced his reputation by his clever pen drawings in the style of Mortimer, under whom it is supposed he studied for a short time while in London. His productions display bold originality and careful elaboration, and fully justify the opinion of his contemporaries that he would arrive at a high position in his profession. This anticipation was unfortunately disappointed by his early death on the 31st of January 1784.

WILLIAM ALEXANDER, who was born in Maidstone on the 10th of April 1767, left his native town at the age of fifteen to study drawing in London, and in 1784 was admitted a student of the Royal Academy, where he received the approbation of Sir Joshua Reynolds. He was in 1792 appointed draughtsman to Lord Macartney's embassy to Pekin, and the outcome of this engagement was the publication of his "Costumes of China," works consisting of highly finished coloured etchings, illustrative of the dress, architecture, and habits of the Chinese, with a descriptive account of each plate. Alexander was professor of drawing at the Military Academy at Great Marlow in 1802, and subsequently one of the resident officials of the British Museum. He died at Maidstone in July 1816. The inscription to his memory in Boxley Church aptly claims that "his pencil introduced into Europe a better knowledge of the habits and manners of China than had been before obtained," and the obituary notices which appeared at the time of his death testify to his worth and popularity. His drawings are scarce and prized.

WILLIAM HAZLITT was born in Earl Street on the 10th of April 1778, being the youngest son of William Hazlitt, minister of the Unitarian congregation, who, as stated in a former chapter, removed from Maidstone in 1780. The biographical notices of this brilliant and thoughtful writer are so numerous and so accessible to every reader that it is unnecessary to retrace in these pages the familiar outlines of his life. It will suffice here to reproduce the graphic but little known portrait of Hazlitt drawn many years ago by a competent pen. "Morbidly self-conscious, touchy, morose, he believed that his aspect and manner were strange and disagreeable to his friends, and that every one was perpetually insulting him. He had a magnificent forehead, regular features, pale as marble, and a profusion of curly black hair, but his eyes were shy and suspicious. As seen when not at his ease, Mr. P. G. Patmore describes him as worthy of Apemantus himself. He would enter a room as if he had been brought in in custody. He shuffled sidelong to the nearest chair, sat down on the extreme corner of it, dropped his hat on the floor, buried his chin in his stock, vented his usual pet phrase on such occasions, 'It's a fine day,' and resign himself moodily to social misery. If the talk did not suit him, he bore it a certain time, silent, self-absorbed, as a man condemned to death; then suddenly, with a brusque 'Well, good morning,' shuffled to the door and blundered his way out, audibly cursing himself for his folly in voluntarily making himself the laughing-stock of an idiot's critical servants. It must have been hard to bear with such a man, whatever might be his talent; and yet his dying words were, 'I've led a happy life.'" He died in 1830.

CHAPTER XVIII.

RECENT PROGRESS.

Old and New Roads—Houses on the Bridge—Population in 1821—Introduction of Gas—The Coaching Days—Railways—Alexander Randall—Water Supply—The New Bridge—Drainage of the Town—Population in Decennial Periods—Conclusion.

IN bygone times, when road and river were the great arteries of traffic, and the giant of steam had not yet commenced his triumphant course, it seems strange that so little attention was paid by public bodies to the state of the highways. But so it was. Old writers often complain of the disgraceful condition of the roads radiating from Maidstone. Newton says that in his time they were the greatest blemish to the neighbourhood; and we know that in George the Second's reign they were torn up into deep ruts, and so unequal in width that at certain parts two vehicles could scarcely pass each other. But shortly after George the Third's accession they were not only much improved, but new roads to Cranbrook, Wrotham, and Tunbridge were formed. The London Road, previous to 1781, passed by St. Peter's chapel and the entrance to Newark House—which still exists, embedded in the Gas Works, though its pleasant lawn that amid drooping willows and other foliage sloped to the river's edge, is effaced—and by a sharp turning, ascended the flank of Rockyhill. At a point about eighty yards beyond Maidstone bridge, the Tunbridge Road swerved abruptly to the left, and led across where is now the South Eastern Railway Station yard, thence up the hill and through the Grammar School site, to where Bower Terrace was erected; the existing thoroughfare was made in 1814. The triangular space between this and the London Road, as far westward as the entrance to Bower Place, was a meadow, crossed by a footway in the line of the present road in front of Rockyhill Terrace. In this meadow the Militia, called out for the first time after the peace, were exercised in May 1831.

Previous to 1808 the width of the roadway over the bridge—that is, the space between the parapets—was only 19ft; but in that year it was increased to the extent of nearly 8ft., and the waterway was confined within five arches, instead of seven, as before. The six cottages which projected from the south side of the bridge had disappeared; but a row of ancient houses, running into the High Street, occupied its eastern end. Two sketches of this group of buildings are herewith given, the "East View" showing in the extreme distance the butter market and shambles at the west end of the Town Hall. The rage for innovation in domestic architecture had not yet set in, and the High Street retained, in its general features, much of the aspect which had for centuries characterised it. Even now several of the houses in this part of the town, hidden behind their modern fronts, are far older than is commonly supposed; but at the beginning of the century there were undoubtedly many that had seen the flash of Wyatt's sword as he spurred along the street on his way to Rochester.

Houses at East End of Bridge.--- East View.

King Street, especially at its main entrance, was one of the narrowest public lanes in the town. It consisted, for the most part, of quaint houses, projecting over first a low-browed shop, then with an overhanging story, and higher a gabled story, whose bolder projection invaded the upper area of the street. Whit Monday and other gala-day processions almost brushed the projecting gables. A five-bar gate was the demarcation between King Street and a footway which led to the Artichoke. In Hasted's map of the Hundred the chief road to Ashford is laid down as by King Street and the Queen Anne public-house, passing a short distance along the Huntsman Lane, and then joining the present Detling Road, with which it coincided as far as Penenden Heath, where it turned eastward as the London and Ashford Road. But this route must soon after the date of Hasted's map have gone out of use, a road to Ashford having been constructed from Wren's Cross. This road led from Stone Street, almost in a straight line, by Pole Mill, through the centre of what is now the Mote gardens, across the Otham Mill Road, and past the front of Maginford House. The existing road from King Street was made in 1815.

During the first decade of the present century the population increased slowly. In 1801 there were 8,027 inhabitants, living in 1,346 houses. The number of inhabitants in 1811 was 9,443, as many as 404 houses having been erected in the interval. When the census was taken in May 1821, the population had increased to 12,508, and the number of houses was 2,234, of which 103 were uninhabited. Some details of this census are given in the subjoined table:—

	Inhabited Houses.	No. of Families.	Persons employed in Agriculture.	In Trade.	Males.	Females.
High Street, &c.	314	353	63	248	905	1,026
King Street, &c.	218	242	37	132	598	665
Tovil	93	114	19	77	278	253

	Inhabited Houses.	No. of Families.	Persons employed in Agriculture.	In Trade.	Males.	Females.
Union Street, &c.	481	555	154	339	1,246	1,300
West Borough	226	215	117	34	594	594
Stone Street, &c.	340	375	—	7	968	1,138
Stone Borough	66	70	48	—	180	174
Week Street, &c.	374	405	--	334	1,265	1,233
Loddington	19	19	13	3	49	42
	2,131	2,348	451	1,174	6,083	6,425

It was about this time that gas was introduced into the town by a Mr. Gosling. He sold his works in 1823 to several of the inhabitants, who obtained an Act of Parliament to enable them to carry on their operations, and who were thereby incorporated as the Maidstone Gas Light and Coke Company—a designation which was retained until 1858, when the name of the Maidstone Gas Company was adopted.

The manners and customs which prevailed when several of the streets were thus for the first time illuminated with gas are fast passing out of living recollection. The chief magistrate filled a larger space in the public eye than now. The mace-bearers, wearing cocked hats and gold-braided coats, attended at his worship's house on the Sunday mornings to precede him, in his gown, and wand in hand, to church, where the maces were stuck up on the pew in front of him. Police had not yet been called into existence, and three or four beadles, with long pewter-buttoned blue coats and switches or canes, performed day duty, while watchmen perambulated the streets during the night, and called the hour and the weather thus, "Two o'clock! a fine frosty morning!" Dress too was a curious characteristic of the time. The horse soldiers of the Depôt came out for their walks with flat curved swords clanking behind them, and wearing short red jackets, with broad brass epaulets. Carpenters wore white flannel jackets, and country labourers

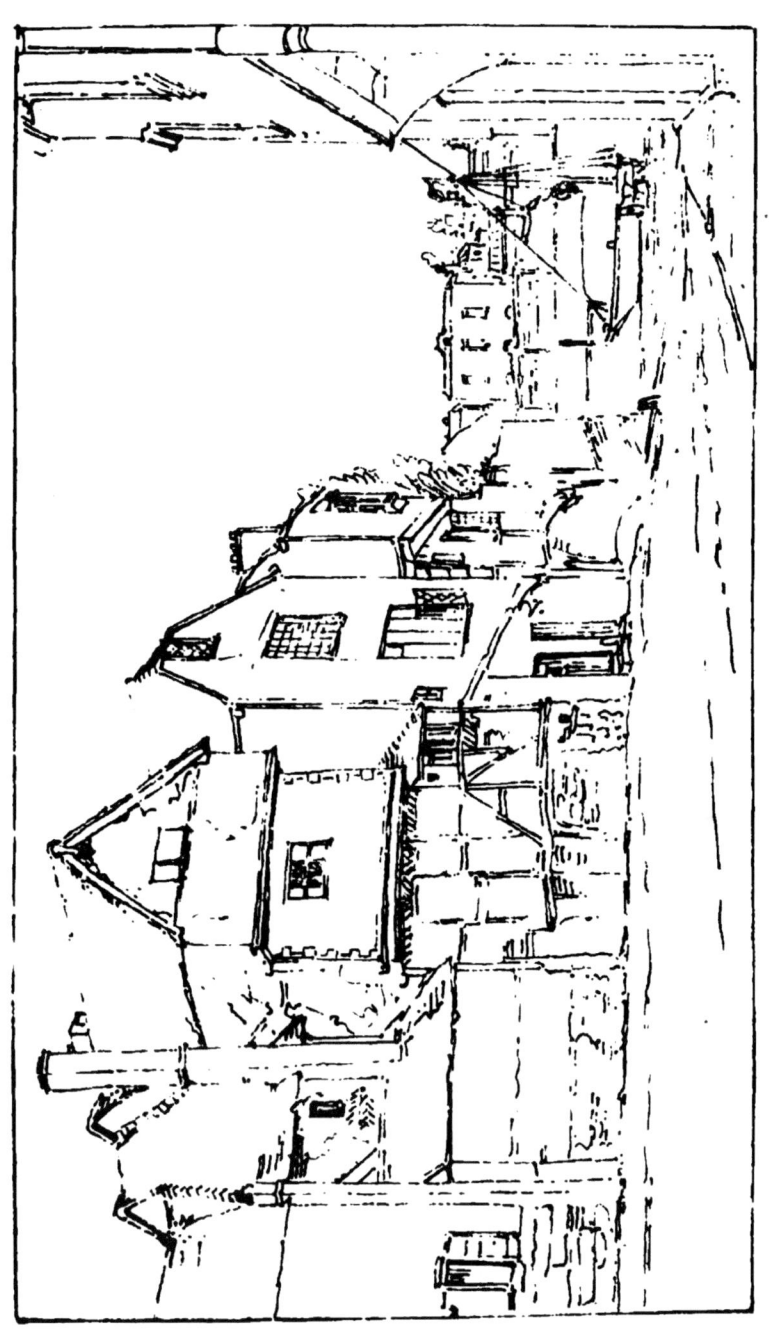

frocks or gabardines, white or green. Ladies appeared in enormous feathered bonnets, and gentlemen who travelled donned uncomfortable hats, very broad at the top, with shirt collars up to their ears, and great-coats with impossible outside pockets, which were so tight that nothing could be got in or out of them.

But in those days distant excursions, for persons of moderate means, were comparatively rare. Travelling was by coach, postchaise, gig, or waggon. Postchaises had in 1781 been advertised for hire from the Bell hotel at 9d. per mile; but though fares were dearer at the time of which we write, these rapid vehicles, which were generally painted a bright yellow, and made to carry two persons, were in considerable demand. Several postboys—often grey-haired—were usually to be seen in front of the Bell and Star, attired in long white smock frocks, booted and spurred, and ready at the first call to run up the yard and reappear in red jackets, striped waistcoats, and the high yellow-white hats peculiar to their class. Saddle horses and gigs were a less expensive kind of locomotion. Heavy waggons for goods travelled on all the main roads. These were at first called caravans; then two balloon waggons—great capacious receptacles, with semi-circular coverings of canvas, and drawn by six or eight horses—took their place, and went from Maidstone to London twice a week, carrying also a few passengers at 2s. 6d. each. Balloon waggons were, about the year 1835, superseded by light vans, which competed with the stage coaches in conveying parcels. In 1839 six coaches ran daily, one on Sundays, and one three times a week, between Maidstone and London. Every night at nine o'clock, Sundays excepted, the mail for the Metropolis, with a too-tooing horn, rattled along the High Street. There were also coaches to Ashford, Canterbury, Tunbridge Wells, Hastings, and other towns.

The introduction of railways into Kent sealed the fate of the stage coach and postchaise. When the scheme of the South Eastern Railway Company was projected in 1836, the recommendation of George Stephenson, the engineer, and the desire of the promoters, was to take their main line from London to Dover by way of Maidstone. This was unfortunately resisted here, on the ground that the proposed railway would be detrimental to certain existing interests, chief of which was the Medway trade. But though the advocates of this purblind policy were successful in pushing the main line away from Maidstone, they succeeded for a few years only in confining local traffic to the possibilities of barges and stage coaches. A branch line from Paddock Wood to Maidstone was opened in 1844, and, two years after, was made a double line. This line was in 1856 joined to the North Kent Railway at Strood. The railways did not, as had been predicted, ruin the river trade, but contributed in a hundred different ways to the prosperity of the town. Another aid to local enterprise was supplied in 1874, when the London, Chatham, and Dover Railway Company extended its system from Otford to Maidstone; this was made a double line in 1881.

The history of the parish during the last forty or fifty years is singularly devoid of incident. It is mainly a record of quiet, uninterrupted progress, socially and commercially, marked by many costly and beneficient public improvements, and by the carrying out of works for the health of the people on a scale beyond the dreams of our forefathers. These changes may not have been rapid—the development may seem measured, and even slow; but none the less is the gain substantial and, as far as can be forseen, permanent. A County Lunatic Asylum for 168 patients was built on Barming Heath in 1832; and the large additions which have since been made to the building give accommodation for nearly thirteen hundred patients. In 1851 Baths were provided for the borough at an outlay of more than £6,000; and in 1858 twenty acres of waste land, situated near the junction of the Sutton Valence and Loose Roads, were purchased, and have since been converted into one of the prettiest and best kept cemeteries in the kingdom.

For a long series of years the town obtained its chief water supply from springs at Rockyhill, whence the water was conveyed in pipes across the Medway. The Commissioners of Pavements in 1819 increased the supply, and laid down new iron pipes, transmitting daily about thirty thousand gallons to seventeen public conduits. A scheme for supplying the town from the chalk hills was proposed in 1858, but owing to a conflict of interests two years elapsed before any improvement in this direction was effected. In 1860 the present company acquired an Act of Parliament to supply the town. The pumping station is in the parish of East Barming, at East Farleigh bridge, and the water, which is collected from a number of springs within a distance of two miles from the engine house, is pumped to the reservoir at Barming at an altitude of about 300ft. The present consumption is above three million gallons per week. The springs at Rockyhill still yield a supply of about thirty thousand gallons per day.

A drinking fountain, surmounted by a canopy enclosing a marble statute of the Queen, was in 1862 presented to the town by Mr. Alexander Randall. From 1835 to 1859 Mr. Randall was a member of the Town Council; and in 1861 he served the office of high sheriff of the county. In the last-named year, as the result of a public subscription amounting to six hundred guineas, his portrait was painted by Sir Francis Grant, and now adorns the Town Hall. Mr. Randall died on the 5th of April 1870. His life was marked by traits that render it worthy of commemoration. Intellect, fortune, graced by sociality and kindness, enabled him to exercise great influence in the town and neighbourhood, and although at times he must have been compelled to guard the interests he represented, he was ever zealous in promoting the welfare of others, and, as a system, deemed it incumbent on him to uphold in his projects and disbursements the prosperity of the town and trade of Maidstone. His popularity was general, and little envied, for though, as magistrate and county gentleman, he was conscious of his rise, his sense and sympathies steered him clear of the meanness of the hoarder and the offensive bearing of the upstart. The architectural ornament which he erected near the site of the old Market Cross, designed in the fleeting fashion of the day as a fountain, was probably not an innate notion, but it well may direct in time to come question or search as to the career of him whose name it bears.

Within the last few years two important public works have been carried out—the erection of a stone bridge over the Medway, and the draining of the town. The traffic passing across the river has enormously increased during the past forty years. To meet the requirements of the workpeople employed at the Tovil paper mills, and the rapidly increasing population in Fant, a light iron bridge for passengers was in 1871 erected over the Medway opposite Tovil. Three years later, Maidstone bridge was reported to be in an unsafe condition; and finding that in order to repair the ancient fabric a considerable sum of money would be required, the Local Board of Health subsequently authorised Sir Joseph Bazalgette, the engineer of the Thames Embankment, to prepare plans for a new bridge. The first pile was driven on the 24th of October 1877, and a new bridge of three arches, giving a clear water-

way 149ft. wide, or 32ft. more than that of the old bridge, was opened on August 6, 1879, in presence of the Mayor and Corporation, the borough members, and a great assemblage of people, including five thousand school children, each wearing a medal which had been struck in honour of the occasion. The cost of the bridge and its approaches amounted to upwards of £55,000, towards which £24,000 was voted by the Bridge Wardens of Rochester.

The old bridge, which spanned the river on the south side of the new structure, only a few inches separating them, was demolished in the autumn of 1879. During the demolition its original width, parapets included, was ascertained to have been 11ft.; at some later period 11ft. 3in. of breadth had been added to it; and the augmentation, already referred to, of 1808, had made the entire width, including parapets, 30ft. The accompanying sketch is from a painting by Samuel Drummond, A.R.A., now in the possession of Mr. Hodsoll, of Loose Court, earlier in that of J. Newington Hughes—a charming piece of colouring, which conveys the idea of quietude that no doubt marked the locality in 1797.

A sewage scheme for Maidstone was adopted by the Local Board in October 1875. The sanitary condition of the town had often been the subject of complaint, and it was felt that an efficient and comprehensive system of drainage could not be longer delayed. The first tender for the execution of the work was accepted in 1877, and the last in 1880. After being conveyed into tanks at Allington, the sewage is clarified and precipitated into the Medway. This salutary work was completed at an outlay of £60,000.

At no period in the history of the town has the progress been so great or so manifest as during the last half century. By the census of 1831 the population of the parish, with an area of 4,576 acres, was 15,387. The enumeration of 1841 showed a population of 17,805, or an increase of 2,418. In the fifth decade the increase was 2,996; in the sixth, 2,215; in the seventh, 3,180. The number of inhabitants in 1881 was 29,632. Of these, 29,608 were living within the municipal area, which comprises 4,008 acres. The number of houses in this area was 5,658, the population residing at a mean elevation of 70ft. above the sea level. And the community has not only much augmented, but it is now far better housed and educated than it was fifty years ago. It was then ravaged by zymotic and other diseases, arising from the neglect of sanitary precautions; the causes which produced and propagated these diseases have to a great extent been removed, and the death-rate for the year 1880 was 18·83 per thousand inhabitants.

This record of the origin and progress of Maidstone, its hopes and fears, its joys and sorrows, its dimly remembered worthies, may awaken a keener interest in the local vestiges of the past, and stimulate in others a spirit of historical research in a neighbourhood which is peculiarly rich in the monuments of great families and the traditions of individual character; and wherever a road has been cut, a locality named, and smoke has curled from the meanest hearth—wherever men have been born, have suffered, and have died, there may be that which ought never to be buried and forgotten.

APPENDIX.

No. 1.

MEMBERS OF PARLIAMENT FOR THE BOROUGH.

1562 Nicholas Barham	1640 Sir Francis Barnham	1708 Sir Thomas Culpeper, Bt.
Henry Fisher	Sir Humphrey Tufton	Sir Robert Marsham, Bt.
1570 Thos. Walsingham	COMMONWEALTH.	1710 The same
Nicholas St. Leger	1660 Thomas Twisden	1713 Sir Robert Marsham, Bt.
1571 Nicholas St. Leger	Robert Barnham	Sir Samuel Ongley
Thomas Danet	1661 Sir Robert Pierce	1714 Sir Robert Marsham, Bt. ‡
1584 Thomas Randolph	Robert Barnham	Sir Thomas Culpeper, Bt. §
Nicholas Saunders	1678 Sir John Tufton, Bt.	1722 Sir Barnham Rider
1585 John Astley	Sir John Darell	John Finch
Thomas Randolph	1679 Sir John Tufton, Bt.	1727 John Finch
1588 The same	Thomas Fane	Thomas Hope
1592 Sir Thomas Fludd	1681 The same	1734 John Finch
Levin Bufkin	1685 Archibald Clinkard	Wm. Horsmonden Turner
1596 Sir Thomas Fludd	Edwin Wyatt	1741 Lord Guernsey
Sir John Leveson	1688 Sir Thos. Taylor, Bt	John Bligh
1600 The same	Caleb Banks	1747 Robert Fairfax
1603 Sir Francis Fane	1690 Sir Thos. Taylor, Bt.	Wm. Horsmonden Turner
Lawrence Washington	Thomas Rider	1754 Lord Guernsey ‖
1614 Sir Francis Fane	1695 Sir Thomas Taylor, Bt.*	Gabriel Hanger
Sir Francis Barnham	Sir John Banks, Bt.	1761 William Northey
1620 The same	1698 Sir Robert Marsham, Bt.	Rose Fuller
1623 Sir George Fane	Thomas Bliss	1768 Charles Marsham
Sir Francis Barnham	1700 The same	Edward Gregory
1625 Edward Maplesden	1702 Heneage Finch	1774 Lord Guernsey ¶
Thomas Stanley	Thomas Bliss †	Sir Horace Mann
1626 Sir George Fane	1705 Sir Thomas Culpeper, Bt.	
Sir Francis Barnham	Thomas Bliss	
1627 The same.		

* On Taylor's decease, Thomas Rider was chosen.
† Sir Robert Marsham and Sir Thomas Roberts, Bart., were returned, but declared unduly elected.
‡ On his elevation to the peerage, Sir Barnham Rider was chosen.
§ On his decease, John Finch was elected.
‖ He succeeded his father as Earl of Aylesford in 1757, when Savile Finch was chosen.
¶ In May 1777 he succeeded to his father's title, and Charles Finch was chosen.

1780 Sir Horace Mann
     Clement Taylor
1786 Clement Taylor
     Gerard Noel
     Edwards*
1790 Clement Taylor
     Matthew Bloxam
1796 Matthew Bloxam
     Oliver Delancy
1802 Sir Matthew
     Bloxam
     John Hodson
     Durand
1806 George Simpson
     George Longman
1812 George Simpson
     Sir S. E. Brydges
1818 A. W. Roberts
     George Longman
	1820 A. W. Roberts
	     John Wells
	1826 John Wells
	     A. W. Roberts
	1830 A. W. Roberts
	     Henry Winchester
	1831 A. W. Roberts
	     Charles J. Barnett
	1832 The same
	1835 Wyndham Lewis
	     A. W. Roberts
	1837 Wyndham Lewis
	     Benjamin Disraeli
	1838 J. M. Fector,
	     vice Lewis de-
	     ceased †
	1841 A. J. Beresford
	     Hope
	     George Dodd
		1847 A. J. Beresford
		     Hope
		     George Dodd
		1852 James Whatman
		     George Dodd ‡
		1857 A. J. Beresford
		     Hope
		     Major Scott
		1859 William Lee
		     Charles Buxton
		1865 William Lee
		     James Whatman
		1868 The same §
		1874 Sir John Lubbock,
		     Bart.
		     Sir S. H. Waterlow,
		     Bart.
		1880 Major Ross
		     Captain Aylmer

No. 2.

LIST OF MAYORS.

(The year, in each case, refers to the date of election.)

1548 Richard Heeley
1549 Richard Heeley
1550 Richard Basse
1551 John Mowerst
1552 William Tilden
1553 John Mowerst
     (Charter forfeited
     in 1554)
1559 Thomas Goar
1560 William Green
1561 John Beale
1562 Robert Balsar
1563 William Mowerst
1564 William Smyth
1565 James Busbridge
1566 Nicholas Austin
1567 Clement Lutwick
1568 Ambr. Ippenbury
1569 Robert Balsar
1570 Richard Catlin
1571 Nicholas Golding
1572 John Staylett
1573 Richard Lee
1574 Thomas Beale
	1575 William Haseden
	1576 William Downe
	1577 Gervase Maplesden
	1578 John Balsar
	1579 Thomas Edmonds
	1580 John Bateman
	1581 Thomas Basden
	1582 John Milles
	1583 James Franklyn
	1584 Edward Maplesden
	1585 Robert Tynley
	1586 William Symmonds
	1587 James Franklyn
	1588 John Fremlyn
	1589 Gabriel Green
	1590 Richard Smythe
	1591 Thos. Franklyn
	1592 George Maplesden
	1593 John Romney
	1594 Stephen Heeley
	1595 Matthew Salmon
	1596 John Green
	1597 Robert Goar
		1598 William Plommer
		1599 James Spencer
		1600 Richard Highwood
		1601 Walter Fisher
		1602 James Franklyn
		1603 Gabriel Green
		1604 Edward Maplesden
		1605 John Romney
		1606 Stephen Heeley
		1607 John Green
		1608 Richard Highwood
		1609 Walter Fisher
		1610 Richard Maplesden
		1611 Thos. Swinnock
		1612 Thomas Reeve
		1613 John Crompe
		1614 John Banks
		1615 Gabriel Green
		1616 Edward Maplesden
		1617 Stephen Heeley
		1618 Walter Fisher
		1619 Thos. Swinnock
		1620 Robert Golding
		1621 John Crompe

* Matthew Bloxam elected in July 1788, vice Edwards resigned.
† Fector resigned on petition, but was again elected in June.
‡ William Lee elected in 1853, vice Dodd retired.
§ Mr. Lee retired in 1870, when Sir John Lubbock, Bart., was elected.

APPENDIX.

1622 John Banks	1675 Samuel Wood	1725 Richard Mussery
1623 Gervase Maplesden	1676 John Lanes	1726 William Wattell
1624 Ambrose Beale	1677 George Walker	1727 Daniel Whetland
1625 Thomas Stanley	1678 William Weldish	1728 William Weldish
1626 Thos. Swinnock	1679 Francis Curteis	1729 George Curteis
1627 Thomas Reeve	1680 Garret Callent	1730 William Rand
1628 James Franklyn	1681 Robert Saunders	1731 Thomas Argles
1629 Richard Maplesden	1682 Thomas Bliss	1732 Gervase Heeley
1630 Robert Swinnock	1683 George Peirce	1733 John Tomlyn
1631 Robert Wood	1684 Robert Salmon	1734 John Blunt
1632 John Collins	1685 John Fowle	1735 Richard Flint
1633 Caleb Banks	1686 Thomas Marshall	1736 William Weldish
1634 Samuel Marshall	1687 { Joseph Wright / Oct. 1688, Robert Saunders }	1737 William Weldish
1635 Gervase Maplesden		1738 William Weldish
1636 George Gilliat		1739 Samuel Stevenson
1637 Ambrose Beale	1688 Richard Wattell	1740 Daniel Kirby
1638 Thomas Swinnock	1689 Alex. Osborne	(The Charter forfeited in 1741).
1639 John Bigg	1690 Richard Heeley	
1640 Martin Jeffery	1691 William Weaver	1747 { June, Ed. Hunter / Nov., Jos. Smalvell }
1641 Thomas Stanley	1692 Robert Swinnock	
1642 Robt. Withinbroke	1693 Samuel Wood	
1643 Robert Swinnock	1694 William Weldish	1748 John Mason
1644 Caleb Banks	1695 Francis Curteis	1749 Thomas Argles
1645 { Thomas Crompe (died dur. office) / Robert Swinnock }	1696 Garret Callent	1750 Samuel Stevenson
	1697 George Peirce	1751 John Harris
	1698 Robert Salmon	1752 Richard Mussery
1646 Gervase Maplesden	1699 Thomas Marshall	1753 Edward Argles
1647 James Ruse	1700 Alex. Osborne	1754 Samuel Stevenson
1648 Andrew Broughton	1701 William Weaver	1755 John Harris
1649 Thomas Taylor	1702 John Greenhill	1756 Samuel Stevenson
1650 Richards Bills	1703 Matthew Chandler	1757 Thomas Pope
1651 George Ongley	1704 Stephen Weeks	1758 Jonathan Weldish
1652 John Saunders	1705 James Sherbourne	1759 Daniel Polhill
1653 Robert Heath	1706 William Weldish	1760 George Post
1654 James Allen	1707 Francis Curteis	1761 John Pope
1655 Jonath. Troughton	1708 Garret Callent	1762 William Roots
1656 Caleb Banks	1709 George Peirce	1763 Robert Lacy
1657 James Ruse	1710 Thomas Marshall	1764 Richard Holloway
1658 Gervase Maplesden	1711 Alex. Osborne	1765 George Post
1659 { And. Broughton / June 1660, Rich. Bills }	1712 Matthew Chandler	1766 Richard Holloway
	1713 James Sherbourne	1767 { John Pope (died Jan. 13, 1768) / David Polhill }
	1714 { John How (died Jan. 17, 1715, aged 80). / William Weldish }	
1660 Richard Bills		
1661 John Cripps		
1662 Michael Beaver		1768 George Post
1663 Thomas Fletcher	1715 George Curteis	1769 William Roots
1664 John Goar	1716 George Curteis	1770 Richard Holloway
1665 John Callant	1717 William Rand	1771 William Mercer
1666 John Beale	1718 Thomas Argles	1772 John Brenchley
1667 John Cripps	1719 Gervase Heeley	1773 Wm. Wrentmore
1668 Gervase Heeley	1720 John Tomlyn	1774 Robert Pope
1669 Daniel Collins	1721 Matthew Chandler	1775 Wm. Wrentmore
1670 Robert Brooke	1722 { Marriott Pett (died Nov. 13), / John Blunt }	1776 Tobias Hammond
1671 John Cripps		1777 George Bishop
1672 John Dunning		1778 Sir William Bishop
1673 Thomas Venman	1723 Richard Flint	1779 Thomas Argles
1674 Arthur Harris	1724 Stephen Page	1780 William Mercer

1781 John Brenchley	1815 John Argles	1848 John Mercer
1782 Tobias Hammond	1816 John Brenchley	1849 Charles Scudamore
1783 Jacob Stone	1817 John Day	1850 Joseph Tootell
1784 Tobias Hammond	1818 Wm. Henry Stacey	1851 William Haynes
1785 Robert Pope	1819 John Mares	1852 Henry Winkles Joy
1786 George Bishop	1820 John Wise	1853 William Laurence
1787 Sir Wm. Bishop	1821 George Burgess	1854 Henry Simmonds
1788 Thomas Argles	1822 Courtenay Stacey	1855 Henry Argles
1789 Jacob Stone	1823 Robert Tassell	1856 John Whichcord
1790 John King	1824 John N. Hughes	1857 George Wickham
1791 Edward Argles	1825 John Wise	1858 Charles Arkcoll
1792 Flint Stacey	1826 John Mares	1859 Jno. Cribb Stephens
1793 Thomas Day	1827 Wm. Henry Stacey	1860 Charles Ellis
1794 George May	1828 Courtenay Stacey	1861 William Haynes
1795 Thomas Poole	1829 Robert Tassell	1862 George Edmett
1796 William Jefferys	1830 John N. Hughes	1863 James Clifford
1797 Edward Argles	1831 Thomas Day	1864 Charles Ellis, jun.
1798 John Stone	1832 Walter Hills	1865 William Laurence
1799 John Blake	1833 John Mares	1866 Horace R. Cutbush
1800 John King	1834 Wm. Hy. Stacey	1867 George Edmett
1801 Flint Stacey	1835 Wm. Hy. Stacey	1868 Charles Arkcoll
1802 Edward Argles	1836 { Jan., Chas. Ellis / Nov., Thos. Pybus }	1869 William Haynes
1803 Thomas Day		1870 Frederick Pine
1804 Thomas Poole	1837 Thomas Pybus	1871 John H. Hills
1805 John Stone	1838 William Hussey	1872 Charles Ellis
1806 John Blake	1839 John Mercer	1873 James Clifford
1807 Henry Cutbush	1840 Thomas Franklyn	1874 Henry Hughes
1808 George Burr	1841 Alexander Randall	1875 William Page
1809 George Burgess	1842 Thomas Edmett	1876 George Youngman
1810 Thomas Day	1843 Thomas Day	1877 William Haynes
1811 James Poole	1844 Edwin Stacey	1878 Charles Ellis
1812 Thomas Poole	1845 Henry Argles	1879 William Day, jun.
1813 John Stone	1846 Thomas Franklyn	1880 Alfred Spencer
1814 Philip Corrall	1847 John Whichcord	1881 E. B. Smith

No. 3.

TOWN CLERKS.

(The first five were Recorders and Town Clerks.)

1560 Henry Fisher	1640 Michael Beaver	1817 George Burr, jun.
1562 Nicholas Barham	1705 John Barrington	1823 Charles Hoar
1583 Alexander Fisher	1736 John Mason	1836 Clement Taylor Smythe
1590 John Smythe	1753 Samuel Eastchurch	
1599 William Gull *	1772 Thomas Punnett	1838 John Monckton
1607 Henry Dixon	1785 George Burr	1874 Herbert Monckton

* He continued as Recorder till 1634.

No. 4.

FROM THE PARISH REGISTERS.

In Quinquennial Periods.	Burials.
1570	359
1575	259
1580	343
1585	280
1590	350
1595	441
1600	467
1605	508
1610	437
1615	539
1620	519

In Decennial Periods.	Baptisms.	Marriages.	Burials.
1682	1343	249	1425
1692	1263	335	1213
1702	1195	253	1225
1712	1206	350	1132
1722	1281	381	1358
1732	1309	423	1502
1742	1405	484	1498
1752	1462	449	1309
1762	1469	460	1406
1772	1742	533	1549

No. 5.

MAIDSTONE TOKENS.*

(R, *reverse*; O, *obverse*; E, *edge*.)

SEVENTEENTH CENTURY.

O. WILLIAM · WEB · MERCER—The Grocers' Arms.
R. IN · MAIDSTON · 1649—W. E. B.
O. RALPH · WARDE · IN—A castle.
R. MAIDSTONE · 1656—R. E. W. ....Farthing.
O. JOHN · HOAD · IN—A windmill.
R. MEADSTONE · 1657—I. H. ....Farthing.
O. RICHARD · WALKER—The Grocers' Arms.
R. OF MAIDSTON · GROCER—R. W. 1658 ....Farthing.
O. JAMES · WOLBOLL—The Grocers' Arms.
R. OF MAYDSTONE · 1664—I. W. ....Farthing.
O. JAMES · WOLBALL—The Grocers' Arms.
R. OF MAYDSTONE · 1664—I. W. ....Farthing.

* This list is the result of a careful collation with the previously published lists, and of corrections kindly supplied by the Rev. T. S. Frampton, of Platt, near Sevenoaks.

O. THOMAS · BOND · IN—The Grocers' Arms.
R. MAYDSTONE · IN · KENT—T. L. B. as a monogram · 1666 ....Farthing.
O. THOMAS · WALL · 1667—The Salters' Arms.
R. MAIDSTONE · HALFE · PENNY—(In four lines, across the field).
O. JONATHAN · TROVGHTON The Grocers' Arms.
R. IN · MAIDSTON · 1668—HIS HALF PENY ....Halfpenny.
O. JONATHAN · TROVGHTON—The Grocers' Arms.
R. IN · MAIDSTON · 1668—I. M. T.............................Farthing.
O. WALTER · WEEKES · 1669—HIS HALF PENY.
R. IN · MAIDSTONE · WEAVER—The Weavers' Arms ....Halfpenny.
O. ROB · BROOKE · IRONMONGER—HIS HALF PENY.
R. IN · MAIDSTONE · 1670—R. W. B. ....Halfpenny.
O. JOHN · WATSON · AT · THE—A bell.
R. IN · MAIDSTON · 1670—HIS HALF PENY ....Halfpenny.
O. ROBERT · HEATH · OF—The Grocers' Arms.
R. MAYDSTONE · GROCER—R. H. ....Farthing.
O. GERVIS · MAPLISDEN · OF—Arms: a cross pattée fitchée.
R. MAIDSTONE · MERCER—HIS HALF PENY ....Halfpenny.
O. JAMES · RVSE · IN—The Grocers' Arms.
R. MEYDSTONE · IN · KENT—I. B............................Farthing.
O. THOMAS · SWINOKE—Three men with astronomical instruments, standing round a globe.
R. IN · MAIDSTONE—T. X. S. ....Farthing.
O. ELIZABETH · WEBB—The Grocers' Arms.
R. OF · MAIDSTONE · GROCER—E. W........................Farthing.
O. STEVEN · WEEKS · OF—The Weavers' Arms.
R. MAIDSTONE · WEAVER—S. A. W. ....Farthing.
O. RICHARD · WICKING—The Grocers' Arms.
R. IN · MAIDSTONE · GROCER—R. E. W. ....Farthing.

EIGHTEENTH CENTURY.

O. The Arms of Maidstone, with two savages as supporters. *Maidstone Halfpenny*, 1795.
R. A figure of Justice, with sword and scales. *The spring of Freedom, England's Blessing, Kent.*
E. *Payable by Henry Olivers.*
O. The Arms of Maidstone. *Maidstone Halfpenny.*
R. A building representing a paper mill. *Payable by J. Smyth at Padsole Paper Mill*, 1795.

ERRATA AND ADDENDA.

Page 79, line 30, for "mendicant" *read* "monastic."
,,   136, line 18, for "pen" *read* "pew."
,,   147, line 6, *omit* " (N.S.)"
,,   148-9.—John Gifford was not connected with the Royalist rising of 1648, but with a less successful affair in the spring of 1645. This is referred to in an ordinance issued in the last-named year by the Parliament, "for constituting commissioners and council of war for trial of all persons in the late rising in the county of Kent." The ordinance states that "divers ill-affected persons have traitorously assembled themselves together in a war-like manner, and as well by secret practices and contrivances as by open force, attempted to levy war against the Parliament, and made uproars and raised seditions." The commissioners were thirty-nine in number, including Colonel Thomas Blunt (who captured Gifford and his companions), Captain Beale, and Captain William Skinner, brother to Augustine Skinner, of West Farleigh. They were authorised to "sit in some convenient place within the said county, and to proceed to the trial of all such persons as have offended, as aforesaid, or which shall offend in like manner, and to inflict upon them such punishments, either by death or otherwise corporally, according to the course and custom of war." A copy of this ordinance, printed in 1645, is in the library of Mr. Hovenden, of Croydon. The rising here referred to has been strangely overlooked by all writers on Kentish history.

Pages 152, 155.—A pedigree drawn up in 1801, now in the possession of Miss Pine, of Earl Street, gives details as to the Pine family. Simon Pine was a fuller at Tovil. John, his eldest son, is supposed to have been a paper-mould maker. Thomas Pine, who died in 1757, aged eighty-two, was a grocer at Maidstone, and "got into the business of paper-making, to which he brought up his eldest son," who carried on the business first at Loose, and afterwards at Tovil. The connection of the Pine family with the Tovil mill ceased in 1824.

Page 208, line 17, for "civil" *read* "criminal."
,,   235, line 30, for "Dean and Chapter" *read* "Ecclesiastical Commissioners."

Page 299, line 15.—Robert Fergusson was incarcerated in the King's Bench Prison. He was subsequently known as the Right Hon. Robert Cutlar Fergusson. He practised at the Indian bar, and became a Privy Councillor, dying at Paris on the 16th November 1838, in his seventieth year. His remains were interred at Craigdarroch, in Dumfriesshire, the family estate. The reader is referred to Froude's "English in Ireland," vol. iii., pp. 312-23, for remarks on the trial of O'Connor and O'Coigley.

Page 362.—A recent overhaul of the parochial library has disclosed the fact that Walton's Polyglot Bible is not now in the collection.

INDEX.

Abjuration of the realm, 18-19
Abergavenny, Lord, repels Wyatt's followers in Blacksole Field, 55; assembles two thousand men at Maidstone, 59
Actors, travelling, 5, 226-7, 232
Aierste, Thomas, bequeaths money for purchase of Calvin's "Christian Religion," 111; mentioned, 176
Alexander, William, 397-8
Allin, Edmund, and his wife, burnt at Maidstone, 106-7
Allington Castle, its present state, 44; its ancient owners, 45; Cardinal Wolsey at, ib.; large walnut trees at, 224-5—see Wyatt and Astley
Almshouses, 165, 170, 223, 224-5, 379, 380, 381, 382, 383
All Saints' Church, its associations, 4; chantries, 98; ceases to be a collegiate church, 99; sale of plate, bells, and vestments, 99,102; a perpetual curacy, 99, 102; its ministers, 102-4, 111, 116, 118-22; altar, 105, 108; regulations, 109; monuments defaced, 114-5; Commonwealth survey, 117-8; a vicarage, 123; building, 124-8, 129; roof, 130-1; re-pewed, 131; spire, 133; brasses, 136; other monuments, 137-9; order referring to funerals, 140
Appleby, Walter, and his wife, burnt at Maidstone, 106-7
Assizes, commotion at, 246-51; in sixteenth century, 276-8; generally held at Maidstone, 280, 287; cases at, 284, 290, 303; provision for, 303-4
Astley, John, master of Queen Elizabeth's jewel house, 68, 137, 220, 347; Thomas, 347; Sir John, 137, 347-8; Baron, 137, 348, 389-91; family, 348, 349
"Astley" House, not connected with Astley family, 349-51

Attendance, church and chapel, 145, 161
Awger, Richard, first perpetual curate of All Saints', 104
Aylesford, annual value of manor in Domesday Book, 12; parliamentary soldiers at, 252
Aylesford, Earl of, 204, 208, 212

Ball, John, his connection with Wat Tyler's rebellion, 37; his death, 39
Banks, Sir John, 230, 338; benefaction by, 379
Baptists in prison, 152; their meeting houses, 155-6, 161, 151
Baraguay d'Hilliers, the French general, at Maidstone, 368-9
Barming, annual value of manor in Domesday Book, 12; Hall-Place, 178; borsholder for, 235
Barham, Nicholas, 127, 141, 187, 341, 356; Arthur, 356, 360
Barracks, erection of, 368
Barrell, Robert, minister of All Saints', 111-4, 191
Beale, William, 40, 169, 184, 185; Thomas, 186; Ambrose, 189, 195, 314; John, 222, 233, 357; family, 136, 343
Bear Ringle, 226
Bells, All Saints', 100, 102, 134-6, 140, 167
Benefit of sanctuary, 18-9
Bliss, Thomas, lessee of rectorial tithes, 122; jurat, 197; his contest for seat in Parliament, 202-3; his house, 350; notice of, 351-2; benefaction by, 379
Blue Coat School, 141
Boleyn, Thomas, master of College, 85
Books on Maidstone, 1
Booth, Sir Charles, lessee of rectorial tithes, 122; benefaction by, 381-2; monument, 139
Borsholders, 209 n., 235
Bower, name of, 240, 352-3

Boxley, annual value of manor in Domesday Book, 12 ; Rood of Grace, 103-4 ; Abbey, 104 *n.* ; borsholder for, 235 ; fuller's earth, 216
Bread charities, 384
Brenchley, John, 340, 381, 385 ; Julius Lucius, 359, 360-2
Brewing, 325
Bridge, the old, its origin, 29-30 ; cottages on, 165 ; width of, 400, 407 ; the new bridge, 406-7
Brockman, Sir William, in the fight at Maidstone, 261, 272 ; taken prisoner, 264, 267
Broughton, Andrew, his family, 192-3 ; clerk of High Court of Justice, 193 ; mayor, *ib.* ; reads sentence to Charles I., 194 ; his disappearance, 195 ; proclaimed a regicide, 196 : dies in Switzerland, 197 ; house in Earl Street, 354
Brown, Peter, his flight to the Continent, 105 ; bequest for purchase of Bible, 110
Buckland estates, 337-9
Butchers, petition by, 314
Butler, Sir William, of Barham Court, 252
By-laws, amusing, 187, 232 ; curious, 190
Cade, Jack, heads a rebellion, 40 ; names of insurgents, 40-1 ; his demands, 41 ; defeats the royalist forces at Sevenoaks, *ib.* ; attacks London bridge and is repulsed, 42 ; his flight and death, 43
Camden, his description of Maidstone, 225
Carr, Robert, minister of All Saints', 111
Carter, Major, wounded in Maidstone fight, 263, 267
Carter, Mrs., benefaction by, 383
Carter, Matthew, his description of Maidstone fight, 264 *n.* ; mentioned 254, 257, 263 *n.*
Chamberlains, duties of, 187 ; accounts, *ib. n.*
Champneys. Justinian, 199
Chap-books, 293
Chapels, ancient, 142-3—*see* St. Faith's
Charles I., Kentish petition to, 250 ; his reply, 251 ; a Maidstone witness against, 271 : sentence, 194 ; head of, 271

Charles family, 357-8
Charter of Incorporation, the first, 184 ; second, 186 ; third and fourth, 188-9 ; surrendered, 197 ; fifth, *ib.* ; sixth, 205-6.
Churchwardens' accounts, 135-6, 235
Cloth-weaving, 309-11, 315, 318
Cockfighting, 243
College of All Saints founded, 74 ; endowments, 74-5, 79 ; objects, 80 ; description of building, 80-3 ; masters, 83-6 ; suppressed, 86 ; sources of revenue, 87-9, 92-3 ; site and lands granted to Lord Cobham, 91
Comberton, John, master of College, 85
Conduits, 227, 232, 239
Congregationalists, 158, 159-60, 161
Convent of Franciscans, 24-5
Cornhill, William de, rector of Maidstone, 70
Corporation order concerning commonalty, 189-90 ; manner of announcing meetings. 191-2 ; discharge of members, 198 ; dissolved, 204 ; re-constituted, 207 ; feasting, *ib.*, 208-10, 211 ; place of meeting, 207-8 ; dispute with commonalty, 210-1 ; rent-roll, 212-3 ; effect of Municipal Corporations Act, 215-6
Corpus Christi Fraternity founded, 162-3 ; hall in Earl Street, 164 ; number of members, *ib.* ; rent-roll, 165 ; accounts, 3, 166-7 ; chantry in All Saints' Church, 167 ; festivals, 168 ; names of wardens, 169 ; suppressed, hall and lands sold, 169-70
Courtenay, Archbishop, founder of the College, 74 ; his death, 75 ; place of burial, 76-9
Court-leet, 209 *n.*, 220, 235
Coxheath, military camps on, 366, 367, 368, 373-4 ; beacon on, 373 ; workhouse, 381
Crump, John, minister of All Saints,' 118-9
Cucking-stool, 278-9
Culpeper, Richard, joins Cade's rebellion, 40 ; Thomas, 66 ; Lady Elizabeth, 164 ; William, of Hollingbourne, 199, 200, 202 ; Thomas, of Park House, 199, 200, 201 ; Sir John, of Leeds Castle, 253, 258, 262 *n.* ; Thomas Lord, 273 ; Preston Hall branch of, 336

Cutbush, Thomas Robert, benefaction by, 383-4
Cutt, Henry, 336, 377

Darrell, John, master of College, 85
Davis, John, minister of All Saints', 119
Davy, John, physician, 138, 176
Day, John, incumbent of All Saints', 104, 108, 109-10
Dealtry, Archdeacon, vicar of All Saints', 122
Denley, John, burnt at Uxbridge, 105-6
Denne, Rev. Samuel, remarks on Courtney's place of burial, 78-9; John, incumbent of All Saints', 122, 236, 288, 289
Dering, Sir Edward, 246, 247, 250; Richard, 341
Detling, chapel annexed to St. Mary's Church, 72; to the College, 74; granted to Sir Thomas Wyatt the younger, 102; tithes, 88, 93, 109, 117; borsholder for, 235
Digons, mansion of, 340-1
Disraeli, Mr., anecdote relating to, 344
Distilling, 325-6
Dominican friar at Maidstone, 110-1
Dudley, Sir Gamaliel, governor of Maidstone, 259, 263; taken prisoner, 264, 267
Duffield, William, master of College, 85
Duke, Mrs., benefaction by, 382
Dutch settlers, their place of worship, 142, 146-8; trade, 309, 318; number, 310

Earls Place, 354-5, 387, 388
Earthquake, shock of, 364-5
East Farleigh, annual value of manor in Domesday Book, 12; tithes annexed to Hospital of Newark, 23; inhabitants concerned in Tyler's rebellion, 39; tithes annexed to College, 75; borsholder for, 235; Fairfax at, 258, 260, 265
East Lane, manor, 221, 235; change of name, 240
Edmett, Thomas, 384, 385
Elections, parliamentary, 202-203, 205, 212, 214-5; municipal, 210, 215
Executions, changes as to place of, 306

Fairfax, General Lord, heavy march of, 253; ordered to suppress Kentish rising, 256; rapid march to the Medway, ib.; strength of his force, 257; crosses the river, 260; his bravery at Maidstone, 262, 266; defeats Royalists, 264; his description of Maidstone fight, 267-8; order against plundering, 269 n.; family, 273; correspondence, ib.
Fair Meadow, 90 n., 226, 232, 236, 332; seven persons burnt, 107
Fairs, 311, 329
Fant, 353
Fergusson, Robert, 297, 299, 415
Filmer, Sir Robert, 250, 282; Sir Edward, 250, 251
Fire, precautions against, 190-1
Fisher, John, 40; Alexander, 50, 66, 101, 377; Henry, 187; Walter, 189, 377; William, 222; family, 353
Fortnightly court, early, 189
Fox, Charles James, at Maidstone, 295
Freemen, creation of, 185, 188, 192; order concerning, 189; maintaining their rights, 210-1; non-resident, 213, 215; number, 214
Fremingham, family of, 335, 339
Freston, John, master of College, 85
Fruit growing, 323-4
Fulling, process of, 315-6

Gifford, John, 149, 415
Gill, William, benefaction by, 381
Goring, Lord, leader of Kentish Royalists, 259, 267; his indecision, 262, 263 n.; life saved by casting vote of Speaker, 270
Grammar School founded, 172-3; regulations, 174, 177; benefactions, 173, 175-6; masters, 173, 174, 176-7, 180; eminent scholars, 178-80; endowments, 180-1; new school, and scheme for administration of, ib.
Grattan, Mr., at Maidstone, 296
Green, William, 66, 166, 184, 186; Henry, 150; John, 170, 189, 345; Gabriel, 189
Grocyn, William, master of College, 86, 90 n., 153 n.
Ginder, Sergeant, wounded in Maidstone fight, 261; appeals for relief, 272
Gunsley, John, 165; Robert, benefactor, 175, 377

Hales, Edward, agrees to lead the Kentish Royalists, 255; superseded, 258-9; mentioned, 265
Half Yoke manor, 339
Hall family, 341, 356
Hall, John, an eminent surgeon, 67
Hazlitt, William, Nonconformist minister, 159; William, author, 398
Harper, Sir George, joins Wyatt's rebellion, 52; his treachery, 56, 58, 63; property, 66; discharged from the Tower, 67
Hell Fire Jack, horse-stealer, 301
Heron, Roger, master of College, 85
Hewitt, William, benefaction by, 377
Hewson, Colonel, despatched to Canterbury, 253; in Maidstone fight, 263, 266; at Westminster, 271
Hollingworth, Thomas Robert and Finch, 296, 297, 327
Holond, John, master of College, 85
Holy Trinity Church, 143, 306
Hops, their cultivation, 311-2, 319-22; appearance, 322; bags, 318
Hospital of Newark founded, 22; its masters, 23-4; dissolved, 75 *n*. West Kent General Hospital, 384-6. Ophthalmic Hospital, 386
Horne, Bishop, 178
Howard, John, at Maidstone, 290-1
Hughes, John Newington, 193 *n*., 273, 285, 344
Hundred of Maidstone, extent of, 16; ancient abuses, 19-20; tenure of land, 20
Hunter, Edward, 344; benefaction by, 383

Innes, Gilbert, minister of All Saints', 120, 235
Inns, signs of, 241-3; list of, 244; early by-law concerning, 188, 190; mentioned, 111, 238, 246, 343, 344, 393
Isley, Sir Henry and Thomas, 52, 66, 67, 339; Roger, 335

Jacobins, house for, 243
Jefferys, William, 346, 396; James, 396-7
Jenkins, Herbert, Nonconformist minister, 160; John, 389
Jinkings, Edmund, Nonconformist minister, 160
Jordans Hall, 341-2
Jurates, right of electing, 203-5, 206

Justices Itinerant, their mode of procedure, 16-7; case before, 338

Kean, Edmund, 346
Kent, population of at Domesday period, 13; early civil divisions of, 15-6
Kingsley, Colonel, 340; General, *ib*.
Knyvett, Anthony, 50, 53, 64, 65, 66, 67

Lamb, William, benefactor, 173; Henry, *ib. n*.
Law suits in reign of Edward II., 31
Lease, John, last master of College, 86
Leeds Castle, 253-4, 273-4, 367
Lee, John, master of College, 85; Richard, 165, 388; Edward, 387-8
Leland, John, visits Maidstone, 217, 241
Len bridge, 263, 342
L'Estrange, Roger, interview with Edward Hales, 255; his remarks concerning Lord Goring, 262 *n*.
Library, parochial, 121-2
Linton tithes annexed to Hospital of Newark, 23; inhabitants participating in Tyler's rebellion, 39; tithes annexed to College, 75; borsholder for, 235
Loddington tithes, 92, 109, 118 *n*., 120; manorial tenants in, 219
Loose, inhabitants connected with Tyler's rebellion, 39; chapel annexed to St. Mary's Church, 72; to College, 74; granted to Sir Thomas Wyatt the younger, 102; tithes, 88, 93, 108, 117; borsholder for, 235
Lower Court House, 207, 276-7, 279-80, 287
Lubbock, Sir John, 180-1
Lynde, Humphrey, minister of Boxley and Maidstone, 119

Maces, 185, 195 *n*., 197
Maidstone, situation of, 2; derivation of name, 9-10; old seal of, 10; persons designated from, 22 *n*., 25-7; sanitary condition of, 223, 225, 239, 407
Mainy, Sir John, conducts defence of Maidstone, 259, 260, 263; slain, 264, 267; mentioned, 250, 251
Mallet, Sir Thomas, 246, 247, 248, 249

Malling, annual value of manor in Domesday Book, 12; men collected at, to oppose Sir Thomas Wyatt, 54; incumbent of, 151; trade of, 311
Manors, small, 221
Manor of Maidstone, annual value in eleventh century, 11: probable extent of, and number of persons employed on, at Domesday period, *ib.*; notice of, in Domesday Book, 12; illegal seizure, 21; annual value in 1291, 27; manor house, 70; becomes the property of the Crown, 89; rent-roll, 219; survey, 219-20; extent, 220; grant of, *ib.*, 235
Mansell, John, the pluralist, 28, 74
Mansfield, Lord, 349; his opinion of Mayor and Jurates of Maidstone, 211
Mantell, Walter, of Monk's Horton, 66, 67; Walter, of Canterbury, *ib.*
Maplesden, George, 52, 356; Peter, 66, 141, 184; Richard, 189; Edward, *ib.*; Gervase, 195, 349; family, 138, 340, 356, 360
Market Cross, 279, 314, 329-30
Markets, 27, 314, 329-31
Marsham, Sir Robert, 129, 202, 335; Sir John, 335
Mayor, salary to the, 207; summoned to Westminster, 248; list, 410
Medway, jurisdiction of Corporation over, 186, 209 *n.*, 313-4; trade on, 312-3, 328-9
Melville, Viscount, at Maidstone, 371
Members of Parliament, right of town to elect, 186; sympathy with Long Parliament, 248; list of, 409
Mills, Benjamin, Nonconformist minister, 158
Monster found, 363-4; child, 364 *n.*
Mortality in sixteenth century, 222; in 1782, 237 — *see* Plague and Smallpox
Mote estate, 333-5; grand review of Volunteers, 369-72
Museum, 129, 355-62

Newman, John, burnt at Saffron Walden, 105
Newspapers, first Maidstone, 293, 344
Newton, Rev. William, 1

Nonconformity, 118, 146-61, 198
Norton, Anthony, 50
Nuts, cultivation of, 324

O'Coigley, trial and execution of, 293, 294-9
O'Connor, Arthur, trial of for high treason, 293, 294-8
Organs in All Saints' Church, 128
Otham, 112, 115, 119, 178

Packington, Patrick, burnt at Uxbridge, 105
Palace rebuilt by Archbishops Ufford and Islip, 70-1; archbishops at, 96-7; Leland's reference to, 218; owners, 346-8; present state of, 348
Paper-making, when first commenced, 326; number of mills, 327-8, 317, 319, 415
Parish, ecclesiastical divisions of, 143
Parish register commenced, 102; statistics from, 222 *n.*; 271-2, 413
Park House, 336-7
Pastimes, 225-6, 281
Peculiar, Court of, 276
Penenden Heath, 13; famous court on, 14-5; polling on, 214, 305; soldiers ordered to, 253; parliamentary troops on, 269; executions, 283, 289, 290, 293, 298-9, 299-301, 306; shire house, 305-6; last great county meeting on, 374; enclosed, 306
Penyton, Thomas, master of College, 86
Pepys, Samuel, visits Maidstone, 233, 241
Petitions, Kentish, 246-50, 198-202
Petty Treason, instance of, 290
Pillory, 279, 301-2
Pimpe, family of, 165, 339
Pine family, 152-3, 155, 206, 415
Pitt, Mr., at Maidstone, 371; at Coxheath, 374
Plague, 223, 224-5, 229-31, 233, 272
Political parties, state of, 202-3, 204-5, 212, 215
Poor, benefactions to, 227-8, 376-84; cost of, 234, 379
Pond, John, astronomer, 180
Population in sixteenth century, 222; in seventeenth century, 234; in 1695, 235; in 1782, 236-7; in nineteenth century, 401, 407-8